mySAP® CRM

SAP PRESS

SAP PRESS is issued by
Bernhard Hochlehnert, SAP AG

SAP PRESS is a joint initiative of SAP and Galileo Press. The know-how offe-red by SAP specialists combined with the expertise of the publishing house Galileo Press offers the reader expert books in the field. SAP PRESS features first-hand information and expert advice, and provides useful skills for pro-fessional decision-making.

SAP PRESS offers a variety of books on technical and business related topics for the SAP user. For further information, please visit our website: *www.sap-press.com*.

Norbert Egger
SAP BW Professional
2004, 450 pp., ISBN 1-59229-017-5

Christian Krämer, Christian Lübke, Sven Ringling
HR Personnel Planning and Development Using SAP
2004, approx. 570 pp., ISBN 1-59229-024-8

Gerhard Oswald
SAP Service and Support
2003, 208 pp., ISBN 1-59229-015-9

A. Rickayzen, J. Dart, C. Brennecke, M. Schneider
Practical Workflow for SAP
2002, 504 pp., ISBN 1-59229-006-X

M. Missbach, R. Sosnitzka, J. Stelzel, M. Wilhelm
SAP System Operations
2004, 355 pp., ISBN 1-59229-025-8

Rüdiger Buck-Emden, Peter Zencke

mySAP® CRM

The Official Guidebook to
SAP CRM 4.0

SAP PRESS

Contents

Foreword   **15**

1   **Introduction: The Customer—The Most Important Business Partner**   **17**

2   **What Makes a Company a Market Leader?**   **19**

2.1   Customer-Oriented Value 19
     2.1.1   Product Leadership 21
     2.1.2   Operational Excellence 22
     2.1.3   Customer Intimacy 23
2.2   Relationships Between Value Focus Points 25
2.3   Business Focus as a Foundation for Success 25

3   **What Is Customer Relationship Management?**   **27**

3.1   The Customer Was Not Always the Focus 27
3.2   Characteristics of Close Customer Relationships 28
3.3   One-to-One Marketing and CRM 28
3.4   Customer Satisfaction as a Business Objective? 29
3.5   Profitable Customers Are the Difference 29
3.6   CRM as a Strategic Business Task 30
3.7   Data Protection Creates Trust 31

4   **Software Solutions for Customer Relationship Management**   **33**

4.1   Value Expectations of the Company 33
4.2   Value Optimization in Integrated, Dynamic Relationship Networks 33
     4.2.1   Integration Example: Sales 35

4.3	Four Basic Requirements of CRM Software Solutions	37
	4.3.1 Connected CRM	37
	4.3.2 People-Centric CRM	37
	4.3.3 Collaborative CRM	37
	4.3.4 Industry-Specific CRM	38
4.4	Structure of CRM Software Solutions	38
	4.4.1 Operational CRM	39
	4.4.2 Analytical CRM	40
	4.4.3 Collaborative CRM	41
4.5	Industry- and Country-Specific Configurations	42
4.6	The Market for CRM Software Solutions	43

5 mySAP CRM—Customer Relationship Management as Part of the Integrated mySAP Business Suite 47

5.1	Enterprise Services Architecture	47
5.2	Business Applications at SAP	48
	5.2.1 Cross-Industry Solutions	49
	5.2.2 Industry Solutions	53
	5.2.3 Packaged Composite Applications	54
5.3	Integration and Application Infrastructure	54

6 Digression: Business Scenarios and Business Maps 57

6.1	SAP Solution Maps	58
6.2	SAP Collaborative Business Maps	60
	6.2.1 Business View	61
	6.2.2 Component View	62
	6.2.3 Collaborative Business Maps as a Basis for Business Profitability Calculation	63
	6.2.4 SAP Business Case Builder	64
6.3	Potential Benefits of Business Scenarios	64

7 mySAP CRM—Applications for the Customer Interaction Cycle 67

7.1	The Four Phases of the Customer Interaction Cycle	67
7.2	Marketing	69
	7.2.1 Marketing—Software's Last Technological Conquest	69
	7.2.2 Market, Customer, and Consumer Analysis	78

	7.2.3	Marketing Planning	80
	7.2.4	Customer and Consumer Segmentation	82
	7.2.5	Campaign and Consumer Promotions	83
	7.2.6	Trade Promotions	87
	7.2.7	Lead Management	89
	7.2.8	Personalization	90
	7.2.9	Campaign Monitoring and Success Analysis	94
	7.2.10	Use Case: Using mySAP CRM in Marketing	95
	7.2.11	Recommendations for Successful CRM Projects in Marketing	97
	7.2.12	Scenario Overview and Potential Benefits	98
7.3	**Sales**		100
	7.3.1	Overview	100
	7.3.2	Sales Planning	102
	7.3.3	Territory Management	103
	7.3.4	Account and Contact Management	105
	7.3.5	Activity Management	107
	7.3.6	Opportunity Management—Overview	110
	7.3.7	Opportunity Management with Structured Sales Methodology	112
	7.3.8	Quotation and Order Management	118
	7.3.9	Product Configuration	124
	7.3.10	Contract Management	130
	7.3.11	Leasing	133
	7.3.12	Incentive and Commission Management	136
	7.3.13	Sales Analytics	137
	7.3.14	Use Case: Using mySAP CRM in Sales Including Sales Order Processing	140
	7.3.15	Recommendations for Successful CRM Projects in Sales	143
	7.3.16	Scenario Overview and Potential Benefits	143
7.4	**Sales Order Processing**		146
	7.4.1	Overview	146
	7.4.2	Availability Check	147
	7.4.3	Payment Processing and Credit Management	151
	7.4.4	Shipping	154
	7.4.5	Transport	156
	7.4.6	Billing	157
	7.4.7	Claims Management	160
	7.4.8	Monitoring and Analyzing Sales Order Processing	161
	7.4.9	Distributed Sales Order Processing (Extended Order Management)	162
	7.4.10	Recommendations for Successful Projects	162
	7.4.11	Scenario Overview and Potential Benefits	163
7.5	**Service**		163
	7.5.1	Overview	163
	7.5.2	Customer Service and Support	165
	7.5.3	Service Contract Management and Service Entitlements	172
	7.5.4	Managing Organizational Knowledge	176
	7.5.5	Managing Customer Installations	177
	7.5.6	Order Management and Resource Planning	180
	7.5.7	Professional Services	187
	7.5.8	Integrated CRM Concept for Service Employees	189

7.5.9 Service Analytics 189
7.5.10 Use Case: Using mySAP CRM in Service 192
7.5.11 Recommendations for Successful CRM Projects in Service 193
7.5.12 Scenario Overview and Potential Benefits 194

7.6 People Shape Relationships—Workforce Management with
mySAP CRM 196

8 On-Site Business Processes—Support for Mobile Users by mySAP CRM 205

8.1 From E-Business to M-Business 205

8.2 Business Benefits Provided by Mobile Applications 205
8.2.1 Sales Employees in the Field Sales Force 206
8.2.2 Service Technicians in the Field Sales Force 207

8.3 Criteria for Use of Mobile Applications 208

8.4 Mobile Applications in mySAP CRM (Field Applications) 209
8.4.1 Solutions for Laptops 210
8.4.2 Solutions for Tablet PCs 214
8.4.3 Solutions for Handhelds 215
8.4.4 Mobile Applications in Industries 217
8.4.5 Case Study: Activity Management for Mobile Sales Employees
with mySAP CRM 218
8.4.6 Recommendations for Successful CRM Projects in Mobile
Applications 220

8.5 Scenario Overview and Potential Benefits 220

9 E-Commerce with mySAP CRM—The Internet as a Sales and Interaction Channel 225

9.1 Electronic Commerce Beyond the Electronic Shopping Basket 225

9.2 Strategic Competitive Advantage through Electronic Commerce 227
9.2.1 Integration of the Sales Process in the Value Chain 227
9.2.2 Inclusion of the Internet in the Company's CRM Strategy 230
9.2.3 Personalization of Interaction with Customers 230
9.2.4 Gaining Business Intelligence 231

9.3 Selected E-Commerce Scenarios 232
9.3.1 Business-to-Consumer (B2C) 232
9.3.2 Business-to-Business (B2B) 233
9.3.3 Business-to-Business Mall (B2B mall) 233
9.3.4 Distributor & Reseller Network (Channel Commerce) 234

9.4 E-Commerce with mySAP CRM 235
9.4.1 One-to-One Marketing 236
9.4.2 Catalog Management and Product Selection 239
9.4.3 Purchase Order and Order Processing 242
9.4.4 Additional Sales with Internet Auctions 246

9.4.5	Self-Service for Customers	247
9.4.6	Interactive Customer Support (Live Web Collaboration)	249
9.4.7	Business Intelligence through Powerful Web Analyses	250
9.4.8	Functional Web Design	252
9.4.9	Implementation Options for E-Commerce with mySAP CRM	253
9.4.10	Successful E-Commerce Projects with mySAP CRM	254
9.4.11	Use Case: E-Commerce with mySAP CRM	256
9.4.12	Recommendations for Successful CRM Projects in E-Commerce	258

9.5 Scenario Overview and Potential Benefits ... 259

10 Customer Interaction Along All Communication Channels—mySAP CRM for the Interaction Center 263

10.1 Introduction ... 263

10.1.1	The Call Center in Transition	263
10.1.2	SAP's Solution	264

10.2 Key Elements of the Interaction Center ... 265

10.2.1	Messages for Agents	265
10.2.2	Preformulated Interactive Customer Dialogs	265
10.2.3	Channel Integration	266
10.2.4	Workforce Planning	266
10.2.5	Workflow Management	267
10.2.6	Knowledge Management	268
10.2.7	The User Interfaces of the Interaction Center	270

10.3 Central Processes of the Interaction Center in Detail ... 271

10.3.1	Telemarketing	271
10.3.2	Telesales	271
10.3.3	Teleservice	272
10.3.4	Interaction Center Analytics	272
10.3.5	Use Case: Problem Solving with the mySAP CRM Interaction Center	273
10.3.6	Recommendations for Successful CRM Projects in the Interaction Center	275

10.4 Scenario Overview and Potential Benefits ... 276

11 Channel Management with mySAP CRM— Controlling Marketing, Sales, and Service Partners Efficiently 281

11.1 Challenges of Indirect Channels ... 281

11.2 Competitive Advantages Through Efficient Channel Management ... 282

11.2.1	Integration of Partners in Customer Relationship Management	282
11.2.2	Using Best-of-Breed Partners to Gain Competitive Advantage	283
11.2.3	Software Support for Better Partner and Customer Relationships	283

11.3   mySAP CRM Channel Management 284
     11.3.1   Overview 284
     11.3.2   Partner Management and Analytics 286
     11.3.3   Channel Marketing 288
     11.3.4   Channel Sales 291
     11.3.5   Channel Service 294
     11.3.6   Channel Commerce 296

11.4   Industry-Specific Enhancements 298
     11.4.1   Automotive 298
     11.4.2   High-Tech 298
     11.4.3   Telecommunications 299
     11.4.4   Use Case: Channel Management with mySAP CRM 300
     11.4.5   Recommendations for Successful CRM Projects in Channel
         Management 301

11.5   Scenario Overview and Potential Benefits 302

12   Decision-Making Support for Employees and Managers—The Analytical Applications of mySAP CRM   305

12.1   Introduction 305
     12.1.1   Main Challenges for an Analytical CRM Solution 306
     12.1.2   Potential of Analytical CRM Solutions for Adding Value 307

12.2   Analyzing and Planning with mySAP CRM 309
     12.2.1   Overview 309
     12.2.2   Customer Analytics 311
     12.2.3   Example: Customer Valuation and Scoring 316
     12.2.4   Product Analytics 317
     12.2.5   Interaction Channel Analytics 317
     12.2.6   Marketing Analytics 319
     12.2.7   Sales Analytics 320
     12.2.8   Service Analytics 320

12.3   Analytical Applications for Customer-Oriented Enterprise Management . 321
     12.3.1   Example: Integrated Planning in CRM 322
     12.3.2   Example: CRM Analytics 322
     12.3.3   Recommendations for Successful CRM Projects in Analytics 325

12.4   Scenario Overview and Potential Benefits 326

13   Implementing mySAP CRM in the Enterprise   329

13.1   Business View 329
     13.1.1   Experience Gained from CRM Projects 329
     13.1.2   Return on Investment for CRM 330
     13.1.3   Methods for Fast ROI 336

13.2 Project View 337
    13.2.1 CRM Software Implementation as a Big Bang? 337
    13.2.2 Challenges and Success Factors 338
    13.2.3 Methodical Software Implementation 340
    13.2.4 Preconfigured CRM Systems 347
    13.2.5 Services, Consulting, and Training 350

14 The Integration and Application Platform—SAP NetWeaver   353

14.1 Technology Development at SAP 353

14.2 Integrated Platform Suites 353

14.3 SAP NetWeaver Overview 354

14.4 People Integration 356
    14.4.1 SAP Enterprise Portal 356
    14.4.2 SAP Mobile Infrastructure 359

14.5 Information Integration 361
    14.5.1 SAP Master Data Management 361
    14.5.2 SAP Business Information Warehouse 363
    14.5.3 SAP Knowledge Management 364

14.6 Process Integration 365
    14.6.1 SAP Exchange Infrastructure 365

14.7 Application Platform 366

14.8 Lifecycle Management 368
    14.8.1 SAP Solution Manager 369
    14.8.2 Security Services 371
    14.8.3 Globalization Services 373

14.9 Composite Application Framework 374

15 Architecture and Technology of mySAP CRM   377

15.1 Overview 377

15.2 The People-Centric User Interface 378
    15.2.1 Pattern-Based Interactive Design 379
    15.2.2 Portal Services for the People-Centric User Interface 381
    15.2.3 Interface Implementation Following the
              Model View Controller Approach 382
    15.2.4 Interface Configuration and Personalization 383

15.3 Multi-Channel Interaction for mySAP CRM 385
    15.3.1 Mobile CRM Solutions 385
    15.3.2 Interaction Center 386
    15.3.3 Internet 389

15.4	Message-Based Component Integration	390
	15.4.1 Fundamental Tasks	390
	15.4.2 Integration Services in CRM Middleware	392
15.5	Configuration and Extension	396
	15.5.1 Configuration Settings	397
	15.5.2 Extension Tools	399
15.6	Running my SAP CRM	399
	15.6.1 International Operation	399
	15.6.2 Multiple-Client Operation	400
	15.6.3 Data Archiving	400
	15.6.4 Backup and Recovery	401
	15.6.5 Operation with Multiple Applications on One Database	402
15.7	System Landscape Options with mySAP CRM	402
	15.7.1 Isolated CRM Solution (Standalone)	403
	15.7.2 Integration with an SAP R/3 Back-End System	404
	15.7.3 Integration with Industry Solutions	404
	15.7.4 Groupware Integration	405
	15.7.5 Integration with Third-Party ERP Systems	407
	15.7.6 Multiple-System Landscapes	408
	15.7.7 Cross-Enterprise CRM Scenarios	410

Appendices

A Technical Component View of mySAP CRM 411

A.1	Software Components of mySAP CRM	411
A.2	R/3 Edition for Internet Sales and Mobile Users	414
A.3	Short Description of Software Components	414

B Data Exchange Between CRM and Back-End Systems 423

B.1	Customizing Data	424
B.2	Master Data	426
	B.2.1 Business Partners	426
	B.2.2 R/3 Plants	427
	B.2.3 Products	427
	B.2.4 Service	428
B.3	Condition Data	428
B.4	Transaction Data	430
	B.4.1 Sales Orders	430
	B.4.2 Service Documents	430
	B.4.3 Billing Documents	430

B.5   Data Exchange for Industry Solutions 430
        B.5.1   Media (SAP for Media) 431
        B.5.2   Telecommunications (SAP for Telecommunications) 431
        B.5.3   Utilities and Waste Disposal Industry (SAP for Utilities) 431
B.6   Technical Details 432
        B.6.1   Data Exchange Between the R/3 Back-End System and
                the CRM Server 432

C   Literature   435

D   The Authors   443

        Index   451

Foreword

With the release of SAP CRM 4.0, SAP's customer relationship management solution—mySAP CRM—has been rounded off with many new functions, business scenarios, and industry-specific features, and is now available as a complete package that covers all enterprise requirements.

In addition to further extensive development, for example, for campaign management and trade promotions in marketing, SAP CRM 4.0, with its channel management capabilities, offers a completely new application for cross-company collaboration with marketing, sales, and service partners. SAP NetWeaver—the technical foundation for SAP CRM 4.0—ensures that all integration and platform requirements connected with CRM can be fulfilled.

With this book, we would like to introduce the mySAP CRM solution in its entirety, including all the new developments and innovations available with SAP CRM 4.0. After introducing you to the fundamental aspects of CRM, we present each application of mySAP CRM in detail, using examples to explain specific business situations. Additionally, we discuss the benefits of the approximately 130 business scenarios and business scenario variants delivered with mySAP CRM, as well as how to assess the profitability of investing in CRM. Because the mySAP CRM solution is based on the SAP NetWeaver integration and application platform, we have also included a detailed presentation of all aspects of the technical architecture and operation of mySAP CRM.

This book would not have been possible without the help of the many SAP colleagues who were involved in this project. We would especially like to thank the head of the CRM business unit, Dietmar Saddei, whose constant support, coupled with his great enthusiasm and many ideas, proved to be invaluable. We would also like to thank all the authors, who, in addition to their numerous daily tasks, found the time and commitment to prepare their respective contributions: Achim Appold, Gero Auhagen, Daniel Beringer, Jochen Böder, Christopher Fastabend, Tomas Gumprecht, Volker Hildebrand, Frank Israel, Fabian Kamm, Stefan Kraus, Peter Kulka, Mark Layden, Claudia Mairon, Wolfgang Ölschläger, Jörg Rosbach, Gabriele Roth, Andreas Schuh, Erik Tiden, Stein Wanvik, Thomas Weinerth, and Rainer Zinow.

Similarly, we want to thank all those colleagues who contributed in various ways to make this book possible. They include: Thomas Anton, Doreen Baseler, Marcus Behrens, Boris Bierbaum, Monika Bloching, Marion Blum, Karin Boeckh, Bernhard Brinkmoeller, Michael Brucker, Marc De Gibon, Renee Ebert, Stephan Endrich, Ramine Eskandari, Dominik Feiden, Jörg Flender, Annette Fuchs, Suzanne Geall,

Marco Gleiter, Uwe Grigoleit, Barbara Haas, Matthias Haendly, Roland Hamm, Ulrich Hauke, Bernhard Hochlehnert, Julia Homann, Jörg Kaufmann, Leslihan Kismir, Jutta Knell, Susanne Kollender, Sabina Krüger, Axel Kurka, Georg Leffers, Kristian Lehment, Siegfried Leiner, Dietmar Maier, Ursula Markus, Matthias Melich, Wilfried Merkel, Arno Meyer, Stefanie Müller, Volker Müller, Christoph Nake, Andrea Nowak, Anja Pusch-Dedeke, Annette Rawolle, Cornelia Röhlich, Birgit Sabaschus, Wolfgang Schaper, Tanja Schindewolf, Tom Schroeer, Nora Schrotz, Hans-Heinrich Siemers, Helmut Stefani, Mark Tate-Smith, Susanne Trimpin, Jochen Vatter, Joachim Vogelgesang, Jutta Weber, Matthias Weber, and Ariane Willenbücher.

Special thanks to those responsible for the English translation: Jacqueline Bornfleth, Ronald Brown, Ben Callard, Steve Coombs, Jane Daykin, Kate Dowle, Rebecca Jones, Kate Roberts, and Matthew White.

Finally, we would like to thank the publisher Galileo Press, in particular, Wiebke Hübner, for constructive and inspiring teamwork.

Rüdiger Buck-Emden, Peter Zencke
Walldorf, March 2004

1 Introduction: The Customer—The Most Important Business Partner

Dr. Peter Zencke, Member of the Executive Board, SAP AG

Today, three important factors determine the financial success of an enterprise: market-driven products, profitability, and satisfied customers. Understanding these factors as a continuous and integrated cycle—and not as areas of conflict—is the basis for a successful business strategy both now and in the future.

Customer relationship management (CRM) plays a vital role in this scenario. Continuous and efficient customer service—as well as knowledge of customer requirements—forms the basis for market success and long-term business value. If enterprises want to maintain and build on their market positions, regardless of their current financial situations, they must endeavor to improve their relationships with existing customers and work hard to acquire new customers.

It's the customer's choice—today's information society and the globalization of the economy now enable the customer to compare products and services from across the globe in detail. While the importance of products and services differs from individual to individual, the most important decision-making factors are product quality, availability, price, delivery reliability, and service. — *Hygiene factors*

Direct customer dialogue alone no longer ensures success: enterprises now must focus their entire organization on the demands and activities of their customers. Moreover, enterprises must constantly be able to recognize changes in customer behavior and market developments and be able to adapt their resources and business processes accordingly. Customer relationship management provides the know-how and the processes necessary to support this requirement efficiently.

Customer relationship management has long since outgrown the direct customer contact of the front office. SAP's integrated CRM approach considers the close interconnection of customer-specific processes with all aspects of enterprise management. In this way, an organization's knowledge of customer requirements and complaints can be used directly in product lifecycle management (PLM) to help provide competitive offers that are in line with market requirements at any time. The close links with supply chain management (SCM) and financial accounting provide quality of delivery and fulfillment.

However, customer requirements do not simply determine an enterprise's internal processes; they influence all business relationships. For example, e-selling platforms make collaboration easier for customers while they improve efficiency for the enterprise. Therefore, improving the exchange of information with sales partners—partner or channel management—plays a decisive role in many business areas. For example, in the automotive industry, numerous direct and indirect communication and sales channels coexist. These channels require coordination and must also deliver important customer information. The business processes, in turn, build on customer and partner knowledge and permeate the supply chain to ensure quality, performance, and profitability in procurement and logistics.

This widely used network of customer, partner, and supplier relationships as well as business processes requires an efficient technological infrastructure, which must be able to consolidate information from different sources and make this information available at the touch of a button. It must offer both security and openness to support transparent business processes across the boundaries of the organization. The infrastructure must also be flexible enough to accommodate new developments at any time, such as changes to business processes, new technology, and expansion. In this way, for example, new application architectures are making it possible to use Web services to organize processes and changes quickly and across the organization. A CRM solution must be flexible enough to incorporate such innovations in a way that allows enterprises to profit from them.

This book reflects the new findings, requirements, and trends in customer relationship management, which are implemented in the latest version of mySAP CRM. Some issues that have been the subject of public CRM discussion in recent times, such as the "new economy," are not the focus in this work. On the other hand, aspects such as integration, fundamental technologies, and collaboration across organizational boundaries have become more important.

mySAP CRM offers a very broad range of functions and uses, which are described in detail in this book—starting with the general concept of the solution, before moving on to the technological foundations, integration aspects, and functional descriptions, all of which are supported by examples and recommendations for implementation. This book is intended to help you understand customer relationship management as a vital part of business strategy and align CRM projects with business requirements so that they attain a successful outcome: competitiveness, profitability, and customer satisfaction.

2 What Makes a Company a Market Leader?

*"Customer Relationship Management is no longer just a good idea.
Instead, it's becoming a matter of survival."*
Gartner Group [Nelson/Comport 2003]

2.1 Customer-Oriented Value

Why are market leaders such as Mercedes-Benz, Dell, or Wal-Mart more successful than their competitors? Do these companies obtain their market advantage through superior products, lower prices, or better service? What is the basis of their business success? Our answer is that all these companies are characterized by an uncompromisingly customer-oriented competitive strategy that dictates all the enterprise's operational processes. A closer examination of the individual market leaders also reveals that their competitive strategies can focus on very different value areas, that is, on different areas within the enterprise. In their best-seller, *The Discipline of Market Leaders*, Michael Treacy and Fred Wiersema specifically identify the following focus points of customer-oriented value:

▶ Product leadership

▶ Operational excellence

▶ Customer intimacy

We will look at each of these three values in more detail in the following sections.

However, before we do this, let's look at the following. Each reader knows from his or her own experience as a customer that customers want their vendors to perform well in all three disciplines at the same time; that is, they want vendors to provide them with the perfect product, at the lowest price, and as part of the best solution, given their personal preferences. Unfortunately, the customer-oriented disciplines contradict one another regarding their goals and the means used by the enterprise to reach them. Therefore, it isn't surprising that there is hardly a company that can fulfill the high customer expectations in all disciplines simultaneously.

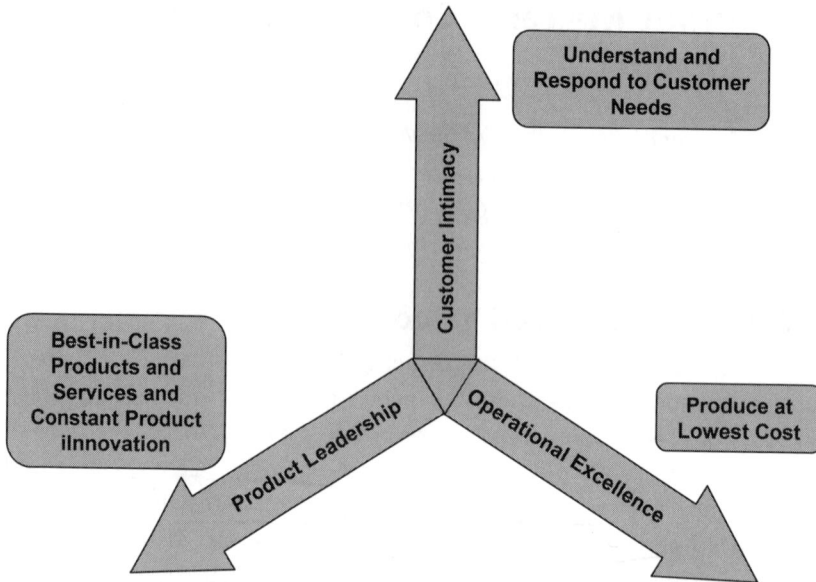

Figure 2.1 Customer-Oriented Value Disciplines for Market Leaders
[Treacy/Wiersema 1995]

To reach a leading market position, a company must be significantly better than the competition in at least one discipline (without, however, neglecting the other disciplines). It can then preserve and continue to improve its market advantage according to the following market principles [AlphaBrand 2001]:

▶ Customers prefer market leaders (leading brands)

▶ It is easier for market leaders to enter new markets

▶ Strong market leaders represent a high market entry barrier for new competitors

▶ Market leaders can negotiate attractive agreements with business partners, which hinders market entry for potential competitors

▶ Market leaders are able to achieve higher market margins

▶ Market leaders can use their market presence to dictate the rules for contesting market share in their favor

Market leaders can take advantage of the aforementioned benefits as long as they are flexible enough to satisfy constantly changing customer expectations with attractive products and services. After all, every reader knows that the customer's expectations increase exponentially with each obligation the vendor fulfills.

2.1.1 Product Leadership

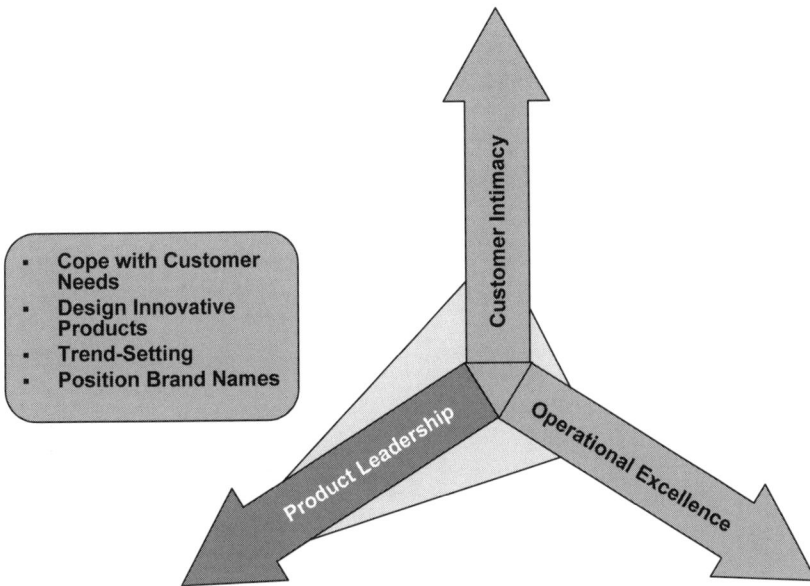

Figure 2.2 Market Leadership through Superior Products [Peppers 2002]

Product leadership means that a company is in a position to offer products or services that are superior to those of its competitors. Companies that base their competitive strategy on product leadership first need a strong, flexible research and development organization with employees who think and act innovatively, can develop visions into products, can quickly adapt to changing conditions, and know the market, competitors' products, and potential development partners.

A typical example of a product leadership company from the automotive industry is Mercedes-Benz. *ADAC-AutoMarxX*, a survey carried out twice a year by the German automobile club ADAC, awarded Mercedes-Benz first place as the best automobile brand in June 2003.

The questions asked of the car makers included, among others, the best possible safety standards, the highest quality, superior driving ability, innovative design, and the top position in automobile research and development. Mercedes occupied one of the top positions in each of these categories and emerged as the overall winner of the survey [Dudenhöffer/Krüger 2003].

In 2002, Mercedes-Benz invested nearly $3600 million research and development to defend and extend its product leadership [Daimler-Chrysler 2002]. One focus point of research is the variability of the vehicles, which in future will combine the qualities of convertibles, sedans, pickups, and estates in one. The vehicles should be able to be converted as required to form SUVs, sedans, small vans, or camper vans. The new development of drive systems is concentrating on fuel cells and electromotors that work with regenerative fuels and produce few emissions. The development of uses for integrated communications systems with mobile Internet technologies for cars is aimed at providing improved safety concepts, navigation aids, and in-car entertainment [Mercedes-Benz 2003].

2.1.2 Operational Excellence

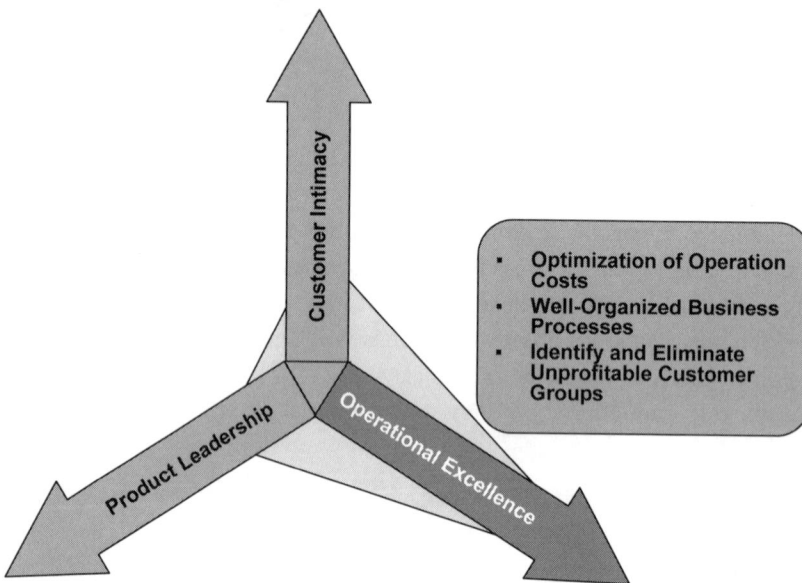

- Optimization of Operation Costs
- Well-Organized Business Processes
- Identify and Eliminate Unprofitable Customer Groups

Figure 2.3 Market Leadership through Operational Excellence [Peppers 2002]

Companies that are characterized by an exceptional operational and organizational structure achieve competitive advantages by establishing effective production, sales, and service processes, and by being able to offer products that are competitively priced and less error-prone. Prerequisites for companies acknowledged to have such operational excellence are extremely standardized, simple, and integrated business processes that are centrally planned and strictly controlled, allowing little room for employee creativity.

A company distinguished by operational excellence is, for example, Volkswagen. VW uses very few technical platforms to produce many different vehicle models. As part of this strategy, there are different platforms only for small, compact, medium-, and upper-class vehicles, with which all car models of the four core brands, VW, Audi, Seat, and Skoda, are manufactured. For example, the platform for the compact class integrates the production of the VW Golf, Bora, and New Beetle, the Audi A3 and TT, the Seat Toledo and Leon, and the Skoda Octavia.

The reduction in the total number of different assembly modules across all four platforms brings with it a reduction in the complexity of the production processes, which means that the manufacture of automobiles at VW is more transparent and easier to control. In addition, VW can use the same assembly groups and sub-modules for all vehicle models manufactured on the same platform, independent of the vehicle brand. The company therefore requires only a few component suppliers and can leverage synergies by making the purchasing process the same for all automobile models, while also making it cheaper.

With the platform concept, VW can realize cost advantages by mass-producing the same parts, taking advantage of existing production capacities, and avoiding idle time. These economies of scale mean that fixed costs are distributed across a larger production volume, thus lowering unit costs for each vehicle manufactured. Raising the quantity of units also has an indirect effect on the time requirements and the error rate of sub-processes, which cannot be performed completely by machines. The greater the number of automobiles produced, the greater the employees' experience and know-how; tasks can be completed in a routine fashion in less time and with higher process quality.

2.1.3 Customer Intimacy

Companies with a great deal of customer intimacy do their best to provide their customers with the exact products or services they require within the context of a tailored overall solution. A prerequisite for this kind of customer intimacy is a corporate culture that treats customers differently according to their individual requirements and is interested in finding specific rather than general solutions. This kind of corporate culture seeks to forge long-lasting customer relationships and is based on a corporate structure in which decisions are often made by individual employees working very closely with customers.

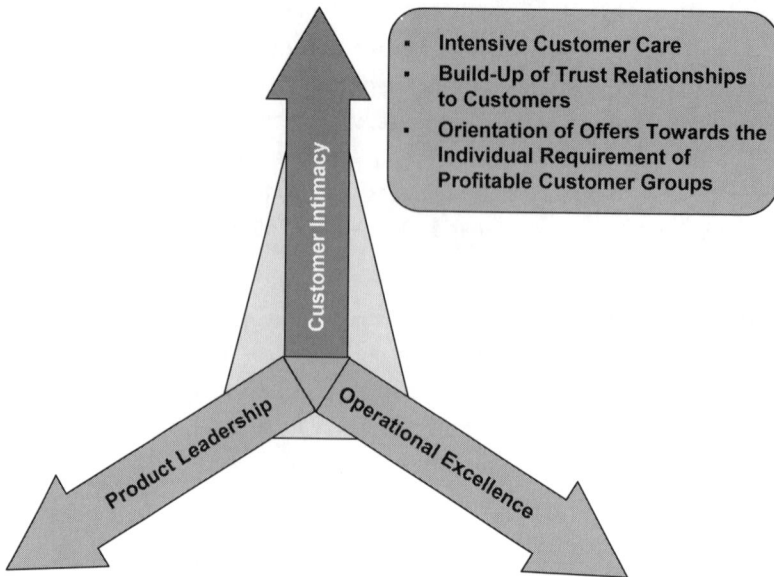

- Intensive Customer Care
- Build-Up of Trust Relationships to Customers
- Orientation of Offers Towards the Individual Requirement of Profitable Customer Groups

Customer Intimacy

Product Leadership

Operational Excellence

Figure 2.4 Market Leadership through Uncompromising Customer Orientation [Peppers 2002]

A close customer relationship, however, does not mean that a company should treat each customer with the same degree of attention. This approach would most likely be counterproductive to the company's success. Companies that derive their competitive advantage through close customer relationships must focus on the more potentially profitable customers to reach their business objectives.

An example of a highly customer-oriented company is the automobile manufacturer Rolls-Royce. Customers who buy a Rolls-Royce want the vehicle to be made according to their wishes. The price of the vehicle is less important. A high amount of manual labor turns each Rolls-Royce into a unique vehicle. The low production figures allow Rolls-Royce to maintain a close relationship with an exclusive clientele. The possible options for the luxurious bodywork far exceed the choices available for engine, finish, interior color, as well as those for additional safety features or technical components. Even more unusual requests, such as an exceptional amount of entertainment electronics or the choice of unique cushioning or upholstery materials, are considered. Therefore, Rolls-Royce does not use web-based self-services that allow potential buyers to generate their own dream cars using a product configurator in a Web shop; instead, they prefer to rely on personal consultation with exclusive customers.

2.2 Relationships Between Value Focus Points

The following chapters show how companies can use successful customer relationship management (CRM) to generate a close relationship with their customers, which can contribute to company success. However, we should not forget that the two other customer-related value disciplines, "product leadership" and "operational excellence," can also profit from good CRM.

The nurturing of customer relationships, which is the starting point for all central business processes, thus becomes even more of an obligation. For example, when a company introduces an integrated, customer-oriented fulfillment system, the internal business processes must be optimized in such a way that reliable statements about deadlines and the ability to deliver can be made.

Such operational reorganization is recognized as a value by the customer and leads to improved customer relationships. The same applies for product leadership. Good CRM and the customer intimacy it brings enable new customer requirements to be recognized earlier and satisfied by suitable products or services more quickly than by other companies. In this way, effective CRM strengthens product leadership and simultaneously boosts customer satisfaction and readiness-to-buy because of superior products.

2.3 Business Focus as a Foundation for Success

Regardless of whether companies obtain their leading positions due to superior products, better operational processes, or closer customer ties, one important quality that market leaders possess is the ability to plan with a strategic focus on particular value disciplines and the ability to pinpoint the measures necessary to implement this plan. This focus can be confirmed by the fact that these companies can deliver clear answers to the following questions [AlphaBrand 2001]:

▶ Who are my customers?

▶ Why do my customers choose my products?

▶ What makes my offer unique for my customers?

▶ Where is my main target market?

▶ Which measures do I need to take and what effort is required to become market leader in the desired target market?

▶ Where are my secondary target markets? What chances of success do I have in these markets?

▶ What is the competition like in each market segment in which my company is active?

- ▶ How does my company differ from the competition?
- ▶ Which internal and external measures are necessary to reach the company goals?

Companies can achieve a leading market position when they are continually able to create an actual value for a well defined target customer group within the market. Prerequisites for defining a target customer group include a detailed knowledge of the customers, their expectations, and their buying habits, and a close relationship with profitable customers and prospects that positively influences their buying behavior.

3 What Is Customer Relationship Management?

"CRM in four words:
Treat different customers differently."
Don Peppers [Peppers 2002]

3.1 The Customer Was Not Always the Focus

Originally, customers were not the focus of company strategies as they are today. If you look back at the last 20 years, you'll see that the way in which companies view their customers has changed dramatically.

In the past, marketing strategies followed a predominantly inside-out approach and concentrated primarily on the products that were offered. Many companies still believe that the most important strategy is to win market share through product-oriented mass-marketing. Profitability and revenue are then generated—one hopes—by themselves through economies of scale. As early as the 80s, the increased competition in global markets and the declining turnovers of companies that relied solely on product-oriented mass-marketing, prompted companies to consider how they could ensure business success in the long term via improved customer relationships and increased orientation towards customer needs [Grönroos 1989]. However, customer satisfaction—initially identified as the factor to be optimized—quickly proved insufficient. Companies can only profit financially from their customers' satisfaction when it leads to loyal buying behavior. In the 90s, this new awareness sparked increased efforts by companies to improve customer loyalty, for example, by implementing customer retention programs with customer cards, customer clubs, and so on [Reicheld 1996, Bruhn/Homburg 2003]. The success of these programs varied considerably [Homburg 2000], one of the reasons being that each customer had his or her own personal wishes and expectations. Eventually, it became apparent that companies could only reach their financial goals with customers if they tailored each individual relationship to reflect the customer's needs by adopting the following measures:

► Personalized customer contact

► Customer-specific product catalog and catalog views

► Customer-specific prices and conditions

► Customer-specific product configuration (mass customization)

► Customer-specific product recommendations

► Customer-specific user interfaces in e-selling solutions

Innovative companies have quickly recognized the transition from seller to buyer markets—created by the globalization of markets and the rise of the Internet—and have implemented this new approach in their customer-oriented business processes.

3.2 Characteristics of Close Customer Relationships

Unlike anonymous, product-oriented mass markets, customer-oriented markets are characterized by close relationships between customers and companies. These relationships can be described as follows:

▶ Both customers and companies benefit measurably from these relationships.

▶ The relationships are iterative in nature. Processing business transactions becomes easier with each transaction. Customers continue to return to a vendor when the vendor makes it as convenient as possible to process recurring business transactions. For example, companies such as Amazon.com offer their registered customers the option to purchase and sell products by entering a minimal amount of information.

▶ Trouble-free relationships create mutual trust. In the course of the relationship, the willingness to disclose personal and sensitive information grows. In this way, vendors gradually become valued and trusted advisors for their customers.

Companies that want to draw long-term financial benefit from close customer relationships need to consider all three aspects listed above.

3.3 One-to-One Marketing and CRM

Since the 1990s, in personalized customer service concepts, the heart of all business activities lies with the individual customers and the information about these customers (see also Section 3.1). Don Peppers and Martha Rogers coined the term *one-to-one marketing* to describe this relationship [Peppers/Rogers 1993]. We use this term in our book in its narrowest sense to refer to e-marketing (see Chapter 9). On the other hand, *customer relationship management* (CRM) has established itself as the generic term for the management of individualized customer relationships. Generally speaking, CRM is a collective term for processes and strategies regarding individualized relationships between enterprises and customers, prospects, and business partners (for marketing, sales, and service) with the goal of winning new customers, extending existing customer relationships across the entire customer life cycle, and improving competitiveness and business success by optimizing the profitability of individualized customer relationships.

3.4 Customer Satisfaction as a Business Objective?

In the heyday of the new economy, many founders of companies thought they could sidestep the principles of classical economics. Semi-plausible business ideas for selling over the Internet were enough to generate risk capital and send share prices through the roof. In many cases, it seemed as if the goal of the company was no longer to be profitable and make profit, but, rather to run the risk of loss, no matter how great.

Today, the picture has changed drastically. Turnover, profitability, and profit have once again become primary business objectives. The close relationships between customer and company, which are discussed here, also must be compared with these goals. Customer satisfaction alone does not create value for a company. Value comes only from profitable business generated as a result of customer satisfaction. In summary, close customer relationships that don't contribute to a company's financial goals are not expedient from a business point of view; they can even incur damaging costs.

3.5 Profitable Customers Are the Difference

"Ten to fifteen percent of the customer base is unprofitable, consisting of buyers who absorb the company's resources and do not provide a return."
[Slywotzky/Morrison 1998]

Customer-specific business services are not free. Companies that want to be successful—as a result of individual customer offers—must make significant investments in business processes, equipment, employee training, and so on. Bearing these costs in mind, you should ask yourself the questions:
"To what extent should individual customer wishes be considered?" and "Should each customer receive the same level of attention?" Ultimately, it is these questions—regarding profitable or potentially profitable customers—that can determine the future success or failure of the company.

Therefore, companies should be able to answer critical questions about their customer strategies [Simkovits 1998], especially regarding the company's business goals, such as:

▶ Should we convert each prospect into a customer?
▶ Should we offer each prospect the full range of products and services available?
▶ Should we offer each customer the same product quality with the same level of service?
▶ Should we use all means available to satisfy and retain each customer?

Companies that can answer several of these questions in the affirmative are in a good position to attract many customers and prospects. However, these companies may unnecessarily commit company resources, thereby foregoing possible profit, and thus, potentially jeopardizing the success of the company. This potential loss of profit can be avoided if the truly profitable or potentially profitable customers can be identified and all company activities are directed only towards this target group. According to Adrian Slywotzky and David Morrison in their bestseller *The Profit Zone* [Slywotzky/Morrison 1998], the best advice is:

> *"Understand what's most important to customers and where your company can make a profit with them; then work to gain market share in that finite arena."*

3.6   CRM as a Strategic Business Task

"CRM success lies in strategy and implementation, not in software."
Gartner Group [Hagemeyer/Nelson 2003]

"Customer-specific action requires the enterprise to modify its organization, processes, and metrics."
Don Peppers [Peppers 2002]

The goal of modern day customer relationship management is to win new customers, extend existing customer relationships, and increase competitiveness and company profitability. For this to happen, all communication channels and business transactions with each customer must be personalized in such a way that only the "shop around the corner" could otherwise do. Therefore, CRM is more than just software-supported process automation in marketing, sales, service, and management. It is also more than a collection of methods on how to increase the efficiency of this process. Customer relationship management for a company means being well-informed and being able to interact with profitable or potentially profitable customers while taking their individual needs into consideration.

In this way, CRM is a business philosophy and is in no way limited to the implementation of any particular kind of CRM software solution (see Chapter 4). The successful anchoring of customer relationship management in a company is based on the coordinated interplay of the following elements (see also [Homburg 2000, Radcliffe 2001, Hagemeyer/Nelson 2003]):

▶ A business vision for CRM that considers value optimization not just for the company, but for the customers, employees, and business partners

▶ A corporate strategy for realizing the CRM vision

▶ An organizational culture that anchors customer orientation as a value within the company and in the attitude and behavior of the employees

- The organizational realization of the CRM business strategy as a company-wide task with business processes whose goal is to satisfy individual customer needs that transcend departments
- A powerful CRM software solution with an appropriate technical system landscape
- Information logistics ensures that all CRM information is consistent and easily accessible to the employees concerned
- Customer data belongs to the company and must not be buried in the heads or hidden in the notebooks of its employees
- The introduction of metrics and processes to determine the success of the implementation of the CRM business strategy

Experiences from many CRM implementation projects (see Chapter 13) show that the potential to improve company results through customer relationship management can only be fully realized by a comprehensive company initiative that includes all these aspects we have named thus far.

3.7 Data Protection Creates Trust

Personalized customer relationship management is based on the founding principle of treating different people individually. This applies both to private customers (Business-to-Consumer, B2C) as well as to business buyers (Business-to-Business, B2B). To reach this goal, individual data about each person must be entered and stored. It is imperative that this data be protected against any misuse so as not to endanger the success of a CRM initiative. Only if customers can be assured that their personal data is protected and their privacy is respected will they be willing to disclose the data required for successful customer relationship management.

Companies should therefore go to great lengths to show their customers that they take data protection very seriously. To do this, we recommend that you produce a written and binding commitment to respect customer privacy, which also informs customers how their personal data will be used and furthermore, explains that no personal information will be passed on to third parties. In addition, companies can use certificates from non-profit organizations such as TRUSTe (Trusted Universal Standards in Electronic Transactions), BBBOnLine (Council of Better Business Bureaus), or Euro-Label to ensure that they have made their data protection policy universally accessible and that adherence to this policy is being monitored by these organizations.

Don Peppers, one of the leading authorities on CRM, gave the following advice regarding data protection [Rageth 1999]:

1. First, you must determine what information about individuals should be recorded (economy of data collection).

2. Furthermore, you must define how this information is to be used.

3. An assurance by your company regarding how this information will not be used will generate additional trust on the part of your customers.

4. Everyone should be informed of the benefits he or she will receive by having the data recorded. This includes the following points:

   ▶ Faster service

   ▶ Lower costs

   ▶ Personalized offer

5. All users should be shown how to preserve their data protection interests and how to minimize the risk of their data being misused.

6. Another factor to consider is that individuals can modify personal data that has been saved.

7. It should also be explained in which circumstances people are to be notified regarding such critical occurrences as mandates, hacker attacks, and other possible violations of their personal data.

8. It is vital to name an employee as the person responsible for ensuring data security within the company so that customers can contact that person in the event of questions or problems.

9. Companies should also define situations in which they accept or reject responsibility for damages that resulted from a breach in data protection.

10. Everyone should know how to prevent someone else from accessing his or her data, or how to delete personal data if necessary.

Even company employees can, intentionally or unintentionally, contravene data protection regulations. Therefore, adequate measures that affect company employees are also important. These measures include funded employee training on how to deal with sensitive data and an organizational decision as to which employees in which role are entitled to access personal data.

At the end of the day, all questions about data security must be satisfactorily answered. In particular, all necessary precautions must be taken to prevent the loss of, fraudulent use of, or unauthorized access to stored personal data (compare [Eckert 2003]).

4 Software Solutions for Customer Relationship Management

4.1 Value Expectations of the Company

In a study conducted by the Gartner Group market research institute [see Nelson 2000], companies named the following goals as instrumental in their decision to introduce a CRM software solution to support customer relationship management:

▶ Increase in sales

▶ Increase in profitability

▶ Improved customer loyalty

▶ Achievement of competitive advantages

▶ Reduction in costs

▶ Access to new customer communication channels (contact channels)

The primary challenge companies face when introducing a CRM solution is to achieve these goals through the balanced interplay between CRM information technology, CRM company strategy, and organizational measures.

Studies, however, have shown that a too strong internal view during the motivation and introduction of CRM is counterproductive [Nelson/Eisenfeld 2002]. Ultimately, what matters most is creating win-win situations with value optimization for all concerned, that is, for companies, business partners (customers, suppliers, marketing, sales, and service partners), and employees. For example, you need to know that the implementation of a sales force automation solution—with its goal of offering management improved reporting and evaluation possibilities—is less important from a customer or employee perspective. On the other hand, the introduction of an efficient call center solution—with its potential to reduce customer waiting times and enable customer questions to be answered faster and more accurately by trained specialists—offers direct value for everyone involved. Lastly, the increased customer and employee satisfaction that results because of the implemented CRM solution directly helps the company to achieve its business objectives.

4.2 Value Optimization in Integrated, Dynamic Relationship Networks

Customer relationship management, production, and purchasing can no longer be viewed as isolated company activities. Value creating processes have changed since the start of the 90s, driven by globalization of competition and the increasing networking between companies and business partners. Individual customer requirements became the starting point of extensive value chains, and collaboration between companies became a decisive success factor. Nowadays, buying and selling processes can be combined across companies, where both procurement activities on the buyer's side (up until goods receipt and payment) and order processing on the seller's side (up until delivery and settlement) run completely automated and are mirrored in connected software systems.

> A customer calls the car manufacturer of the car he ordered a few days prior, because he now wants more expensive car seats. The customer is connected to the call center. In order to answer the customer's questions, the call center employee needs the customer data and the order data, which are in separate databases. A supply chain management (SCM) system is used to check whether it is still possible to fit different car seats. Because the order can still be changed, the new car seats are ordered, and this new data is sent to the car seat supplier.

By using innovative solutions to manage the entire logistics chain, companies can integrate their customers, sales partners, and suppliers in a virtual, customer-centric process network. Individual customer requirements trigger extensive business processes during which the software systems involved exchange relevant information such as demand, forecasts, availability of stock, and production capacity in real time. Two core company tasks—maintenance of customer relationships and optimization of logistic chains—become more and more intertwined and can no longer be viewed as independent processes as they were a few years ago.

Because value processes now increasingly occur in dynamic company and relationship networks, an adequate relationship management is required, which in turn yields a new view of software solutions that support the operational processes connected with these relationships (see Figure 4.1). The current trend is moving towards the development of integrated solutions as part of the further development and combination of specialized relationship management software solutions for CRM (customer relationship management), SRM (supplier relationship management), PRM (partner relationship management), and ERM (employee relationship management). These solutions—in close connection with powerful ERP (enterprise resource planning) and SCM systems—allow mutual value optimization for companies, business partners, and employees to be placed at the center of the company strategy (Value Optimization for the Extended Enterprise, see also [Kumar 2001, Zencke 2002]). Only the seamless access, for example, from the CRM system to real-time data of the ERP and SCM systems—in other words, to stock levels, production capacities, payment behavior of individual customers, or to the business partners' ability to deliver—makes it possible to overcome the operational insecurities that are inextricably tied to an isolated front-office system. One example of this is the processing of marketing campaigns (front office), which can be successful only if the demand generated is synchronized with the availability data (back office).

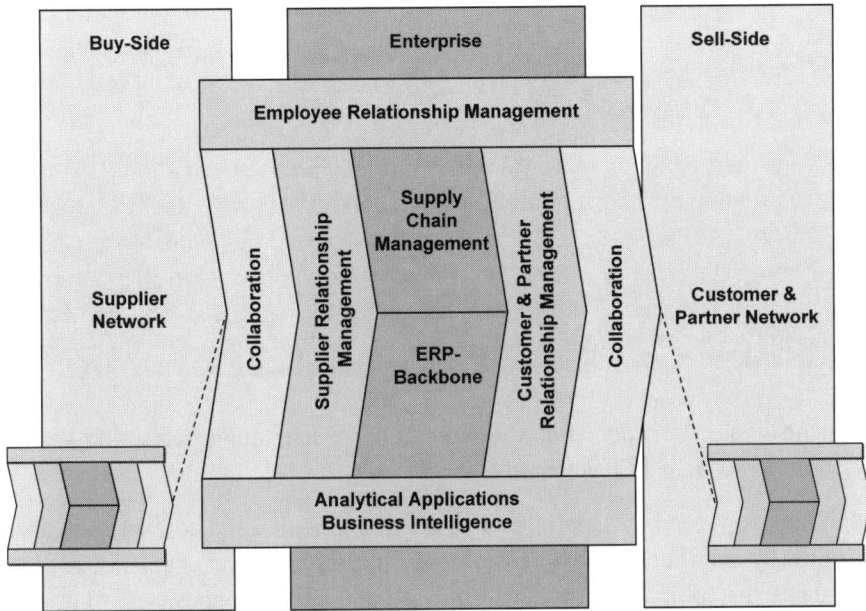

Figure 4.1 Value Optimization in Dynamic Relationship Networks

4.2.1 Integration Example: Sales

The first CRM software solutions of the 90s, which were often marketed under the name of SFA (Sales Force Automation)—also known as CAS (computer-aided selling) in Germany—focused on supporting sales employees with their daily work in the following areas:

▶ Contact management

▶ Management of sales activities

▶ Management of opportunities (new sales possibilities)

▶ Analyses

▶ Product and customer information

In particular, information management for field sales employees, who are constantly on the move and cannot always access the company network, needed improvement. It is only in recent years that people have realized how important it is to view sales not as an isolated area, but rather as an area that is connected to all other business units, which are also in constant customer contact. To a certain extent, marketing and service departments have the same need for information and deliver important background information for the sales employees.

After a detailed analysis, the marketing department of the company PC4YOU began a price reduction campaign to improve the market position of product 4711. The marketing department's collaboration with sales, however, occurs only at the management level.

The sales representative Mike Smith has carefully prepared for a long-planned visit to an important customer to close a contract for product 4722. Only at the start of his talks does he realize that the customer would like to learn more about product 4711, having been convinced of this product's worth by a report in a marketing brochure. Mike, however, cannot say anything about the value of this product.

This kind of situation demands the integration of marketing, sales, and service functions in advanced CRM systems.

Although a big step has been taken by integrating people and software solutions that directly communicate with customers and prospects, this is still not enough to provide the company with a well-rounded and homogeneous view of its customers. In fact, even the company areas that don't have any customer contact must be involved in customer relationship management, because their contribution is also critical to sales success.

Let us assume that the company PC4YOU has introduced a recognized CRM system. Marketing, sales, and service applications were successfully integrated. Of course, Mike knows about the campaign for product 4711 and is suitably prepared. The deal is closed. However, later PC4YOU cannot deliver on time because a supplier, unexpectedly, couldn't provide the necessary number of units.

The second example shows that sales can only truly act in a customer-oriented manner if it is integrated with SCM systems. This means that, during the acceptance of an order, an availability check along the entire logistics chain can be performed in real time to determine the possible delivery date.

4.3 Four Basic Requirements of CRM Software Solutions

In the past, CRM software solutions that were designed as general, front-office applications were often unable to meet a company's high expectations. Eventually, it became clear that CRM software solutions had to meet both individual and industry-specific requirements, as well as ensure tight integration with back-end systems. Experience has given credence to the belief that a successful CRM solution must be built on a broader foundation that considers the following basic company requirements:

▶ Integration with the other company applications, such as ERP and SCM

▶ Focus on the end user's needs

▶ Support of cross-company collaboration

▶ Alignment with the specific requirements of individual industries

These four pillars of CRM software solutions are also known as *connected CRM, people-centric CRM, collaborative CRM,* and *industry-specific CRM.*

4.3.1 Connected CRM

Companies that assume that customers maintain only marginal relationships to sales representatives or the service department are wrong. Customer relationships span the entire company! All company areas and communication channels must interact to provide customers with a uniform, synchronized view of the company. Front-end and back-end information must be directly available to serve customers individually. In this respect, front office and back office combine to form one office.

4.3.2 People-Centric CRM

The acceptance of the CRM software solution by the end user is of paramount importance for the success of CRM projects. Many CRM implementation projects have failed by underestimating the importance of this requirement. End users— employees as well as customers—who don't discern any recognizable benefit to their work from a CRM software solution, don't use the system in the way in which it was intended by management. An intuitive, easy-to-learn user interface that allows end users to perform their individual work faster, more efficiently, and with less effort can pave the way for wider user acceptance.

4.3.3 Collaborative CRM

In CRM solutions, integration does not simply mean the combination of product data and end-user information; for example, it also implies the close linkage of business processes both within the company and across company boundaries, such as with sales partners and suppliers. By using shared customer data, company-wide business processes can be handled efficiently.

4.3.4 Industry-Specific CRM

Taking customer orientation seriously also means paying attention to the individual customer and company requirements from each industry. Service provider customers have different requirements from those of an industrial manufacturing company. Individual industries differ specifically in the products they produce (mass products, configurable products, services, and so on) and in the characteristics of their preferred distribution channels. CRM software vendors should recognize these differences and take them into account in their solutions.

4.4 Structure of CRM Software Solutions

CRM software solutions must have functions to address all phases of the customer relationship, from generating buying interest (Engage), to the sales (Transact) and fulfillment process (Fulfill), and finally to service (see Figure 4.2). The solutions must support various customer communication channels and encompass the basic requirements descibed in Section 4.3. For clarification, we have classified the following CRM functions into the sub-areas *operational CRM*, *analytical CRM*, and *collaborative CRM*.

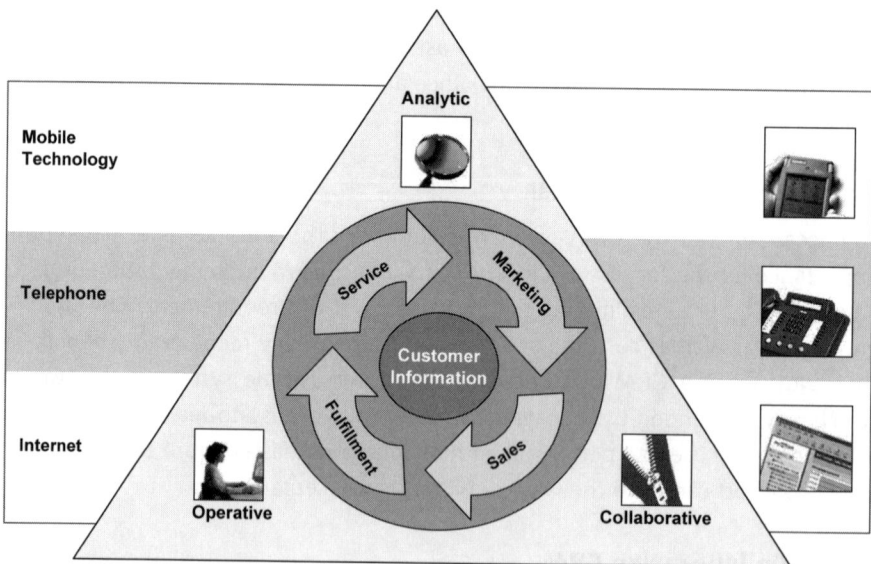

Figure 4.2 Operational, Analytical, and Collaborative CRM Across All Phases of the Customer Relationship

4.4.1 Operational CRM

Operational CRM supports the business processes that are directly aimed at the customer in the areas of marketing, sales, service, and company management.

Marketing applications simplify, for example, the planning of marketing activities and the execution of marketing campaigns, and therefore lay the foundations for identifying prospective buyers (lead generation). To also be able to address specific customer requirements, the sales market must be split into customer segments in which particular products and services can be offered. Trade promotion management serves, in particular, sales and merchandising promotions in the consumer goods industry.

Sales applications concentrate on the planning of sales activities and the management of quotations, orders, and purchasing and leasing contracts. The goal of sales is to guide qualified leads to the dotted line of the contract (opportunity management). To this end, sales employees in each region maintain customer relationships and agree on deadlines for customer contracts. The starting points for negotiations stem from either the product price or from changes to the product specification. If a contract is signed and if it is necessary, sales initiates the delivery, the invoicing, as well as the processing of payments or reminders, and calculates the commission earned on the contract.

Service applications support the processing of service queries and requests that occur after the contract is signed, either as part of a service contract or due to a customer complaint. Services carried out are invoiced, which includes the processing costs for payments and the processing of reminders. In the planning and forecasting of demand for service employees, both service contracts as well as complaint management data are used. When solving problems, the maintenance and management of customer installation data helps, as do solution databases that document known difficulties and how to solve them.

The operational daily business of CRM is no longer limited to receiving customer calls and producing written responses to questions and requested offers. Instead, marketing, sales, and service employees use all available *communication channels* and proactively approach potential prospects and existing customers. Interaction center agents carry out telephone-based telemarketing campaigns, distribute products via telesales activities, and answer service queries as part of the help desk. Field employees are equipped with mobile devices and use mobile marketing applications (for example, in the context of trade promotion management), sales applications from sales force automation, and service components, for example, to carry out inventories of replacement parts in a service vehicle. The Internet has a permanent place as a 24-hour communication channel.

Management uses the figures from the operational areas to carry out continuous planning for finance, sales, and resources that is aligned with customer needs. The current key performance indicators (KPIs) and their comparison with planned values form the basis for management decision-making. Here, non-monetary factors come into play which, with the help of multidimensional controlling tools such as the balanced scorecard (BSC) [Kaplan/Norton 1996], can be combined with monetary values to create an aggregated performance measurement system.

4.4.2 Analytical CRM

Analytical CRM aids the preparation, support, and optimization of customer-oriented decision processes—internally and externally. "Do the right thing" is the motto here. The basis for this is a detailed customer database in connection with data warehouse and OLAP (online analytical processing) functions, as well as further planning, optimization, and simulation functions. The goal of analytical CRM is to gain a solid understanding of customer satisfaction and possible future customer behavior, to deliver the basis for decision-making in sales and marketing, to support customer-related planning, and to optimize operational processes such as marketing and promotion activities. In this sense, analytical CRM does not constitute a specific application for selected employees, rather, it is a daily tool for everyone involved with customer-oriented processes.

Typical evaluations and key figures that analytical CRM applications might deliver as the basis for strategic business decisions include:

▶ Market share

▶ Number of customers

▶ List of customers generating the most revenue

▶ List of most profitable customers

▶ Satisfaction index (key figure for customer satisfaction)

▶ Loyalty index (key figure for the extent of customer ties to the company)

▶ Customer retention rate (proportion of customers who return to buy from the company)

▶ Share of customer potential (share of wallet, proportion of total company expenditure used for a particular product group)

▶ Rate of return (reaction rate of target group to particular marketing measures)

▶ Customer-specific key figures, such as customer lifetime value (total value that can be gained from one customer), which is used to direct marketing and sales activities at the right customers, for example

The key figures and methods of analytical CRM create a sound basis for predicting, planning, measuring, and optimizing all customer-centric business processes.

4.4.3 Collaborative CRM

Collaborative or cross-company CRM enables companies, business partners, and customers to work together in the areas of marketing, sales, and service. Examples of technical platforms for this kind of collaboration include the Internet and electronic marketplaces. Examples of collaborative scenarios supported by CRM software solutions are Internet-based processes for e-marketing, e-selling, and e-service, as well as channel management and distributed order management.

E-marketing focuses on the introduction of new products to the market (product launch) with the close collaboration of manufacturers, traders, market research companies, and customers. E-marketing also looks at the planning and execution of marketing campaigns together with marketing service providers. These collaborative partners provide personalized product demos and training on the Internet, offer a platform for online chats, and support virtual communities of customers, suppliers, and business partners (Internet communities).

E-selling is directed either as a B2B scenario (Business-to-Business sales process) to business customers or in B2C sales (Business-to-Consumer sales process) to consumers. B2B sales connects customer and supplier fulfillment systems and optimizes the processes via direct data exchange and interactive query functions between the sales process (quotation, order, bill of delivery, goods issue, invoice, receipt of payment) on the supplier side and the complementary buying process (request, order, goods receipt, invoice check, payment order) on the buyer side. B2C scenarios are personalized self-services for customers with interactive services for catalog search, product configuration, availability check, price determination, and order status check. Collaborative sales processes involving customers, traders, and manufacturers enable, for example, customer-specific product design or mutual processing of key accounts by manufacturers and traders.

The collaboration in the area of *e-service* ranges from the provision of online services as self-service offers, to running a joint solution database, to collaborative processing of customer complaints by service providers, traders, and manufacturers.

Channel management helps to build up and maintain indirect customer sales channels through sale traders, resellers, distribution centers, service providers, marketplace providers, hosting and outsourcing partners, and so on (see Chapter 11). Functions for partner selection, registration, analysis, and monitoring help to find the right partners and to measure their contribution to the company's success.

Sales partners, for example, receive access to jointly-used customer, prospect, product, and marketing information, or specific partner training units.

Extended order management enables the coordination of orders across all software systems involved. One can no longer assume that orders are processed using a single, central fulfillment system. On the contrary, increasingly used are several fulfillment systems linked together in one comprehensive relationship network, spanning companies, branches, and business partners (see Section 7.4.9).

4.5 Industry- and Country-Specific Configurations

"The vertical market will get 'white hot.'"
Gartner Group [Nelson/Marcus 2002]

The core philosophy of customer relationship management is to optimize company profitability by building up and maintaining personalized relationships with individual customers. After various CRM software vendors tried to reach this goal in the past by adopting a generic approach, it has been accepted in recent years that industry-specific requirements need to be considered when building up individual customer relationships. This applies to the following three categories:

▶ Support of the typical products for a particular industry

▶ Support of the distribution channels used by the particular branch

▶ Support of the industry-specific, customer-oriented business processes

In addition to providing support for these industry-specific requirements is the need for integration with industry-specific back-end systems, for example, for meter billing in energy providers or financial calculations in banks and insurance companies.

To get closer to reaching the goal of industry-specific CRM software solutions, it is not enough merely to enhance a generic software product with a few superficial industry-specific characteristics. What is needed is a solid understanding of industry-specific processes that can be implemented in the software.

Industry analysts agree that industry-specific configurations for CRM software solutions will determine the market in the years to come. We have already seen that generic CRM solutions are often insufficient. A financial institution's customers simply have different service requirements than supermarket shoppers, or employees of a public authority.

Along with the industry-specific configuration of CRM software solutions, the consideration of different country requirements plays a large role in customer relationship management. In addition to formalities such as supporting local languages, currencies, and units of measure, this also means observing local business practices including country laws for invoicing and tax calculation (see also Sections 14.8.3 and 15.6.1).

For a detailed representation of industry-specific customer-oriented business processes, please refer to [Buck-Emden/Böder 2004].

4.6 The Market for CRM Software Solutions

"...there are clear benefits to buying CRM from an ERP vendor."
Forrester Research [Schmitt/Walker/Dorsey 2002]

"Enterprise suites will dominate CRM spending."
Gartner Group [Thompson/Radcliffe 2003]

The CRM software solution vendors of today come from quite different development backgrounds, which are still reflected in their products:

▶ The first CRM software solutions were created with the goal of supporting field sales employees. In those days, the term *sales force automation (SFA)* was coined. The pioneer and leading vendor in this area was the company Siebel [Siebel/Malone 1996].

▶ Even the vendors of call center solutions (*customer interaction center, interaction center*) recognized the need for individualized customer relationships early on, and therefore, developed more extensive CRM software solutions. An example of this is the former Nortel subsidiary Clarify, which is now part of the company Amdocs.

▶ An important part of CRM is the evaluation and analysis of all data relevant to optimizing customer relationships. Some vendors of analysis software, such as Teradata/NCR, are now enhancing their products step-by-step to become more extensive CRM software solutions.

▶ Even vendors of e-commerce solutions who use the Internet to introduce and sell products are striving to enhance their products with additional CRM functionality. However, pure e-commerce solutions without close integration with the value chain, which stretches from supply to transport logistics, have often failed. Examples of vendors of pure e-commerce solutions are Intershop and Broadvision.

▶ Finally, vendors of company-wide ERP software solutions such as Oracle, PeopleSoft, and SAP, have enhanced their extensive business application suites with powerful CRM front-office functions and can now offer their customers an integrated solution for all aspects of business data processing. These integrated solutions offer the user the following advantages:

- Harmonized, uniform business solutions, which seamlessly connect the front-office applications to the back-office applications, including order processing, reporting, and human resources management
- Controllable project costs and project runtimes with considerably less integration effort when compared with best-of-breed solutions

The market for CRM solutions as a whole will continue to grow in the coming years, because, unlike business back-end solutions, all-encompassing CRM solutions are implemented only in a few companies. Market analysts from Current Analysis [Spang 2000] estimated in the year 2000 that only 5% of potential CRM software customers were implementing CRM solutions. The market research institute Gartner Group [Topolinski/Eschinger/Kumar 2002] expects the global market for CRM solutions to grow at an average rate of 9.8%, from 3.7 to 6 billion U.S. dollars from 2002 to 2006, thereby becoming the fastest-growing segment for enterprise software.

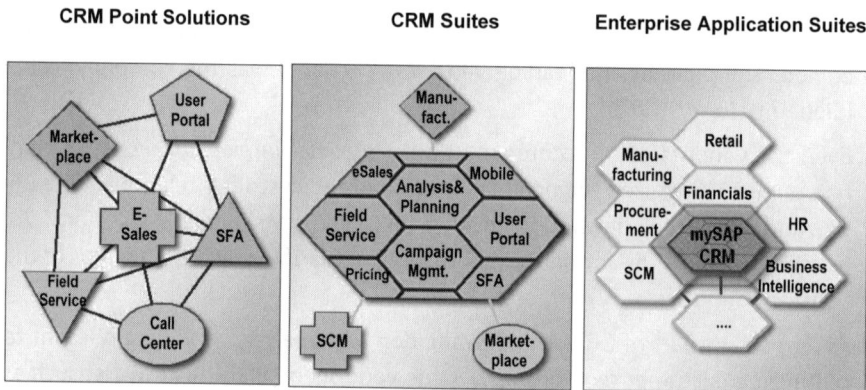

CRM Point Solutions   **CRM Suites**   **Enterprise Application Suites**

Figure 4.3 CRM Solutions from CRM Point Solutions, CRM Suites, and Enterprise Application Suites Vendors

Currently on the vendor side, the market for CRM solutions can be divided as follows (see Figure 4.3):

- Specialized vendors that sell products for particular application areas (sales force automation), for particular markets (small and medium-sized businesses), or for selected industries (CRM *point solutions*)
- Vendors of extensive front-office solution packages for customer relationship management (*CRM suite vendors*)
- Software companies that have been creating business application solutions for many years and offer CRM as part of their solution platform (*enterprise application suite vendors*)

Important CRM software vendors are currently the CRM suite specialist Siebel, the enterprise application suite vendor SAP, Oracle, and PeopleSoft, as well as, Microsoft (in particular, for smaller and medium-sized businesses), and the CRM point solution vendors, Onyx and Pivotal.

Since the introduction of a CRM software solution is a long-term investment, a company should ensure that its software vendor is a stable company that can guarantee the maintenance and further development of its software throughout the software life cycle. It is the smaller, more specialized CRM software vendors that are endangered. In the coming years, market observers expect a significant shift in CRM software investments in favor of enterprise application suite vendors [Thompson/Radcliffe 2003].

5 mySAP CRM — Customer Relationship Management as Part of the Integrated mySAP Business Suite

"Customer Relationship Management is [...] starting to merge with such closely related applications as Supply Chain Management and Enterprise Resource Planning."
Gartner Group [Nelson/Comport 2003]

5.1 Enterprise Services Architecture

Isolated solutions for customer relationship management or logistics management, however powerful they may be, are not enough to map and optimize cross-application and cross-system business processes completely. Companies need applications that integrate seamlessly with others and enable system users to access information and functions required through a standardized interface. The implementation, administration, and customizing of these cross-application and cross-system processes represent a great challenge.

SAP has met these challenges with the service-oriented concept of Enterprise Services Architecture (ESA, see Figure 5.1), which addresses all levels of integrated application solutions, that is:

▶ Business scenarios and processes (business solutions)

▶ Business applications

▶ Integration and application infrastructure

▶ Computing infrastructure

For an in-depth description of ESA, please see [Woods 2003a]. We will concentrate on those aspects of Enterprise Services Architecture that affect mySAP CRM, in particular, the associated business scenarios, processes, business applications, and the integration and application structure.

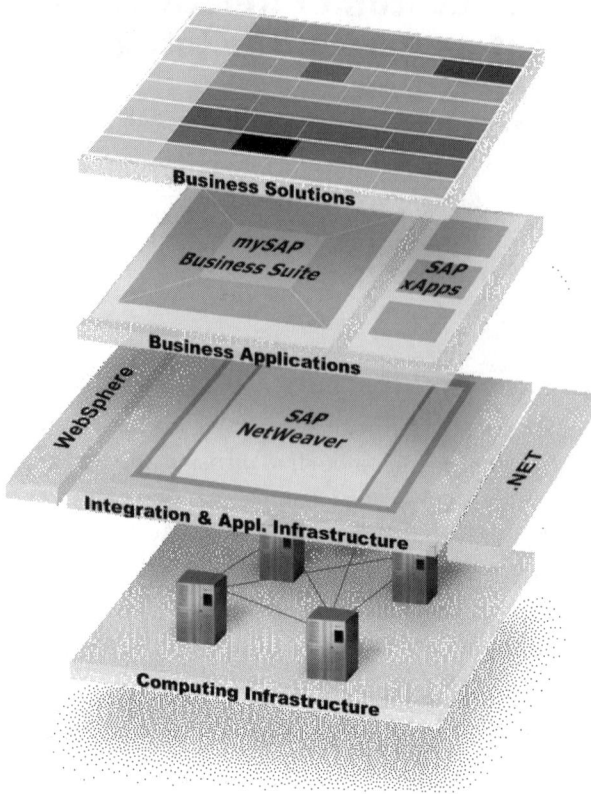

Figure 5.1 Enterprise Services Architecture (ESA)

5.2 Business Applications at SAP

The mySAP Business Suite comprises the large, cross-industry SAP business application solutions (see Figure 5.2). The following SAP business applications are also available:

- ▶ More than 20 industry-specific solutions
- ▶ mySAP All-in-One and SAP Business One as solutions for medium-sized businesses and subsidiaries (SAP Smart Business Solutions)
- ▶ New, cross-application solutions based on software services (SAP xApps)

All SAP solutions (with the exception of SAP Business One) run on the integration and application platform SAP NetWeaver (see Chapter 14).

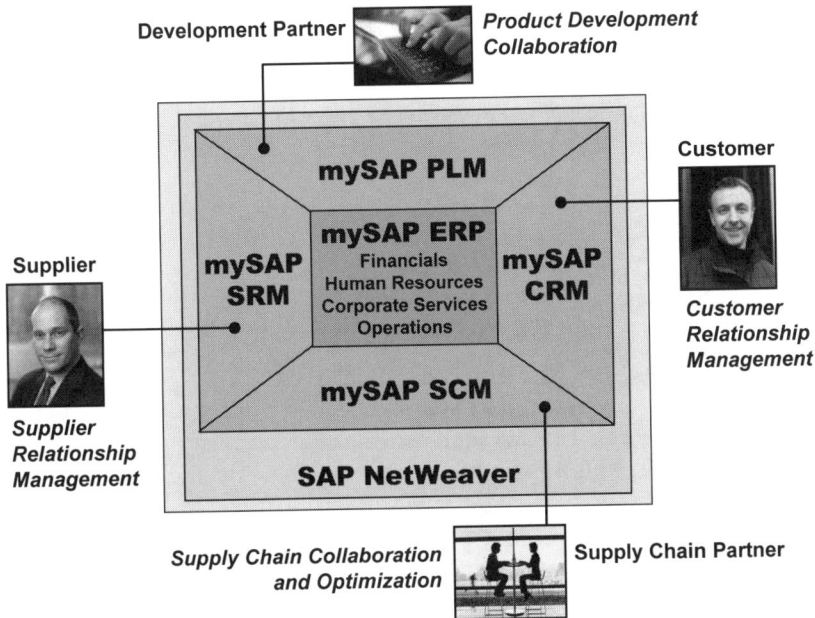

Figure 5.2 The mySAP Business Suite

5.2.1 Cross-Industry Solutions

The following company requirements are covered by the cross-industry solutions of mySAP Business Suite:

▶ **mySAP Customer Relationship Management**
Customer-centric services for planning, creating, and maintaining customer relationships, giving particular consideration to new possibilities using the Internet, mobile devices, and multi-channel interaction. mySAP Customer Relationship Management (mySAP CRM) supports customer interaction in all phases of the customer interaction cycle—from first contact to closing the deal and on to order management and follow-on services. To enable analytical evaluations, mySAP CRM is tightly connected with mySAP Business Intelligence (mySAP BI) and integrates the functions of SAP Business Information Warehouse (SAP BW).

▶ **mySAP Supply Chain Management**
With mySAP Supply Chain Management (mySAP SCM), customers, manufacturers, distribution partners, and suppliers can be included in cross-company logistics chains (see Figure 5.3). mySAP SCM delivers transparency for stock, orders, forecasts, production planning, and performance key figures, which improves customer service (on-time delivery, online availability of order status

information, and so on), manufacturing efficiency, the ability to react to changes in demand, order processing time, and the amount of manufacturing capacity. The planning and optimizing component, SAP Advanced Planner and Optimizer (SAP APO), is a core component of mySAP SCM.

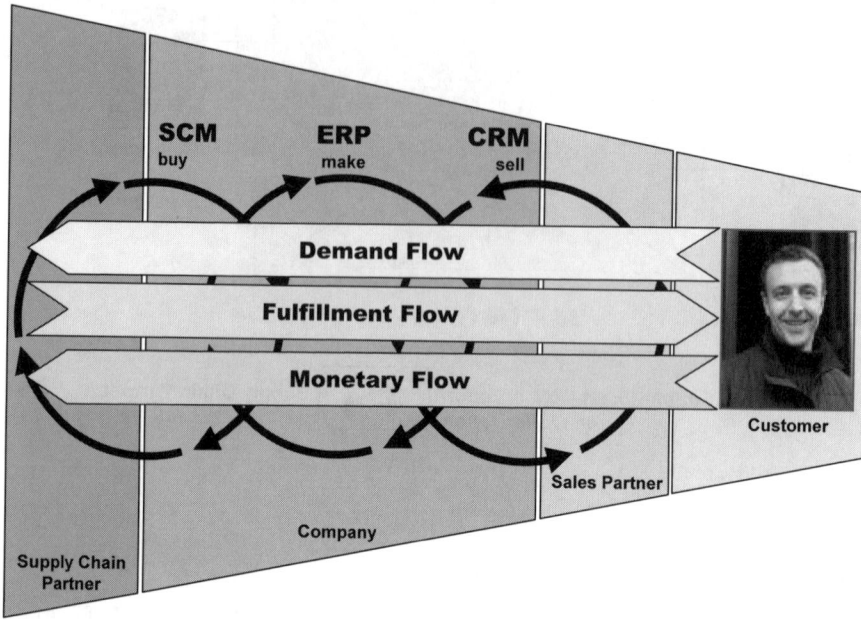

Figure 5.3 CRM as the Starting Point for Central Company Processes

▶ **mySAP Product Lifecycle Management**
mySAP Product Lifecycle Management (mySAP PLM) is SAP's solution for cross-company product planning, product development, and asset management on the basis of common product and project data. All parties involved in product development, service, and maintenance—such as product designers, suppliers, manufacturers, and customers—are provided with one simple point of entry for all relevant product information.

▶ **mySAP Supplier Relationship Management**
mySAP Supplier Relationship Management (mySAP SRM) is a comprehensive and integrated solution for both ad-hoc and strategic procurement in the B2B area. Based on the Enterprise Buyer procurement solution, mySAP SRM delivers functionality for purchasing direct and indirect goods. Buyers can use Enterprise Buyer to purchase products and services from their PC directly over the Internet. A simple connection to electronic marketplaces is also ensured.

▶ **mySAP Business Intelligence**

mySAP Business Intelligence is SAP's solution for collecting and managing internal and external data. Its goal is to transfer this into business knowledge using data warehouse and analysis tools. mySAP BI consists of the components SAP BW, SAP Strategic Enterprise Management (SAP SEM), and SAP Knowledge Management (SAP KM). The components of mySAP BI are tightly integrated with mySAP CRM.

▶ **mySAP Enterprise Resource Planning**

mySAP Enterprise Resource Planning (mySAP ERP) offers companies an all-encompassing solution for accounting, human resource management, business management, and company-internal services. SAP R/3 Enterprise, the latest version of SAP R/3, is an integral part of mySAP ERP, as are the functions of the SAP solutions mySAP Human Resources (mySAP HR) and mySAP Financials (mySAP FI). mySAP HR and mySAP FI are the well-known standard SAP solutions for all human resource management and financial reporting requirements (as compared with, for example [Brinkmann/Zeilinger 2000, Lübke/Ringling 2004]). Both are tightly connected with mySAP CRM, for example, for dealing with workforce management or invoicing issues.

▶ **mySAP Mobile Business**

With mySAP Mobile Business, the mySAP Business Suite breaks away from the world of desktop PCs and local networks. Mobile devices, such as laptops or handheld devices, allow users to access all solutions of the mySAP Business Suite at any time and from any place. mySAP Mobile Business is the basis for the mobile mySAP CRM applications. Examples of mySAP Mobile Business are:

▶ Mobile CRM (field sales and field service employees)

▶ Mobile Business Intelligence (mobile access to analysis and data warehouse information)

▶ Mobile Procurement (direct purchasing for employees in the field)

▶ Mobile Travel Management (access for mobile employees with central travel management services)

▶ **mySAP Enterprise Portal**

mySAP Enterprise Portal is SAP's customizable, role-based enterprise portal for all users along the length of the value chain. An easy-to-understand, easy-to-use, and easy-to-customize browser interface enables users to access all company-internal and company-external information, as well as applications and services that they need in their personal work environment. The screen layout of mySAP Enterprise Portal is tailored to the individual user role in the company. Each user can have more than one role and can switch between these roles as required.

▶ **mySAP Marketplace**

mySAP Marketplace is a complete infrastructure for building virtual, electronic marketplaces that can serve as platforms for processing Internet-based business transactions within virtual buyer and seller communities. These marketplaces are a prerequisite for dynamic n:m business relationships instead of static 1:1 contacts between predefined business partners. mySAP Marketplace supports electronic auctions, automated bid invitations, sourcing, procurement by self-service, as well as catalog and content management.

Users access mySAP Marketplace from mySAP Enterprise Portal. The purchasing and selling systems connected to mySAP Marketplace are connected by open interfaces in XML (Extensible Markup Language).

Finally, we should also mention SAP R/3 Enterprise, the current software version for existing SAP R/3 customers and a core component of the mySAP ERP solution. Company-internal processes, such as human resource management, accounting, product development, or inventory management, are mapped in SAP R/3 Enterprise. SAP R/3 Enterprise is seamlessly integrated with other solutions of the mySAP Business Suite, for example, with mySAP CRM.

SAP R/3 Enterprise consists of three large functionality areas:

▶ Functionality from the previous release (SAP R/3 4.6C), combined in SAP R/3 Enterprise Core

▶ Functional enhancements that are packaged in SAP R/3 Enterprise Extensions

▶ The technological platform SAP NetWeaver which, along with a stable application server, offers tools for integrating people, information, and processes

Unlike earlier SAP R/3 versions, SAP R/3 Enterprise is based on the new technology *SAP NetWeaver*. Moreover, it offers a flexible enhancement concept thanks to SAP R/3 Enterprise Extensions. Although the application kernel of SAP R/3 Enterprise is mostly unchanged when compared to the previous versions—notwithstanding the enhancement of current legal regulations regarding the American requirements for handicapped-accessible software (Rehabilitation Act Section 508)—new functionality is delivered in the form of additional enhancement packages, which can be activated individually. These enhancements are available for the following application areas:

▶ Human resource management (HR)

▶ Travel management (TM)

▶ Accounting (FI)

▶ Product development/Product Lifecycle Management (PLM)

▶ Logistics (SCM)

Another new development with SAP R/3 Enterprise is the ability to group individual configuration settings in logical units, *business configuration sets*, which can be easily transferred to other SAP R/3 systems within the company. The company-wide roll-out of SAP R/3 Enterprise across all areas thus becomes significantly easier.

5.2.2 Industry Solutions

Alongside the mySAP Business Suite, SAP offers specialized solutions with specific business processes and functions for more than 20 industries *(industry solutions)*.

The following industry solutions are currently available:

▶ **Discrete industries**

  ▶ SAP for Aerospace and Defense

  ▶ SAP for Automotive

  ▶ SAP for Engineering, Construction, and Operation

  ▶ SAP for Industrial Machinery and Components

  ▶ SAP for High Tech

▶ **Process industries**

  ▶ SAP for Chemicals

  ▶ SAP for Mill Products

  ▶ SAP for Pharmaceuticals

  ▶ SAP for Oil and Gas

  ▶ SAP for Mining

▶ **Financial services**

  ▶ SAP for Banking

  ▶ SAP for Insurance

▶ **Consumer industries**

  ▶ SAP for Consumer Products

  ▶ SAP for Retail

▶ **Service industries**

  ▶ SAP for Professional Services

  ▶ SAP for Media

  ▶ SAP for Service Providers

  ▶ SAP for Telecommunications

  ▶ SAP for Utilities

- ▶ Public services
  - ▶ SAP for Healthcare
  - ▶ SAP for Higher Education and Research
  - ▶ SAP for Public Sector

For more information about SAP's industry-specific solutions, please see [Kagermann/Keller 2001] and [Buck-Emden/Böder 2004].

5.2.3 Packaged Composite Applications

SAP xApps are an innovative type of application that combines the services of existing, heterogeneous applications and systems to create new, cross-functional applications known as *composite applications*. The xApps delivered with an SAP standard solution are known as packaged composite applications [Woods 2003]. SAP xApps have the following characteristics:

- ▶ SAP xApps are based on the existing application systems. SAP xApps build on investments already made and increase their value.
- ▶ Services from various application areas, for example, CRM, SCM, or ERP, are merged to form new business processes.
- ▶ SAP xApps combine transactional applications with functions such as team collaboration, content management, and business analytics.
- ▶ SAP xApps run on the technological platform SAP NetWeaver.

SAP xApps are particularly suitable for quickly addressing cross-functional application requirements for which no standard application exists, for example, corporate mergers or project resource management.

5.3 Integration and Application Infrastructure

mySAP Business Suite uses SAP NetWeaver technology, an enhancement of the trusted mySAP Technology, to form an extensive integration and application platform. SAP NetWeaver makes it easier to manage total IT costs (total cost of ownership, TCO) in the company by simplifying implementation, ease of operation, and centralized monitoring of all involved systems, applications, and processes.

SAP NetWeaver is structured in the following functional levels:

- ▶ People integration
  - ▶ Portal for individual, role-based access to transactional and analytical applications and Web content

- Different technical communication channels such as telephone, fax, chat, mobile devices, or email for interaction with the applications (multi-channel access)
- Tools for system-based collaboration, within and outside the company and in teams (collaboration)

▶ **Information integration**

- Data warehouse and analysis tools for combining internal and external structured data to obtain business knowledge (business intelligence)
- Uniform retrieval of unstructured information from various sources, such as document management systems or file servers, including search functionality (knowledge management)
- Homogenization of product and business partner master data within the system landscape of a company (master data management)

▶ **Process integration**

- Infrastructure for the operative collaboration between applications and secure exchange of business data (integration broker)
- Tools for configuring, managing, and monitoring business processes (business process management)

▶ **Application platform**

- Scalable application server for ABAP- and J2EE-based applications (SAP Web Application Server)

▶ **Lifecycle Management**
with extensive services for implementing and operating mySAP Business Suite applications

▶ **Development and runtime environment**
for service-based applications using standardized application services (xApps)

For a detailed description of SAP NetWeaver, see Chapter 14.

6 Digression: Business Scenarios and Business Maps

Companies expect their business software solutions not just to support individual business functions, but also to support complete business scenarios—including sub-processes and process steps. The terms used here have the following meanings:

▶ **Business process**

A *business process* consists of a number of logically related business activities that can be executed to achieve a predefined result [Davenport/Short 1990]. A business process can involve several software components from different manufacturers.

▶ **Business process step**

Business process steps represent the fundamental activities that are performed within business processes. Each business process step is performed either by the user or the system and takes place within a single software component.

▶ **Business scenario**

A *business scenario* is a collection of logically related business processes that defines a complex company task, which is largely independent of other processes. Examples of business scenarios are campaign management in marketing or quotation and order management in sales.

The sequence of the individual business processes within a business scenario represents a complete, continuous business process with a visible business benefit. If required, process variants for individual business scenarios can be defined. As a rule, business scenarios refer to business units or central functional areas in the company, although business partners from other companies can also be included.

Even when we speak of *software solutions* and *software components*, the actual business processes and scenarios that are performed by the employees and supported by the software must be at the forefront when implementing and running new software in the company. SAP provides detailed scenario descriptions and SAP Business Maps, which can be accessed from SAP Solution Manager, SAP Service Marketplace, and SAP Help Portal.

Two types of SAP Business Maps are used to display and evaluate business scenarios:

▶ *SAP Solution Maps* for the display of processes and functions of SAP solutions at different levels of detail

► *SAP Collaborative Business Maps* (C-Business Maps) for describing cross-company scenarios with views that vary according to requirements

SAP Business Maps can be individually created or modified to complement the standard offer, for example, for customer-specific modifications. This can be achieved by using the PC-based tool *SAP Solution Composer*. In addition, you can assess the quantitative customer-specific benefit that you expect—from the implementation of mySAP Business Suite solutions—with the aid of *SAP Business Case Builder*, a Web-based tool based on C-Business Maps.

6.1 SAP Solution Maps

SAP Solution Maps provide a quick overview of business processes and functions of SAP solutions. This applies both to general applications of the SAP Business Suite and to industry-specific solutions. In total, more than 40 SAP Solution Maps are available.

SAP Solution Maps are structured hierarchically. On the highest level, the most important processes and properties of a solution—the key capabilities—are displayed with context or in partial views. The lower levels present more detailed views of the respective functionalities. All descriptions are from a customer- or industry-oriented view and utilize the appropriate terminology.

The following key capabilities were identified when structuring the solution map that describes mySAP CRM:

► **Functional key capabilities**

  ► Marketing

  ► Sales

  ► Service

  ► Analytics

► **Channel-oriented key capabilities**

  ► Field applications

  ► E-commerce

  ► Interaction center

  ► Channel management

► **Architecture-and-technology-related key capabilities**

  ► Generic application services

  ► Architecture and technology

Figure 6.1 shows an overview of the individual key capabilities in mySAP CRM.

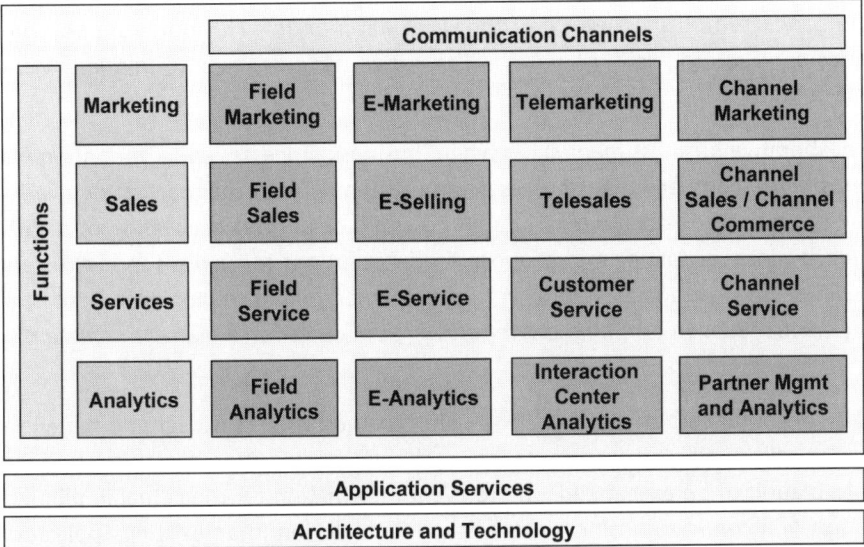

		Communication Channels		
Marketing	Field Marketing	E-Marketing	Telemarketing	Channel Marketing
Sales	Field Sales	E-Selling	Telesales	Channel Sales / Channel Commerce
Services	Field Service	E-Service	Customer Service	Channel Service
Analytics	Field Analytics	E-Analytics	Interaction Center Analytics	Partner Mgmt and Analytics
	Application Services			
	Architecture and Technology			

Figure 6.1 mySAP CRM Key Capabilities

For each of the key capabilities named, there is a detailed partial view in the solution map. An example of the highest level of the solution map for the functional key capabilities is shown in Figure 6.2.

Marketing	Marketing Planning	Customer Segmentation	Campaign Management	Trade Promotion Management	Lead Management	Personalization
Sales	Sales Planning and Forecasting	Territory Management	Account and Contact Management	Activity Management	Opportunity Management	Quotation and Order Management	Contract Management and Leasing	Incentive and Commission Management
Service	Service Planning and Forecasting	Customer Service and Support	Resource Planning and Optimization	Service Operations Management	Professional Services
Analytics	Customer Analytics	Product Analytics	Marketing Analytics	Sales Analytics	Service Analytics	Interaction Channel Analytics

Figure 6.2 Solution Map for mySAP CRM (functional key capabilities)

6.2 SAP Collaborative Business Maps

Collaboration both within and outside the company is of increasing importance in the connected business world of today. To describe this collaboration, SAP provides specific models—known as *collaborative business maps* (*C-Business Maps*) [Hack 2000].

Collaborative business maps show where business processes and information systems in the company meet processes and systems from other parties involved in the process. They document in detail possibilities of joint processing of distributed business scenarios and propose model solutions for various industries and business application areas (for example, customer relationship management, supply chain management, financial reporting, human resource management, and so on).

The collaborative business maps look at both the business aspect and benefit as well as all aspects of process design, including organization structure, business information to be exchanged, and relevant information for the actual implementation of a common business process and its inclusion in an existing application landscape. The goal of collaborative business maps is to show—using an easy to understand figure, that is, a correlation—how the different companies and participants work together, and to document the resulting value potential. This collaborative mapping enables companies to recognize qualitative and quantitative potential within a value chain and, therefore, to achieve the greatest benefit for all parties.

On the basis of implementation experience, customer talks, and independent expert analysis, the business benefit of the collaborative business scenarios was identified, documented, and quantified as a central part of C-Business Maps. The collaboration and integration across company boundaries can generate the following benefits for all business partners involved:

▶ Competitive advantages through shortened time-to-market cycles

▶ Innovative business models and processes

▶ Growth potential through, for example, customer-specific service offers

▶ Faster information exchange

▶ Higher quality of information

▶ Cost advantages (see also [Brandenburger/Nalebuff 1996])

Collaborative business maps are described by their different views. In particular, the business-oriented *business view* and the software-component-oriented *component view* should be mentioned.

6.2.1 Business View

The business view provides information on the business partners involved and offers an overview of the extent and the sequence of the collaboration between the participants. Furthermore, the business view documents the business arguments and the value potential that can be realized by the participants. These form the basis for calculating the investment and the rate of return. Figure 6.3 describes the business relationship between the participants within the collaborative business scenario *Campaign Management using a correlation*. The scenario shows how three potential participants in marketing campaigns—an external data provider, a manufacturer, and a mailing provider—can work together to execute a marketing campaign jointly and successfully.

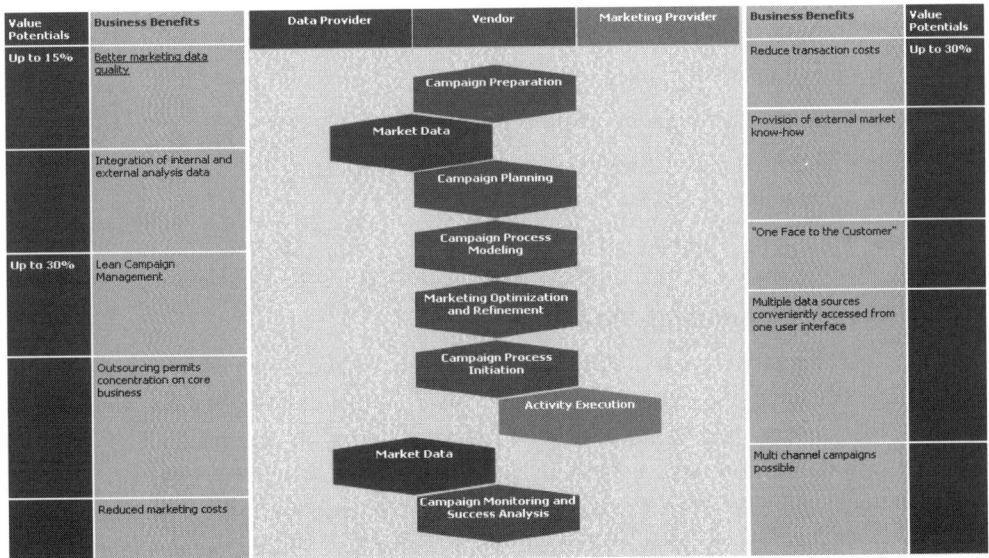

Figure 6.3 Business View of Collaborative Business Map "Campaign Management"

The marketing manager in charge of initiating a marketing campaign first obtains an overview of the current sales figures using SAP Business Information Warehouse (SAP BW). The external analysis data delivered by a market research institute is also included in the analysis. Keeping in mind the market development, the marketing requirements, and the potential competitor behavior, the marketing manager identifies the products whose turnover will be increased by a marketing campaign. The marketing manager defines the campaign name and outlines its start and end dates. Like the marketing manager, the sales manager defines the campaign target group by selecting customers or prospects.

Finally, both managers check and discuss the campaign and its target group one more time and confirm the start of the campaign. After this collaborative effort, the mailing activities are generated and forwarded, using an external *mail shot provider* (a service for sending e-mails). The marketing manager monitors the status and execution of individual mail shots. At the end of the campaign cycle, the marketing and sales managers can evaluate the effectiveness of the campaign and use this experience in the next campaign.

As shown in Figure 6.3, various qualitative and quantitative improvements occur during the course of business. They include:

▶ Improved quality of data through data consistency

▶ Reduced transaction costs through improved collaboration

▶ Integration of external and internal analysis data

▶ Use of external market know-how

▶ Lean campaign planning and execution

▶ Concentration on core business tasks by outsourcing the campaign execution

▶ Presenting a unified image ("one face") to the customer

6.2.2 Component View

The component view unifies the IT application landscapes of business scenario participants in one consistent display. It describes the application components that are required to support the business process. The activities are divided up into relevant individual steps that are executed within the appropriate applications. Moreover, the component view contains information on release requirements and is the basis for the subsequent technical implementation (see Figure 6.4).

These different views—which are customized to meet the information requirements of various recipients (management, specialist department, IT specialists)—ensure that there is a consistent transition from business context to component implementation in an IT application landscape.

For more information on models for cross-company cooperation networks, including all C-Business Maps for mySAP CRM, please see SAP Service Marketplace under *http://service.sap.com/C-Business*.

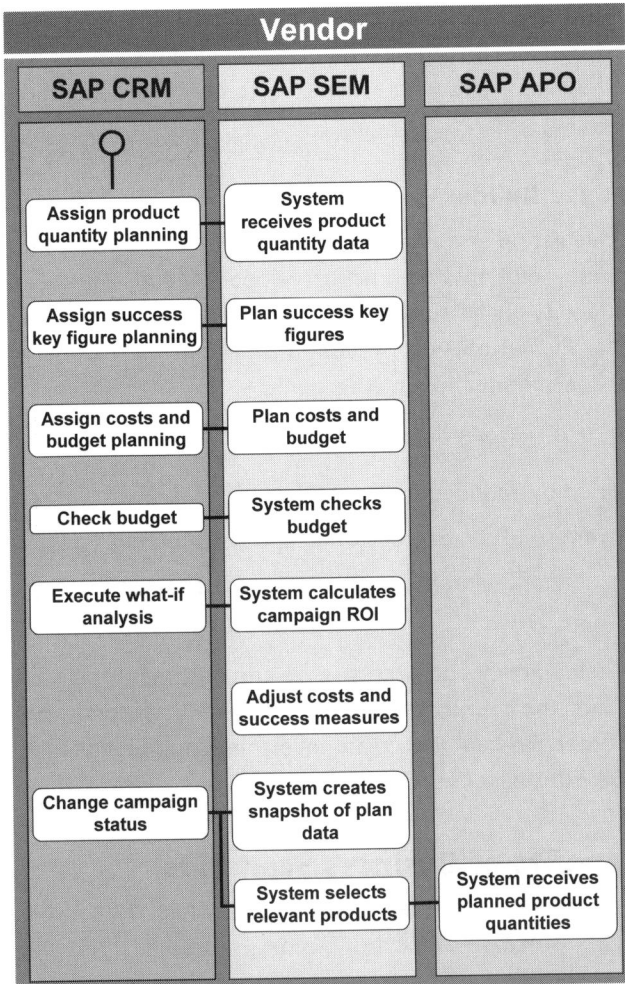

Figure 6.4 Component View (Excerpt) on Collaborative Business Map "Campaign Management"

6.2.3 Collaborative Business Maps as a Basis for Business Profitability Calculation

The advantages of integrated common business processes are documented as business benefits and as value potential on both pages of the business view of a C-Business Map. For example, up to 30% reduced transaction costs are estimated for the business scenario *Campaign Management*. Savings are measured as a percentage, which enables the improvement potential (for example, up to 20% increase in turnover through cross-selling) to be applied to each individual company situation. In this way, before they implement a C-Business business, business partners can check how high the possible return on investment (ROI) can be when realizing such a business process using appropriate business application software. The expected potential for improvement and percentage figures is investigated and validated through talks with experts, customer projects, or independent analyses.

6.2.4 SAP Business Case Builder

To enable a quantitative calculation of the expected customer-specific value from using mySAP Business Suite solutions, SAP has developed *SAP Business Case Builder*. As part of a profitability analysis (a *business case*) for a planned software solution, *SAP Business Case Builder* offers a structured procedure for calculating ROI, taking the customer-specific situation into account.

SAP Business Case Builder is structured in three parts:

▶ Industry analysis (provided by an independent vendor)

▶ Identification of a software solution for a customer-specific situation

▶ Creation of an investment appraisal (return on investment) as part of a business case

With SAP Business Case Builder, companies can analyze and document their specific situations and compare their requirements with the solution portfolio of mySAP Business Suite. Companies can also create investment appraisals for the selected solutions using SAP Business Case Builder.

6.3   Potential Benefits of Business Scenarios

Companies always pursue one or more of the following goals, which must also be the focus of optimization and software support of business processes:

▶ Increase turnover and market share

▶ Increase profitability and lower costs

▶ Satisfy customers to generate business advantages

Various business scenarios can help to facilitate your reaching these goals. Therefore, at the end of the detailed descriptions of the individual applications of mySAP CRM, we have included a useful overview that does the following: lists the important business scenarios of the affected sub-applications, succinctly outlines their functionality, and breaks down existing potential benefits into turnover, profitability, and customer satisfaction.

The primary use for a scenario is indicated by a double tick, for example, ✓✓ for the scenario Campaign Management, which primarily intends to increase turnover. A further use in other categories is shown by a single tick.

Scenario	Short Description	Potential Benefits		
		Revenue	Profitability	Customer Satisfaction
Campaign Management	Optimization of campaign processing from market analysis to result validation	✓✓	✓	✓

Table 6.1 Categorization of Potential Benefits of Business Scenarios Using the Example Campaign Management

In this way, companies that strive for improved turnover, profitability, or customer satisfaction can easily find the most suitable scenarios for each application area of mySAP CRM.

7 mySAP CRM—Applications for the Customer Interaction Cycle

7.1 The Four Phases of the Customer Interaction Cycle

The development of customer relationships runs in customer interaction cycles that include the phases *marketing, sales, order management*, and *service,* and which, when successful, repeat frequently. The goal of fostering customer relationships along recurring interaction cycles is to maintain long-term customer business relationships and strengthen them when possible.

A customer relationship is initiated by the first contact with a prospect who has decided to buy a product or take advantage of a service. According to their impressions of the first business transaction, the customers are open to further business relationships or lose interest in the vendor. If the customer's expectations are fulfilled or even exceeded during the first purchase, a long-term trusting relationship with the vendor can emerge. In this case, the customer would remain loyal to the vendor, which means that the customer believes in the vendor's competence, shows little readiness to change vendors, and plans to return to that same vendor for the next purchase. Later, these ties are strengthened by re-buying or cross-buying can lead to long-term turnover success for the vendor [Homburg/Bruhn 2003].

The effect that customer relationship management (CRM) has on the customer's perception of the vendor—and how this estimation manifests itself in the customer's buying behavior—can encourage the vendor to build on and further develop the customer relationship via purposeful interaction (see Figure 7.1).

Each time a customer interacts with a company, the customer has certain expectations of the products and services. These expectations are either confirmed satisfactorily, exceeded, or disappointingly not met. Each interaction loop contains the risk that the company will not meet customer expectations and, therefore, won't have the opportunity to generate follow-on business. The greater the ties between customer and company, the less the potential for losing a customer after a one-time mistake. However, if a company fails to meet customer expectations even once, this can—especially given today's market conditions—cause long-term customers to move over to the competition. Therefore, the activities surrounding each business transaction are critical for the long-term success of the company.

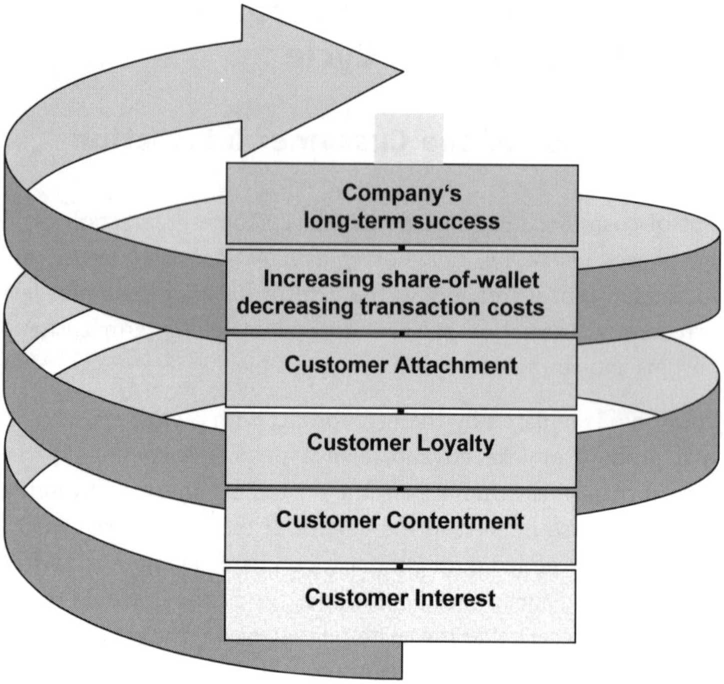

Figure 7.1 Effect Chain of Customer Relationship Management

In each loop, the customer interaction cycle continues with marketing, sales, order processing, and customer service. Marketing recognizes potential customers, draws their attention to the company, and arouses their interest in its products. The marketing department uses appropriate offers to develop prospects (leads) into actual sales possibilities (opportunities). After sales closes the business agreement, the delivery and service commitments are fulfilled and billed during the order processing phase. The after-sales area provides services and supports customers after they make their purchases. In further interaction cycles, marketing contacts regular or occasional customers, submits them specific offers, or suggests additional or higher-value products. Sales monitors the individual customer status, for example, long-term contracts or special discount margins, during the quotation creation. After order fulfillment, customers can use the services offered as part of the service contracts or receive special services given to longtime customers loyal to the vendor. The basis for successful interaction cycles is created by an information pool that integrates all relevant customer data and makes it available to authorized employees in each phase of the customer interaction cycle (see Figure 7.2).

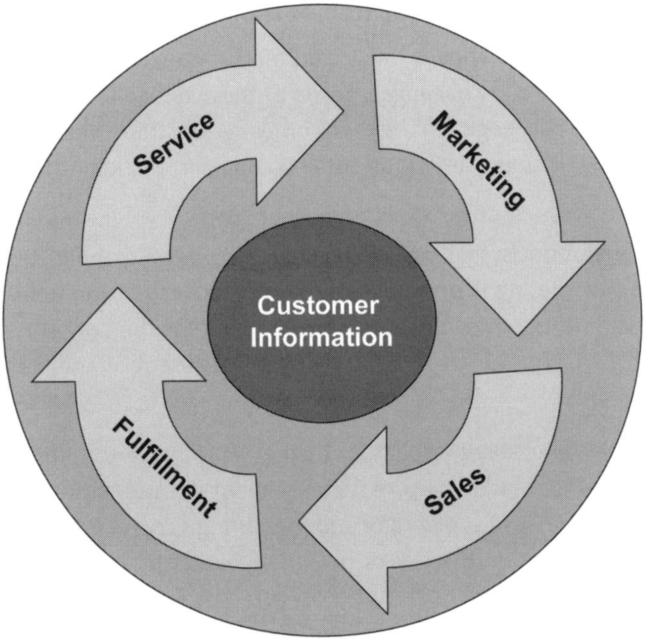

Figure 7.2 Customer Interaction Cycle

mySAP CRM helps to develop all phases of the interaction cycle in the sense of optimizing customer relationship management, including customers, employees, and business partners. This is outlined for each component of mySAP CRM in the following chapters.

7.2 Marketing

"Business has only two basic functions: marketing and innovation. Marketing and innovation produce results. All the rest are costs."
Peter F. Drucker [Drucker 2001]

7.2.1 Marketing—Software's Last Technological Conquest

Marketing is the last new area to use process-optimized information technology (IT). After re-engineering, optimization, and automation of financial accounting, administration, human resources management, supply chains, and, increasingly, sales and customer service, it is now marketing's turn. Companies that gain this new territory can reap rich rewards. Marketing is a decisive strategic driving force for company success, a fact confirmed by the ever-increasing number of successful companies that invest heavily in extensive global marketing management [Marcus 2003, Blumstein/Wardley 2003].

The Difficulties of Changing the Perception of Marketing

Despite its potential to improve company value and market capitalization, marketing faces its own difficulties and challenges. Some of these difficulties are surprisingly different from the challenges that other company functions must confront. The most astonishing discovery is that, in some companies, marketing is not taken seriously.

The reason for this perception is that marketing does not have to hold itself accountable. Moreover, marketing is one of the few—perhaps, even the only—enterprise functions that has its own easily accessible budget. It is the only enterprise function that neither knows exactly what its budget was spent on, nor how efficiently it was spent.

Another important reason for a lack of respect for marketing is the very culture of marketing. For example, when marketing professionals resist the use of modern, tool-supported business processes for planning and measuring success because it stifles marketing creativity, they run the risk of being laughed at by other enterprise functions that could no longer exist were it not for today's constantly improving and IT-supported business processes.

There is still no solution for this schism between marketing and the other departments of a company. There is also no secret recipe to measure exactly, for example, the contribution margin of an advertising campaign. What we do have, however, is a growing range of increasingly mature and usable tools that support marketing professionals, marketing organizations, and enterprises. The answer to the many challenges facing marketing is in the implementation of efficient business processes that are based on powerful IT solutions.

We will first address these marketing concerns by listing them, beginning with the operational and organizational challenges that confront marketing organizations and their employees. We will show how you can use IT solutions to meet these challenges and therefore be successful against your competition.

Operational Challenges

If we analyze the most important operational challenges facing marketing departments today, we must consider the following five points:

▶ Optimization of resources for marketing activities

▶ Increasing brand value

▶ New customer acquisition

▶ Optimization of consumer and customer demand

▶ Management of the offer portfolio

These challenges affect all industries, although their characteristics and focus, with the exception of resource optimization, are heavily dependent on the individual business activity. Marketing for business directly with the end consumer is different from marketing for business via distributors. Companies from the consumer goods industry (consumer packaged goods (CPG)) optimize consumer demand by their ability to increase brand recognition, execute consumer and trade promotions, and continuously develop their product portfolio. Utilities companies proceed in the same way and also contact their customers individually through direct marketing, tailoring their offers to suit each customer.

Many companies also differ in intensity and focus of their media-based mass marketing. *Brand- or product-oriented marketing*, which concentrates on mass marketing techniques, is dominant in the consumer goods, high tech, pharmaceuticals, and textiles industries. Conversely, *individual relationship or direct marketing*, which is customized for each recipient, plays a large role for financial service providers, telecommunications, retail, and travel companies. However, consumer goods companies also maintain individual relationships using call centers for consumers, focus groups, and wholesalers. Alongside direct marketing, banks also invest heavily in brand value and consumer promotions, such as limited interest cuts. Marketing is a truly "horizontal" discipline that is performed in all "vertical" industry sectors.

This begs the question, "How can companies that spend relatively little on direct marketing still remain competitive and operate the latest technology in this specialized marketing discipline?" The same applies for companies that perform comparatively little mass marketing and brand maintenance. Part of the answer to this question is that it is part of SAP's role as a vendor of marketing software solutions to work together with leading companies in each marketing discipline to incorporate state-of-the-art processes, methods, and functions into its software solutions. In particular, industries with little experience in marketing benefit from this working arrangement.

Optimize Resources

In a study conducted by Accenture in 2001, 175 marketing managers from England and the U.S. were asked about their greatest marketing challenges [O'Halloran 2001, Marcus 2003]. The study showed that the main problem was measuring the profit generated from investing in marketing campaigns. Only those marketing managers who know which marketing activities were efficient and which weren't can optimize the use of resources in the future.

"Half the money I spend on advertising is wasted. The trouble is, I don't know which half."

This famous quotation, attributed to the American department store pioneer John Wanamaker (1838–1922), may be amusing, but it no longer applies today. Of course, it is still no small matter to determine the exact contribution margin of a particular series of advertisements or the efficiency of an individual imaginative marketing event. However, one should at least know the objective of each marketing investment made. For which products or brands in which regions and for which target groups was money spent? Additionally, it is now possible to determine the exact contribution margin for an increasing number of marketing activities such as campaigns, trade promotions, and events.

Increase Brand Value

Brand value is a fearsome concept for many technocrats. It is based only on perception! Unlike brand recognition, it is difficult to measure directly. Nevertheless, the brand is the capital that differentiates market leaders from the rest of the competition. Being in the decision-maker's (consumer's or customer's) mind at the moment of decision is the most important value of a brand.

However, building up a successful brand does not just mean constantly and consistently exceeding customer expectations. Securing long-term success through increasing brand value means spending each dollar available for marketing optimally to improve continuous advertisements and marketing programs, and to carefully monitor markets and competitors. This requires consistent marketing planning, efficient campaign management, and precise success analyses.

Acquire New Customers

As far as customers are concerned, there are two growth dimensions for a company to consider:

▶ Growth within the existing customer base through increased share of wallet. See also Section 4.4.2 and Chapter 12.

▶ Growth through new customers

Concentrating solely on the admittedly important existing customer base has clear limits. The acquisition of new customers is therefore a key factor for the long-term success of a company. But which customers should be acquired? And where? Companies must consider the risks involved if they want to expand by acquiring new customers. For example, banks don't want to attract new customers with a poor credit history. Similarly, companies in the consumer goods industry will hesitate before expanding in new regions where there is already strong local competition.

Three procedures often come into play when acquiring new customers:

▶ Finding new customers with a similar profile to existing customers who contribute to making the company profitable

▶ Expanding to new customer segments

▶ Expanding in new geographical regions

Before they can find new customers with a profile similar to that of existing customers who add to the company's profitability, companies must know which of their customers actually contributes to profit. A guideline is the old rule of thumb: 80% of the profit comes from 20% of the customers. The challenge is, therefore, to determine which customers belong to this 20% and which new prospects have a similar profile to customers who contribute a profit to the company. To do this, you need a complete view of the customer base, supported by advanced segmentation and analysis tools. You also need a way to obtain information on prospects with similar characteristics to those of the existing customers who add profit to the company. Lastly, you must have the means by which to attract these potential customers, i.e., a convincing service offer.

The expansion into new market segments also offers possibilities for growth. For example, in this way, a normally conservative bank can use a convincing Internet offer to persuade busy young workers to purchase its core products. A diaper manufacturer can use technology to open up new markets and target groups, such as incontinence products for senior citizens. Factors such as careful analysis of market possibilities and price as well as production capacity influence the decision on whether to expand into new customer segments.

Finally, geographical expansion offers possibilities of acquiring new customers. Questions about product localization, local competition, acquisition, and distribution must be systematically evaluated in order to weigh the advantages and the disadvantages of expanding into new geographical markets.

Optimize Consumer and Customer Demand
One of the main tasks of marketing is optimizing demand. This begs the question, "What is optimal demand?" Sometimes it is the highest demand; sometimes, however, it is also the demand created by particular conditions that arise from production, logistics, and certain implementation restrictions. In this case, tight integration with the corresponding company functions is indispensable.

The interaction of supply and demand can be optimized only if there is a working bridge between marketing or promotion planning and demand planning in the supply chain. Effective analysis and segmentation applications that support the identification of customer segments with significant increase potential are also part of the technological software answer to the challenges of demand optimization. Another part is the powerful product proposal functionality (cross- and up-selling).

Manage the Offer Portfolio

Companies must constantly use innovative offers to reflect customer and consumer needs and therefore maintain their long-term competitiveness. This is nothing new; however, we are currently in an age of unprecedented choice for customers and consumers. The explosion of these choices leads to another bitter fact: product lifecycles are becoming shorter and time-to-market is becoming an increasingly important factor in predicting a successful outcome. It is therefore even more important for companies to manage offers proactively.

To make decisions based on solid information, companies must have an accurate and complete overview of their offers and contribution margins. Without this precondition, decision-making is arbitrary at best. Of course, there will always be some products that are launched and others that aren't, but that's business. However, information technology can help to shorten decision cycles and increase the success rate.

Organizational Challenges

In addition to the operational tasks that we addressed, there are also organizational challenges that marketing must confront. The five most important organizational challenges are:

▶ Management of knowledge

▶ Coordination of sub-organizations within the company

▶ Coordination of the marketing supply chain

▶ Use of technology without stifling creativity

▶ Integration of marketing with other business processes in the company

These organizational challenges can be overcome by the interplay of first-class IT solutions and change management within the company. As the bitter experience of past marketing projects gone awry has shown, IT solutions must be aligned with change management. The use of some kind of popular technique alone isn't enough to solve the tasks at hand.

More and more leading market-oriented companies are becoming aware of this fact. They're looking for solutions that don't only selectively improve the efficiency of different marketing activities, but also ensure that marketing expenditures are no longer hidden, as well as raise the efficiency and profitability of the entire marketing organization. The marketing solution thus becomes a strategic catalyst for business success.

Knowledge Management

"Marketing is done by two-to-four-year-olds." This often circulated statement refers to the fact that marketing is one of the business function areas with the highest labor turnover rate. The common turnover rate for an employee in marketing is two to four years. Just when marketing employees start to become truly productive, they change jobs.

Yearly variations of one and the same thing are typical for marketing organizations. A high-tech company attends the same trade fairs each year to identify potential buyers; a clothing company organizes a promotion each fall before school begins; a mail-order company carries out a campaign each year at Christmas. The questions often remain: Which of these measures was really successful and which was not? Was it the discount coupons or the promotional display in the shop? Were enough qualified leads identified at this event in the last three years to justify a repeat? If they exist at all, the answers to these questions can be found only in the heads of the employees. If these marketing talents leave every two years, it is very difficult to build up experience and use this accrued knowledge in the long-term.

This fact creates one of the greatest challenges in marketing: knowledge management and learning from experience. So, how can companies with such a "revolving door culture" keep knowledge within their doors and learn from experience? The solution is to transfer knowledge and experience to the IT-supported marketing systems. Companies do themselves a great favor when they equip their marketing employees with standardized, IT-supported methods for carrying out campaigns or trade auctions. This means that employees don't waste valuable time guessing and can concentrate on profitable activities instead of reinventing the wheel each year.

Coordinate Sub-Organizations

"How much did we spend last year on advertisements in the most important large town markets?" "How much have we invested this year in customer events in Latin America?" "As director of marketing for eastern Europe, how can I justify my budget to headquarters?" "Do my local goals match the company goals?"

Companies operating in multiple regions are confronted with these and similar questions every day. Answers are often found only after long meetings after-hours and laborious processing of extensive spreadsheet tables. Coordinating marketing across regions and business areas can be very challenging. With the help of standardized methods and IT solutions, however, leading marketing organizations are gradually starting to master global company-wide planning, budgeting, and reporting. The combination of a top-down and bottom-up approach during planning, budgeting, and reporting means that directives can be given from top to bottom for centrally determined goals, which can then be modified from bottom to top by a planning process. The entire process leads to cooperative individual sub-organizations, which, in turn, provide each person involved with a greater degree of responsibility, accountability, and the opportunity to learn from one another.

Coordinate Marketing Supply Chain

"We have just changed our company logo and slogan; do all of our subsidiaries and partners know this and are they using the correct advertising material?" "Did the sales booth arrive on time at the supermarket?" "Who has the up-to-date list of the participants and speakers at our next event?"

Interestingly, marketing—although previously an isolated unit within the company—is a very active area with respect to coordinating activities with external partners. Advertising agencies, graphic designers, suppliers, distribution channel partners, event organizers, and mail shops are just a few examples of partners that work together with marketing. In the past, however, the coordination with external partners was only supported loosely by information technology, usually in the form of emails with attachments. This procedure is often comfortable, but also has its disadvantages, for example, when version or authorization checks are needed. Once an email is sent, one can no longer control its content and final destination.

Implement Technology Effectively without Stifling Creativity

Marketing professionals are naturally creative and are often reluctant when it comes to using technology to support their work. Consequently, marketing software must not only be easy to use, but must also be seen as adding value to daily work without impeding individual creativity.

Winning the acceptance of the user is therefore an important piece of the puzzle when implementing software systems. Identifying and utilizing "quick wins" (things that enable the end user to carry out his or her daily work more easily) helps to secure the long-term success of software projects. Here are some examples of marketing quick wins:

► **Change from spreadsheets and file servers to planning applications and data warehouses**
The transition from a planning and reporting infrastructure based on spreadsheets and file servers to a system environment characterized by data warehouse and reporting tools can greatly reduce the time marketing needs to produce reports. Such a process also makes it possible to perform comparisons with the past, for example, with last year's campaign success. This enables marketing organizations to use experience effectively for future activities.

► **Segmentation tools for the standard marketing employee**
Graphical segmentation tools shift the task of segmentation from IT employees to marketing staff, where it belongs. Marketing can use these tools to obtain knowledge of the customer base, in areas that might not have even been noticed.

► **Marketing calendar with graphical display**
A clear graphical calendar in which all campaigns and promotions are displayed gives the marketing employee a good overview of all activities. The marketer can see at a glance when which products are advertised in which regions. Trade and consumer promotions are displayed in the same calendar and can be coordinated, although they are planned by different departments. The calendar enables the marketer to work interactively with graphical elements: promotions can be created, moved forward or back in time, and have their duration modified at the click of a mouse button. A solid overview and quick, interactive working methods make the work of the marketer both more efficient and more satisfying.

These are just three examples of how easy-to-use tools can support marketing employees to work more efficiently, without robbing them of their creative freedom.

Integrate Marketing with other Business Processes

Of course, selected, isolated marketing solutions can have their uses for individual companies. However, the true benefit of a marketing solution becomes apparent only if it is integrated with other business processes. For example, an enterprise will not benefit from scheduling a telemarketing survey for next week when the call center does not have capacity. If a promotion is set to start in ten weeks, it might be advantageous to first check whether production can cope with the expected rise in demand. And wouldn't it also be a good idea if the planned and approved budgets were automatically linked to the enterprise's financial systems? Generating buying interest is all very well, but wouldn't it also be desirable to make the sales pipeline visible in order to be able to check whether the sales employees have time to deal with the potential buyers and convert them into turnover?

An isolated marketing procedure means that these questions are not answered until it is too late, which leads to lost opportunities and dissatisfied customers. On the other hand, an integrated procedure can make overall relationships visible and release latent organizational potential.

Marketing Application Areas in mySAP CRM

mySAP CRM offers a comprehensive, open, modular, and individually enhanceable solution for the entire marketing process. It includes application services that reflect actual customer scenarios for the following functional areas:

- ▶ Market, customer, and consumer analysis
- ▶ Marketing planning
- ▶ Customer and consumer segmentation
- ▶ Campaign and user promotions
- ▶ Trade promotions
- ▶ Lead management
- ▶ Personalization
- ▶ Campaign monitoring and success analysis

SAP's marketing solution is tightly integrated with all other functions of mySAP CRM and can be accessed through all interaction channels. In particular, the comprehensive reporting and analytical functions of mySAP CRM, which can be used for extensive marketing analyses, should be emphasized.

The individual marketing applications of mySAP CRM are discussed in detail in the following sections. Unlike the transaction-oriented applications of sales (see Section 7.3) and service (see Section 7.5), we start here with the market, customer, and consumer analysis, because it is these analyses that form the decision-making basis for all subsequent operational activities.

7.2.2 Market, Customer, and Consumer Analysis

Companies amass large amounts of information and endeavor to understand and use them. The analysis and reporting tools needed for this are frequently completely separated from the operational tools companies use to contact their target groups. This obviously causes difficulties for the operational use of the analysis results.

SAP has another method—solid analysis and reporting tools that are integrated with the operational marketing tools, even at a conceptual level. Of course, isolated reporting can also take place for the sake of reporting, and operational activities can be carried out without analyses. However, the combination of both tools offers companies significant competitive advantages. SAP offers marketing a range of developed analytical functions for analyzing customers, consumers, segments, competitors, products, marketing channels, trends, profitability, and marketing data from third parties. The foundation for these are laid by the analysis functions of mySAP Business Intelligence—SAP's combined solution for data warehousing and data evaluation, which is an integral part of mySAP CRM.

Sound analysis functions help companies to plan better and to develop more opportunities. In addition, they support companies in monitoring, following, and measuring all marketing activities. Since mySAP CRM is an integrated solution with direct access to all data concerned with transactions, financials, and operational processes, companies have a complete overview of their marketing activities at all times (see Figure 7.3).

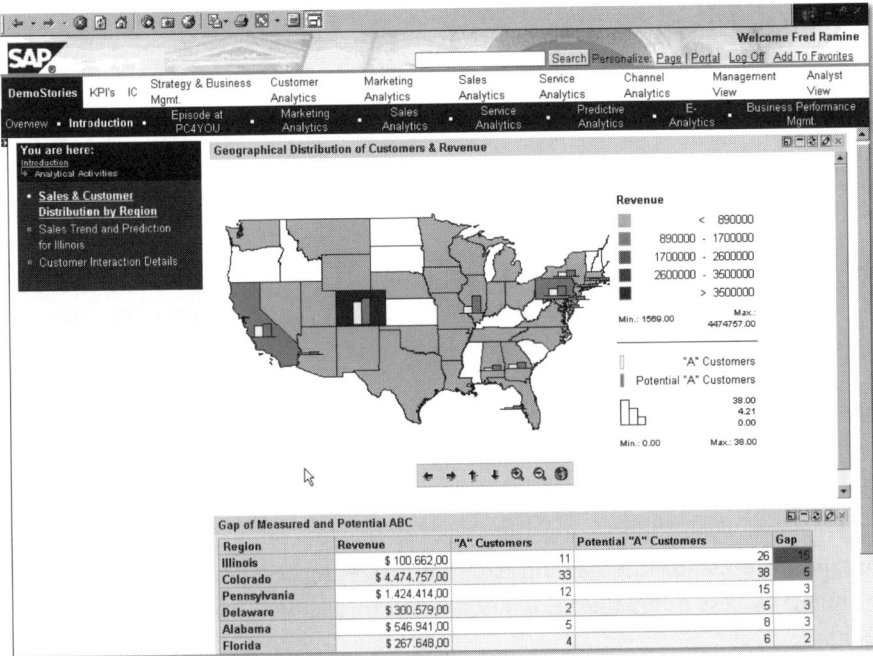

Figure 7.3 Marketing Analysis Cockpit

mySAP CRM offers companies all the market analysis functions they need to be able to analyze and report on customer-related information, which is necessary to give them a better understanding of customer behavior and value. Companies can use this information to plan campaigns, promotions, and events, make their customers better product proposals, increase customer satisfaction, raise the use and profitability of products, and retain customers in the long run.

Among the most important marketing analysis functions of mySAP CRM are:

▶ Proactive alarm messages for problems and possibilities, combined with proposals for how to react best

▶ Providing important performance indicators that enable the company to measure customer satisfaction, loyalty, and value

▶ Advanced data mining functions that allow companies to model customer behavior, prevent customer churning, analyze product proposals, and improve customer satisfaction and loyalty

- ▶ Analysis of the efficiency of communication channels, which allows the company to contact customers at the right time and using the right channels
- ▶ Portfolio analysis for a greater understanding of the company's own product and service offers
- ▶ Analysis of customer relationship value over its entire duration to secure long-term profitability
- ▶ Web site monitoring to improve the effectiveness of Web-based marketing
- ▶ Integration with financial reporting systems for proper ROI reporting
- ▶ Orientation of campaigns to goals

By providing marketing with integrated analysis and reporting tools, companies can manage their knowledge more effectively and can learn from experience to make better decisions and achieve the right results.

7.2.3 Marketing Planning

Large, complex enterprises must plan and organize their marketing initiatives on different levels, for example, company level, area level, product level, brand level, and regional level. Global companies can use this functionality to coordinate and optimize the use of internal and external marketing resources. The rationalized planning process offers the flexibility needed to deal with ever-changing market trends.

The marketing planning of mySAP CRM allows enterprises to plan marketing activities centrally and transparently across all levels involving all people concerned, including external partners. Since mySAP CRM is integrated, it uses all relevant customer, financial, product, and market data for its marketing planning. In this way, mySAP CRM bridges the gap between the supply and demand chains, improves the customer service at the front office, and optimizes the cost efficiency at the back office (see Figure 7.4).

Important functions of mySAP CRM for marketing planning are:

- ▶ Collaborative, rationalized planning functions with embedded marketing workflows and approval processes for faster planning cycles and reduced planning and execution costs
- ▶ Interactive and personalized marketing calendar functions to manage campaigns, marketing planning, and trade promotions
- ▶ The ability to deal with complex and ever-changing requirements by enabling companies to react quickly to demand changes with access to centralized marketing plans

▶ Integration in supply and demand chains for higher efficiency and accuracy

▶ Simulation of different supply chain scenarios

▶ Proper ROI reporting functions based on current financial data and not on estimates

▶ The possibility to formulate and communicate marketing strategies company-wide

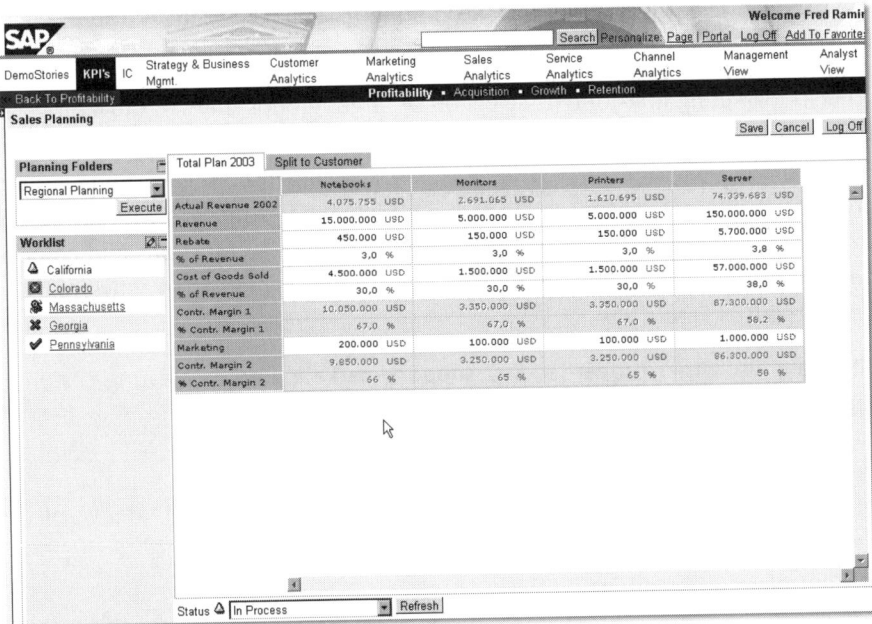

Figure 7.4 Integrated, Cross-Brand Planning of Key Performance Indicators

▶ The possibility to coordinate and optimize the use of internal and external marketing resources and initiatives across the company

▶ The availability of snapshots—versions of modified marketing plans—which offer detailed budgeting functions as well as better understanding of plan modifications over a particular time period

▶ Individualized planning of key performance indicators to enable planning on a financial, supply logistics, and product level

▶ Flexibility in distributing and coordinating plans, which allows companies to perform top-down and bottom-up planning

An integrated planning procedure can help companies to coordinate company objectives with those of their subsidiaries. It also encourages companies to move from the chaos of spreadsheets and file servers to a more disciplined concept for planning, measuring, and reporting. Only by adhering to this concept, which can clearly outline integrated marketing planning, can companies become more successful in the long run and learn from past failures and successes.

7.2.4 Customer and Consumer Segmentation

Segmentation is a decisive core task of marketing. Without a targeted procedure for customer and consumer retention, companies are just throwing money out of the window. What is the point of attempting to gain a potential customer who will probably not respond?

To help marketing fine-tune its selection of target groups, mySAP CRM offers all the tools required for analytical and ad-hoc segmentation. Business users can create targeted segments for customers, partners, organizations, prospects, and groups and integrate them seamlessly with marketing campaigns without having to wait for support from the IT department. Data display functions and embedded forecasting analysis functions allow all customer segmentation activities to be optimized (see Figure 7.5).

There are also other properties that support marketing when creating customer segments:

▶ Embedded functions for optimizing response rates
▶ Random selection of smaller customer groups that are representative of the entire customer base but can be analyzed faster for sampling
▶ Control group functions
▶ Simplified operation through personalized attribute lists for each user
▶ Analytical segmentation functions, including clustering, decision trees, and other data mining technologies
▶ Real-time determination of the number of business partners that correspond to selection criteria for the purpose of more precise planning and segmentation (counter function)
▶ Access to partial quantities of customer and consumer data to enable a personalized view on the data base
▶ View on individual customer data records for quality assurance and to enable modifications

In this way, users can model target group segments for optimized, goal-oriented campaigns quickly and easily. By using sophisticated segmentation functions with an easy-to-use user interface, marketing can make quick decisions when necessary to optimize marketing processes without involving the IT department.

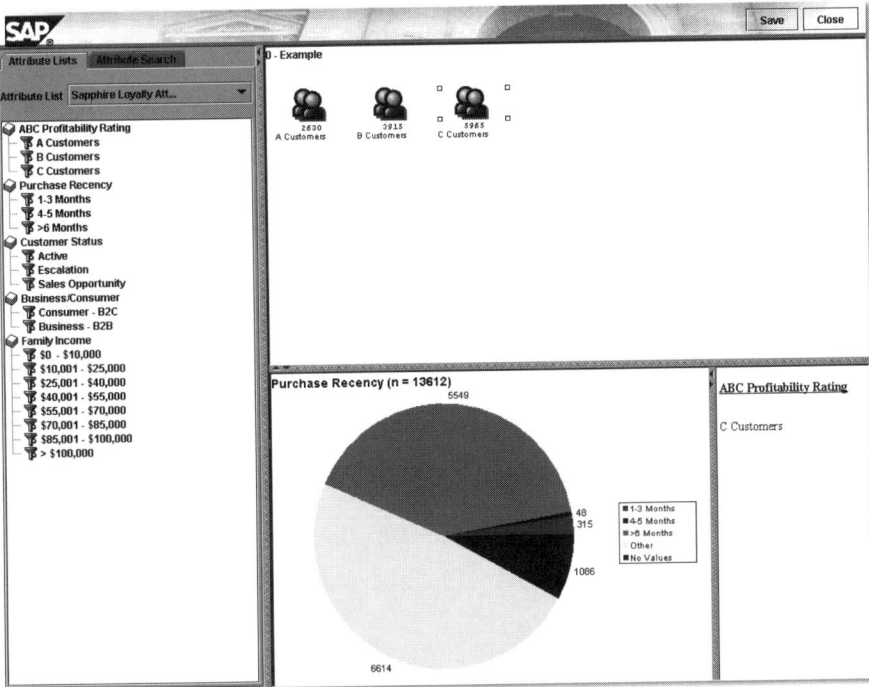

Figure 7.5 Customer Segmentation

7.2.5 Campaign and Consumer Promotions

In the past, mailing campaigns with a high circulation and a minimum response rate of 2% were not a rarity. Offers were often distributed using the shotgun principle, where the turnover made could not cover the high total costs. This kind of undifferentiated marketing not only leads to high costs, but also often annoys the customer. Today, campaign management is much more than posting offers to potential customers.

mySAP CRM provides companies with complete control over the campaign process, from conception to execution, coordination, optimization, and monitoring. Companies can create goal-oriented, personalized campaigns via all communication channels, including the field, call center, letter, email, fax, Internet, and mobile devices.

It is also possible to monitor the profitability company-wide at program, product, customer, and partner level. In addition, you can plan and execute indirect communication with consumers, for example, using print media and television. The integration with financial accounting and the data warehouse empowers companies to measure the actual success of not only direct communication campaigns, but of indirect consumer promotions as well.

With the campaign automation and optimization functions of mySAP CRM, companies can develop communication flows visually and intuitively and trigger events from defined customer reactions (see Figure 7.6). To overcome the complexities presented by customer segmentation, mySAP CRM contains embedded simulation and optimization functions that help users without any technical knowledge to create the channel, customer, and offer mix for each campaign. For example, the RFM (*Recency, Frequency, Monetary*)-analysis enables companies to exclude customers who would probably not respond to the campaign, assuming that customers who purchase frequently will have purchased recently; that is, those who buy in bulk are more likely to respond to a campaign.

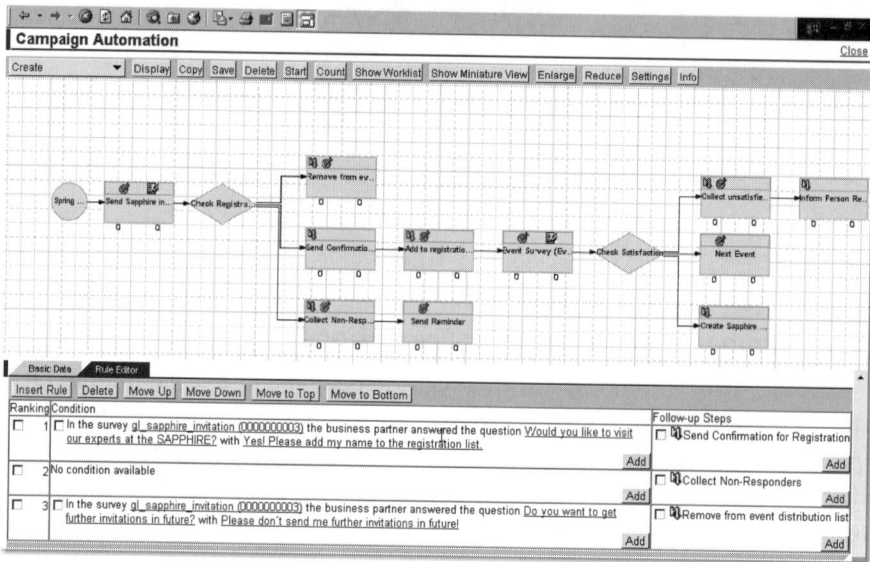

Figure 7.6 Campaign Automation

The marketing calendar functionality offers a comprehensive overview of all marketing activities. Companies can view their plans, trade promotions, and campaigns from several perspectives (for example, by brand, customer, or product groups) and can use aggregation, drill-up or drill-down methods, as well as print functions. Marketing plans are visualized on a daily, weekly, or monthly basis and are given a color code to make them easily recognizable (see Figure 7.7).

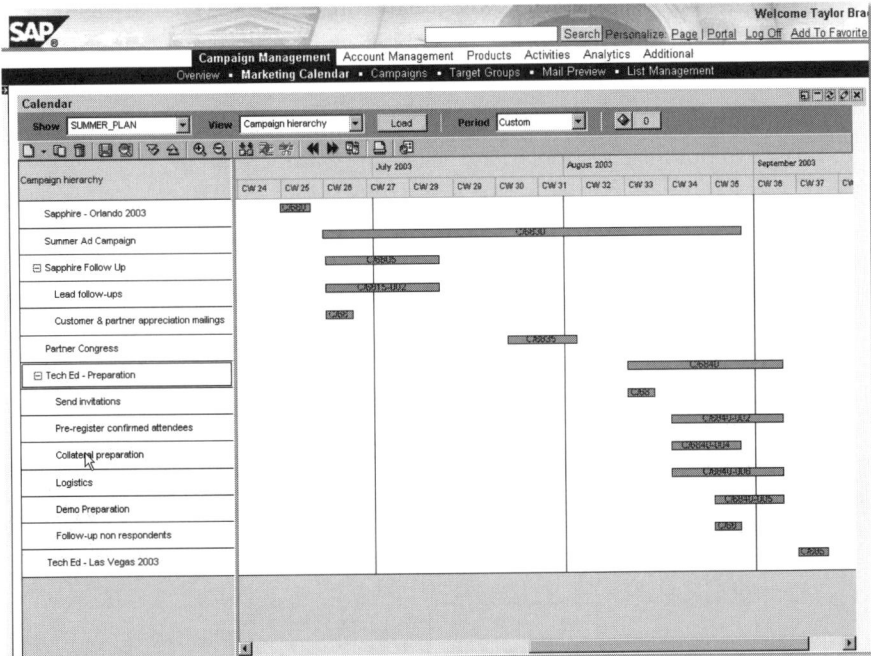

Figure 7.7 Marketing Calendar with Display of Customer Events

Important components of Campaign Management in mySAP CRM are listed below:

▶ Campaign manager portal, which offers a personalized, role-based point of entry that can be used by all users to gain access to all relevant information, applications, and services

▶ Complete multi-channel functions, including letter, email, Web, telephone, SMS (short message service), fax, face-to-face, and mobile devices

▶ Embedded functions for campaign planning, which enable optimized processes with low implementation costs and short planning and development cycles, and also promote trouble-free campaign execution

▶ Calendar functions that offer a complete view of marketing activities

▶ User-friendly design that enables users without a technical background to create sequential campaigns and activities that promote dialogue with the customer and make communication more effective

▶ Efficient reading of external lead data that can be used in all marketing campaigns and initiatives

- Marketing report function with which marketing activities, such as campaigns and promotions, can be quickly assembled in PDF format for internal and external communication

- Coordination and visibility of product assignments and planning in a marketing campaign to optimize resources and accelerate product delivery

- Analytical functions that companies can use to determine the value of their customers

- Personalized e-marketing functions (permission-based, i.e., already accepted by the recipient)

- Tight integration with financial, supply chain, and logistics applications, as well as analytical data warehouse systems

- Dynamic offer generation in real time to improve product proposals

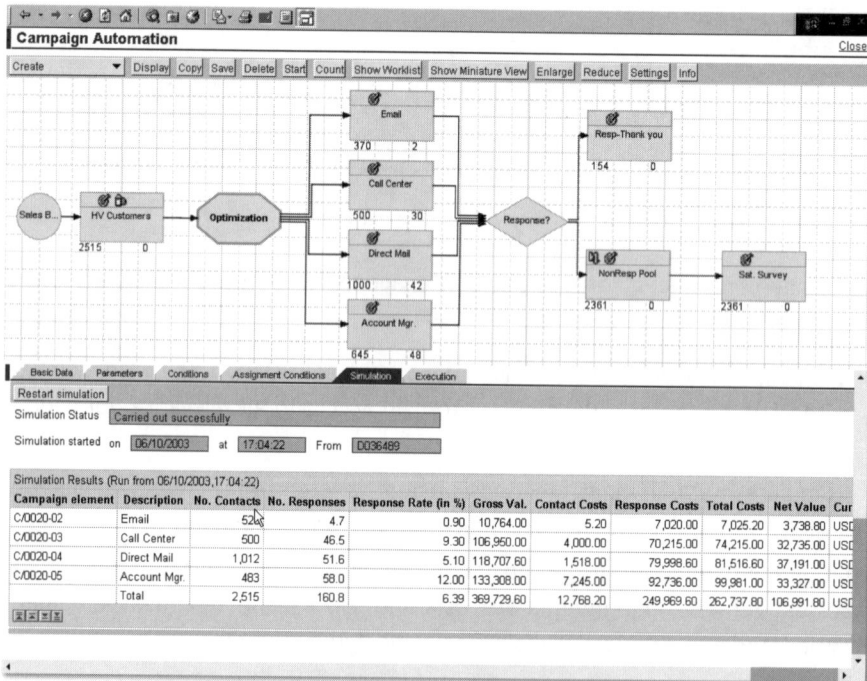

Figure 7.8 Campaign Optimization

Integrated campaign management that is linked with the supply chain and financial systems helps marketing organizations to optimize resources and coordinate activities across the organization (see Figure 7.8). Moreover, with mySAP CRM, marketing managers receive a definitive answer to the age-old question of the actual business use of a particular campaign (ROI reporting).

7.2.6 Trade Promotions

No other industry offers a broader product spectrum than the consumer goods industry: from food and drink products to household goods and cosmetic and drugstore articles to shoes and electronic appliances. The competition in these markets is fierce. The customer is usually contacted in three different ways:

▶ By media (radio, TV, print media)

▶ Directly as a consumer (mailing, product presentations at home with friends or neighbors)

▶ During trade promotions (displays, demonstrations, sample stands, price events)

The component *Trade Promotion Management*, which is outlined below, supports the entire sales promotion process. Trade Promotion Management forms a closed loop with the following process steps:

▶ **Strategic sales planning**
Management determines the sales volume targets and the advertising budget. It also determines the framework for customer-specific trade promotion planning (retail structure, products, discounts).

▶ **Field sales force planning and sales talks with retailers**
Based on the sales volume targets and the budget, retail structure, products, and discounts, the account manager creates sales planning for his or her customers. To achieve the sales targets, the account manager can plan trade promotions with his or her customers. In sales negotiations, details about trade promotion duration and discounts are agreed upon. To optimize the planning and support the sales negotiations, the account manager can use the analysis functions of SAP Business Information Warehouse (SAP BW). The account manager also has access to delivery and consumer data to enable him or her to choose optimum timing and an appropriate volume. This *fact-based sales* step contributes to optimizing the sales promotion. The costs arising from sales promotion activities are contrasted with the additional revenue gained.

From the planning, activities are generated for the field sales employees, and their calendars are updated. This enables field sales employees to promote sales on site, for example, by positioning the products in the shop for better visibility or by having retailers order larger product amounts in time for a planned promotion.

▶ **Processing and validation**
After the planning is complete, the trade promotion is processed: orders are received and carried out, customer deliveries are made, the goods issued are posted and subsequently invoiced. After invoicing, the order data is forwarded

to cost accounting, financial accounting, and SAP BW. Once the data has been transferred to SAP BW, it is available for future trade promotion planning.

Field sales employees carry out the validation on site. They use a questionnaire to verify that the retailer has upheld all agreements and that the payment of bonuses is justified.

► **Evaluation and analysis**

The following questions are used during evaluation and analysis:

- ► Were the targets reached with respect to volume, consumption, market share, and profit?

- ► How do the actual figures for sales volume and profitability compare to the planned figures?

- ► What conclusions can be drawn from this?

- ► Does this require changes to be made to the planning of the next trade promotion?

Consumer goods manufacturers use a larger and larger proportion of marketing expenditure for trade promotions. For this reason, marketing, sales, and purchasing departments are tightly integrated with the marketing process. SAP Trade Promotion Management supports the entire cycle of the business process and enables faster planning, processes integrated seamlessly in the company, and efficient reporting with the best possible analyses (see Figure 7.9).

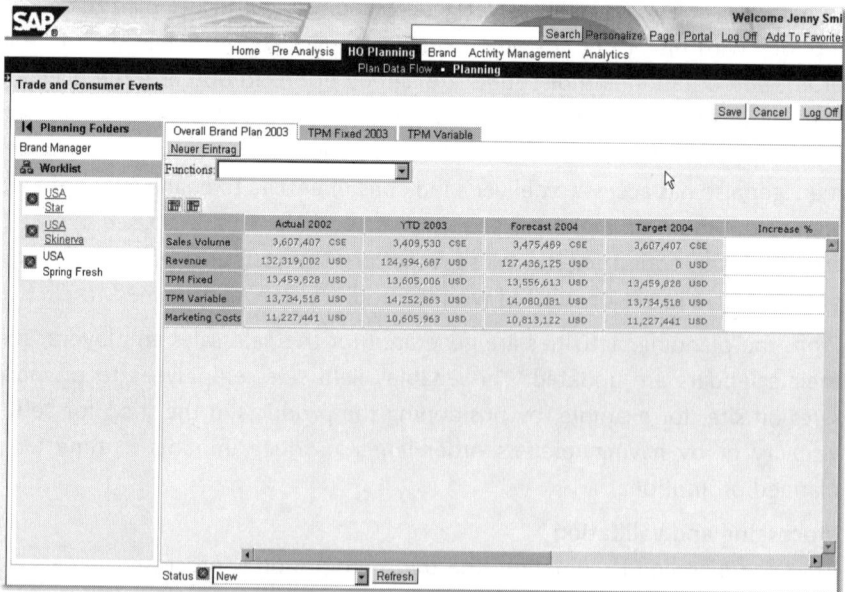

Figure 7.9 Trade Promotion Planning

7.2.7 Lead Management

With lead management, potentially valuable existing customers or new sales prospects can be identified. Lead management enables a company to keep an eye on existing customers, obtain new customers, and identify their interest in a product or service. Lead management paves the way for sales. Leads are potential customers of tomorrow or today's customers that companies would like to interest in a different product range.

Solid lead management functionality doesn't just help companies to increase the share of profit of existing customers; it also opens the door to invite business with new customers. The company-wide sales channel strategy can also be improved by opening the lead qualification for business partners.

Before a lead can become an opportunity, it needs to be qualified. Only leads that lead to turnover contribute to company profit. Lead management in marketing enables companies to convert qualified leads quickly into paying customers and eliminates time wasted on bad leads.

The lead management functions of mySAP CRM are used by marketing professionals to collect, qualify, and distribute leads and to give sales employees the best opportunities to capitalize on a lead. With collaborative lead management functions, companies can extend the lead process to internal and external staff.

When generating leads, an important piece of the puzzle is to identify potential buyers by name. To do this, companies must acquire lists of names from external providers; then, these lists can be compared with the customer data-base to identify the truly promising customers. As part of the list procurement process, companies must know which lists have yielded the best results in the past. Precise analysis of the list performance helps companies to improve their search for the best external lists.

Important lead management functions of mySAP CRM are:

▶ Lead manager portal, which offers a single, personalized, and role-based point of entry that provides the lead manager and lead qualifier with access to relevant information, applications, and services

▶ Functionality for managing external lists, including reading potential leads and the execution of specific subsequent marketing activities

▶ Lead qualification to increase conversion rate and revenue

▶ Lead forwarding to bring the right leads to the right sales employees or business partners

▶ The ability to create a survey for fast lead qualification

► Duplicate check for leads, that is, filtering of duplicate customer addresses to ensure data quality

► Comprehensive monitoring functions to follow the progress of each lead

7.2.8 Personalization

Personalization allows companies to create better customer relationships and to use these relationships to retain customers and increase the share of that customer's business.

With the personalization functions of mySAP CRM, enterprises can offer the right products to the right customers at the right time. Data mining technology offers product proposal functionality that ensures that companies get the greatest benefit from each customer interaction. Companies can create personalized product proposals for each interaction, independent of the communication channel used.

Important personalization functions of mySAP CRM are:

► Dynamic personalized product recommendations

► Personalized bestseller lists for each customer

► Personalized communication (see Figure 7.10)

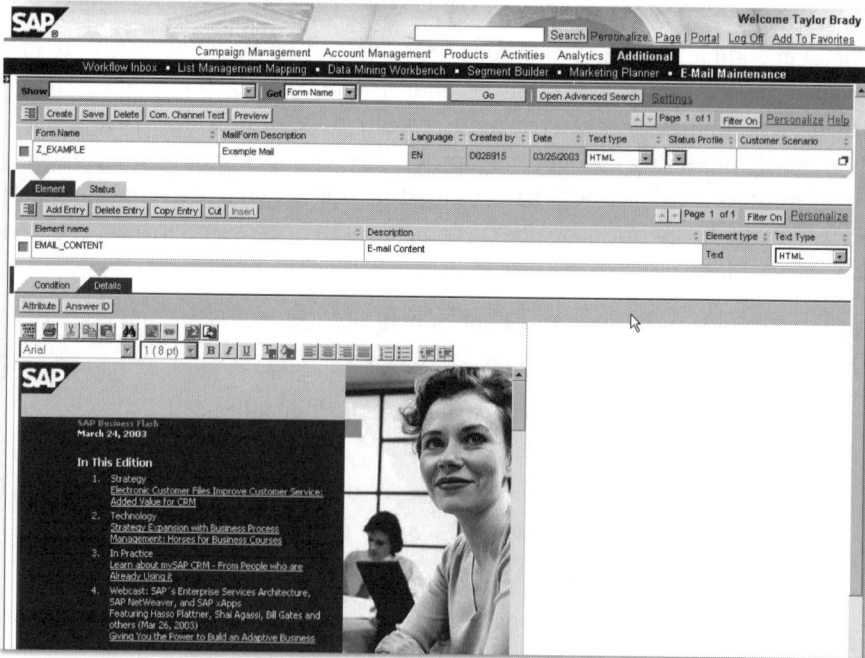

Figure 7.10 Definition of a Personalized Email

Product Proposals

The world of electronic retailing is El Dorado for marketing experts. The catchment area of Web shops is always global and the number of potential customers can be measured in millions. Companies that can give their target group a distinct profile can contact their customers directly and personally make a tailor-made offer. Even with this personalized effort, the company has by no means exhausted the customer potential until the next order.

On the contrary, the company must now keep the acquired customer, increase customer satisfaction, generate long-lasting customer ties, and sound out the customer's turnover potential. The mySAP CRM marketing application Product Proposals supports all of these goals across the communication channels— telesales, interaction center, and mobile sales. It not only automates cross-selling scenarios and up- and down-selling activities; it also groups together a particular number ("n") of products in "top-n-product lists."

Product Association Rules

This automatic product proposal function has proven to be a highly effective tool in online scenarios and in the interaction center. How does it work? The relationship between different products can be defined by using *product association rules*. These rules contain all products for which one or more other products are recommended as well as the already suggested (dependent) products. In addition to (or instead of) an already selected product, further product proposals can be made using this invisible link.

Examples of Using Product Association Rules

Cross-selling
A customer orders a new computer. The customer is also offered a printer or a useful software package: Maybe the customer needs a new printer right now.

Up- and down-selling
A customer orders a fax machine. The customer is offered a more expensive fax machine with a built-in scanner. Maybe the customer didn't know that multifunction fax machines exist. Or, perhaps the fax machine is too expensive, and to avoid losing the customer, a simpler (and cheaper) device is recommended. A customer with lower turnover is better than a customer lost to the competition.

Product association rules can be freely defined. The most frequently used rule is probably "If A is chosen, B is also suggested"; however, more complex variants are also possible. If A and B are chosen, but not C, only product F is suggested.

You can combine several product association rules in one method schema to automatically generate cross-selling proposals. These rules can be automatically read and evaluated and the products determined can then be combined in a special process. The cross-selling proposals can automatically be displayed in a Web shop as soon as the customer has selected a product; Of course, the proposals can also be displayed on the screen of a telesales agent or in the handheld PDA display of a sales employee.

Product Lists

Another way of offering customers additional products are *product lists*. Based on which attribute set they belong to (for example: "20 to 30 years old"), business partners can be assigned to one or more target groups displaying this attribute. The evaluation of sales data from SAP BW enables you to create a list of the most frequently purchased top products for each target group (bestseller list) and display it for all customers from each target group.

The creation of a top-n product list—be it a top 10 or top 50 list—seems random, yet it is based on actual sales figures. It reflects the product preferences of all customers from a target group that displays a particular attribute. It may seem strange that some men who buy baby diapers also buy a six-pack of beer at the same time; however, recorded sales figures actually support the likelihood of this occurrence. At the end of the day, the product combination in a top-n product list is as random as the contents of a shopping basket. However, since it reflects the product preferences of a very large number of customers (with at least one identical attribute), one can infer that it does signify tendencies.

Alongside top-n product lists, whose makeup can change in a relatively short space of time, "permanent" product lists can also be maintained. They can contain products for which no sales data exists, or warehouse stock to be sold cheaply ("offer of the month").

Personalized Communication

The antiquated and impersonal address "Dear Sir or Madam" is enough to make any marketing professional's hair stand on end. There is hardly anything worse than giving customers the impression that they're merely anonymous figures in the sales process. On the contrary, the customer personally deserves the undivided attention and esteem of the enterprise. Today, the customer has a different standing in deregulated industries and globalized markets—the customer is the absolute center of attention. And marketing experts know this adage by heart: The customer is king and wants to be treated like one.

As the last functional link in the process chain of marketing or campaign planning, personalization is of particular importance. After careful cost and appointment planning, painstaking segmentation of business partners, optimized allocation planning, and sophisticated product proposals, the campaign is started and the customer is contacted directly. In *Marketing Planner,* it is determined which communication channel should be used to address the customer: telephone, fax, letter, SMS, or email.

The scope of personalized communication is helpful to the user. The following options are available:

▶ **Creation of mail templates**
Using various tools, the content and layout of templates—created in plain text or HTML format—can be configured and sent as an email, fax, letter, or SMS. Mail templates enable a visually appealing layout of messages.

▶ **Creation of mail forms (personalized standard letters)**
The content of the message can be suited to the recipient's customer profile. To do this, placeholders representing the customer profile attributes are added to the text blocks that make up the message. The data underlying the attributes is not replaced by the current valid values until the form is output ("Congratulations on your 40th birthday!"). A typical personalization can mean, for example, contacting each customer in his or her native language, an important feature in global marketing.

▶ **Preview and test of mailings**
The preview function can be used to check that a mailing meets the requirements of content and layout before it is finally sent out. The test function shows whether emails are correctly output.

▶ **Monitoring mailings**
Mailing lists can be used to check whether mails were correctly sent and integrated links to other Web sites were clicked, or whether the delivery failed, for example, due to an invalid email address.

▶ **Tracking emails**
When links (for example to a Web shop) are integrated into emails, a "tracking ID" is included, which records whether the recipient visits the Web site connected by the link. The customer can then be personally greeted when visiting the site, for example (see Figure 7.11).

Figure 7.11 Personalized Email Preview

7.2.9 Campaign Monitoring and Success Analysis

In order to fully assess the success of a campaign, you must have all the information pertaining to responses, actual sales revenue, and costs. mySAP CRM offers comprehensive Web cockpits and evaluation tools that present all information relating to campaign success and response rates. Campaign managers receive all information relevant for decision-making, in particular, the actual financial campaign success, based on actually posted values. The excellent back-office integration of the SAP solution particularly helps companies in this area. SAP provides a special account assignment object for the systematic cost and revenue monitoring of marketing campaigns. In the profitability analysis (SAP R/3 CO-PA), the campaign-specific revenues (i.e., customer orders created for a campaign) can be grouped with the campaign costs already assigned to an account (for example, material withdrawal or incoming invoices for a campaign) and made available in SAP Business Information Warehouse (see Figure 7.12).

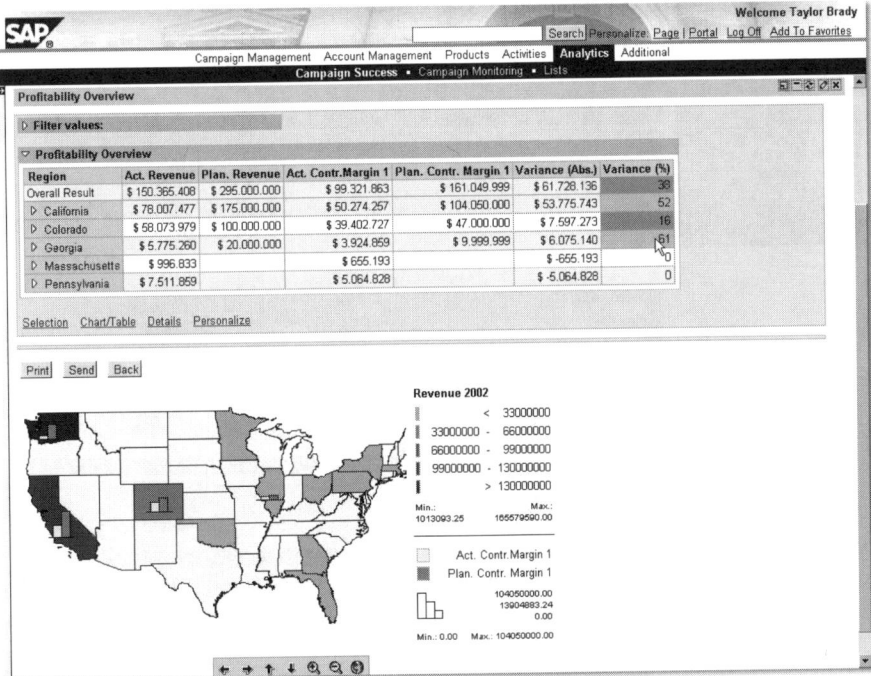

Figure 7.12 Campaign Monitoring and Success Analysis

7.2.10 Use Case: Using mySAP CRM in Marketing

The company PC4YOU has presented its hardware products at the CeBIT trade fair and gathered information about potential leads. After the trade fair is over, PC4YOU's marketing manager, Taylor Brady, evaluates the number of leads generated by CeBIT in the sales pipeline. He notices that the sales figures for 2003 have already been exceeded by more than 22%. He also notices that the budget for follow-up campaigns in 2003 has not yet been fully used. Since only $18,000 of the planned amount has been spent, $43,000 is still available, which, in Taylor's experience, is enough for an email campaign (see Figure 7.13).

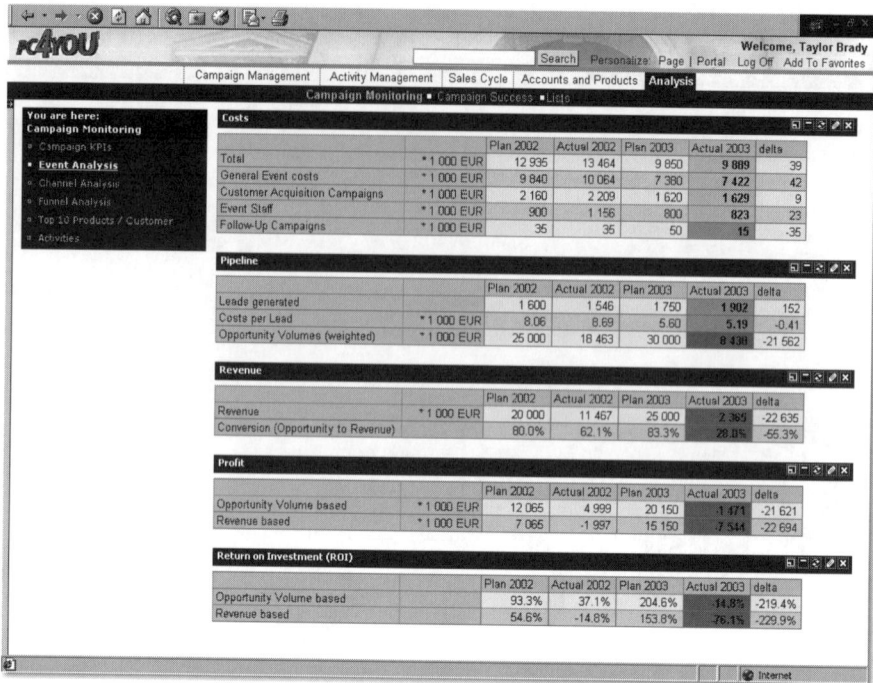

Figure 7.13 Lead Analysis in Campaign Monitoring

After Taylor has obtained an overview of the marketing campaigns planned for the near future, he creates a follow-up campaign, during which the leads from CeBIT are written to via email to restrict their area of interest and generate actual sales opportunities. PC4YOU's interaction center will then contact interested customers who respond to the email query. Taylor expects many of the mailed leads to show a firm interest to buy after further talks. He assures himself that the planned budget for follow-up campaigns has not been exceeded by the email promotion and, after awhile, he checks the results of the email campaign.

He sees that the endeavor has been successful. Through the campaign and the follow-up activities of the interaction center, 412 of the 506 CeBIT leads could be classified, 240 of them as hot leads. Of these, 179 leads can be viewed as actual sales opportunities. Taylor recognizes that the number of leads classified with the follow-up promotion could be increased to 82%. This exceeds even the planned success expectation of an increase to 75%. The proportion of opportunities generated from the leads also increased because it was 35% higher than the expected rate of 30% (see Figure 7.14).

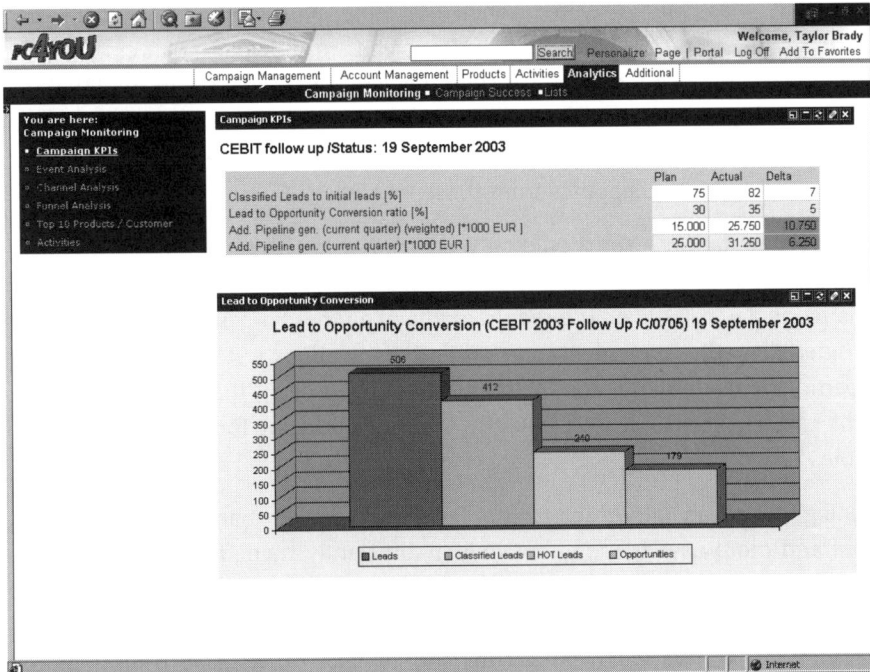

Figure 7.14 Result Analysis of Follow-Up Campaign

7.2.11 Recommendations for Successful CRM Projects in Marketing

Technology plays a more and more important role in the successful implementation of marketing strategies. However, using the correct technologies is only half the struggle: To lead a CRM project in marketing to success, additional factors must be considered. These factors are outlined below.

Support at management level is crucial; however, on its own, it cannot guarantee the success of a marketing project. The employees responsible for the operational marketing processes should be actively involved in the definition of business processes and should therefore be included in the blueprint phase. An important factor for success is anchoring the responsibilities for the marketing project at the operational level of the marketing organization.

It is also imperative that the marketing departments of an international marketing organization be involved in the planning process at the country and regional level. How can regional and global reporting needs be coordinated? Are campaigns processed in different ways in different countries? Can the individual marketing organizations learn from each other and jointly assemble a catalog of tried and tested business processes from which everyone profits? These are just a few of the questions that must be answered when implementing international marketing projects. Only when the various groups involved are allowed to participate in the development of business processes from the very start, can it be ensured that differences and possible synergistic effects are considered, compromises are made, and advantages are recognized. If this does not occur, the entire planning can meet with a lack of acceptance from those involved.

The implementation team should be organized across all functions. How is marketing integrated with accounting and finance? What is the collaboration with production and sales like? The requirements of all these areas must be noted and considered by the implementation project. If this does not succeed, marketing departments risk a silo effect. With an isolated approach, the marketing department can be seen to work efficiently for itself, but not for the company as a whole.

Training is also an important factor. Technology-based marketing is becoming more and more user friendly, but only a sufficiently trained team can lead the project to success. It must be ensured that a sufficient training budget is planned and that training doesn't appear as an "also ran" in the project planning. Training measures for the various user groups should take place in all project phases because the users provide important feedback necessary to fine-tune the solution.

Lastly, the benefits that the new solution brings should be transparent for all groups concerned. Typically, changes represent a challenge and some groups will probably have to make concessions for the good of the company. The advantages must be evident for all involved. If a technology with no discernible advantages is forced upon a marketing department, this poses a large obstacle for the overall success of the company.

7.2.12 Scenario Overview and Potential Benefits

The marketing applications of mySAP CRM enable the efficient execution and automation of planning, budgeting, implementation, and analysis of all required marketing measures. Important cross-industry business scenarios are listed in the following table, sorted by their focus:

Cross-Industry Scenarios	Short Description	Potential Benefits		
		Revenue	Profitability	Customer Satisfaction
External List Management	Use of externally procured datasets as marketing lists for lead generation in the marketing process	✓✓	✓	
Campaign Management	Optimization of campaign processing from market analysis to result validation	✓✓	✓	✓
Lead Management	Automation of steps for sales preparation Concentration on the most promising leads and opportunities	✓✓		✓
Marketing Planning	Planning and control of all marketing activities from budgeting to result analysis		✓✓	
Product Proposal	Generation of recommendations and proposals for customers based on top-n product lists or cross-/up-selling information	✓	✓	✓✓
Customer Segmentation	Division of customer base into segments for differentiating and personalizing the product and service offer (without extra programming)	✓	✓	✓✓

All of the scenarios mentioned above can also be used within industry solutions. SAP also provides the industry-specific scenarios listed in the following table.

Industry-Specific Scenarios	Short Description	Potential Benefits		
		Revenue	Profitability	Customer Satisfaction
Trade Promotion Management for Consumer Products	Planning and execution of sales promotion measures (trade promotions)	✓✓	✓	

Industry-Specific Scenarios	Short Description	Potential Benefits		
		Revenue	Profitability	Customer Satisfaction
Campaign Management for Media	Particular function of campaign management to support advertising measures and obtain subscribers	✓✓	✓	✓
Campaign Management for Utilities	Enhancement of campaign management with campaign execution using industry-specific communication channels (for example, marketing with bill supplement)	✓✓	✓	✓

7.3 Sales

7.3.1 Overview

The second phase of the customer interaction cycle is devoted to sales. In close coordination with *marketing, sales order processing,* and *service,* business processes in this area aim to establish and enhance business relationships with customers. The following planning, implementation, and management activities are supported by the mySAP CRM sales solution.

▶ Sales Planning

▶ Territory Management

▶ Account and Contact Management

▶ Activity Management

▶ Opportunity Management

▶ Quotation and Order Management

▶ Contract Management and Leasing

▶ Incentive and Commission Management

▶ Sales Analytics

Figure 7.15 shows that sales represents an individual, closed cycle within the customer interaction cycle. However, on a daily basis, the various stages of a business process rarely continue directly one after the other. Complex requirements, as well as disruptions and dependencies, frequently have to be addressed in the individual phases. Additionally, there are individual cycles within each phase which in and of themselves consist of planning, action, and analysis. Interfaces between sales management and other business areas, but also for partners and competitors, must equally be taken into account. Information and data about orders and sales prospects, and sales organizations, teams, and territories, come into play in the planning phase. At this stage, strategies are developed—possibly with the support of the marketing order—to provide the sales representative with all the necessary instruments and information required to reach a successful conclusion. After the conclusion of a contract, all contract details are recorded and can be used for analysis and evaluation. On this basis, planners and decision-makers can, for example, determine which products were successful in which regions, how often "opportunities" (see Section 7.3.6) became orders, and in which segments additional sales resources or initiatives are required.

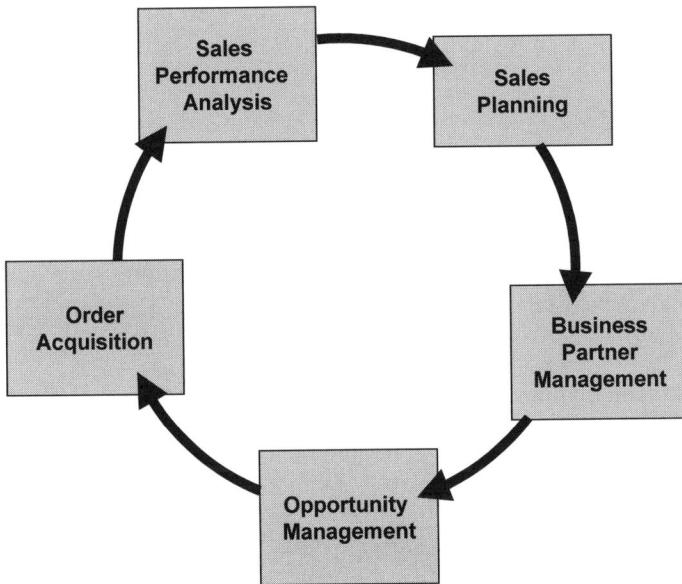

Figure 7.15 Sales in the Customer Interaction Cycle

Integration of All Interaction Channels

Sales can be successful today only if the high communication demands of potential and existing customers are met. This is true in particular for the interaction channels supported. Nowadays, almost everyone can be contacted via the Internet and mobile phones. It goes without saying that customers also expect this type of interaction from their suppliers. Furthermore, customers want to be able to choose their communication channel freely. They might, for example, place an order over the Internet today, then call up tomorrow and, in the event of making more critical decisions and dealing with higher purchase prices, expect direct contact with the field sales representative.

The greatest challenge here is the ability to change interaction channels as a process is running. For example, a customer places an order over the Internet, but calls the very next day to increase the quantity ordered. This is the moment of truth that will determine whether customer reach a reality. Does the employee in the call center have the same information as the customer? Or does the employee have to ask again for all the information that the customer entered the night before on the Internet? The call center employee who has access to all sales order data before starting the conversation can seamlessly continue the interaction that began the night before on the Internet.

In mySAP CRM, all interaction channels are integrated on the basis of a joint dataset. Every employee has access to the information required for each individual customer interaction in a consistent and complete form.

7.3.2 Sales Planning

Sales organizations can focus on customers, customer groups, and products that generate profit through effective sales planning, simulation, and forecasting, for example with regard to sales volumes, profit margins, visit frequency, and so on. This helps the sales department to make existing customers more profitable customers, and to decide which sales prospects could become potential profit-generating customers.

The following sales planning functions are available with mySAP CRM:

▶ Multidimensional planning with flexibly designed planning levels for strategic and operative sales targets

▶ Planning tasks personalized according to the area of responsibility for individual sales employees

▶ Comprehensive toolbox with planning methods for modifying and restructuring plans, such as top-down distribution, evaluations, simulations, and copying functions

▶ Integrated account planning as part of Account Management (see Section 7.3.4)

▶ Integrated opportunity planning as part of Opportunity Management (see Sections 7.3.6 and 7.3.7)

▶ Integration with other plans, such as strategy and financial planning

Planning can take place top-down or bottom-up. With top-down planning, requirements are specified right down to the smallest sales unit. In contrast, bottom-up planning condenses plan figures upward along the sales organization hierarchy. Structure information from Territory Management is used for bottom-up planning. Bottom-up and top-down planning, together with individual planning for individual customer contacts and activities, constitute the best prerequisites for lasting sales success. Sales planning is supported by sales analysis figures (see Section 12.2.6). This means that it is possible to determine, for example, which products were successful in which regions, and which customers contributed the most to profitability. On the basis of this information, you can forecast sales figures and make decisions regarding the assignment of individual sales employees.

7.3.3 Territory Management

Successful sales organizations divide up responsibilities in such a way as to win sales prospects and customers on the market with as few sales employees as possible and bind them to the company in the long term.

Organizational Model

The structure that is illustrated by the organizational model of mySAP CRM describes organizational units such as sales organization or sales office, as well as their interdependencies. All sales employees are assigned to an organizational unit in this model. If the human resources solution mySAP HR (Human Resources) is also in use and information relevant to the organization has already been collected, this information can be loaded and synchronized automatically. In this case, maintenance of this data takes place directly in mySAP HR.

Territories and Territory Hierarchies

Territory Management is a tool that can be used to structure and organize the market into individual territories according to different criteria, for example, postal codes, products, customers, customer groups, and so on.

The *Territory Hierarchy* describes the structure of territories. The following table shows an example of one way to create a hierarchy according to levels and attributes. Territories can be assigned at each level of the territory hierarchy.

Territory Hierarchy	Attribute
Level 1: Product group	Software, hardware
Level 2: Country	France, England, Germany
Level 3: Customer group	A001-A999

With reference to this example, territory '4711' could then be responsible for all business processes with the following attributes:

- ▶ Customers interested in software
- ▶ Customers based in Germany
- ▶ Customers who belong to customer group A110

While the organizational model represents the structure of sales, Territory Management portrays the market. The connecting link between the two is the *sales employee*, who, from the point of view of the organizational structure, for example, belongs to the sales office, and, from the point of view of Territory Management, is responsible for a particular sales territory.

Sales employees are not assigned directly in the organizational model, but rather by position, so that vacation and sickness coverage and staff turnover can be processed in the system as effortlessly and smoothly as possible. The position is a sort of placeholder in the organizational model for each individual employee. Every post within a company (whether occupied or unoccupied) is defined by a position.

Territory structure, territories, and assignments are time-dependent, that is, they can be planned in advance and entered in the system, but only become valid at a defined point in the future. This means that reorganizations or personnel changes can take place without hitches.

In some industries, for example, the pharmaceutical or consumer goods industries, there are standardized sales territories for which market share and sales statistics are available.

Third-party administrators calculate optimal Territory Management hierarchies and structures with the assistance of mathematical processes. Therefore, in addition to the maintenance of territory hierarchies and territories, mySAP CRM also offers an open interface so that this data can be transferred directly into Territory Management.

Territory Determination

In Territory Determination, each sales transaction (activity, opportunity, quotation, or order) is assigned to the corresponding territory. Here, there are basically two possibilities:

- ▶ The sales employee is found, and then the accompanying territory is determined
- ▶ The territory is determined, and then the sales employee assigned to that territory is found

The rules for territory determination can be flexibly defined according to each business process, which means you can automatically assign sales transactions quickly and effectively to the correct employees. As the territories themselves and their assignment to the individual business processes can be used in reporting, all types of analysis can be carried out regarding the territories (see Section 7.3.13).

Workflow Management

SAP's Workflow Management uses the data from the organizational model and Territory Management for automatic forwarding of business processes.

A lead (potential sales opportunity) is generated by direct mailing. mySAP CRM uses the rules defined in Territory Management to determine the appropriate sales territory from the company's postal code. The appropriate telesales agent is automatically determined by the position assigned to the territory. Because an important customer is involved, an automatically generated workflow is also sent to the agent, who can then call the sales prospect in order to qualify the lead, or rather to determine whether it is a genuine sales opportunity.

If the outcome is positive, mySAP CRM automatically determines the key account manager responsible for this customer. This person then receives the lead in his or her inbox, and knows that this sale must be processed with high priority. The account manager can see the last time there was contact with this customer, and what was discussed at that time, i.e., what information was already sent to the customer.

7.3.4 Account and Contact Management

mySAP CRM Account and Contact Management manages all relevant information about the customer, also in the context of cross-company cooperation.

Information about different people involved in the sales process can be managed in Account Management, including:

▶ Customers
▶ Sales prospects
▶ Sales partners
▶ Employees
▶ Competitors

Data is saved centrally as business partner master data. Duplicate checks ensure that each business partner is stored only once in the system, even if the business partner plays several roles in the company. The information held in master data includes address, contact person, relationships between different people, as well as credit, payment, and delivery information, and freely definable marketing attributes, for example, (according to requirements) the business partner's sales volume, number of employees, personal interests, and hobbies.

All employees have direct access to a wide range of information during their customer interactions. When, for example, a customer calls the Interaction Center, the agent can check this customer's telephone, email, and address data and update it immediately if necessary. The agent is not required to leave the on-screen working environment or inform other employees of any changes made. Individual employees can also be stored in the system alongside business partners. This provides a quick overview of employees' qualifications, knowledge, and experience, in addition to address and communication data. With the assistance of organizational management and Territory Management, the suitable employee can then be assigned to the right customers, projects, or sales activities.

Navigation in Account Management

Account Management equips sales managers with comfortable, portal-based access to the abundance of information on business partners. The following functions are available in Account Management:

▶ Search for and list important business partners

▶ Contact history with all business-partner-specific documents over the last *x* number of days (orders, quotations, activities, opportunities, complaints, and so on)

▶ Fast entry of activities and opportunities in Account Management

▶ Fast entry of contact persons in Account Management (a new business partner is generated in the background and the relationship "is contact person of" is created for the account)

▶ Important logistical and financial information (from SAP R/3 Enterprise or equivalent systems through defined interfaces)

▶ Business-partner-specific analysis

With this information, employees have immediate access to all past transactions, such as deliveries or payments. Before they call a customer to offer a new product, they therefore know that, for example, this customer has experienced delivery problems, and can prepare for the conversation accordingly.

The information presented in Account Management can be adapted to meet the information needs of a variety of employee groups. In this way, agents in the

Interaction Center receive information that is important when processing questions or problems raised by customers during calls. This means that all employees, regardless of how or where they work, are always informed about all relevant aspects of each customer's entire contact history.

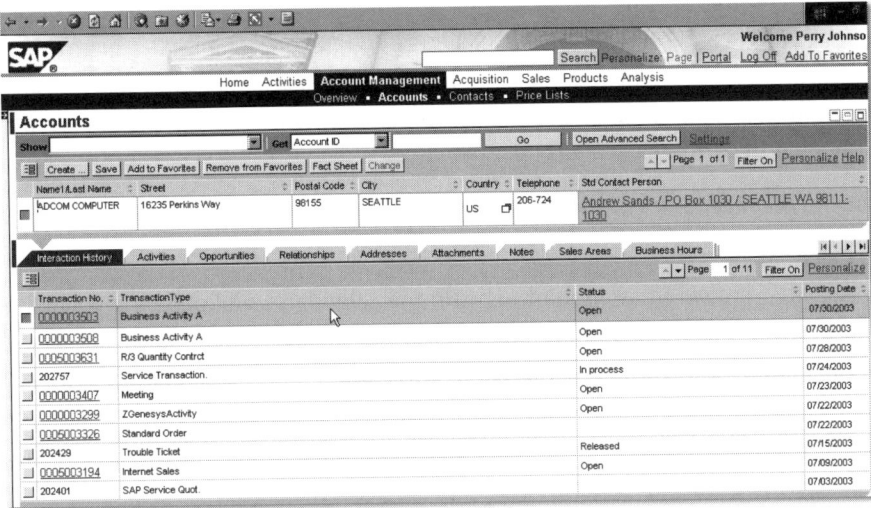

Figure 7.16 Interaction History in Account Management

Integrated Sales Planning in Account Management

In order to meet particular requirements in Account Management, SAP delivers integrated sales planning as part of Account Management.

Account managers have a good overview of the sales pipelines of their companies' products with their key customers. In many cases, the account manager and customer—for example, the buyer for a warehouse chain—give mutual consideration to the development of sales volume and sales quantity. Planned figures, historical, market, and customer data, as well as product hierarchies, prices, and campaigns, form the basis for planning. The planning layout that is integrated into Account Management for this purpose is tailored to meet the needs of the account manager.

7.3.5 Activity Management

Activity Management is not only available in sales; it is a general component of mySAP CRM that supports employees in organizing their daily work. Several interactions between companies and customers are recorded as business activities. Furthermore, employees can use the same transaction to manage both upcoming tasks and private appointments.

Typical questions that Activity Management can answer are:

▶ Which appointments do I have next week?

▶ When should I plan to visit Ms. Smith?

▶ Who can step in for a sick colleague in export trade?

A sales employee can, for example, view the results of a telephone call after the first customer visit. Activity Management offers the sales manager a succinct and simple overview of all activities that have occurred within a certain time frame within the department.

Activity Management consists of the following elements:

▶ **Calendar**
Activities are saved as appointments in the calendars of all people involved in a given business transaction.

▶ **Documents for business activities**
Documents contain information on business partner addresses, times, and dates, as well as related documents such as product information, letters to customers, and marketing brochures.

▶ **Results and reasons for activities**
For the purpose of analysis, it is important to know what happened with an activity and why. Therefore, the reasons for carrying out an activity, its status, and whether it was successful can all be recorded and evaluated in that activity.

It is often necessary to be able to create and evaluate specific information in a structured manner. Two tools are available in an activity for this:

▶ **Activity Journal**
Product reference often has to be recorded in an activity. In the pharmaceuticals industry, for example, drugs that have been discussed and medication tests sent to doctors are recorded. In the consumer goods industry, promotion sales prices and the number and location of listed products on the shelf are recorded. Using the Activity Journal, any number of key figures can be generated with product reference and later evaluated.

▶ **Survey**
In addition to the Activity Journal with actual product reference, it is also possible to create surveys centrally and to assign corresponding activities. This, for example, allows suitable customer surveys to be managed in parallel with a marketing campaign. Then, the appropriate survey is assigned to all activities that are created as a result of the campaign (customer visits or calls). This

means, for example, that it is possible to ensure that only those customers who have actually ordered a given product are asked questions about it.

Any number of surveys can be assigned to an individual activity. This allows you to deliberately use surveys for certain interaction channels or customer groups.

All information that is gathered in a survey or using the Activity Journal can be analyzed in detail and can, for example, be drawn upon for target group definition in a marketing campaign.

Activities can be created as follow-up documents for a large range of other business transactions, which affect, for example, opportunities, leads, sales orders, or contracts. Each activity also offers a quick link to Account Management (see Section 7.3.4) with the data and history of the customer interaction.

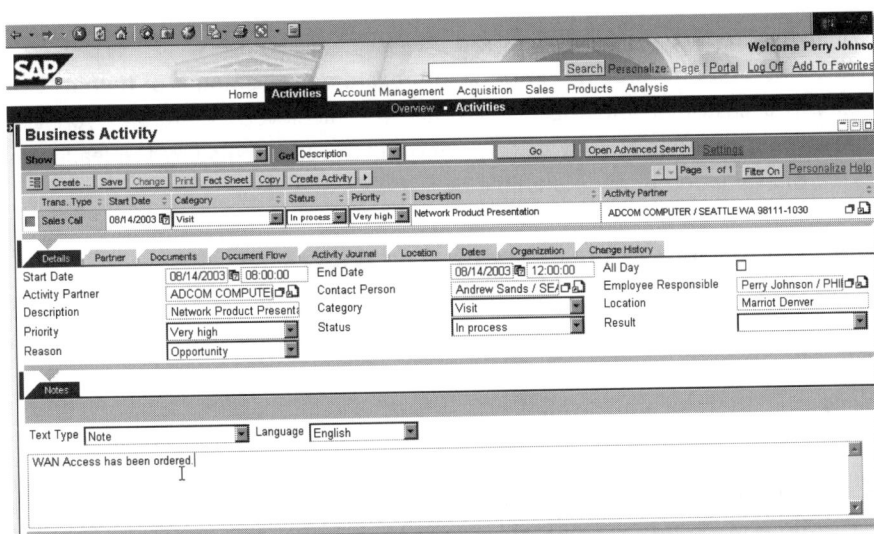

Figure 7.17 Activity in Activity Management

Working with Activities

Activities are associated with all aspects of daily sales processes. They can be created at any time in order to document an interaction with a customer. Activities appear automatically in the calendars of all employees who are entered as partners in the activity. This means that all employees involved are always kept up to date on discussions, customer visits, and results. You can also determine which employee came into contact with a certain business partner, when this contact took place, and what status the corresponding activities have for each available connection to Account Management in each activity.

Monitoring Activities

Together with other documents, activities offer a reliable history of the results achieved by employees as well as the possibility of forecasting future tasks. mySAP CRM provides reporting tools with which individual activities can be followed in detail. Two types of reports are available:

▶ **Operative report**
This type of report delivers, for example, all open business activities for a particular business partner or all business partners that have not been contacted in the last month. The appropriate employee can call up these reports directly in the system and view them in his/her portal. In this way, the employee learns what has to be planned for the coming weeks, or where and when it is necessary to take action.

▶ **Analytical report**
This type of report provides information regarding the amount of time it took to win a customer and the results that were achieved. Therefore, you can determine whether it was worth the effort involved in pursuing the lead. This kind of evaluation is made possible by SAP BW.

7.3.6 Opportunity Management—Overview

An opportunity is a *qualified sales chance*, or a verified chance for a company to sell a product or service. Opportunities can either be created from leads, or directly by a sales employee, for example, as a result of a trade show discussion, a sales promotion, or a bid invitation.

A sales employee is informed by his PDA about a new, extremely interesting opportunity that must be processed immediately. He searches for the sales prospect in the Business Partner Cockpit and finds out which service, marketing, and sales activities have already taken place. Using the Internet, the sales employee quickly discovers the most important competitors. He then sends an email to request more information about the market situation from the marketing department, and stores this information as an opportunity to be pursued.

In mySAP CRM, all opportunities are comprehensively documented, including:

▶ Description of the sales prospect
▶ Description of the products and services inquired about
▶ Budget of the sales prospect

- Potential sales volume
- Estimated sales probability

As the sales cycle progresses, this information can be altered, confirmed, completed, and finally sent to mySAP Business Intelligence (SAP BI) for evaluation.

Opportunity Hierarchies

It is possible to set up opportunity hierarchies so that sales projects can be mapped out even more effectively. This means that for every product belonging to a sales project, a separate opportunity is created and linked to the higher-level opportunity. A considerable amount of data is transferred from the higher-level opportunity and expected sales volumes are cumulated.

For sales projects with large companies it is also possible to divide up the entire sales project, for example, according to individual sectors. In this case, the accompanying opportunities are not linked by individual products, but rather directly with one another.

The structure of the opportunity hierarchy can be as deep as required, and makes it easier for sales managers as well as for employees involved to retain the bigger picture.

Opportunity Planning

The opportunity establishes the window of time for the sales project. At the closing date, the opportunity is either won or lost. Frequently, the sales volumes of an opportunity are received in several payments over a longer period. However, a simple opportunity can only post the expected sales volume by the closing date. This would mean that the sales volume forecast could only be mapped out very roughly. Using opportunity planning, however, you can record a more exact sales volume forecast. In an opportunity-specific planning table (planning layout), all important key figures are defined and then made available in Opportunity Management.

In opportunity 4711 with closing date 10/31/2003, a sales volume of $610,000 is expected. The sales volume is spread between two products.

| 100 PCs | $122,000 | 10/31/2003 |
| 200 Laptops | $488,000 | 10/31/2003 |

Any further data that is important for the sales volume forecast can now be stored in opportunity planning. For example, some laptops are to be delivered in advance on 10/31/2003, while others should be delivered at the time of the new software's productive start, and thereafter at three-month intervals, in parallel with the rollout of the software. The 100 PCs are intended to replace old PCs independently of the project and should be delivered in batches of 25, as installation is time-consuming.

Simple planning might look something like the following table:

	11/01/2003	03/01/2004	06/01/2004	09/01/2004	12/01/2004
Laptops	$48,000	$73,000	$122,000	$122,000	$122,000
PCs		$30,000	$30,000	$30,000	$30,000

7.3.7 Opportunity Management with Structured Sales Methodology

According to analysis carried out by Swiss Infoteam Sales Process Consulting AG, the real reasons behind a great many failed sales projects lie in companies' own sales processes [Kreindler/Lutz 2002]. Frequent key problems are:

▶ The focus is on the wrong people; the real decision-makers are identified and contacted too late

▶ Resources are wasted due to insufficient project assessment and qualification

▶ The sales team is uncoordinated

▶ The solution offered lacks convincing, people-centric argumentation of the benefits, meaning the cost does not seem justified

▶ Instead of learning from past mistakes, excuses are made

To avoid similar problems in the sales process, mySAP CRM implements a structured sales methodology that is applied in the Sales Assistant component. With this methodology, sales projects can be managed, documented, and monitored from the very outset.

Sales Assistant

The Sales Assistant guides sales employees through a structured sales process and supports them in the planning of their activities, without restricting their freedom to make decisions. It offers an activity plan, including a checklist with recommended activities and tasks, which sales employees should carry out in each phase.

The Sales Assistant can be adjusted to meet the needs of the specific sales processes of each company. If, for example, various sales cycles are implemented—one for existing customers and one for new customers—then special activity plans can be stored for each cycle with mySAP CRM.

Sales employees can elect to view the recommended activities for each phase and copy them into their personal activity plans for the sales project. They can also use their own ideas to customize their plans.

For each activity, sales employees have tips and background information at their disposal that are based on tried and tested sales practices. A tip for the activity *First Visit At Sales Prospect* might, for example, contain key questions and subjects that should be discussed during the visit. The activity plan might note when an activity should take place, which employee is responsible for orchestrating the activity, and whether the activity has already been completed. If an activity is overdue or not yet completed, an icon is automatically displayed to remind the sales employee.

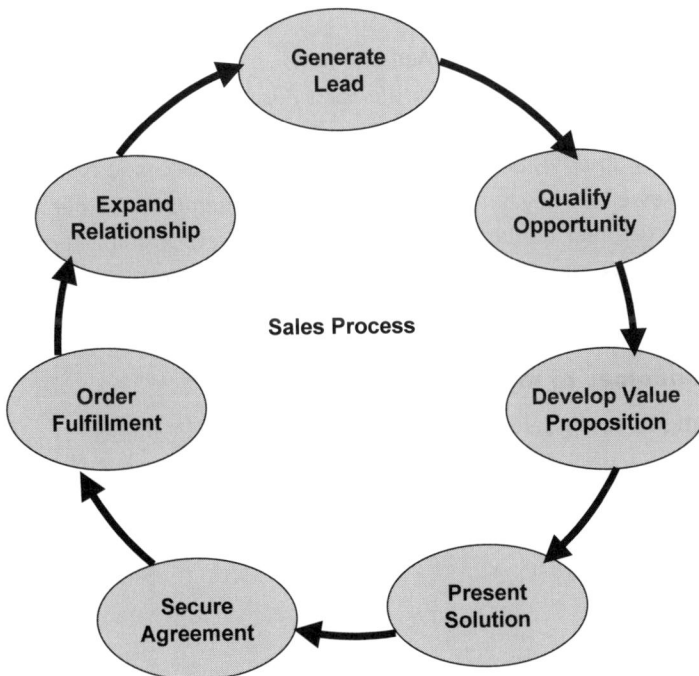

Figure 7.18 The Sales Process Supported by the Sales Assistant

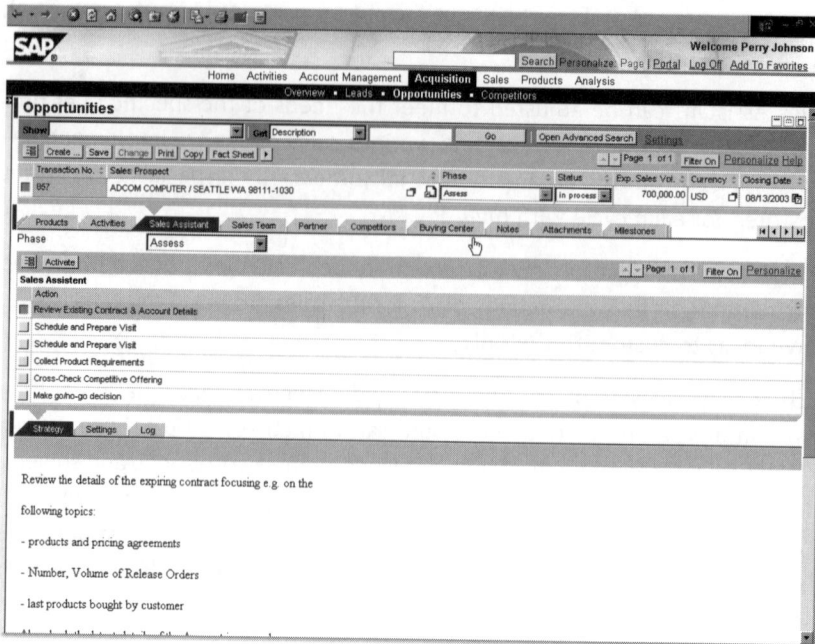

Figure 7.19 The Sales Assistant in Opportunity Management

Integration with mySAP CRM Activity Management

The personalized activity plan provided by the Sales Assistant is closely linked to mySAP CRM Activity Management. All activities from the personalized activity plan (for example, customer visits, telephone calls, emails, or discussions) can be called up and processed at any time from Activity Management. Partner data (such as customer, customer contact person, or employee responsible), remarks or notes, and other texts are automatically copied from an opportunity into an activity.

The Sales Methodology of mySAP CRM

Fundamental elements of the sales methodology of mySAP CRM are:

▶ Project goal description

▶ Buying center

▶ Analysis of competition

▶ Opportunity assessment

▶ Opportunity plan

▶ Analysis and reporting

All of these elements are described in the following sections.

Project Goal Description

In order to establish whether and how a customer can benefit from a sales offer, it is important to understand the requirements of the customer and what results are expected. Furthermore, the sales employee must clearly define short- and long-term goals vis-à-vis this customer. Goals can be defined both from customer and sales perspectives, and are then accessible to all employees involved in the sales process.

Buying Center

In order to sell successfully, the organizational structures and all important decision-makers of the customer must be known early on. Many sales projects fail because this factor is underestimated. The project buying center incorporated in mySAP CRM Opportunity Management offers support in answering questions, such as:

▶ Who makes the final decision at the customer end?

▶ Who is responsible for approving the project? How is the relationship network?

▶ Who benefits from the solution being offered?

▶ What are the key attributes for each individual involved, such as his or her opinion of the solution offered and what he or she feels can be gained from it?

mySAP CRM offers as standard a host of predefined sales categories that play a part in the sales process, namely:

▶ **Endorser**
Gives the final go-ahead and can increase or decrease the budget.

▶ **Decision-maker**
Recommends to the endorser which of the solutions offered to buy. This person is responsible for the success of the project and adhering to the budget.

▶ **User**
Benefits from the purchase decision and judges the solution offered with respect to its use for his or her own work processes.

▶ **Assessor**
Assesses other possible solutions from a technical point of view.

▶ **Coach**
Offers support and guidance throughout the sales process. Furthermore, this person delivers information and pointers that are important to the success of the sale, for example, if important people have been overlooked.

Additionally, you can define further, customer-specific roles.

It is not only the people involved in the sales process who are important; the relationships between the people involved are also very significant. In order to make a successful sale, this intertwined relationship—which can go well beyond the official hierarchy—must be understood. The following relationship types are definable for the individual people in the buying center:

▶ Formal relationships based on the enterprise structure (person A informs person B)

▶ Informal relationships that depend on personal relationships and influences (person A influences person B)

Relationship types can be defined in Customizing according to the individual requirements of the company.

As soon as the primary decision-makers and their influence on the purchase decision are known, the next step should be to work out the added value that the solution offered will bring to the customer. At this stage, people often make the mistake of placing functionality in the foreground, instead of presenting the benefits in a people-centric fashion. Awareness of the following factors makes for a convincing argument in favor of the benefits:

▶ Importance and urgency of the project from the point of view of each person

▶ Personal and business-related goals and decision criteria of all people

▶ Knowledge of how individual people rate the solution

All known information can be stored in the opportunity description for each person so that gaps or areas where there is a need for action can be identified early on. Additionally, other appraisal factors that are important for the sales process can be defined. Risks and shortages of information can be highlighted by warning indicators. This information makes it possible to adjust sales campaigns to meet the exact needs of customers. Knowledge of business goals and decision criteria are extremely useful when, for example, creating customer-specific presentations.

Analysis of Competition

Sales employees should know their competitors, including both their strengths and weaknesses. To provide support in an actual sales project, the following information on competitors can be gathered and used in the development of a counter-strategy in Opportunity Management:

▶ Solutions offered by competitors

▶ Competitors' strategies

▶ A coach at the customer end, who can answer open questions relating to competitors

Opportunity Assessment

Before an enterprise goes to greater sales expense for an actual project, it must be clear on whether the expected sales volume and chance of success are justifiable given the investment required. If this matter is addressed early on in the sales process, risks can be identified in advance and, if necessary, eliminated before any investment is made in a cost-intensive sales project. Figure 7.20 shows an example of an opportunity assessment.

To calculate a sales project's chance for success, a computerized survey (the *Survey Tool*) is integrated into mySAP CRM. With this tool, you can rate questions and answers on opportunity assessment and, based on the answers of the sales employees, determine the chance for success, and thus provide a forecast of the outcome. Alternatively, the employee can also enter his or her own forecast based on a personal evaluation of the project.

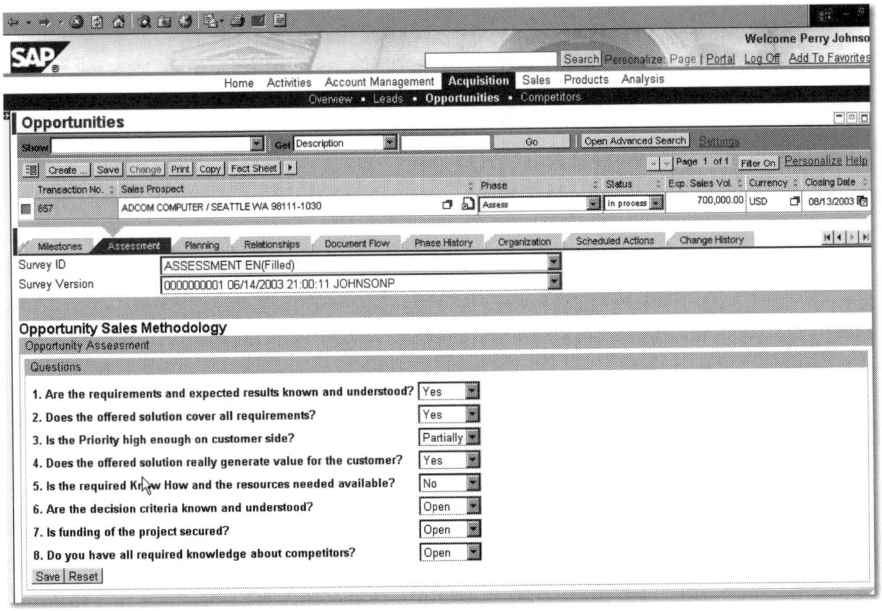

Figure 7.20 Assessment of an Opportunity

Opportunity Plan

An opportunity plan is drawn up for each opportunity. This pulls together all key information that is attained with each opportunity.

▶ **Project Overview**

Expected sales volume, customer budget, chance of success, current phase in the sales cycle, closing date, sales team, project goals for customer, sales goal

- ▶ **Product Overview**
  Products, quantities, expected product value

- ▶ **Buying Center**
  The organizational chart of the customer, that is, sales prospects with key peo-ple and definitive attributes for influence, opinion, decision criteria, and per-sonal benefits argumentation

- ▶ **Analysis of Competitors**
  Strengths, weaknesses, strategies of competitors

- ▶ **Opportunity Assessment**
  Evaluation of the chance for success with the help of sales employees and the chance for success as determined by the system

- ▶ **Activity Plan**
  Overview of all activities, employees responsible, and level of completion

The opportunity plan offers a comprehensive overview of the stage a project is currently at. It serves as a basis for presentations and discussions in internal project meetings and can be displayed, printed, or emailed at any time.

Analysis and Reporting

Opportunity Management uses SAP BW for the purpose of analysis. Here, ready-made queries are available which make it possible to gain a comprehensive over-view of all opportunities, thus forming the basis of detailed sales planning and simulation. The opportunity pipeline delivers, for example, information about the current status of all opportunities and allows you to monitor short- and long-term sales volume possibilities.

7.3.8 Quotation and Order Management

The Quotation and Order Management phase in the sales process pertains to the exchange of sales documents between the vendor and the customer as soon as the customer has decided on actual sales negotiations. If an opportunity was not created beforehand, an inquiry or a quotation regarding the purchase of products or services can exist at the start of the actual negotiations. Once the conditions have been agreed upon, the quotation is copied into a customer order or contract at the end of the sales process.

Inquiries, quotations, and orders can be created using any communication chan-nel, for example, by an agent in the Interaction Center, a sales employee at the customer, or by the customer himself or herself on the Internet. Once a customer has decided to purchase a product, all customer data is seamlessly entered in the required documents. Since all documents in a single business transaction are linked, it is possible to automatically transfer information from one document to another. In doing so, you can determine which data is copied into the other document, such as organizational data and partner functions, and the assigned business partners (for example, ship-to and bill-to party) or product and price information.

Integration with systems makes it possible to run credit and product availability checks in real time, and ensures that relevant information is forwarded to the responsible employees. Prices, taxes, and product availability checks are automatically determined from the gathered data, and displayed and saved in the business process.

> The customer Mrs. Brown places an order by telephone for x number of a particular product. The system stores the following information: Mrs. Brown should receive a 10% discount. Once the order is taken in the Interaction Center, the system assimilates the data and automatically calculates the discount on the goods ordered by the customer.

Content of a Sales Document

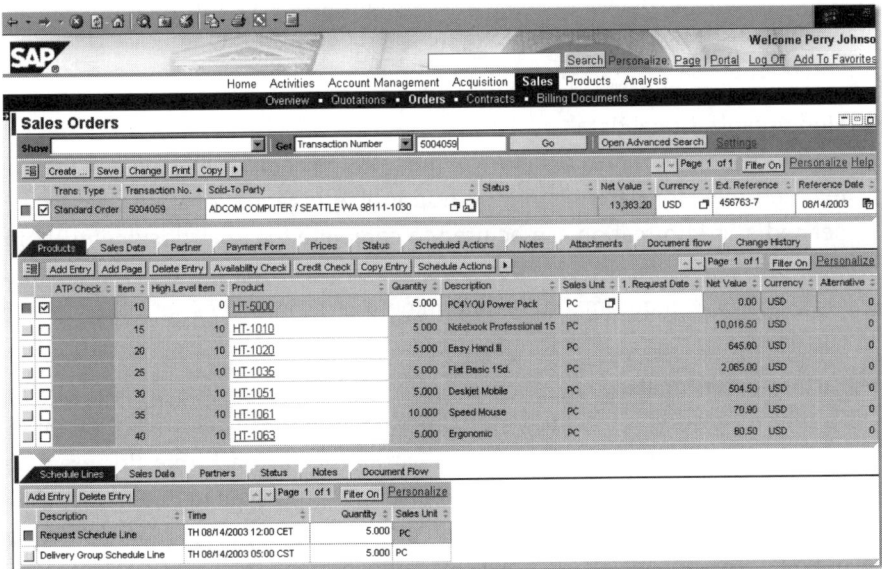

Figure 7.21 Sales Document

A sales document (inquiry, quotation, order, contract) is divided into the two following sections, which can be further broken down by tab pages:

► **Header**

The document header contains all important data relating to the entire document, for example type (inquiry, quotation, or sales order), number, and status of the transaction. It can also contain information on the campaign through which the business transaction was originally triggered. Additionally, it is possible to determine campaign-specific pricing conditions (for example, discounts or other price reductions), or to evaluate at a later stage the number of sales orders that were won using a certain campaign. Furthermore, information on shipping, payment, and delivery conditions, as well as tax data, organizational, administrative, and partner information and texts can all be stored here.

► **Items**

This section contains details on each individual document item, including schedules, prices, conditions, texts, order information, as well as partner, delivery, payment, and organizational data. Products can be configured at item level. The item details offer a comprehensive overview of all ordered products, their prices, and delivery conditions.

General Functions for Documents

A wide range of general functions are available for sales documents (business transactions). These general functions are listed below in the order in which they are used in the sales process:

► **Find organizational data**

When the organizational structure of the sell-side company is stored in the system and rules for determining the responsible organizational unit have been defined, this information can be used to complete the sales documents. If, for example, a sales order is created, and the name of the customer is entered, mySAP CRM can automatically determine the responsible sales office for this customer.

► **Partner determination**

Partner processing is used to determine which partner roles are important for which transactions, and which task is carried out by each role (for example, ship-to party, bill-to party, or contact person). It is possible to determine which partner roles should appear in a document and whether they are mandatory or optional. As soon as these settings have been made, mySAP CRM automatically enters the necessary partners into the documents. A sales order can, for example, contain a sold-to party, a contact person, and a ship-to party. The fields for entering these people automatically appear on the screen as soon as a sales document is created. When the name of the contact person is entered, mySAP CRM determines the names of the sold-to party and ship-to party. If necessary, these fields can be changed manually.

▶ **Listing and assortment**
A listing or an assortment is a combination of business partners and products that is valid in predefined scenarios for a certain time period. It can contain a list with the important products and services for a particular customer, or specify products that should not be sold to a particular customer, perhaps because the price is not suitable for this customer.

▶ **Product determination**
In order to save time when entering products, product keys can be stored in the system. As soon as this key is entered in the business transaction, mySAP CRM automatically determines the desired product and completes relevant fields, such as product number and description.

▶ **Product configuration**
You can get a technical view of configurable products that have many possible variants, for example, cars or machine tools. Possible product attributes such as color, equipment, special accessories, and their dependencies are stored, and the actual product is then assembled in the sales document (see also Section 7.3.9).

▶ **Pricing**
The pricing function automatically calculates all relevant pricing conditions in a business transaction. Various kinds of pricing elements can be combined, for example, material prices, surcharges, or discounts. This is how gross and net prices and taxes are calculated. When required, you can use exchange rate information to convert currency. Pricing is centrally implemented in the CRM system and linked to the relevant business process so that current and reliable price information is available at all times throughout the sales process.

▶ **Free goods**
In addition to the various pricing conditions, it is also possible to offer "free goods." These free goods can be either inclusive or exclusive bonus quantities of the same product or another product. Examples are:

  ▶ When you buy 10 PCs, you pay for only nine.

  ▶ When you buy 10 PCs, you get eleven.

  ▶ When you buy 10 PCs, you receive a laser printer free of charge.

▶ **Availability check**
The availability check offers the following services in the sales transaction:

  ▶ Check the ability to deliver for a product.

▶ Reserve products in the required quantity. This enables the sales team to make reliable promises during order entry.

▶ Forward requirements to the production or purchasing departments.

The availability check runs in *SAP Advanced Planner and Optimizer* (SAP APO) or in *SAP R/3 Enterprise*. Furthermore, there is an open interface so that you can connect to non-SAP systems. Further details on the availability check are included in Section 7.4.2.

▶ **Date management**
Using date management, you can store any number of dates in documents, for example, planned and actual dates of activities, or the start, end, and validity period of a contract. Dates can also be determined according to rules, for example: "The validity period for a contract always runs for 12 months from the start date."

▶ **Credit check**
The credit check allows you to reduce financial risks when a sales transaction is being processed. This check does not take place in mySAP CRM itself; rather, it is triggered by a function call in the system (see also Section 7.4.3).

▶ **Text management**
In text management, transactions or objects can be described in detail, and separate notes or documents can be created and linked to the business transaction. These texts relate either to the business transaction as a whole—in which case, they are linked to the document at header level—or to a particular item.

▶ **Attachments**
Additional documents—also in special formats such as presentations, product descriptions, information brochures, or hyperlinks to the Internet—can be included in a transaction as attachments at either header or item level. Each business transaction has its own list with attachments.

▶ **Output**
The output format for documents can be chosen freely from the various output channels (print, fax, email). Each document contains selected information from the business transaction, such as address, ship-to party, operational data, sales texts, and order items.

All phases of order processing support EDI (Electronic Data Interchange).

Sales Documents in the Process

Managing and monitoring sales processes is made easier by the following document flow-related functions:

- ▶ Create promotions/actions
- ▶ Copy sales documents
- ▶ Display document flow
- ▶ Manage status

These functions automatically trigger entire event chains when required, and make it easier for sales employees to support their customers effectively.

Actions

Actions support the planning and triggering of the next steps in the business process as a reaction to certain conditions, and serve to automate sales and service processes. They are started automatically as soon as the corresponding conditions are fulfilled. In this way, subsequent documents can, for example, be generated automatically, or documents that have already been processed can be changed, printed, or sent by fax or email. You can define the type and schedule of actions according to the needs of your customers and your own company's processes.

You schedule actions in a document manually for a business process. Every document (business process) has a tab page called *Actions* on which the user can see which actions are planned, as well as which actions have started or ended.

Actions can be scheduled automatically by implementing a method. In the method *Create a Quotation*, for example, you can define that the system automatically generates an activity for the responsible sales employee two weeks later, so that this employee reminds the customer of the quotation by telephone and answers any questions that might have arisen.

Actions can also trigger *Workflows* for more complex processes, such as creating follow-on documents for which approval is required. It is, for example, possible to define that the system automatically sends a customer a quotation to renew a contract four weeks before the existing contract runs out. The contract should be forwarded to the responsible credit representative beforehand using *WebFlow—* SAP's workflow component—so that he or she can check whether the customer's credit status is in order.

Copy Documents and Display Document Flow

Both mySAP CRM applications and its users can copy business transactions—that is, all accompanying documents—or create subsequent documents for particular transactions. This ensures that certain information is always consistently passed on to other documents so that data only has to be entered once in the system. This saves working time and minimizes the likelihood of errors occurring.

Copying documents means that while work is being done in a given business transaction, a new transaction of the same kind and with the same header and item details can be created, such as a new order generated from the original order. In doing so, the system does not establish any reference between the two documents.

Data from one or more transaction documents can be copied using *Follow-on Business Transactions*. After the transaction type for the follow-on document has been selected, the system copies the header data. Items that are to be used can then be selected or new items can be added. The new document is linked to the original document via a *document flow*, which allows the connection between the business transactions to be displayed. For example, when an opportunity is created with two activities and a sales order is in the process of being finalized, all four documents are listed in the document flow.

mySAP CRM applications can also copy documents or generate follow-on documents themselves. This helps sales employees by creating automatic workflows that make available the required documents at the right time.

Status Management
mySAP CRM differentiates between system status and user status.

A *system status* is automatically assigned to a business transaction internally by the system. It informs you that certain business processes are complete, for example, that a new document has been created or a document contains errors.

A user status, on the other hand, is assigned manually by the user or set by customer-specific workflows (for example, "Two days remaining until quotation expires"). The user status provides certain additional information, such as still *being checked*, *to be released*, *released*, or *rejected*.

Workflows or actions can also be triggered by the status. If, for example, a contract receives the status *canceled*, an activity can automatically be created in the form of an email, which informs the sales manager of this incident.

7.3.9 Product Configuration
The increasingly common expectation of customers to have their specific demands met when they purchase a product means it is necessary to make the spectrum of products flexible, with the option to modify products to meet each customer's needs. Accordingly, the product range must be extended to include new variants, which not only take into account product modernization and market trends, but also cater to customer-specific, country-specific, and regional demands. Consequently, the potential for variation within a product range is rap-

idly expanding, and products are becoming faster moving and more complex. It is becoming more and more important for the various sales channels to receive the most current information about new products and their potential for being modified and combined.

▶ The product configurator—*SAP Internet Pricing and Configurator (SAP IPC)*— helps the user to find the most suitable product, and, due to its advisory nature, frequently supplements the product catalog and search functions available within it.

▶ The configurator supports the individual customer adaptation of a product by presenting the end user with the range of available product options in a dialogue, such as different air conditioning systems, colors, and engine sizes of a car, and then checks the selected product configuration against a predefined set of rules for completeness and consistency.

▶ Product options can be linked to corresponding increases and decreases in the base price, as well as to images with explanatory texts, which help the end user to select the required options.

▶ SAP IPC ensures the integration between the sale itself and order processing so that exactly what was ordered is also delivered and billed for.

With mySAP CRM, the product configurator can be used in all sales scenarios across all channels of communication. Depending on each case, either the customer configures his or her products, or the configurator supports the sales employee or sales partner when creating a quotation or order, or during the consultation discussion. In the following section, three business processes are described in detail.

Business-to-Consumer (B2C) on the Internet

In B2C retail, the customers (the end users) expect the Web shop to help them find the optimal product or service as a solution to their problems. By answering specific questions posed by the product configurator, the customer is presented with only valid product variants, options, and possible combinations.

A doctor who buys a PC on the Internet doesn't order a standard PC; instead, she orders a complete package put together to match her requirements, consisting of a PC, monitor, printer, fax machine and paper to go with it, applications, installation, and startup in the existing local network, as well as maintenance services.

The SAP configurator determines which PC models are offered in this region with on-site installation, which hardware components the doctor needs to use the network, which printer meets her requirements, and which monitors are best suited for her PC. All options or components are accompanied by a detailed description, an illustration, and a price range for the high and low end. Even without having intimate knowledge of the product, the customer can describe relatively complex product requirements with the assistance of the product configurator. Before she sends in her complete order, she can also verify whether her requested delivery date can be met without even having to pick up the telephone.

Business-to-Business (B2B) Customer on the Internet

The business process that takes places between two companies (Business-to-Business), unlike the transaction that occurs between a business and an end user, often results in the building of a long-term business relationship. Accordingly, the customer sometimes requires the same detailed product information as does the internal employee.

A European, medium-sized producer of access control systems has given its business customers direct access to the product configurator, and in so doing, has achieved several goals; the architect currently searching online for the right access control system for a management office is pleased that the "product advisor" knows several product series in detail and can offer support in finding a solution that is technically and financially optimal. The orders created via the product configurator contain far fewer errors than orders that were previously sent in by fax. Ultimately, it becomes apparent that the capacity of the sales-oriented product specialists can be put to better use, as they are required only in particularly difficult cases.

The information advantages that the product configurator offers to professional purchasers lead to greater customer satisfaction, which, in turn, results in greater customer retention and increased sales volumes with existing customers. As customers ask the sales team fewer questions, but nevertheless make fewer mistakes when placing orders, the costs involved in order processing are reduced. A service provider for banks, which uses the SAP product configurator as a part of SAP Internet Sales, has even reported a dramatic 90% reduction of order processing costs.

Product Configuration for Sales Employees

In this case also, the first priority is to find the optimal solution for the customer, independently of whether the customer calls and deals with an Interaction Center agent, is visited by a field sales representative on site, or is advised by a sales partner. Here, the same product knowledge and consistent product information must be available throughout all sales channels.

An office furniture manufacturer operating internationally has made the SAP product configurator available to his sales offices and sales partners as part of a CAD application, so that they can call up in detail which product options and components can be combined with one another. The product configurator also provides explanations for certain options that cannot be selected concurrently. The current configuration of office equipment with desks, shelves, cupboards, partition walls, and tables is, in this case, always represented graphically.

This transparency in the product offer makes it possible for sales offices and partners to serve their customers themselves, and considerably reduces the number of queries that product experts receive per telephone or in written form. The error rate in orders taken by sales partners was drastically lowered by the introduction of the SAP product configurator, while the time required to bring new, consultation-intensive products onto the market was cut from one or two years to just a few months.

Sales employees use the product configurator to familiarize themselves more quickly with new product ranges, products, and product variations, as well as to become better qualified in offering more products and product combinations, and to become better at advising their customers.

Order Scenarios

In the area of supply, SAP has prepared various sales processing scenarios to meet different requirements. Some scenarios are aimed at make-to-order manufacturers; other scenarios are applicable to consumer goods and services.

▶ **Ship-to-Order/Deliver-to-Order**
This is the scenario for simple products. Here, the configuration can be linked to a search for suitable products that can be delivered in the desired configuration (for example, from the warehouse) as soon as the order is entered. This applies to services, PCs, game consoles, clothing, cars, electric motors, pumps, and transmission systems, for example.

▶ **Make-to-Order**
This is the scenario for products that must first be assembled or completed in

some other way. This is a common scenario in engineering or high-tech sectors or the automotive industry. For example, the components required for geared motors are generally prefabricated, and groups of components are preassembled at the supplier site. The completion of units for sale rarely takes place without an order, as the number of possible combinations is simply too great.

▶ **Engineering-to-Order (ETO)**
Engineering-to-Order is relevant when engineering efforts are required after a sale. SAP customers from branches such as elevator and power station construction, as well as manufacturers of switchboards and carriages, work with this scenario. It is possible for a switchboard manufacturer to prepare a few variants for sales transactions. However, with a new product range, the effort required to construct all components necessary for completion of all variants would be too great. Therefore, as soon as an order is accepted, the engineering department must develop all of the required components before they can be completed and assembled.

The product data can be gathered and maintained using the component *Change Management* in mySAP Product Lifecycle Management (mySAP PLM).

All sales-relevant data, for example, product, sales-relevant options, rules, and pictures, are replicated to mySAP CRM. Later data can then be added here. Depending on the sales organization, different specifications are possible for a product. For cars, for example, this might be in the form of country-specific options packages. For Scandinavia, a winter package including snow chains, auxiliary heating, and air conditioning might form part of the offer, while in Spain a beach package with air conditioning, tinted windows, and a sunroof might be developed.

The master data required for production is transferred to mySAP Supply Chain Management (SCM). In this way, tight integration between the sale and production is ensured. For certain scenarios that don't require production processing in an SAP system, you can carry out all product maintenance in mySAP CRM. The SAP product configurator can also use configuration models that are present from SAP R/3 so that separate modeling is not required in mySAP CRM.

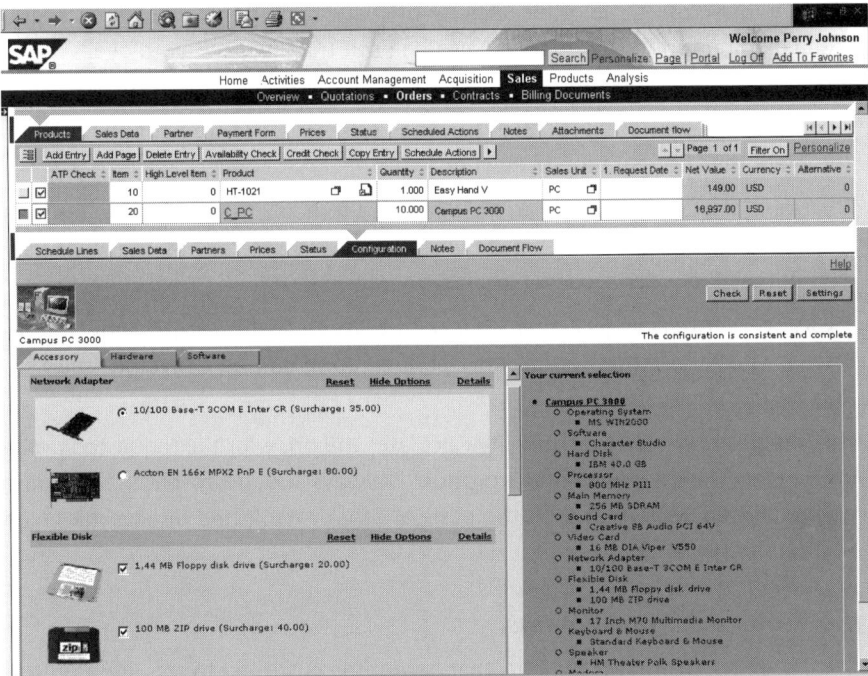

Figure 7.22 Functions of the Product Configurator

Functions and Characteristics of the Configurator

The illustrated examples of how the product configurator can be used have shown that the SAP product configurator is not limited to only certain sectors or individual product groups, but can be used for both smaller configuration requirements as well as complex tasks, for example, in the production industry or service sector. This flexibility is in large part due to the number of generic functions and characteristics that constitute the SAP product configurator:

▶ During the first phase of the customer contract, the configurator can record a description of the customer problem for which a solution is required. It can record this problem electronically in a standardized format and use it to determine the optimal product or solution.

▶ The product configurator checks whether the selection made is complete and consistent, for example, whether the service can be offered or the product can be built as requested, or whether the chosen combination of products and services is possible.

▶ The configurator can also explain why certain combinations are not allowed; for example, when configuring a car, you might not be able to order a CD player and a cassette recorder because of space limitations. This function aids with customer understanding and also helps in training sales employees.

▶ If the customer has not filled in or checked off a required entry (for example, when ordering a PC, no processor has been selected), the configurator helps to complete the configuration using a dialogue.

▶ The result of a configuration can be forwarded to downstream systems through standardized interfaces so that downstream processes receive the necessary data entries for order processing.

▶ mySAP CRM offers an availability check so that the customer can know immediately when the requested product configuration can be delivered (see Section 7.4.2).

▶ The integrated pricing functionality calculates the price for the requested product variant. The total price of the product is always kept up-to-date, depending on the chosen options and on the basis of other established pricing rules (see Section 7.3.10).

7.3.10 Contract Management

Contracts are long-term agreements that permit the customer to acquire products or services on special terms that are negotiated in advance, for example, special prices. Contracts are an important tool for achieving customer retention, as they help to increase customer satisfaction and loyalty. With their help, you can learn about what customers want and how they behave. These long-term agreements are also advantageous for customers, as they enable customers to acquire goods or services under better conditions.

E-business has intensified the competitive situation between salespersons. Contract Management in mySAP CRM helps enterprises to adjust to these changes by offering a flexible and intuitive solution to create and update customer-specific agreements. The following contract types are available:

▶ Sales contracts

▶ Service contracts

▶ Leasing contracts

Sales contracts and customer orders are very similar. All of the functions of the customer order are also supported in sales contracts. The following sales contract types exist:

▶ **Quantity contract**
An agreement that a customer acquires a certain quantity of a product within a particular time frame

- ▶ Value contract

    An agreement that a customer will order products for a certain value in the course of an agreed-on period

- ▶ Combination of quantity and value contracts

Working with Contracts

Contracts with duration and pricing conditions are generally negotiated between the sales team and the customer over a certain period of time. During the negotiations, the items in the contract retain the status *open* or in *progress*, even when the contract has already been created as a document (business transaction) in mySAP CRM, and, therefore, cannot be called up from the contract.

Only once the final contract conditions have been agreed on, can the contract be released. After this release has taken place, the customer can call up products from the contract. Authorized employees then create sales orders as follow-up documents for the contract. In this way, all relevant documents are always linked to each other. Employees can display the document flow at any time in the system, and thereby keep an overview of the number of products or the value that has already been called up from the contract.

When a customer calls up products, using his or her chosen communication channel, mySAP CRM automatically verifies whether a contract exists for this business partner. If a corresponding contract is found, the agreed-on conditions contained within in it are used as a basis for the order, and the ordered quantity or value is automatically entered in the contract. It is possible to determine if a customer can exceed the agreed-on target quantity or value, and whether the system should automatically set the status of the contract to *complete* as soon as the target quantity or value has been reached.

Special Functions and Their Use in Sales Contracts

The sales contract matches the sales order in both structure and functionality. However, sales contracts have additional attributes that are important.

- ▶ Date Profiles and Rules

    mySAP CRM offers date profiles and rules that are used to define and control the validity period of contracts. The most important dates in a contract are:

    - ▶ Contract start
    - ▶ Contract end
    - ▶ Contract term

You can also add your own date rules; for example, you could choose a default setting for start date and duration of contract, so that all contracts start on January 1st and must run for at least two years. This ensures that all employees pass on consistent information to customers. When an employee creates a new contract, this data is preset—the system automatically works out the contract end date. The employee can, if necessary, and if he or she has the authorization to do so, manually change the suggested values.

▶ **Action profiles**
The status of contracts currently running can be followed up using action profiles. For example, you can automatically generate an activity for a certain employee reminding him or her to contact a customer whose contract is about to expire. Also, when it looks like a customer is not going to call up the agreed product quantity in time, an automatically generated activity can inform the employee responsible. This warning function helps to increase customer satisfaction, as the enterprise is seen to be taking care of its customers and ensuring that customer relationships are more actively defined.

▶ **Cancellation rules**
In the event that a customer wants to cancel his or her contract, mySAP CRM offers a cancellation procedure with which different reasons and rules for a cancellation can be defined and assessed.

▶ **Releasable products**
When a quantity or value contract is created, the corresponding products can be entered manually. However, mySAP CRM also offers predefined product selection, product categories, or a combination of both. This function ensures that all employees can easily work out which products can be called up by which customers.

▶ **Business partners with authorization to call up**
This check is especially important when special price agreements have been made. Partners with authorization to call up are used to precisely control whether the contract is valid for this partner, and whether a discount or price markdown is to be granted for the corresponding order.

▶ **Agreements**
Particular delivery and payment conditions as well as special prices and discounts can be agreed on in contracts. These agreements are automatically identified when a contract is called up.

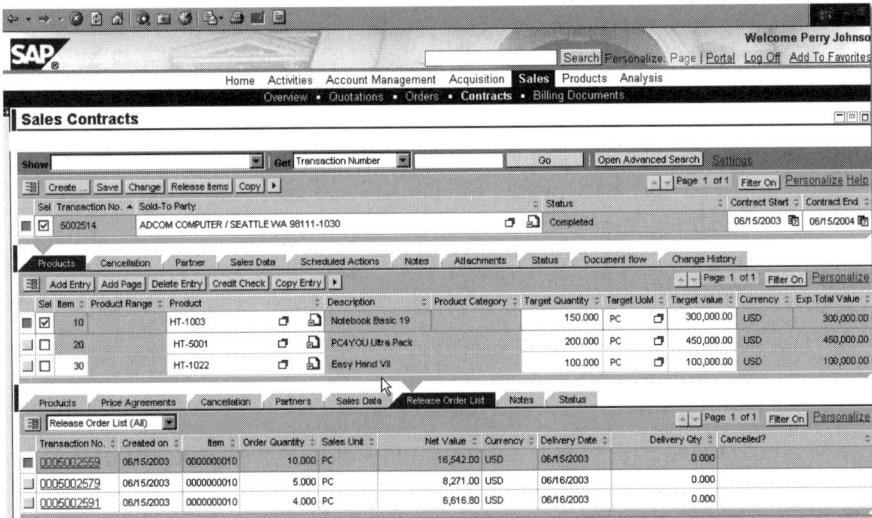

Figure 7.23 Sales Contract in Contract Management

7.3.11 Leasing

Alongside the classic suppliers of leasing and financing models, manufacturers and sales companies can also make use of financing as a means of sales promotion, regardless of whether it is leasing or a classic credit scheme paid back in installments. Furthermore, financing facilitates improved customer retention. While in a sale the process is complete after delivery and payment, in a leasing or credit arrangement, the customer is bound to the financing company for the duration of the contract. This means that additional services can be offered during the term of the contract, and customers can be won over by the same brand through the use of specific offers made at the end of the contract.

▶ Leasing and financing contracts must be carefully calculated in order to be profitable.

▶ A financing contract remains profitable only when transaction costs for the management of the contract are low over its term (usually between one and five years).

▶ Financing contracts and, if necessary, financed objects, must be managed in terms of bookkeeping by the financing company. This process must take place automatically in order to remain profitable.

▶ Customer service is a central element of a financing contract.

Financing companies can process all of their financing business using the leasing solution offered by mySAP CRM. It supports the entire contract life cycle, from initial quotation to the contract itself and management of contract changes, as well as the processing required at the end of the contract. All of the steps involved in contract management are seamlessly integrated into all required back-office processes. Every contract is transferred directly to Accounting. Rule-based software components automatically carry out classification at this stage, and thereafter take care of all necessary postings in general and subsidiary ledgers, and guarantee complete integration into Asset Accounting. Not only are several currencies supported, but the contract can also be displayed simultaneously according to different accounting principles (for example, the German HGB, the IAS, and the U.S. GAAP.

Contract Management

mySAP CRM provides the basis for the entire Contract Management part of the SAP leasing solution. Inquiries, alternative quotations, and contracts can be processed here. Flexible status management, the connection to Business Workflow, and error control, also help leasing companies to manage a multitude of quotations and contracts at low transaction costs.

The browser-based user interface for managing contracts can be integrated easily into a user's work center. Leasing and financing companies can ensure that contracts are properly processed with the help of the roles and extensive authorization concept included in the standard delivery.

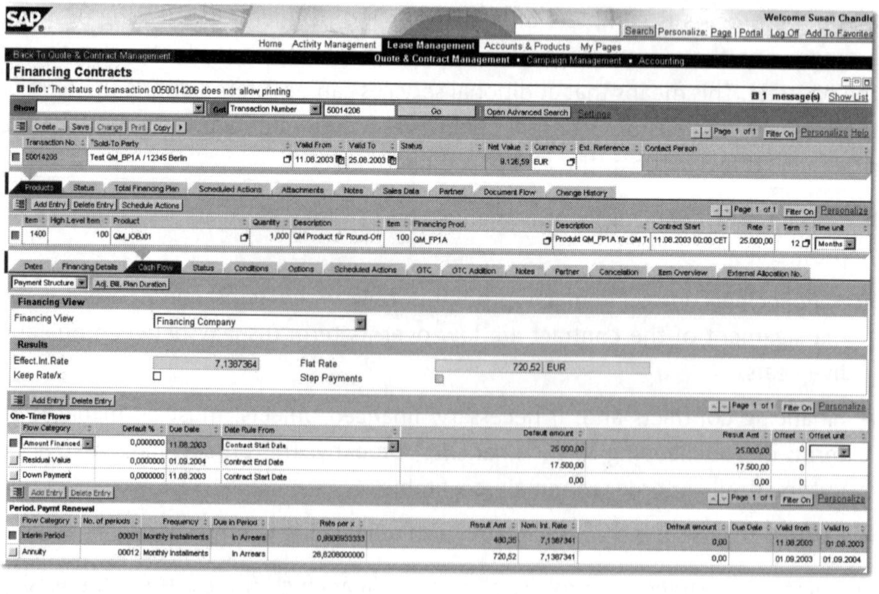

Figure 7.24 Leasing Contract

Financing Products

In addition to actual leasing products, for example, cars, various financing options are also represented within mySAP CRM. Financing products form the basis for financing quotations and contracts, and contain the essential characteristics of the financing plan rules. These products are seamlessly integrated into the product maintenance of mySAP CRM and can be structured hierarchically.

Integration in Marketing and Campaign Management

Campaigns play a central part in the financial services sector. For example, in car financing, particularly favorable financing plans may be offered on certain models for a limited time due to a sales promotion. The complete range of marketing functions offered by mySAP CRM can be used for this kind of sales-promoting leasing quotation. This means that campaigns can control the pricing agreements of individual financing plans, and that customer groups can be specifically chosen for a campaign.

Mathematical Calculation

Very effective mathematical calculation possibilities form an integral part of Contract Management that, in addition to simple leasing and financing contracts, also supports special requirements, such as seasonal repayment schedules, floating rate adjustments, and various views of the payment plan.

Automatic Classification

Leasing and financing contracts are classified automatically. This classification can be carried out in parallel according to different accounting principles. It is a prerequisite for automatic further processing of leasing contracts in the Lease Accounting Engine. Classification is also triggered and updated when changes are made to contracts.

Integration in Asset Accounting and General Ledgers

Numerous activities are linked to leasing and financing contracts in the back office so that they are represented correctly in accounting. The Lease Accounting Engine ensures that leasing contracts always run synchronously from both a customer and financing company point of view, and that all necessary postings take place automatically. For handling leasing contracts from a financing company perspective, the whole of general ledger accounting, as well as matters such as revenue realization and special depreciations, run parallel to Asset Accounting.

7.3.12 Incentive and Commission Management

Incentive and Commission Management (ICM) is an application that an enterprise can use to develop and manage complex remuneration plans, and adjust them quickly to suit economic conditions. Sales employees can track their current activities and work out potential remuneration for their opportunities. As employees can project commission amounts at any time, they are able to recognize the opportunities that will guarantee that not only their personal goals, but also those of the enterprise, are achieved.

ICM supports different commission scenarios spanning the entire enterprise, but is geared primarily for the sales process. This means, for example, that sales representatives can deduce the potential commission for a certain opportunity or a certain sales transaction using a commission simulator. Sales managers can use the valuation function to influence the actions of their sales team by, for example, offering higher rates of commission for the sale of particularly profitable products or for new sales contracts. Sales employees can make use of many functions, including:

▶ Commission simulation for opportunities and sales transactions

▶ Direct access to the commission status for sales representatives and sales managers

▶ Preconfigured templates for general commission scenarios

▶ Functions for controlling commission potential on the basis of transaction attributes such as product or customer

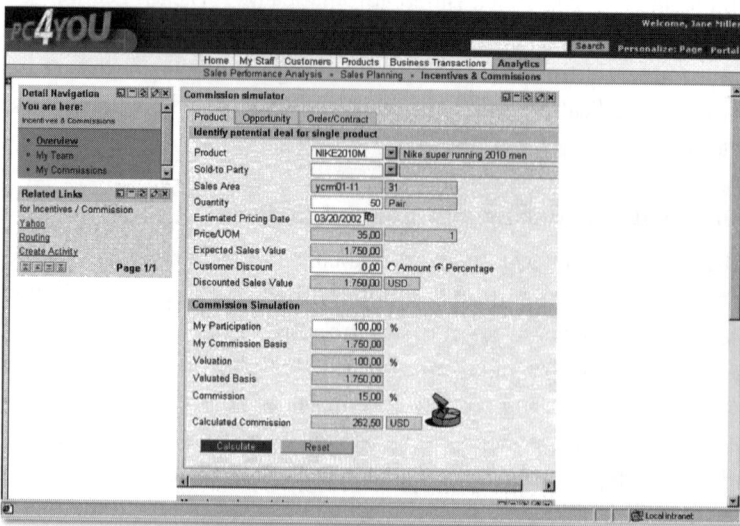

Figure 7.25 Commission Simulator

ICM supports many different commission scenarios, for example, sales commission, channel-specific incentives, and remuneration of internal employees. The scope of functionality covers the complete management of commissions and incentives. In addition to the functions aimed at sales employees, the following tools are also available:

▶ A tool to automatically and precisely calculate remuneration

▶ Tools for flexible modeling, cost simulation, and plan individualization

▶ Administrative functions for processing routine tasks

▶ Accurate cost and activity reporting

7.3.13 Sales Analytics

All data from the sales process is gathered and saved, and can be analyzed at a later stage. mySAP Business Intelligence (mySAP BI) offers flexible data warehouse functionality that can be used to determine exactly how and when data should be analyzed. This analysis can be carried out from various perspectives:

▶ Operational
The status of current sales transactions is checked using *operational* reports. For example, you can determine how many sales orders are open, which contracts are about to run out, or whether there are any delivery delays. Furthermore, information from previous sales transactions can be used for product recommendations.

A sales manager learns from a report which customers are buying which products. Depending on how much money a customer has spent or which type of product he or she has bought, the sales manager can decide to offer that customer an additional (*cross-selling*) or a more expensive (*up-selling*) product. The sales manager enters this information as a product proposal in a partner/product range. The next time the customer contacts a sales employee, the latter automatically receives a note to say that he or she should suggest the products to the customer.

▶ Analytical
Using *analytical* reports, you can measure the achievements of the sales team and the success of the sales strategy.

Sales Analytics Along Hierarchies

Each user has a different perspective on data to be analyzed depending on his or her role and position within an enterprise.

▶ The head of the company views data from an organizational point of view.

▶ The product manager is interested in the success of the product groups and products that he or she oversees.

▶ The account manager analyzes the results along the customer hierarchy.

▶ Sales managers observe the sales success of the individual territories assigned to them.

▶ Sales representatives seek to monitor their own performance.

SAP CRM synchronizes the organizational model, product hierarchies and products, customer hierarchies and customers, territory hierarchies and territories, and all other business partners involved (employees and external partners).

Consequently, all information can be analyzed accordingly.

Funnel and Pipeline Analysis

In addition to sales analysis for activities, opportunities, quotations, orders, and contracts, mySAP CRM offers the following specific reports for cross-application analytics.

▶ **Sales Pipeline Analysis** (analysis of current data):

▷ Detailed information on the leads (in cooperation with marketing), opportunities, and quotations that have been created, which, in turn, provide information on the sales pipeline, or the potential sales volume that can be gained from sales

▷ Values for sales orders and contracts, considering the returns so that the exact total sales volume of incoming orders can be calculated

▷ Comparison of the sales volume expected from an opportunity with the actual incoming order value

▶ **Sales Funnel Analysis** (analysis of old data):

▷ Display sales documents that come either directly or indirectly from a certain opportunity, for example, display quotations and sales orders that were created as follow-up documents for an opportunity

▷ Display sales orders and contracts that come either directly or indirectly from a certain quotation

Sales Performance Analysis

Sales performance analysis was developed especially for managerial positions within sales. It helps the sales manager to gain a comprehensive overview of all of the sales organization's relevant information. For this purpose, sales performance analysis from mySAP Business Intelligence offers various sales-specific analyses from all areas. It isn't limited to analysis from sales; instead, it looks at all areas of the enterprise.

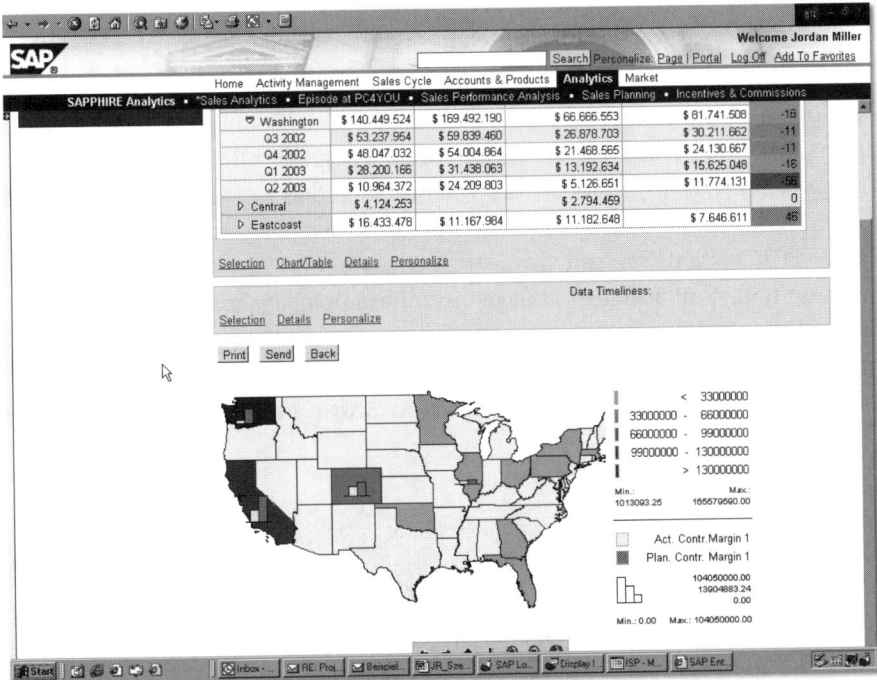

Figure 7.26 Data Analysis in GIS Format: Number of Activities versus Sales Volume

Sales performance analysis is divided into the following four areas:

► **Finances**
Pipeline analysis for opportunities and open contracts provide an overview of current and expected developments. Using sales order analysis, open and incoming order values, and therefore also the potential sales volume, can be analyzed.

► **Customers**
ABC analysis can be used to compare and categorize different customers according to degree of importance. Furthermore, analyses can be conducted on customer value and profitability.

► **Internal Sales Processes**

The business transactions created by the sales team can be followed up here, such as opportunity quantities, success rates, profit and loss comparisons, quotation analysis, and the connection between quotations and contracts or sales orders that are actually won.

► **Employee Development**

Processes that relate to employees and their satisfaction are investigated here. For example, you can analyze staff turnover, the number and costs of courses and the number of participants, sick leave and overtime figures, and employee satisfaction (assessed using questionnaires).

Most of the analyses mentioned can be displayed in detail for individual sales regions with the assistance of a web-based geographical information system (GIS), which makes it possible to view information and key figures for individual regions. Most of the data used in sales performance analysis is supplied by the mySAP CRM system. You can also extract data from an SCM or HR solution and pass it on to mySAP Business Intelligence, for example, analysis of headcount and staff turnover.

7.3.14 Use Case: Using mySAP CRM in Sales Including Sales Order Processing

Perry Johnson is an employee at the company PC4YOU. Every morning, he logs on to the PC4YOU CRM portal. All important information, such as activities, upcoming customer appointments, sales volume analysis, and so on, are automatically presented to him in one view. This allows him to prioritize his many tasks and address the most important tasks first.

All current sales projects can be accessed in the opportunity pipeline. Perry Johnson is pleased to discover that many opportunities in the pipeline are already in the final phase. However, an automatic alert message in his inbox draws his attention to the fact that the opportunity with transaction number 603 at Adcom Computers should have gone into the decision phase two days ago. Perry calls up the details of this opportunity by clicking on the alert message (see Figure 7.27).

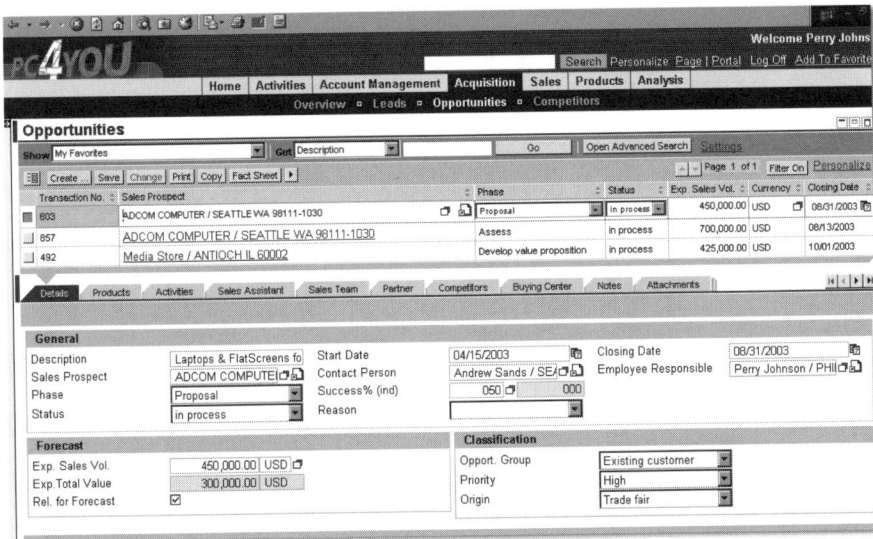

Figure 7.27 Opportunity Details

Perry immediately receives all information gathered in the last few weeks relating to this sales project. The sales probability is currently at 50%. If the order is won, PC4YOU expects a sales volume of $450,000 with a pure product value of $300,000. Perry verifies whether all important activities, including a detailed product presentation, have been finished, collects information about strengths and weaknesses of the competitors, analyzes again the project organization chart, and decides to call the key person at the customer site, Ian Brooks. After a successful telephone call, the go ahead is given to make a quotation.

Perry is successful; the quotation is persuasive. He can sell 220 items of Notebook Professional 17 (model HT-1011) with a quantity discount of $149 per item. The sales volume achieved amounts to more than $518,000, with $44,508.64 in tax and $902 in shipment costs. The determining factor for Ian Brooks is that Perry is able to provide information on the exact date of delivery at the quotation creation stage. Once the order has been accepted, Perry can directly confirm the advised date.

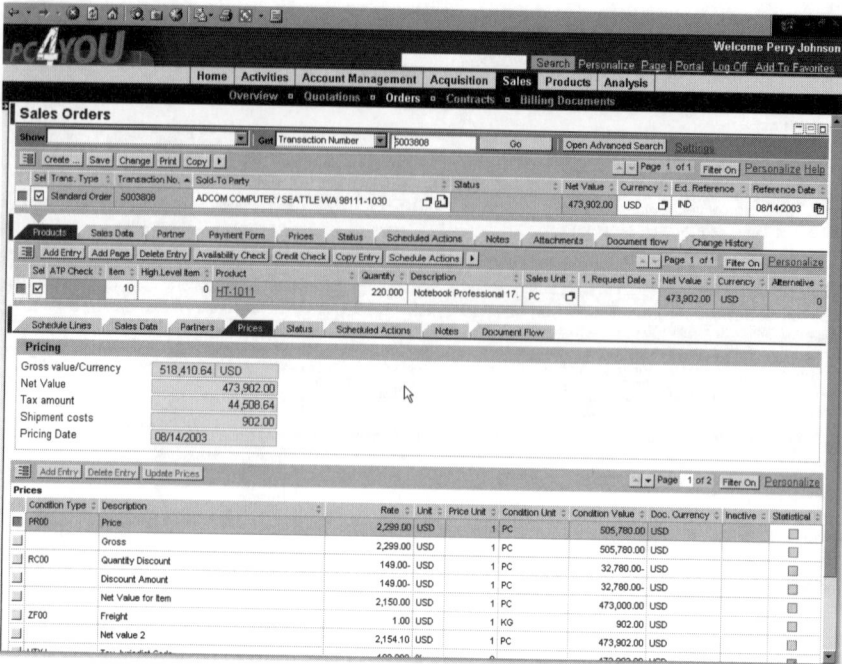

Figure 7.28 Sales Order in the Portal

A few days later, Andrew Sands, contact person at Adcom Computer for PC4YOU, calls and asks if the order quantity can still be changed. Once again, Perry can give an immediate answer. As the sales item in question has not yet been delivered, he can adjust the product quantity straight away.

Figure 7.29 Billing Document with Reference to Order

Thanks to seamless integration with logistical sales order processing, PC4YOU is able to deliver quickly and on time. Perry can also view the invoice in his portal. He can follow up any problems concerning receipt of payment using Revenue Management.

7.3.15 Recommendations for Successful CRM Projects in Sales

It goes without saying that the focus of CRM is the customer; CRM does, after all, stand for "Customer Relationship Management." For this reason, account management forms the basis for all sales support offered by mySAP CRM across all channels. The CRM implementation project should begin with this part of the application. The next step is Activity Management, which is necessary to achieve seamless integration with the customer. Admittedly, sales employees tend to dislike CRM systems; however, they also don't like surprises when it comes to customer appointments. This is where the key to success lies in wedding mySAP CRM to sales. When customer information that is relevant to sales is not buried in the heads of individual employees or on some server somewhere, but is accessible to all people involved in the sale, information that is critical to the sale can be shared. For example, a sales representative can find out at the stage of preparing for a customer visit that the customer was on the last mailing list, has already complained, called invoice verification the day before, and so on. With this kind of transparency of information, sales employees can also, for their part, be amenable to sharing information with others instead of simply storing it in their personal organizers.

Depending on the scope of the sales cycle, early implementation of Opportunity Management offers considerably more flexibility than does Activity Management when it comes to complex sales transactions. It is worth noting that each sales employee has his or her own way of working, or his or her own "sales methodology." Why should this knowledge not be made available to all people involved? Here, the opportunity presents itself to include sales employees in the CRM project from the very outset, thus increasing acceptance of the implementation of the CRM project. It's very easy and straightforward to store their individual sales methodologies in mySAP CRM. Sharing their methodologies ensures that all employees quickly feel at home in the productive CRM system.

7.3.16 Scenario Overview and Potential Benefits

mySAP CRM supports all stages of the sales process, from the initial contact with the customer to the conclusion and fulfillment of the contract, taking all communication channels into account. The business scenarios described in the following table are included in the SAP standard delivery for use in all industries.

Cross-Industry Scenarios	Short Description	Potential Benefits		
		Turnover	Profitability	Customer Satisfaction
Quotation and Order Management	Support for the entire order process, from the inquiry and quotation through to the order, including product configuration, availability check, pricing, and integration with order processing, regardless of the communication channel used to create the order	✓✓	✓	✓
Extended Order Management	Extension of Quotation and Order Management for sales order processing in distributed and heterogeneous system landscapes with SAP and non-SAP systems It is possible to distribute order items to multiple sources, including external suppliers, and to monitor status and invoicing centrally	✓✓	✓	✓
Contract Management	Functions for creating and processing quantity and value contracts, that is, long-term customer contracts granting individual pricing and delivery conditions	✓✓	✓	✓
Leasing	Support of the leasing process, from creating quotations, managing contracts, and changing ongoing leasing agreements, through to end-of-lease transactions for return, extension, or purchase Financing products are also considered	✓✓	✓	✓
Sales Planning and Forecasting	Multidimensional planning, for example, for sales territories, product groups, and customer hierarchies, on the basis of key figures, such as sales quantities, sales volume, or customer satisfaction, with corresponding evaluation options and graphical analysis	✓	✓✓	

Cross-Industry Scenarios	Short Description	Potential Benefits		
		Turnover	Profitability	Customer Satisfaction
Opportunity Management	Accompanies the sales cycle, from identification of sales opportunities to successful conclusion One view of assigned transactions, history, appointments, progress, and responsible decision-makers	✓	✓✓	
Incentive and Commission Management	Remuneration rules for sales employees, partners, or other commission recipients	✓	✓✓	
Activity Management	Planning, executing, and managing sales activities, and organizing daily sales business to conclude sales more quickly		✓✓	✓
Territory Management	Structuring and organizing sales by dividing into territories according to arbitrary criteria such as size, distance, or revenue Hierarchical territory structuring, territory-related definition of sales goals, and assignment of sales employees to territories		✓✓	✓
Account and Contact Management	Providing all important information about customers, sales prospects, and partners for interaction history, pursuit of activities, and analysis of successful or critical business relationships	✓	✓	✓✓

The cross-industry business scenarios are complemented by further industry-specific scenarios.

Industry-Specific Scenarios	Short Description	Potential Benefits		
		Revenue	Profitability	Customer Satisfaction
Sales Management for Commercial and Industrial Customers in the Utilities Industry	Describes the sales process for commercial and industrial customers, from customer acquisition to maintenance of lasting customer relationships	✓✓		

Industry-Specific Scenarios	Short Description	Potential Benefits		
		Revenue	Profitability	Customer Satisfaction
Sales Management for Residential Customers in the Utilities Industry	Supports the sales cycle for residential customers, including service for existing customers and creating service contracts	✓✓		
Contracts and Chargeback for Pharmaceuticals	Managing contracts and prices, acceptance, inspection, and processing of returns, verification of chargeback claims, and determination of chargeback amounts	✓✓	✓	✓
Channel Sales Management for the High-Tech Industry	Functions for incorporating external partners in the sales process of the enterprise	✓✓	✓	✓
Sales Against Contract for the Oil and Gas Industry	Functions for creating and processing long-term customer contracts granting individual pricing and delivery conditions specifically for the oil and gas sector	✓✓	✓	✓
Value-Based Detailing for Pharmaceuticals	Integrated processes for marketing, sales planning, territory and activity management for developing profitable customer segments in times of changing behavior regarding prescriptions, and increasing cost pressures in the health sector	✓	✓✓	
Intellectual Property Management for Media	Offers help in managing intellectual property in rights and licenses, optimizing economic exploitation, and calculating license fees	✓	✓✓	

7.4 Sales Order Processing

7.4.1 Overview

In the past, sales success was often measured by the amount of incoming orders. For many sales representatives, their work was done when the customer had signed the order or contract. Whether the enterprise continued to do business successfully in the long term was decided only when payment was received and the order was processed to the customer's and vendor's complete satisfaction. In this way, profit margins could be lost, for example, if the customer specified incorrect terms of delivery and omitted freight costs, or if freight costs could not be determined correctly in the invoice. Today, credit management must minimize the risk of large outstanding arrears without offending the customer. A deteriorating pay ethic requires claims management, but, as far as is possible, without it having a negative effect on customer satisfaction.

Most CRM solutions make a clean break when order processing is finished and leave further processing to a back-end ERP system. For mySAP CRM, sales order processing is part of the integrated solution. Particularly in the case of distributed sales order processing, this is an indispensable prerequisite for being able to map the business processes at all (see Section 7.4.9).

Sales order processing (fulfillment) begins with the creation of an order or a contract, and includes the following steps:

▶ Availability check

▶ Payment processing and credit management

▶ Shipping

▶ Transport

▶ Billing

▶ Claims management

▶ Monitoring and analysis of sales order processing

For processing a sales order, information on products, delivery data, and payment details are essential. mySAP CRM collects all the necessary product availability data, processes payment information, and checks the customer's credit status. As soon as the order has been confirmed and saved, mySAP CRM sends all information to the system, where, based on need, material planning, shipping, and billing are initiated. Customers as well as employees can query the current status of the order at any time. Additionally, sales management can evaluate and analyze sales order information for an overview of the effectiveness of fulfillment processes.

7.4.2 Availability Check

Before a sales transaction can be confirmed, suppliers and customers must know whether the products in question can be delivered by the requested date. To do this, mySAP CRM offers an availability check: The *ATP (Available-to-Promise)* check. This tool enables you to query the warehouse stock that is valid for the requested delivery date and to reserve goods for inbound sales orders. The ATP verifies all inbound and outbound movements, quantities already reserved for other customers, and current warehouse stock. Additionally, ATP enables you to adjust production or purchasing to fulfill requirements if necessary.

In Figure 7.30, a customer has ordered 100 pieces of Product 4711; delivery is scheduled for October 10, 2002.

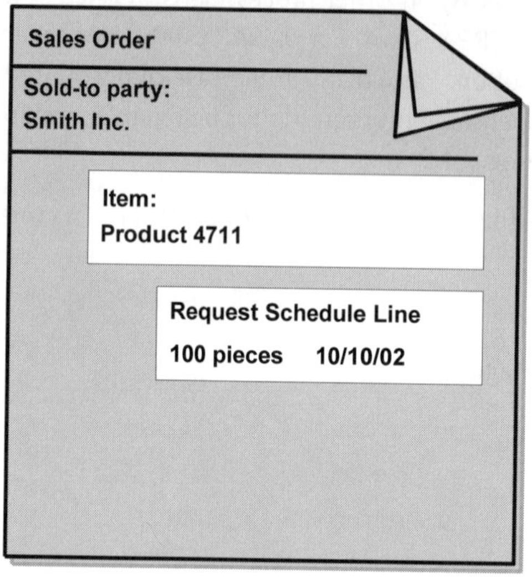

Sales Order

Sold-to party:
Smith Inc.

> **Item:**
> **Product 4711**

> **Request Schedule Line**
> **100 pieces   10/10/02**

Figure 7.30 Sales Order with Requested Delivery Date

In this example, the availability check could produce the following results for the order (Figure 7.31):

▶ 60 pieces by October 10
▶ 40 pieces by October 15

The information in the example above is displayed as a *confirmation schedule line*. As soon as the order has been saved, that is, when the customer has accepted the relevant quantities and dates, the corresponding products are reserved. Reserving these products means that they are temporarily assigned to the relevant order and, therefore, are no longer available for another order.

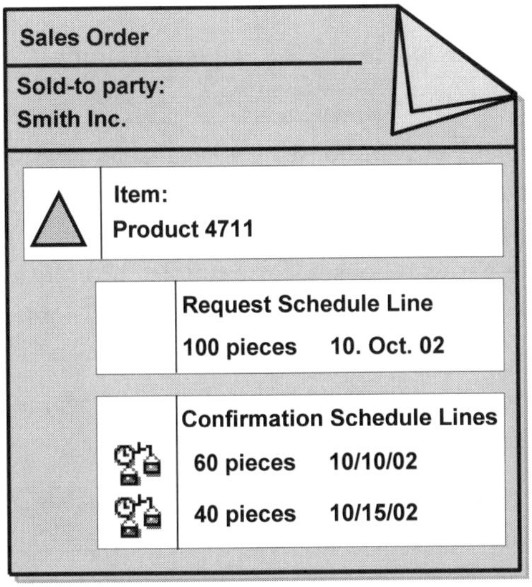

Figure 7.31 Sales Order with Confirmation Schedule Line

However, production, purchasing, and material planning are not triggered yet. When an employee has checked the sales order for errors and has saved it, the temporary assignment is deleted and the product is assigned. Now, material planning can begin because the business transaction is relevant for delivery and shipping from this time forward.

Simulated Availability Check (Availability Information)

In some cases, it makes sense, for informational purposes, to use a simulated availability check. This applies, for example, to orders for which the delivery of specific products on a given date has already been agreed upon; however, the customer has not yet made a binding confirmation. In this case, you can request availability information on the specific products to determine whether they would be available at the requested time. No products are reserved here, and the check also has no bearing on material planning. The follow-up processes named above are triggered only when the offer is converted into a sales order. Availability checks are also useful for probable purchases that have not yet been confirmed. To do this, the system checks the availability of a partial quantity of the sales transaction, which is calculated by multiplying the total quantity by the sales probability. This simulated availability check depicts more precisely the quantity that will be needed later.

When Products Are Unavailable

With mySAP CRM, you can automate sales processes if a requested product is unavailable:

▶ If a product in a specific location (plant or warehouse) is unavailable, mySAP CRM can check whether another plant has the desired product in stock. This check also makes it possible to complete a delivery to a customer by shipping products to the customer from different warehouses, for example, 100 pieces of a product from Plant A and the remaining 50 pieces from Plant B (order split).

▶ If a product is no longer in stock, it can be replaced by a similar or even superior product.

You can also use this type of check for optimizing advertising campaigns, seasonal sales, or up- and cross-selling. If, for example, a sales promotion of the type "Buy a PC and get a DVD writer free" is to run, then, upon receipt of the order, mySAP CRM not only checks whether the PC is available, but also verifies whether the combination of PC and DVD writer can be delivered.

Combining Deliveries

As shown in the previous example, the availability check can yield the following results:

▶ There is different delivery data for different items of the sales order.

▶ There is multiple delivery data for one item.

Sometimes, it must be ensured that all items of a sales order are delivered concurrently or that all products in an order are delivered together. This may be necessary as a result of a customer request, or because the products ordered belong together, or, perhaps, because an advertising campaign promises that the products will be delivered together. To guarantee common delivery, these items can be combined in a *delivery group*. All items in one of these groups are then delivered on the date that the item with the latest availability date becomes available.

Backorder Processing

When customer demand exceeds the offer, or if an important customer is to be granted preferential delivery, it may be necessary to redistribute items that have already been confirmed to existing sales orders. Using back-order processing makes this possible. To do this, all quantities that have already been confirmed but are still open—that is, all quantities that have not yet been delivered—are added back to the available quantities and mySAP CRM gets the results of an updated availability check. The sales orders are automatically adjusted so that employees and customers alike have access to the changed, updated availability information at any time.

7.4.3 Payment Processing and Credit Management

Payment Types

Depending on the scenario in which a business transaction was created — Business-to-Consumer or Business-to-Business — there are the following types of payment:

- Payment card
- Cash on delivery
- Invoice

In the first two payment types, payment is direct, which minimizes the risk for the enterprise that delivers payment. However, in the latter case, the company that delivers payment bears the main risk when accepting a sales order. A credit management process can reduce this risk. mySAP CRM supports all the aforementioned payment types. The solutions shown in the following sections are now available.

Payment Card Processing

Most one-time customers pay by card, particularly when they order over the Internet. This could be a credit card, customer card, or purchasing card. From the trader's viewpoint, using payment cards reduces the risk when dealing with unknown partners, because payment — once the card has been authorized — is guaranteed.

Authorizing Payment Card Transactions

Authorization means a process used by a clearinghouse to guarantee payment of a transaction amount. If a sales order is saved, mySAP CRM contacts the authorization module responsible in the clearinghouse. The clearinghouse then checks the following details:

- **Card Number**
- **Name and Address of the Card Owner**
- **Card Verification Value**
  Three- to four-figure value in the signature field or magnetic strip, which can be used to prove that the card and account belong to a specific customer

► Address Verification System

The address given in the sales transaction matches the data saved by the clearinghouse and the customer is the owner of the card in use

The clearinghouse's response—authorization is granted or authorization is
denied—is noted in the sales order. If authorization is granted, the sales transaction can be processed further. If not, the transaction is halted.

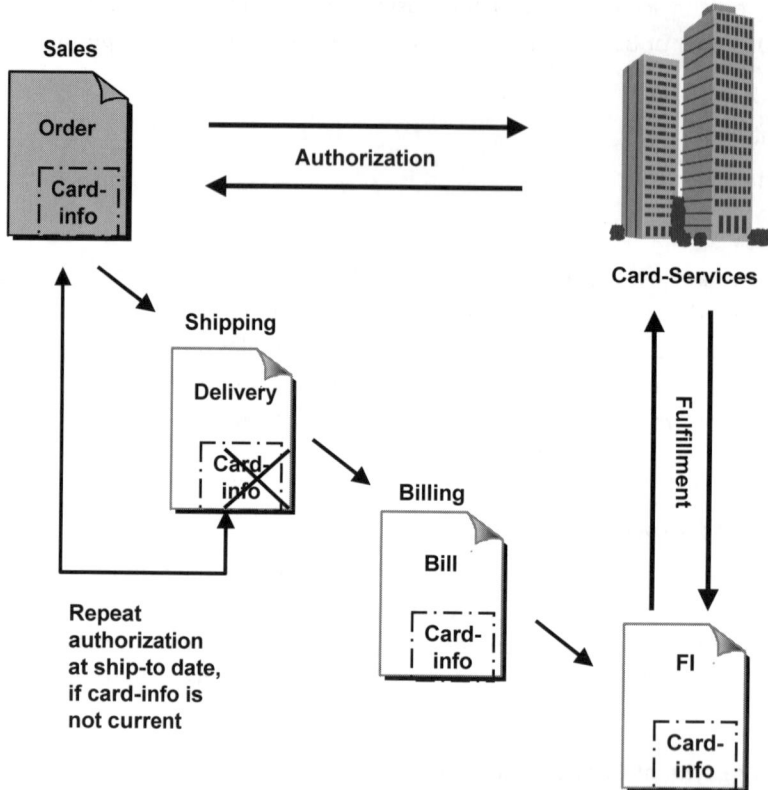

Figure 7.32 Authorization of Payment Card Transactions

Sales Order with Payment Card

If a customer or employee creates a sales order, he or she enters the payment card
data in the order, for example, the card number and the name of the card owner.
If required, preauthorization can be carried out, in which the card data is checked
to see if it is correct. To do this, name, address, and card number are sent to the
clearinghouse and confirmation is received. This can reduce the risk of problems
during actual authorization later. The decision can be made immediately whether
the relevant payment card is to be accepted or not.

As soon as a sales order has been saved, the following happens within mySAP CRM:

▶ The transaction, including verification of the address and payment card, is authorized by the clearinghouse, and the results are entered in the sales order

▶ Card data is encrypted (is still unencrypted) so that it doesn't appear as readable text in the database

▶ The transaction is forwarded for further processing

Authorization Horizon

When goods are first available several weeks or months after the corresponding sales transaction was created, it is not sufficient that the payment card was valid on the day the order was entered. On the contrary, it must be established that the payment card is still authorized up to the agreed upon delivery date, that is, when the customer receives the goods ordered and becomes the owner. In mySAP CRM, you can specify the number of days before the agreed upon delivery date that an authorization check is to be carried out. The number of days between the authorization and delivery date is the authorization horizon. This ensures that a current, valid credit check is present immediately before delivery of the goods (see also Figure 7.32).

Cash on Delivery

Cash on delivery (COD) is another payment option for customers. It is strongly recommended when the products ordered are to be forwarded by a mail-order company, such as the postal service, or by a parcel service. The customer receives the products together with an invoice to be paid upon delivery.

It must of course be ensured that the cash-on-delivery customer agrees to pay in cash. Business partners can then be indicated as cash-on-delivery customers in the business partner master data. Furthermore, a particular mail-order company can be specified as the payer for a particular customer. When a sales transaction is created for a business partner whose payer can pay cash on delivery, then this type of payment is proposed automatically in the sales transaction.

Invoice and Credit Management

The company that delivers bears the most risk when accepting a sales order and makes credit management a critical success factor—this is especially relevant for payment by invoice. mySAP CRM enables all credit information to be recorded in the customer data record, as well as a credit check in real time when placing the sales order. Integration of this data into customer relationship management allows a customer's credit history to be tracked, in addition to the use of *Early*

Warning Lists or *Alerts*, which are warnings issued by the system when a customer places an order and his or her credit limit has already been exceeded. In this way, non-creditworthy customers are recognized and blocked. Furthermore, via analysis of customers, payment history and credit risk can be checked and thereby ensure payment security for the company and customer.

Credit Check

A credit check can be performed as soon as a sales transaction has been entered. The credit check verifies that the customer is creditworthy, that is, the customer has the ability to pay. Among other things, the check determines the credit control area (specifying who is responsible for granting and monitoring credits), the payer's credit account, and the account's risk class. Afterwards, the payer's creditworthiness can be determined and the corresponding credit status is set on header level for each single item and as a general credit status for the entire document. If the credit status is in order when the transaction is saved for the final time, the transaction can be released for delivery and billing.

Informing Employees About Credit Problems

To ensure the trouble-free flow of credit management, employees can be informed in various ways about potential problems. To do this, many enterprises set up a workflow procedure that directly forwards all sales transactions whose credit status is not in order to the employee responsible in credit management. The employee can then appraise each individual transaction and decide whether it should be released for further processing or rejected.

Credit information can also be displayed in Account and Contact Management (see Section 7.3.4) to notify an employee, who is processing the corresponding customer's order at the time, of potential credit problems.

7.4.4 Shipping

Shipping includes all transactions that are required so that the customer receives the products ordered. To ensure that this happens, all relevant sales data is sent by mySAP CRM to the logistics system responsible for shipping.

If mySAP SCM is used as a logistics system, an efficient and automated shipping process with the following functions can be initiated:

▶ Monitoring deadlines for sales documents to be furnished

▶ Planning and monitoring of workflows for shipping activities

▶ Checking material availability and processing of open repeat orders

▶ Monitoring of warehouse capacity

▶ Outbound delivery

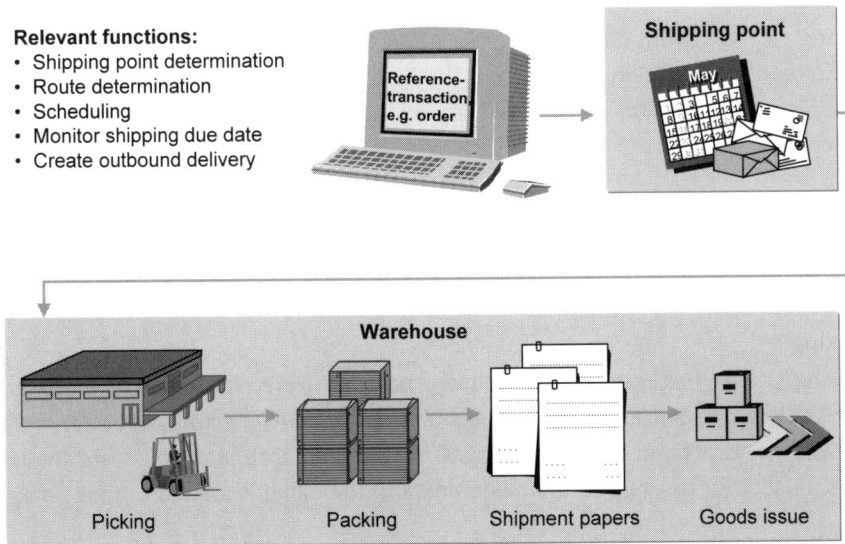

Relevant functions:
- Shipping point determination
- Route determination
- Scheduling
- Monitor shipping due date
- Create outbound delivery

Reference-transaction, e.g. order

Shipping point

May

Warehouse

Picking   Packing   Shipment papers   Goods issue

Figure 7.33 The Shipping Process

Next, we will look at the activities associated with outbound delivery—as part of shipping—in more detail.

Outbound Delivery

Outbound delivery includes the following activities:

▶ Creating and processing outbound deliveries

▶ Picking

▶ Packing deliveries

▶ Printing and transferring shipping documents

▶ Processing goods issued

▶ Taking foreign trade conditions into account

When you create an outbound delivery, the data generated during the shipping process is transferred, and activities such as picking and delivery planning are initiated. You can track the status of all delivery activities at all times.

According to need, outbound deliveries can be created in workflows automatically or manually. Agreements can be made with the customer regarding partial or complete deliveries, or a combination of both forms of delivery. Outbound deliveries can be combined into a single delivery group.

Picking

During picking, goods are taken from a storage location and forwarded in the correct quantity to a picking area where they are made ready for shipping. To facilitate this, picking can be adjusted to the usual system processes in the corresponding enterprise:

▶ Automatically—when creating an outbound delivery

▶ Routinely—at specified times

▶ Manually—after an overview of employees' workflows on a specific day

Packing

Packing is the next step in the delivery process. Here, the delivery items are selected for packing and are assigned to specific *Handling Units*. For example, delivery items are packed in cardboard boxes, the cardboard boxes are loaded onto a pallet for delivery to the customer, and the pallet is loaded onto a truck.

Goods Issued

As soon as the goods leave an enterprise, the business transaction is complete from the shipping viewpoint. mySAP CRM stores this transaction by posting the goods issued. The data required to do this is copied from the delivery document to the document for the goods issued. When posting the goods issued for a delivery, the following functions run on the basis of the document for the goods issued:

▶ Reduction of the inventory by the delivery quantity

▶ Posting of the value change to the inventory accounting's stock account

▶ Reduction of requirements by the delivery quantity

7.4.5 Transport

Effective and economic transportation planning and shipment completion are critical for customer satisfaction; you need only think about delivery on time and transport costs, which play a decisive role in defining the price of a product.

Inbound and outbound transports are planned, executed, and monitored. The costs arising from this are calculated and are settled with the transportation service providers. It is also possible to forward billing for shipment costs directly to customers.

Outbound transports are created and planned on the basis of outbound deliveries (see Section 7.4.4). The following shipment planning and completion tasks are executed in the corresponding shipping document:

- Combine various outbound deliveries that are to be shipped together
- Assign and commission service providers
- Organize means of transport
- Determine the shipment route and shipment stages
- Register the means of transport
- Load, weigh, and post goods issued
- Print the shipping papers required

To have an overview of the planned shipping activities and shipments already underway at all times, a graphical information system and Gantt charts are available.

Shipment Cost Processing

Shipment cost processing includes calculating the costs arising from shipping, transferring these costs to Financial Accounting, and billing the service providers or transferring these costs to the customer billing document.

To calculate the costs automatically, different output values and influencing factors can be referred to, for example, distance, weight, or transportation zone.

7.4.6 Billing

Bills today can contain much more than a simple request for payment. They are often used as an effective method of communicating with the customer; for example, they can contain supplementary information or notifications that are relevant to the customer. Generally, modern billing solutions must cope with raised requirements resulting from increased competitive pressure, such as costs, flexibility, openness of systems, and customer orientation. The mySAP CRM billing solution is directed equally at contract and contract-related billing. It is marked by the following properties:

- Support for the entire billing process
- Ability to integrate with different SAP and non-SAP systems as a source or follow-up application
- Invoicing not only for orders from mySAP CRM, but also from other solutions such as SAP for Telecommunications and SAP for Media

In billing, data supplied by different source applications can be combined, evaluated with prices, and collectively presented in a shared invoice. All transactions that aren't relevant to delivery, such as credit and debit memo requests, are transferred directly for invoicing, whereas transactions that are relevant to delivery are forwarded for invoicing when the corresponding delivery has taken place.

Invoicing Sub-Processes

Invoicing consists of the following three sub-processes:

▶ Input processing

▶ Invoicing

▶ Output processing

Cancellation is also possible. Figure 7.34 illustrates the process for creating and processing invoices.

Input Processing

During input processing, data relevant for invoicing is transferred in the billing due list. To do this, the billing solution adds data (for example, master data) and starts a processing check.

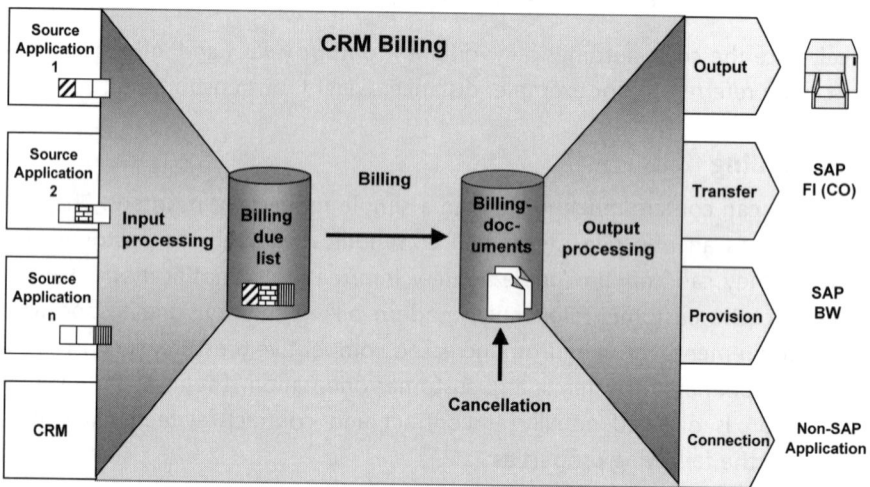

Figure 7.34 Billing Process

Invoicing

In invoicing, CRM billing creates complete billing documents from single billing due list items. This results in *billing documents* (for example, invoices, credit memos, debit memos) with items that possibly come from different CRM business transactions. During invoicing, the system combines as many billing due list items as possible in one billing document. A combination like this is not possible if it is hindered by one or several split criteria. This means, for example, that the system can combine two billing due list items with the same sold-to party but cannot combine different payers in a shared invoice, because each billing document is formatted for one payer only. The payer is therefore defined as a split criterion. If you use the data from the billing due list, the entire billing process can also be simulated, which enables specific invoicing runs to be tested, for example.

Output Processing

Billing supports a range of output media, including printers, fax, email, or external output management systems. The following functions are available:

▶ Creation of invoices in printed, fax, or email form

▶ Optical archiving of invoices by using *ArchiveLink*—the interface between mySAP Business Suite solutions and storage systems

▶ Formatting billing data for the Internet (creation of electronic billing document)

▶ XML interface to external output management systems

By using *Smart Forms*, an SAP tool for processing the graphic structure of forms and documents, you can define different layouts for different types of billing forms, such as invoices, and credit and debit memos. Additionally, tailoring of these forms supports enterprise- or industry-specific needs. So, for example, different layouts can be stored for different customer categories, or different fonts and logos can be included in the forms.

Invoice output can be triggered either automatically or manually according to choice. Automatic output takes place directly after billing or after a specified period of time, perhaps after a week or a month. Furthermore, you can send invoice copies—even time-delayed ones—through any channel to other recipients.

Cancellation

Billing documents can also be cancelled. You have the choice between a full cancellation (that cancels the entire billing document) or a partial cancellation (that cancels a specific part of the billing document, for example, a specific item). CRM billing transfers the cancellation data to the accounting application responsible, for example, to Contract Accounting in mySAP Financials.

Transferring Billing Data to Downstream Applications

For further processing of billing data, interfaces are available for the following downstream applications:

▶ Accounts receivable accounting

▶ Contract accounting

- ► Controlling

- ► Analytical applications (mySAP BI)

7.4.7 Claims Management

Claims management includes all activities in an enterprise that are connected with settling open claims. These activities include processing of incoming payments, processing dispute cases, and dunning.

Processing Incoming Payment

A posted outgoing invoice automatically results in an open item in accounts receivable accounting. Incoming payments from the customer are accounted for against this open item. This processing of incoming payments is supported by a manual procedure by employees in accounting, as well as by electronic input processing.

Processing Dispute Cases

In practice, a customer often reduces the payment amount in an invoice unilaterally and without giving notice. If the invoice reduction is within limits, then the difference is posted as an expense. If, however, the difference exceeds set threshold values, then the invoice reduction must be investigated. To do this, *SAP Dispute Management* provides a component that enables efficient processing of debit-side dispute cases.

If an invoice reduction that cannot be tolerated is discovered when incoming payments are posted, the respective employee for the resulting residual item opens a dispute case immediately. This type of dispute case is a kind of electronic folder in which all information that is relevant to the dispute case processed is entered. Depending on the reason for the dispute case or the customer group, the corresponding employee is automatically assigned to the dispute case. The dispute case can include status, notes, and additional information. Inbound payment posting, credit memos, or other forms of clearing with respect to the dispute case are logged automatically and are linked with the respective documents accordingly.

Typically, a dispute case is processed across several departments. The sequence of processing steps is enterprise-specific and depends, for example, on the reason for the dispute case.

Besides the current processor, a coordinator and a person responsible are assigned to a dispute case. The coordinator controls and checks the dispute case processing. He or she monitors the adherence to processing deadlines, escalates overdue dispute cases, and analyzes and optimizes the process. The person responsible is the person to whom the case can be escalated. For example, if the reason for the invoice reduction is a quality problem, then the quality manager in charge would be responsible.

A dispute case is completed and closed when the case has been clarified and the requested amount has been reduced to zero by corresponding financial accounting. If the planned date for completing dispute processing is not met, the coordinator can also write off the disputed amount automatically.

Dunning

In dispute case processing, or even independently of it, you can use an automatic dunning program. Dunning creates reminders to draw customers' attention to payments due and updates the dunning level (1st reminder, 2nd reminder, and so on) in the proper order for the customer. Dunning blocks can also be set, for example, if a deferred payment has already been agreed upon and a reminder of the payment due would severely damage the relationship with the customer.

7.4.8 Monitoring and Analyzing Sales Order Processing

To give the sales manager and all other authorized employees all the information they need for trouble-free fulfillment processing, mySAP CRM offers a variety of reports and analyses that address the entire sales order processing with shipping, payment processing (including credit management), and billing. As is the case for the sales performance analysis, these reports can be used for operative as well as for analytical purposes. All reports can be assigned different warning functions that indicate different problems.

Operative Reporting enables current business processes to be monitored by specialist employees, as shown in the following examples:

▶ A credit representative can see all customers whose credit status is so bad that they have been blocked from other sales orders.

▶ A service employee can keep an eye on delays in delivery or warehouse problems that necessitate a change in delivery dates.

▶ A processor for invoice processing can track incoming invoices, and credit or debit memos.

Analytical Reporting offers comprehensive options for evaluating sales order processing in the enterprise. For example, the sales manager receives a complete overview of all fulfillment processes by answering the following questions:

- ▶ How reliable are our deliveries?
- ▶ How often do we need to process backlogs?
- ▶ How often do we get returns, and for which reasons?
- ▶ What is the proportion of planned sales figures compared with the actual billed amounts?
- ▶ What is my customers' payment history?

These analyses can be used to target problem areas and develop appropriate solutions for them.

7.4.9 Distributed Sales Order Processing (Extended Order Management)

Today, one can no longer presume that orders are processed exclusively by using a single, central fulfillment system. On the contrary, increasingly more fulfillment systems are involved, which work together in a collaborative relationship network that includes enterprise divisions, plants, and business partners. However, even if an order is fulfilled jointly with several partners, the customer expects just one order document and one invoice, regardless of the partner, international subsidiary, or enterprise division that supplied the individual products. The CRM application *Extended Order Management (EOM)* is confronted with the difficult task of coordinating sales order processing with the different software systems involved, on the basis of uniform master data. Important business aspects include supporting third-party business transactions in which a customer is not supplied directly, but by a business partner or by another plant, the option for an order split, that is, for sales order processing by different suppliers for each order, even if different partners supply the customer.

7.4.10 Recommendations for Successful Projects

In the first implementation phase of mySAP CRM, enterprises should focus on communicating with the customer by using a particular communication channel: Internet Sales, Mobile Sales, or Telesales. All of these options provide you with competitive advantages that offer seamless integration in sales order processing, for example, consistent quotation pricing up to the invoice and binding delivery date information, which is often critical in the sales process. Here, business processes should be as lean as possible. Therefore, enterprises must analyze precisely which of the comprehensive functions offered by mySAP CRM are required in their scenarios, and how to optimize the high degree of integration of mySAP CRM with mySAP ERP. When contrasted with other CRM solutions, this substantially simplifies implementation.

7.4.11 Scenario Overview and Potential Benefits

mySAP CRM Sales supports all sales processing steps from order entry to incoming payment. The business scenarios shown in the following table are offered by SAP as standard for sales order processing across all industries.

Cross-Industry Scenarios	Short Description	Potential Benefits		
		Revenue	Profitability	Customer Satisfaction
Credit Management	Support for risk assessment at all times during sales order processing, in particular during the delivery phase, to minimize accounts receivable		✓✓	
Billing	Accounting for order items and tracking invoice processing		✓✓	✓
Claims Management	Processing and tracking outstanding payments, and user-friendly dunning		✓✓	✓
Availability Check	Enables precise statements concerning delivery dates in real time at the time of order receipt	✓		✓✓
Shipping and Transport	Complete integration of shipping and transport in sales processing, which enables sales to make precise statements regarding delivery dates		✓	✓✓

7.5 Service

7.5.1 Overview

Customer service plays a key role in retaining customers for the long term. No other employees within a company have more direct customer contact than do the agents of an Interaction Center or field service experts. SAP recognizes the importance of customer service through a wide range of applied functionality within the integrated solution mySAP CRM. The mySAP CRM service components support the entire service cycle right from the initial contact with the customer, to the carrying out of services or the shipment of spare parts, to billing.

The mySAP CRM service component is an integral part of the CRM solution and provides:

- ▶ All tools necessary for efficient customer service
  (Customer Service and Support)
- ▶ Access to an adaptable database for solutions to problems
  (Knowledge Management)
- ▶ Central management of existing installed bases with all customer-related data
  (Installed Base Management)
- ▶ Resource planning, control, and management of customer service (Resource Planning and Optimization) using mobile terminals (Field Service)
- ▶ Determination of planned services within service contracts, and forecasting options for ongoing service tasks and spare part usage (Service Planning and Forecasting)
- ▶ All processes and functions required to manage services successfully, which demands the tight integration of logistics and financial processes such as costs and revenue (Service Operations Management)
- ▶ Useful analysis of services and strategic service planning (Service Analytics)

The mySAP CRM service functions are closely related to other application components in the company:

- ▶ The integration of the SAP Business Information Warehouse (SAP BW) with mySAP CRM enables the current analysis of service processes in relation to workload (for example, the workload of specific technicians), quality (for example, orders processed outside of negotiated response times), and cost-effectiveness (turnover, revenues). Other key figures can be defined freely.
- ▶ Connection to financial applications, such as mySAP Financials (mySAP FI), enables the smooth transfer of controlling relevant data between both systems. In this way, the entire value flow of a service process, including costs and revenue, can be analyzed.
- ▶ Human resource components, such as mySAP Human Resources (mySAP HR), complete the integration of mySAP CRM. Data that is relevant to the employee—such as working times or activity reports that can also be sent to the CRM system using mobile terminals—is saved and processed in the ERP system. The ERP system then provides the CRM system with information about time off due to, for example, vacation or sickness. This, in turn, enables the resource planner to see the availability of all field service employees for resource-planning purposes, which means that data has to be created only once and is then available in all integrated applications without time delays.
- ▶ Provided that mySAP CRM is connected to the materials management component of an ERP system, it can check the availability of spare parts and reserve these parts. It can also report spare parts, machines, and tools used by the technician, directly in the ERP system. In material requirements planning, the ERP system can

then trigger repeat orders and control inventory management. Because the stock kept in individual technicians' vehicles can also be monitored, the technicians can see the stock available in their own and their colleagues' vehicles.

7.5.2 Customer Service and Support

Large companies must deal with customers often on a daily basis. It doesn't matter whether the customer stops by personally, calls the Interaction Center, sends a fax or email, chooses to use self-service on the Internet, or requests the callback option from the Internet. The company is always available for the customer, across all channels and around the clock. Customers usually contact the manufacturer of a product or a service provider because they have:

▶ A question

▶ A problem

▶ A request

▶ A complaint

All four scenarios and the response options open to an agent in the mySAP CRM Interaction Center are introduced in the following section, and are illustrated with examples.

Responding to Customer Questions

A customer calls his or her utility company because an item on the last electric bill is unclear. The agent enters the customer name or contract number in the Interaction Center application. The mySAP CRM Interaction Center application provides agents with a user interface that is linked to all necessary system components. It is comparable to a control panel from which follow-up activities can be triggered.

When a customer calls with a question, problem, or other service request, the agent can see at a glance the customer's entire history with that company: for example, when the customer changed contracts or completed a new contract; when and what products or devices the customer registered; which contract partners were involved in a business transaction, for example, for the installation of devices; and which deliveries and bills the customer received. The customer history enables agents to communicate knowledgeably about transactions that they did not deal with personally.

The agent is then in a position to answer the customer's questions promptly. While customers may be surprised because they spoke with a different agent previously, in the event of a technical problem or complaint, they appreciate not having to repeat the entire past series of events with each new contact. The agent is well informed and can immediately answer or resolve the customer's question regarding the electric bill.

Automatic Support for Agents

The alert modeler is an invisible observer that runs in the background and, in specific cases, warns or reminds agents about certain things. If a customer's data matches specific criteria that was defined previously, the alert modeler appears on the agent's screen in the form of a message. Employees of a large car dealership, for example, can use the alert modeler to issue a note for all those customers with a specific type of car: "Inform customer about a special offer for an annual service." The agent for an airline, for example, gets the prompting message, "Offer frequent flyer program," for all customers who have flown more than 100,000 miles in a year and are not yet part of a bonus program.

During the conversation, agents can read additional information from a text field, for example: "Customer is also a commercial electricity consumer." This information is supplied to the alert modeler by an assistant function of the mySAP CRM Interaction Center component. The agent then knows that the customer is not referring to his or her own private household electricity and therefore, can highlight current offers for business customers.

Solving Customer Problems

Customer queries about a bill can usually be answered quickly. However, solving technical problems can take a lot longer. In some circumstances, it is even necessary to involve technical customer service. In each case, the Interaction Center agent takes on the role of problem solver—even in a case where a customer's heating system was only recently installed.

The agent can see the details of the customer installation in the Interaction Center application at a glance. The agent can also tell from the customer-specific Service Level Agreement (SLA), which is automatically displayed from the service contract, that the customer has concluded a service contract with a 24-hour response time for the installed system or that the system is still under warranty.

Additional information about the on-site installation is supplied to the agent by central installed base management (see Section 7.5.5). It's not just installations (appliances) that are mapped in the installed base database, such as is the case for a computer manufacturer; all policies can also be represented, as is the case for an insurance company. Generally, contracts or accounts, machines or vehicles, and buildings or inventory can all be mapped in the installed base database.

The agent has the customer describe the exact problem with the heating system before searching for a solution. Knowledge management supports the agent in the search for a solution (see Section 7.5.4). The customer reports that the heating system display is showing the message "8—Off" and there is a red light lit to the left side of this message. First, the agent consults the list of *frequently asked questions (FAQs)*, which provides an answer to the red light question (for example, "water level too low") but not the message "8—Off."

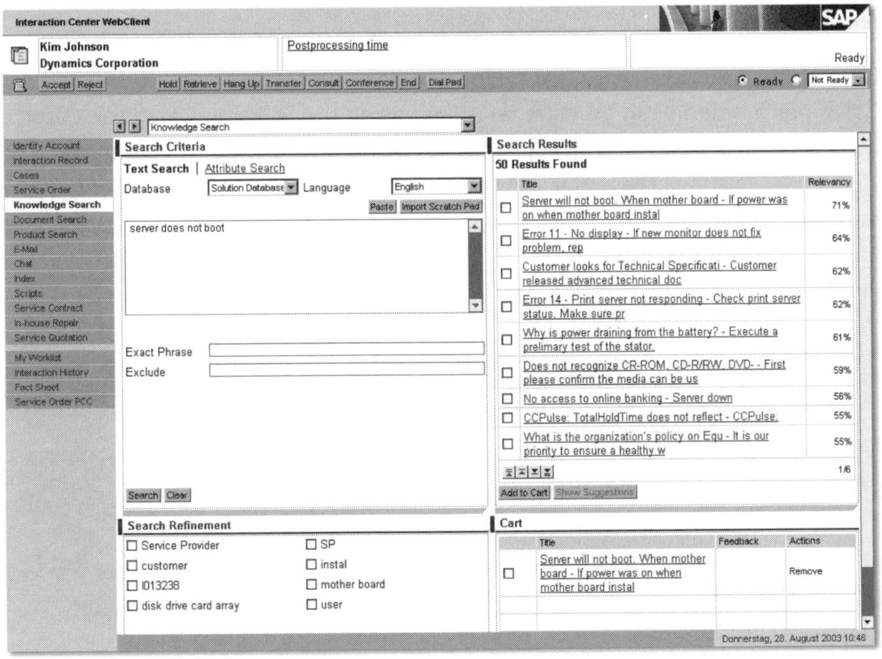

Figure 7.35 Solution Search in the Interaction Center

Solution Database

The agent also consults the *Solution Database*, in which all known error descriptions and related solutions for all products are saved. The agent can limit the solution options that support him or her and thereby refine the search for a solution. The system minimizes irrelevant and repeated search transactions by selecting error descriptions and solutions rated helpful by users.

Although the message "8—Off" occurs infrequently, the database recognizes it and identifies it as an error in the control electronics. The agent creates a service order in the Interaction Center in the mySAP CRM system and automatically proposes an appointment with the customer so that the problem can be resolved in the next 24 hours as agreed in the contract.

In a best-case scenario, the help desk can solve the problem by sending the solution directly to the customer via email along with a short cover letter. The solutions sent are stored in the customer history so that the customer does not receive the same solution twice.

Case Management

Customer problems can't always be solved using the Solution Database. Often a case is created first, in which various types of documents can be stored and viewed at a glance. These documents could be service orders, complaints, sales orders, or Microsoft Word documents. It isn't important whether the case is created first and the documents are assigned later, or whether the documents exist first and are later attached to a case.

If, for example, a pipe bursts in a street, residents of the street call the utility company and report the burst pipe. Usually, these calls are taken by different agents. To avoid having ten workmen sent to the same emergency location, these calls are assigned to the new case "Pipe Burst in Market Street," as is the service order for the repair. All customer calls that are now taken can be assigned directly to a specific case. This means that the agent can immediately inform the caller that a technician is on the way.

There are also many application examples in the automotive industry. A case is created for each new model at the point of sale to group all future problems relating to that model. Then, if a customer has to take the new car to the garage, a case is created to group all activities associated with this specific vehicle. These activities could be repairs, customer calls, or even a complaint made over the Internet to report that something is rattling in the back of the car again. This vehicle-specific case is assigned as a sub-case to the case for the model. The car manufacturer's engineering and development department then has an overview of all the cases and can take measures to improve quality if a specific vehicle's problems increase to the point where the new model becomes unpopular with customers.

Comprehensive functionality is available for maintaining cases. It is particularly important that appropriate processors and contact persons are allocated to a case, that changes made can always be tracked, and that the correlation between cases can be shown. It is often necessary to find specific cases from previous years: "We've had that problem before...there was some trouble a couple of years ago with the milling machine." Comprehensive search functions are available to enable you to track down this type of case successfully, particularly for public authorities where cases can last over a period of many years or are reopened after new information comes to light.

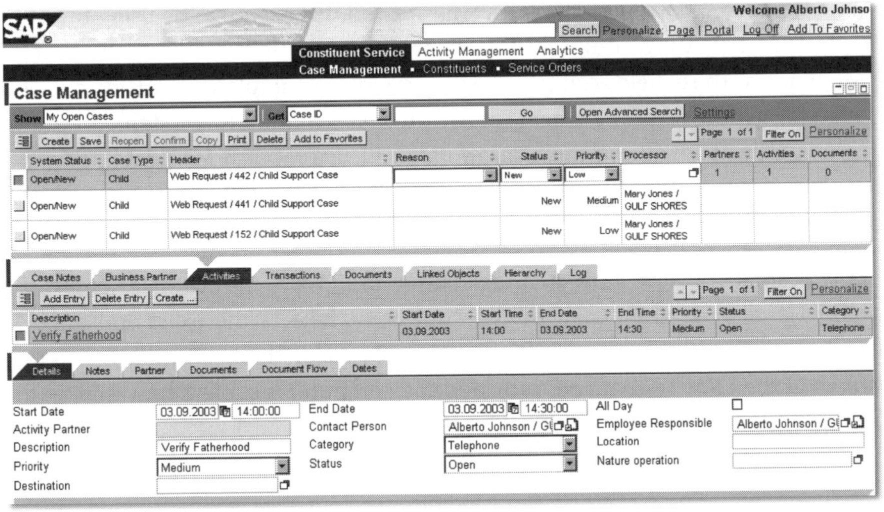

Figure 7.36 Case for Claiming Maintenance Payments

Fulfilling Customer Needs

A company rents an additional building with open-plan offices that are equipped with new computers and printers. The company wants to register this equipment with the manufacturer who will be responsible for servicing the equipment. An employee of the firm registers this request with the hardware manufacturer over the Internet.

The manufacturer's homepage doesn't simply have up-to-date product information; it also provides a variety of electronic forms for requesting additional information, ordering new products, authorizing maintenance work, and even registering products such as the computers and printers the company bought. The Internet as a channel of communication is just as convenient for the manufacturer's customers as any other channel.

This is exactly what manufacturers and service providers intended. They want to offer their customers and potential customers a comprehensive and easy-to-use service, which at the same time is more cost-effective for their companies. Numerous studies show that each customer need that is fulfilled over the Internet is worth cash in hand to manufacturers and service providers.

What a visitor to a homepage doesn't see is the complex functionality behind the Internet pages. Each electronic form was created, for example, by using the *Web Requests* mySAP CRM tool, which defines individual fields with the help of an XML schema. These fields can then be generated in a complete HTML form. Completed forms automatically trigger service processes in the CRM system; for example, a vehicle reservation from a car rental agency, a request for a catalog from a mail order company, or the renewal of a passport at the department of passport services.

In the example regarding product registration used here, the customer enters the product and serial number of the computer and selects the exact appliance to which this information refers in the *Product Type* field. The computer is then registered in the CRM system and, provided the computer is subject to warranty, the warranty period can begin.

The e-service component integrated in mySAP CRM (*Internet Customer Self-Service*) offers much more than just product registration. Self-service through the Internet not only enables customers to see the orders they have placed, but also provides access to company information shared across organizational networks. If a problem occurs, customers can refer to a catalog of FAQs any time of the day or night, or consult the Solution Database. Imagine that a customer with a defective household appliance visits the manufacturer's homepage and, simply by creating a service notification, is informed directly of a date for the repair. This is exactly what the automatic appointment scheduling function integrated in *E-Service* offers. This ensures that only technicians with the required qualifications are dispatched and that they carry the necessary spare parts in their vehicles.

Managing Customer Complaints

After the installation of two new servers for its CAD (Computer-Aided Design) applications, an engineering firm experiences problems when more than three workstations try to access an application simultaneously.

The agent, Jose Vega, enters the customer name and the Interaction Center application provides an immediate overview of all devices installed at this firm. Jose sees when, and by which contract partners, the two servers were installed. He also sees that the engineering firm has reported the same kind of problems twice before during the last four weeks; however, these problems have since been resolved. The servers are still under warranty and the SLA in the contract stipulates that faults occurring on workdays should be fixed within six hours.

Since the customer is angry about the recurrence of this problem, Jose uses the *Complaints* function in mySAP CRM to create a complaints transaction. He enters the subject of the complaint (the two servers) and the reason for complaint (insufficient server performance) in the relevant input fields. He then triggers tasks to try to satisfy the customer as quickly as possible. The complaints transaction provides an entire range of handling options specifically for this purpose. Agents can, for example, authorize a credit memo for the customer, trigger the return delivery of a product and simultaneous provision of a replacement, or, as shown in our example, ensure that a field service employee is sent to address the problem by creating a service order. A few hours later, the field service employee who was assigned by resource planning uses his or her laptop to report to the CRM system that the order has been completed.

From the customer's point of view the complaint has now been addressed. However, the server manufacturer doesn't view the problem as being resolved. The manufacturer's CRM system saves both the subject of complaint and the reason for complaint because the Interaction Center agent usually selects these servers from a predefined catalog. The agent can select reasons such as *Unfriendly Employee, Late Delivery,* or *Malfunction in Product Xy,* or decide on a follow-up action such as *Credit Memo, Substitute Delivery,* or *Return Request.* Weak points can then be identified during a subsequent service analysis and suitable measures can be taken to eliminate them. This could include employee training, the dispatching of additional delivery vehicles, or an order to quality control. No company is ever happy to receive complaints, but a customer-oriented business learns from complaints and uses them to optimize its processes. This optimization process is supported by the *service analysis* in mySAP CRM (see Section 7.5.9). To measure customer satisfaction with the handling of complaints, an agent calls the customer and questions him or her regarding the service that customer received. The customer's responses are then stored in the system.

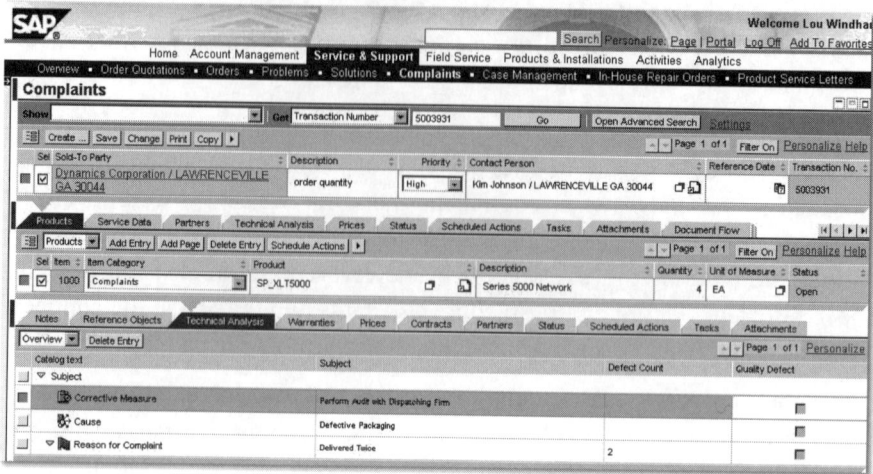

Figure 7.37 Complaint About an Order Quantity—Quantity Delivered Exceeds the Quantity Ordered

7.5.3 Service Contract Management and Service Entitlements

Service contracts principally represent long-term agreements between companies and their customers. Service contracts usually contain agreements that are described as *Service Level Agreements* (SLAs) or *SLA parameters*. The standard SLA parameters *Availability Time* and *Response Time* are integrated in mySAP CRM. However, additional company-specific parameters can also be defined freely and integrated to support specific business processes.

These parameters are not only used to describe specific agreements, they can also be used to control service processing, whereby the CRM system permanently monitors the times specified in the contract. If it seems likely that the specified times cannot be met, predefined company-specific escalation steps are triggered as a proactive measure to try to head off a possible customer complaint. An escalation step could include, for example, giving customers ample warning that the service employee will be arriving later than planned, or informing them about the unavailability of spare parts on a particular date.

If a contract refers to a specific machine or technical installation, the technical equipment is displayed along with the contract. Whenever a service order based on a service contract is triggered, the CRM system automatically compares the services to be performed with the contract conditions.

If, for example, an on-site service within 24 hours is specified in a computer user's contractual agreement, but the user requests a technician within six hours due to an urgent order, the user can then be invoiced separately for the faster response time. All prices for services covered by a contract are defined and stored in a product list in the CRM system. Similarly, it would be possible to note in a maintenance contract that all services performed for a customer installation within a particular period should be free of charge; however, the customer should receive an invoice for the spare parts used.

Service Contracts with Release Quantities

A special form of service contract is one in which release quantities can be defined. A software company has tailored a service package for one of its customers who has just implemented the software. The service package includes a check shortly before the go-live date, three telephone consultations, and a check of the productive system. The company offers the entire package as a service contract and sells it to customers on request along with the software. If a customer purchases this type of contract and then uses one of the telephone consultations listed in the contract, the system automatically reduces the number of open consultations correspondingly until all consultations have been claimed.

Planned Services

Many customers don't think the "Standard Offer" is sufficient for their needs and they request service contracts that are more individually tailored to their requirements. They request, for example, a service contract for an air-conditioning unit extending over two years and including the proviso that the technician carries out the planned maintenance work on the first Monday in February. The contract also specifies that any malfunctions that occur will be corrected within 24 hours.

This type of planned maintenance is represented using service plans. Service plans are an integral part of service contracts. The service plan is used to define which services are to be performed and at what intervals. In this way, all individual requirements are considered.

Imagine that, for legal reasons, all company elevators must be inspected every two years. The inspection must always occur on a Friday because there are no customers at the company on that day.

In this case, the service plan is time-based and a service order is automatically created every two years. If required, the system immediately selects a technician who would be suitable to carry out this service order. In the best-case scenario, this automatic selection is the customer's first choice of technician.

Another example foresees the machine control system of a sophisticated installation regularly sending the most up-to-date counter readings to the CRM system. The counter readings are then stored in the CRM system in a counter that was created especially for this installation. This installation needs to be inspected every 800 hours that it is in service and the inspection must include specific checks. This allows actual counters to be referenced in the service plan and a service interval of 800 operating hours to be entered. When the machine control system reports 800, 1600, and so on hours of service, the system generates a service order in which the items for individual checks have already been entered.

Combinations of time and performance are also feasible (every 20,000 miles, but no later than every three years), as are one-time-only events (a one-time-only check after a year).

Companies that want to see an outline of all the planned services for the next half year, for example, can use the service plans to start a simulation and obtain the required information. The results can also be extracted from the CRM system and transferred to SAP BW where they are displayed as a column for strategic service planning (see Section 7.5.9).

Warranties

Warranties play an important role in service. Usually, warranties are the starting point for service work. Therefore, they should be flexible and lend themselves to being customized for each customer. Customers will only sign service contracts if they're satisfied with the warranty management provided.

A machine builder sells an installation for which he wants to offer specific customer warranties for different parts: three years for the engine, but 10 years for the individual parts that are housed in the engine. In turn, warranties for parts that are prone to wear and tear are based only on the number of hours that they're in service. The firm buys only parts from its own suppliers for the installation.

The supplier provides the company with a warranty for these parts. The machine builder wants to store this warranty in the system, so that, wherever possible, the repair costs incurred during the period of the warranty provided by the supplier are passed on to the supplier (vendor warranty).

In these cases, warranties can be assigned flexibly to the individual components of the installation. It is also possible to assign more than one warranty to each component. Warranty templates can be created for warranties that are used most frequently. These templates can then be found automatically during product registration or they can be assigned manually.

When creating service orders, confirmations, repair orders, or complaints, the system automatically runs a background check to see whether a warranty exists, and if a warranty does exist, assigns it accordingly. When calculating prices for services and spare parts in billing, these warranties can be accounted for through appropriate discounts.

Marketing Services

In mySAP CRM, services are created as products and can be marketed strategically for predefined customer target groups within widespread campaigns. Service products support all types of services: customer service and technical installation, training, and consultation.

A telecommunications company could, for example, plan the following services and offer its Interaction Center or field service over the Internet:

▶ Exchange of connected in-house telephones for portable devices for a fixed price (for devices and assembly). This offer is available only for a limited period of six months and is valid only if the exchange of devices occurs on a Tuesday or Thursday because the field service workload on these two days is less than 70 percent.

All customers with ISDN Internet access are offered faster network access at a flat rate through conversion to broadband if they accept the offer within the next six months. The telecommunications provider advertises this offer to its customers over the Internet, on the monthly statement of charges, and by using country-wide television commercials.

The following examples show that these types of service products are feasible for almost any company that views service as a valuable instrument for strengthening and extending relationships to the customer, and not just as an obligatory product accessory.

▶ A heating firm discovered that more than 85% of its customers requested an inspection of their heating systems in the months of November and December. To try to balance the workload for the technical service team, the firm offers a cheaper inspection in the months of April to June along with a "Winter Warranty" that includes a maximum downtime of six hours.

> ▶ Through its subsidiaries and authorized dealers, a car manufacturer offers its customers a cost-saving holiday check for their vehicles. The check is offered only on Tuesdays. The workload in all of its workshops is significantly lower on this weekday.

7.5.4 Managing Organizational Knowledge

Not so long ago, only specialists could be found working in the support centers of manufacturers of sophisticated software programs or complex technical devices. These specialists were responsible for a particular product range. They knew the technical inner workings and functionality of the products they were in charge of inside out. As a customer with a problem, you were lucky to reach a specialist when he or she was available.

Today, every Interaction Center agent is a specialist for all questions, providing his or her company works with a sophisticated customer relationship management system. mySAP CRM enables agents—and customers using the Internet—authorized access to all organizational knowledge. The term *Knowledge Management* is used to group these functions. Knowledge Management is an effective element of mySAP CRM that not only manages knowledge, but also supplements knowledge through strategic collection and categorization.

The need to search a company high and low to find a specialist who can provide a competent answer to trifling questions is now obsolete. No one employee possesses such a wide range of problem-solving knowledge as does the integrated Solution Database in mySAP CRM, which offers precise, consistent, and tried and tested solutions to complex problems.

All known problem descriptions are saved in the Solution Database. They are entered as free text with attributes (for example, type description) or by using defined codes that describe a problem or damage that occurred. One or several problem solutions are assigned to each problem description, which can contain free text, codes, detailed figures, video clips, or Web pages. The Solution Database uses a variety of information sources to document, save, and map solution options to known problems.

Optimizing Knowledge

Knowledge optimization means that the specialist responsible for the content of the Solution Database is supported by the statistical data preparation that is based on user reports, and by reports from different perspectives and automatically generated proposals. This kind of support enables the content of the Solution Database and the search quality to be continuously refined and improved. The list of FAQs and answers is a collection point for the organizational knowledge bank saved in the database and represents an important source of information for both customer and company employee alike.

7.5.5 Managing Customer Installations

The management of existing customer installations (*Installed Base Management*) includes the maintenance and administration of all relevant information. The following examples are used to explain the details.

Installed Base Overview

In cooperation with several allied partners, a machine tools manufacturer supplies a large part of the technical equipment for the new production facility of an automotive components supplier. Because component parts are delivered just-in-time (JIT) to the car manufacturers, the supplier has finalized service contracts with the machine tools manufacturer to ensure extremely fast response times for equipment that is essential to production.

As the main contractor, the machine tools manufacturer guarantees customer service for the technical equipment that it and its partners supply. In mySAP CRM, this equipment is represented graphically in installed base management.

For Interaction Center agents and every field service employee who can access the CRM data from mobile devices, installed base management provides at-a-glance information showing, for example, that three CNC lathes, two four-axle machining centers, a laser cutting center, and four industrial robots are installed at the automotive components supplier. The clear tree structure also lets you recognize whether the three lathes are of the same type or whether they have different optional features. The visual image of the installation allows the agent to see which machines are supplied by which partner firm of the agent's company. The agent can see immediately whether the machining center is still under warranty.

Because installed base management is integrated in the service process, you can access contracts from installed base management. Field service employees get information about the conditions of the contract agreement with the customer, before making an on-site call with that customer.

In many companies, the CRM system is connected directly to the ERP system, which supports production and delivery. A company produces printing machines, for example, and after completion sends the finished product to its customers. Following the goods issue that is entered in the ERP system, the printing machine that was sold should of course also be available in the CRM system as a customer installation so that service contracts can be created and malfunction reports can be maintained. mySAP CRM provides this out-of-the-box integration with ERP systems and can be used for a multitude of integration scenarios.

Products with "Individual" Features

A property management company offers maintenance and repair services to its business and private customers. Services include the exchange of energy consumption meters and defective thermostats on radiators. The property management firm has created an installation description in its CRM system for each customer (*Installed Base*).

The installed base for a law firm's two-storied office building has the following structure:

Installed base
  Building
    Floor 1
      Room 1
        Radiator
        Radiator
      Room 2
        Radiator
        Radiator
      Room 3
        MAIN SUPPLY
    Floor 2
      Room 1
        Radiator
        Radiator
        Radiator
      Room 2
        Radiator
        Radiator

This installed base description lets you see at a glance how many radiators there are on a floor and in a room. The same information is displayed for each radiator: identification number, thermostat type, and type of energy consumption meter. The component in room 3 stands out. The main supply with integrated hot water heater, a customized product specifically for the office building, was mapped as an individual object due to the irregular amount of information to be displayed, such as device type, year of manufacture, service data, and maintenance intervals. If the main supply was to be interrupted, the property management firm would not send a service technician, but rather a heating specialist.

Installed base descriptions can also be a valuable tool in the service sector. An insurance company could, for example, make each customer's entire portfolio of insurances visible at a glance.

The insurance company could map the portfolio for customer Adams, which is stored as an installed base in the CRM system, as follows:

Portfolio for Mr. Adams

Car insurance
    Policy for car 1
    Policy for car 2

Property insurance
    Policy for house 1
    Policy for house 2

Contents insurance
    Policy for house 1
    Policy for house 2

Any company can tailor mySAP CRM installed base management to meet its individual requirements. For example, this includes options for mapping all customer installations in one single installed base description, grouping several similar customer installations in one description, or creating a separate installed base for each customer.

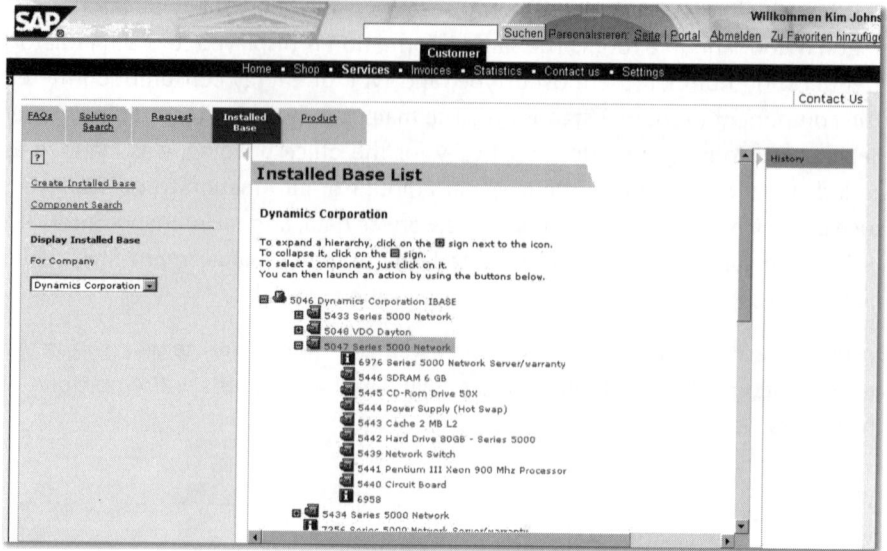

Figure 7.38 Customer Maintains His or Her Installed Bases in E-Service

7.5.6 Order Management and Resource Planning

The functions for field service, resource planning, and optimization provided by the mySAP CRM service components support the entire service cycle from the customer inquiry, to the execution of an order, to billing.

However, when considering field service and resource planning, the subject of "service" should not be restricted to just the traditional range of tasks performed by technical support, that is, maintenance, repair, and the exchange or new installation of an appliance. A field service employee for an insurance company also completes a service task when he or she records the damage inspected on the customer's premises. A health-insurance customer also utilizes service when he or she has a personal consultation before undergoing a rehabilitation procedure. The field service employee of a security firm is offering service when he or she presents new techniques for object security to a customer on request. To the automated service process in mySAP CRM, it is irrelevant whether these types of services are performed under coverage of existing service contracts or are calculated separately.

Technical Field Service

With the help of an order for technical field service, the user-friendly functionality of the *Resource Planning* service component speaks for itself.

Resource Planning and Order Management

The air-conditioning unit at a customer's house has broken down. The customer, Nina Lopez, calls the hotline for the manufacturer's service center from her office at 8:30 a.m. Although the company's headquarters is over 100 hundred miles away, it supports a nationwide network of combined sales and service centers. The provisioning of spare parts occurs centrally from the company headquarters.

Ms. Lopez gives the Interaction Center agent the serial number of the device and describes the problem. The agent checks for possible causes of failure (fuse, level of coolant) by questioning Ms. Lopez. However, this proves unsuccessful. Ms. Lopez responds with, "It would be best if you sent a technician."

The agent creates a service order with the necessary customer data (name, city of residence, type of air-conditioning unit, defect description) in the Interaction Center application and informs the customer that an employee will be in contact shortly to arrange an appointment. mySAP CRM compares, for example, the place of residence and the zip code, and automatically submits the service order for resource planning by the regional dispatcher responsible. The dispatcher, Rodney Washington, then receives an outline or diagram of the field service employees available in his region.

On his screen, Rodney sees that, potentially, eight technicians are available. However, two technicians are currently on holiday, one is on sick leave for the remainder of the week, and four are already busy with other orders on that day, which leaves just the eighth employee available. Rodney can see that this technician is free today from 1 p.m. on and has the necessary qualifications. He calls Ms. Lopez and proposes that the technician call her between 1:00 and 4:00 p.m. He also has an outline of the priority of existing orders, requested-by dates, and latest start times as stipulated in the contracts.

The dispatcher, in this case Rodney, then assigns the order to the manually selected technician who is available today. The CRM system transmits the order to the field service employee's mobile terminal (laptop or handheld device). Rodney knows that some of the technicians enter their service confirmations in the evening offline over mobile devices and transfer them to the CRM system the following morning. They then use this opportunity to accept the current day's orders. This would be too late for Ms. Lopez, the customer with the failed air-conditioning unit. Therefore, Rodney also informs the technician about the order by using an SMS message or contacting the technician's pager. Shortly afterwards, the service employee confirms the new high priority order.

The technician, Seamus O'Hara, reaches the customer at around 1:00 p.m. and sets to work. With the help of a diagnostic tool, he quickly finds the defect in the central control system for the air-conditioning unit. Although he doesn't have a motherboard of this older type with him, he is able to circumvent the defective circuit by installing an additional switch as a temporary solution. This will ensure that the air-conditioning unit can function in the short term, before the motherboard is replaced by a new one.

While still on site, Seamus arranges for a follow-up appointment with the customer to exchange the motherboard. The dispatcher, Rodney, can also see this appointment in the resource planning tool.

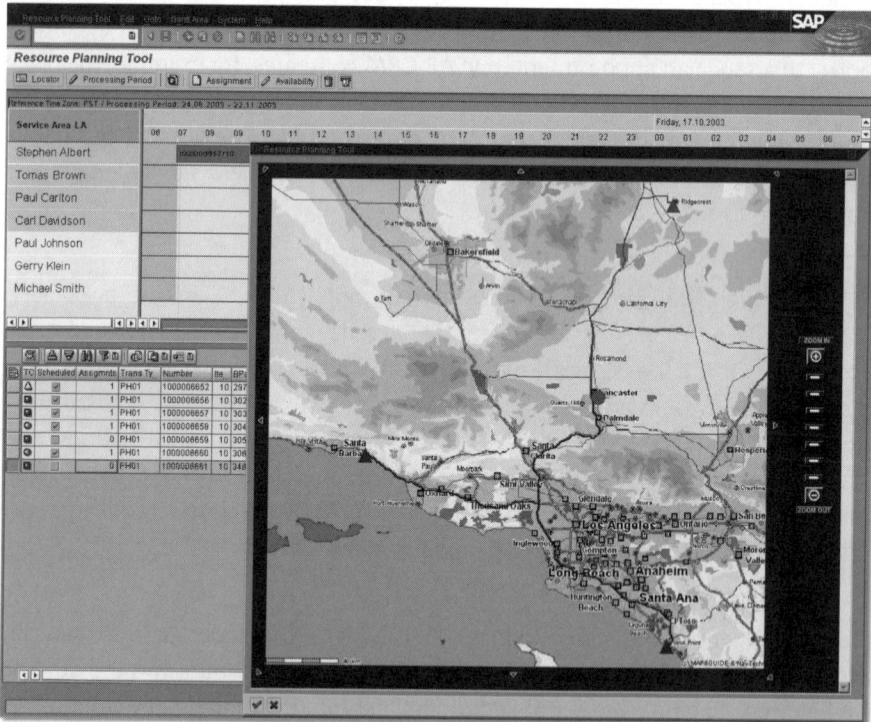

Figure 7.39 Resource Planning with Graphical Route Planning

Automated Order Management

mySAP CRM Service supports completely automated order management.

In such a case, the agent in the Interaction Center proposes to the customer a timeframe within which the order should be completed, or the customer searches for a suitable appointment (*Appointment Scheduling*) in the Internet (e-service)—Thursday between 8:00 a.m. and 12:00 p.m.—and creates a service order with a defect description. mySAP CRM assigns a suitably qualified field service employee to complete this task according to his or her availability. This form of order management is favored by, for example, appliance manufacturers who deal in mass production.

Real-Time Order Confirmation

Services can be confirmed using a variety of communication channels and, if appropriate, can automatically trigger diverse follow-up actions. This has the important advantage that the confirmation can be entered directly at the site of the repair and no further processor is required to enter the information later. Incorrect entries are also reduced to a minimum.

During a repair performed on the customer's premises, the service technician uses the order number to enter the relevant data for the partially completed order in his or her handheld device: time of arrival and time of departure, working time, and materials used. The technician can communicate these details over the telephone to an Interaction Center agent or transmit them to the CRM system online over the Internet. For its part, the CRM system then forwards these details on to the appropriate components of the ERP system (personnel planning and materials management). The process steps that result from this operation run automatically in the ERP system.

▶ A materials management component registers the withdrawal of materials, checks the target stock levels, and triggers extra stock as appropriate.

▶ The CRM system reports the technician's traveling and working times in the Cross-Application Time Sheet (CATS). This application posts the confirmed times to the technician's time account (mySAP HR Payroll). Provided that they are relevant, all invoice items (materials, time) are automatically converted to dollar amounts and are clearly displayed including special price agreements from contracts (service level agreements) or other sources. The customer receives a comprehensive invoice for all individual items.

▶ The costs for the service order are transmitted to Controlling. This involves the costs being assigned to a cost collector (for example, internal order), whereby you can flexibly set in Controlling whether a cost collector should automatically be created for an individual service order, service contract, or project, and then posted to it.

mySAP CRM allows you to create several confirmations for a service order. This could be necessary if a field service employee, as per the example with the defective air-conditioning unit, requires more than one day to complete the task, or more than one employee is involved in completing the same task. You can also enter confirmations for several orders simultaneously. For example, the confirmations are entered offline in a laptop or handheld application and then collectively transferred to the CRM system during the next online connection.

In-House Repair

Not all repairs can be carried out directly on the customer's premises. There are large service centers and repair centers where repairs and planned services are performed for anything from video recorders to excavators. The business generated by spare parts and repairs is often more profitable than the sale of new appliances. That is why in-house repair and the shipping of spare parts occupies an important position in many companies.

Repairs are predominantly reported through an Interaction Center or over the Internet (e-service). In some cases, a complaint precedes a repair order, which results in the customer returning the defective part for repair.

> For example, a customer, Mr. Brian Nielsen, reports to an agent in the Interaction Center that his DVD player no longer works. The agent, Julie Chung, enters the problem in the system and issues Mr. Nielsen a unique RMA (Return Material Authorization) number. Mr. Nielsen writes this number on the delivery note that he returns along with the DVD player. When the return delivery is received by the service center, the employees can assign the DVD player returned by the customer directly to the repair order. Employees at the service center can then check whether a part sent in is still under warranty or is covered by a service contract. A service technician then performs a technical analysis and records the inspection result (causes, measures to be taken, and so on). The technician uses the inspection result to determine the appropriate action to be taken, which means either replacement or repair.

If the technician decides that a repair is to be made, the necessary repair services and spare parts are then planned. An availability check provides information on availability of the spare parts in the repair center stock. Each spare part item generates a reservation that enables a procurement process to be triggered early on.

The system also determines the prices for each repair item. Factors influencing pricing include spare parts and services covered under warranty, customer-specific prices (discounts), and contract-specific price agreements.

If a customer requires one, a quotation can be created for each repair item. If the customer rejects the quotation, the system generates a return delivery of the defective part to the customer. Alternatively, once the product has successfully been repaired, it is returned to the customer.

The repair process ends with billing. This involves billing the customer at a fixed cost rate or according to the actual work involved in the repair.

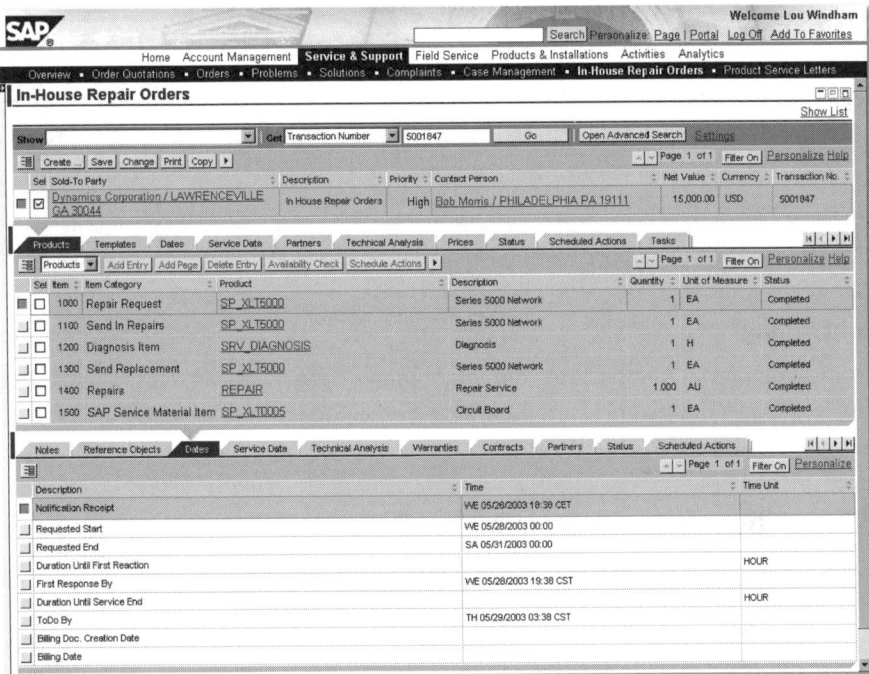

Figure 7.40 Processing the Repair of a Defective Product

Billing

Billing provides all of the functions necessary for invoicing a customer for time, materials, and services (see also Section 7.4.6). Service contracts can be settled periodically, which involves using a billing plan to define which amount or percentage is to be settled. Regardless of whether order confirmation is required in particular cases, you can also bill for individual orders or service assignments following each individual confirmation or the completion of an order.

Before billing the customer, you can decide for each individual service order item whether the customer should in fact be billed, or whether the sum owed should be considered as an act of goodwill. It could be that a customer sends in a part for repair during the period of warranty; however, during the repair, it becomes apparent that the customer is responsible for the damage incurred. In this case, the customer must pay for the repair even though it is performed during the warranty period. The technician can also make this decision when conducting the service confirmation on the customer's premises.

You can also use amount allocation to generate invoices for different bill-to parties for the services performed and the materials used.

> For example, a hydraulic hose on an excavator cracks shortly after the end of the warranty period. After the customer contacts the manufacturer, the manufacturer decides that although the warranty period has ended, it will bear 50% of the costs as a courtesy to the customer. In this case, the costs incurred by the repair are shared. The customer pays 50% and the manufacturer pays the other 50%. You can also allocate costs by directly entering a specific amount.

Controlling

Controlling plays an important role in companies providing services. Controlling can be used to draw conclusions about the efficiency of services provided and to recognize those services that generate the most revenue.

> For example, a company for security doors has concluded service contracts with customers for specific high-security doors. The service contract includes planned maintenance and malfunction reports. A cost collector for these service contracts is created automatically in controlling (mySAP Financials). The company has a clear idea of the profitability represented by the conclusion of a service contract. Controlling provides the company with tools for making the cost and revenue situation transparent, including the analysis of costs from warranty services, goodwill services, spare parts, and additional costs. Receiver costs can be settled or reposted according to the originator. This allows for warranty costs to be settled to a warranty cost center or goodwill costs to go to a sales cost center. Controlling-related reports are supported by Service Analytics (see Section 7.5.9).

7.5.7 Professional Services

Today, service doesn't just mean eliminating malfunctions and performing planned maintenance work. The performance of services is often project-oriented, for example, to give a company the best possible support with the organization and execution of a limited number of specific tasks. Examples of such project-oriented service providers are management consulting or IT consulting companies, IT software vendors, auditors, and law firms.

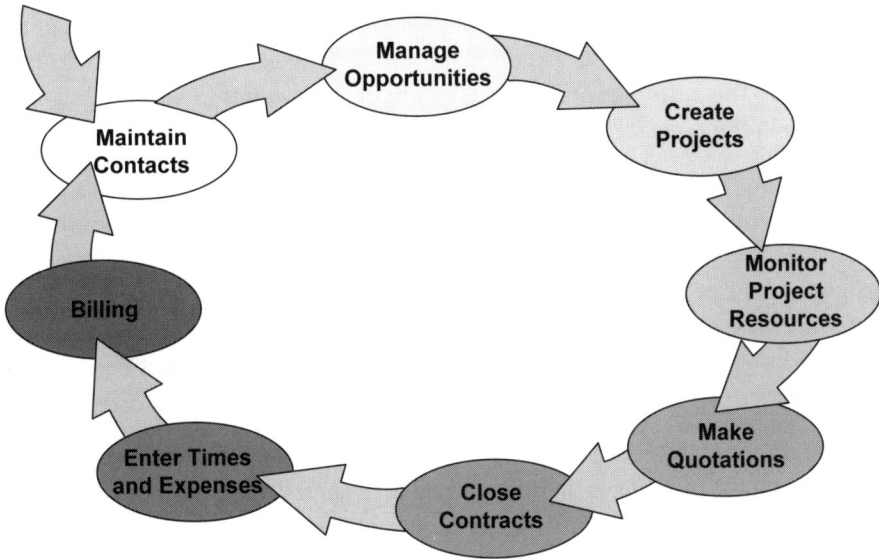

Figure 7.41 Professional Services

Opportunity

In a consulting firm that specializes in advising customers in the pharmaceuticals industry, the planning of consultants wasn't previously supported by a software system. Although this gave the consultants a greater degree of freedom, it meant that they did not have an optimum workload, and project planning involved a great deal of time and effort requiring a lot of coordination over the telephone.

After implementing mySAP CRM, the situation changed. Now, as soon as a customer calls and makes an inquiry about project support, or a sales employee or consultant has an idea for a customer project, an opportunity is created for the possible consulting project and accompanies the entire sales process from this point onward. The opportunity is authorized by consultants or sales employees. The total number of opportunities provides an overview of the pipeline of consultancy projects lined up for the future.

Project Management and Project Resource Planning

Even at this early stage in the sales cycle, a project is created for the opportunity to assess whether the consultancy project at a pharmaceutical firm can be executed according to the conditions named by the customer. The project is structured roughly into phases and tasks, and workloads are calculated. You can then schedule the project and perform the first cost estimate. You can also check the available capacity and the feasibility of the consultancy project. Project roles are used to define the requirements for consultants in terms of qualifications and workload. A search for suitable consultants can then be performed based on qualifications, organizational affiliation, and availability. If central resources are required for the customer project, you can book consultants in advance, even at this stage in the cycle (see also Section 7.6).

If the customer accepts the quotation, the next step is to plan the details of the project to be performed. The planning includes structuring the consultancy project in more detail and expanding tasks and subtasks. The roles are then assigned to the project tasks. Now, it is important to assign the most suitable consultants to the project, that is, the right consultant in the right place at the right time. Once again, you will find that project resource planning will help you in your search for appropriate resources as you review qualifications and availability.

It is important for resource planners to know the availability of their employees. Project resource planning is therefore based on a central availability database that not only manages project assignments for the consultants, but is also integrated with the attendees and absentees in mySAP HR and an employee's MS Outlook/Lotus Notes calendar. This enables the resource planner to know at any point in time which projects the consultants are currently working on. The resource planner can then select available consultants and assign them to the project per mouse click. These consultants are automatically informed about the assignment by an MS Outlook/Lotus Notes task or appointment.

Engagement Management

Controlling and billing requirements for projects are especially high. A fixed price for the project is agreed on with the pharmaceuticals firm. However, additional services that were not described in the specification are billed according to the work and resources involved. All of this is possible. As the project progresses, the consultants enter travel expenses and time spent on the project. They can do this either online (for example, using a browser-based interface) or offline (for example, on a laptop). Project controlling enables the consultancy firm to keep an overview of costs at all times. It can then assess whether the project costs are on target and within budget, or whether they need to be renegotiated. Flexible billing options allow both billing based on fixed prices and resource-related billing. In resource-related billing, billing is based directly on the working times and travel expenses entered by the consultants. You can also perform in-house billing. This is necessary and useful when the project is staffed with other consultants who, from a legal point of view, belong to other independent organizational units.

7.5.8 Integrated CRM Concept for Service Employees

The integrated CRM concept based on mySAP CRM also provides service employees with access to field service functions.

> Had Ms. Lopez, the customer in the example with the defective air-conditioning unit, decided to enhance or modernize her in-house system, the service technician, Seamus O'Hara, could have immediately made real and binding proposals. If this had been the scenario, it wouldn't have been the *field sales team* who generated additional revenue for their firm, but the *technical field service team*, thanks to the technician's on-site assessment of the situation. The concept "Make every service employee a sales person" would have been adhered to. As you can see from this would-be scenario, the old sales adage "Sales makes the first sale, service takes care of the rest" is still valid.

Service employees can, of course, have access to a customer's payment history and any outstanding payments, and use this information to draw appropriate conclusions. The data is displayed clearly and simply in Account and Contact Management (see Section 7.3.4). It not only displays open orders and complaints, but also outstanding payments from reminders.

7.5.9 Service Analytics

Along with their sales colleagues, a company's service and field service employees always have the closest contact with customers. From the customer's viewpoint, *they* represent the company—they are the people with whom you can talk; they're the folks who answer your questions, and who are there to help when problems occur. Customer opinion of a company is unquestionably influenced by the employees with whom customers have personal contact. While the quality of a product or service is little more than one differentiation indicator, customer satisfaction with the service provided is increasingly the factor that distinguishes a company from its competition.

Customer-oriented companies not only keep customer satisfaction at the forefront of their business; they also measure it. mySAP CRM provides the necessary data. *Service Analysis* handles the evaluation and graphical display of this data

(*Service Analytics*), which can supply answers to many questions, including the following:

▶ Which service level agreements (SLAs) are requested most often by customers?

▶ In what percentage of cases was the company unable to meet the agreed SLA times? What were the reasons for this?

▶ Which products cause the most defective reports?

▶ What percentage of complaints refers to the Interaction Center, the Internet customer self-service, or field service?

▶ Which customer segment has the lowest number of complaints (categorized, for example, by age, service contract, or private and business customers)?

▶ Which customer group takes the new product or service offers most often/least often?

▶ Are there regional differences in the degree of customer satisfaction?

The service analysis is divided into the following areas of responsibility:

▶ Strategic service planning

▶ Quality analysis

▶ Contract and order analyses

▶ Warranty analysis

▶ Profitability analysis

▶ Performance analysis

Strategic Service Planning

Strategic service planning utilizes the SAP SEM planning platform belonging to the mySAP BI solution (see Section 5.2.1) to plan future services. Similar to the planning applications in marketing and sales that have already been described, companies also plan the following required key figures, for example:

▶ Planning service revenue

▶ Planning service costs

Quality Analysis

Quality analysis includes all relevant issues starting from the problem report and the handling process, to the completion of the service process, to the customer's satisfaction. The reports range from changes in the quantity and value of service processes and the workload in the different service areas, to the status and success analyses of the responsible service employees. Possible reports could answer the following questions, for example:

▶ How have the service complaints developed for each sold-to party, product, and service employee?

▶ What are the most frequent complaints for each product?

▶ How high is the rate of delayed services and handling times?

Contract and Order Analyses

All contracts and orders are synchronized automatically in real time by using SAP BW. The analysis of related service documents is the basis for all the more extensive analyses. Typical examples are:

▶ Which quantities and values in service contracts have changed?

▶ What is the ratio of cancelled, open, and processed service contracts?

Profitability Analysis

An accurate analysis of costs, revenue, and profit for services performed is of particular importance. Detailed controlling of revenues and costs for each service process is supported by back-office integration with the SAP solution. This provides transparency for financial trends and non-profitable activities, enabling appropriate counter measures to be implemented in good time. Typical examples are:

▶ How have service revenues and costs developed over a period of time?

▶ Which service products and customer segments are the most profitable?

Performance Analysis

SAP provides a ready-to-use analysis cockpit specifically for service managers, supplying all relevant data and key figures. Data ranges from customer information, financial key figures, and key figures for service-relevant processes, to employee-related key figures. The following selection demonstrates the variety of available key figures:

▶ Financial key figures, such as revenue and profit, broken down according to product or service organization

▶ Customer-related key figures, such as customer profitability, customer satisfaction, or delayed services per customer

▶ Process-related key figures, such as processing volumes or services completed on schedule

▶ Employee-related key figures, such as ratio of errors, overtime rate, or sickness

There is scarcely a question that is relevant to service that cannot be answered by a service analysis using the mySAP CRM database or, if appropriate, in cooperation with other internal company sources. The analysis results enable companies to recognize negative trends early on and to respond with appropriate measures. The goal of all analyses is to optimize service processes and to target the customer's needs repeatedly, thus turning satisfied customers into loyal customers.

7.5.10 Use Case: Using mySAP CRM in Service

Dynamics Corporation, a customer of PC4YOU, recently bought a new network from the 5000 series. The IT manager of Dynamics Corporation, Kim Johnson, uses PC4YOU's e-service portal to register the new server and begin the warranty coverage. Shortly after the server installation, Kim notices problems with the motherboard. She revisits the e-service portal and creates a complaint. She wants the server repair to be a high priority complaint.

Tara Lee, an Interaction Center agent with PC4YOU, contacts Kim and informs her that PC4YOU will exchange the server as soon as Dynamics Corporation has returned the defective hardware. Tara also records the exchange activity in the CRM system. Two weeks later, she automatically receives a note in the Interaction Center informing her that the activity is still open and that the server has not yet arrived at PC4YOU. She calls Kim Johnson and asks whether there was a problem with returning the network server. Kim confirms, however, that the server is on its way to PC4YOU.

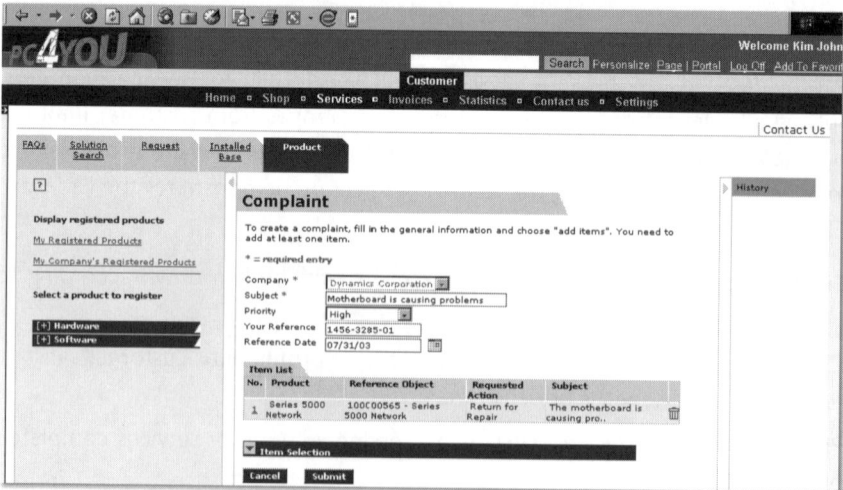

Figure 7.42 Customer Complaint in the E-Service Portal

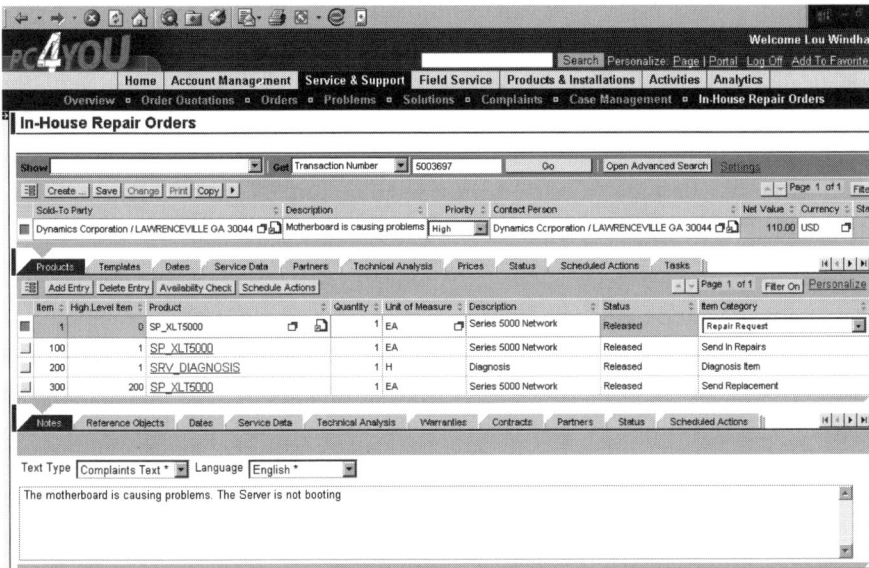

Figure 7.43 Repair Order

> When PC4YOU receives the server, Lou Windham, a service technician with PC4YOU, inspects the causes of the defect and records them in an inspection report. Then he performs the necessary repairs and reports his working time and materials.

7.5.11 Recommendations for Successful CRM Projects in Service

Service as a selling point and a business with a guaranteed future is becoming increasingly important. When companies want to increase customer satisfaction, there are many different scenarios that they can use as a starting point.

First, there is the complaints management scenario that companies can use to support the entire complaints process—from the initial complaint, to complaints processing, to analysis. This enables companies to focus on simple complaints transactions in the Interaction Center. Further communication channels, such as e-service, can be connected later. Just like the communication channels, the complaints processing functionality can be extended step by step. For example, there's an option for automated complaints handling for specific complaints that enables the system to control processes, such as the creation of credit memos for complaints worth up to 125 USD ($125.00).

Another area recommended for initial projects is resource planning for service employees. In many firms, this task is still performed on paper, or by using a blackboard. mySAP CRM users can use the resource planning tool, which is provided by the system, to assign service orders to service employees with the right qualifications. To ensure that service employees are informed directly of the orders that need to be addressed, the next step should be enabling the use of mobile devices. These devices can provide employees with access to all necessary information that pertains to existing orders and customers, even when employees are in the field. After they have completed their work, they can use mobile devices to confirm working times and materials.

Most implementation projects in service, however, begin with the mapping of customer installations (installed bases). Much attention should be paid to this fact because it lays the groundwork for the subsequent operational processes, and retrospective changes are very time-consuming. Companies must consider very carefully before they decide how the actual individual objects (machines, accounts, and vehicles) are to be mapped in the system, and which additional master data, such as warranties and contracts, should be assigned.

7.5.12 Scenario Overview and Potential Benefits

This key functional area from mySAP CRM covers the central processes in service organizations, from the creation of service contracts and the performance of services, to confirmation. The actual cross-industry scenarios are grouped in the following section along with their potential benefits:

Cross-Industry Scenarios	Short Description	Potential Benefits		
		Revenue	Profitability	Customer Satisfaction
Service Order Management	Supports a range of service processes including inquiries and quotations, order creation, spare parts planning, employee resource planning, and fulfillment	✓✓	✓	✓
Planned Services	Processing of recurring services for customers using service plans for time-based or counter-based creation of service orders	✓✓	✓	✓
Service Contract and Entitlement Management	Service order management including automatic check for existing contracts and warranty entitlements, taking parameters such as first response times into account	✓✓	✓	✓

Cross-Industry Scenarios	Short Description	Potential Benefits		
		Revenue	Profitability	Customer Satisfaction
Professional Services	Management of project-based services with project-planning, delivery, processing, fulfillment, and project analysis	✓✓	✓	✓
Service Parts Order Fulfillment	Functionality for sales of spare parts within service processes, including interfaces for capacity planning of spare parts delivery	✓	✓✓	
In-House Repair	Mapping of in-house repair execution, reprocessing, and exchange of defective products, and fulfillment and complaints analyses for customer returns	✓	✓✓	✓
Product Service Letter Management	Implementation of manufacturers' service instructions by service organizations by means of product service letters for product maintenance or recalls to prevent expensive repair measures and to solve repeated technical problems		✓✓	✓
Complaints and Returns Management	Management of complaints processes from the acceptance of a complaint and technical analysis, through to service provision, credit memo creation, and returns processing		✓	✓✓
Case Management	Grouping of all information relating to ongoing transactions for one case and for structuring and monitoring the procedure for processing a case		✓	✓✓

The following additional industry-specific business scenario simplifies the service process in the public sector.

Industry-Specific Scenario	Short Description	Potential Benefits		
		Revenue	Profitability	Customer Satisfaction
Citizen Services in the Public Service Sector	Online services offered to citizens and companies by authorities and public institutions through self-registration on the Internet or through an Interaction Center		✓	✓✓

7.6 People Shape Relationships—Workforce Management with mySAP CRM

What Is Workforce Management?

Whether active in an Interaction Center, service, sales, or another part of the company, all employees perform specific tasks that provide services. The *Workforce Management* (WFM) component is used to plan the work for these employees, in terms of their time and location, and to optimize the use of the workforce. Workforce management must map the company targets for daily business with the number, availability, and skills of the employees. Changing targets are immediately accounted for by reassigning employees to operational tasks.

Workforce management is an essential component of CRM solutions because customer relationship management focuses on *relationships* and relationships are all about people. Therefore, companies can improve customer relationships only by ensuring that the right employee is always in the right place at the right time—just when the customer needs him or her.

Reasons for Implementing Workforce Management

Workforce management solutions principally concentrate on the resource planning of employees, the allocation of tasks, and the creation of motivating performance incentives. Within the *closed-loop concept* (see section 12.2.1), these solutions are extended to include an analytical function that permits effective and timely corrections in problematic situations.

WFM solutions differ from traditional human capital management systems (HCM) in that HCM systems are management systems, while workforce management provides operational scheduling of employees based on real business requirements, for example, shift plans or the allocation of service orders to specific employees. In this way, workforce management enhances traditional production systems such as supply chain management (SCM, see Section 5.2.1). Both applications contribute towards company success by optimizing the best possible implementation of resources. However, while SCM is more object-oriented, focusing on objects such as materials and machines, WFM addresses the largely individual and varied implementation of resources.

When juxtaposed with the operational improvements of business processes that are based on optimized employee planning, the following characteristics make workforce management an attractive investment:

▶ **Savings in Personnel Costs**
Workforce management enables you to save personnel costs by using employees only where they are really needed and have an actual workload. This reduces redundancy and empowers the greatest influencing cost factor in a company, namely, the employees.

▶ **Reduced Management Expenses**
Implementation of WFM solutions usually leads to reduced management expenses.

▶ **Lower Costs and Faster Results**
Workforce management can be implemented as a standalone solution and, because it is a relatively small component of the CRM solution in comparison to other solutions, implementation costs can be controlled and results are more immediate.

▶ **Reduced Process Costs**
Despite its autonomy, workforce management is very tightly integrated with the operating processes in companies; this integration enables process costs to be significantly reduced. For example, an Interaction Center manager can plan the incoming call expenses and the employees required for this based on a general workload forecast. For optimized planning of outgoing calls, the manager requires the close integration of workforce management with marketing campaign management.

Workforce management has its origins in service, which is also its primary focus. Here, the employees represent their company's "product." The relationship between service employees and customers is often critical for the success of the company. Therefore, the implementation of a workforce management solution should be considered first and foremost for departments with direct customer contact.

Workforce Management with mySAP CRM

The WFM solution with mySAP CRM deals with all activities that pertain to workforce planning, whether the employee in question is a consultant, field service employee, service employee, or a combination of all the above. The workforce management activities supported by mySAP CRM include:

▶ Workforce planning for the Interaction Center
▶ Incentive and commission management
▶ Workforce planning in field service
▶ Resource planning for project employees
▶ Workforce planning in the retail sector

The following section provides a brief summary of all the WFM activities mentioned.

Workforce Management for the Interaction Center

The Interaction Center supports customer contact using different communication channels, if necessary, around the clock (see Chapter 10). Workforce Management with mySAP CRM ensures that the necessary personnel resources are available in the right number at the specified time. Managers can also use the following services:

▶ Long-term business and capacity planning
▶ Long-term personnel, budget, and service level planning
▶ The integrated maintenance of employee data using mySAP HR
▶ Short-term planning and the assignment of employees to specific tasks and handling of exceptional circumstances (for example, sickness of scheduled employees)
▶ Real-time monitoring (absence times, waiting times, and so on) and intraday forecasts
▶ Business analysis after period close (taking into account budget, business goals, and employee performance)
▶ Managing several locations
▶ Comprehensive reports and analyses

The Interaction Center application in mySAP CRM delivers all the relevant and current information that is required to create precise and complete work plans for the Workforce Management component.

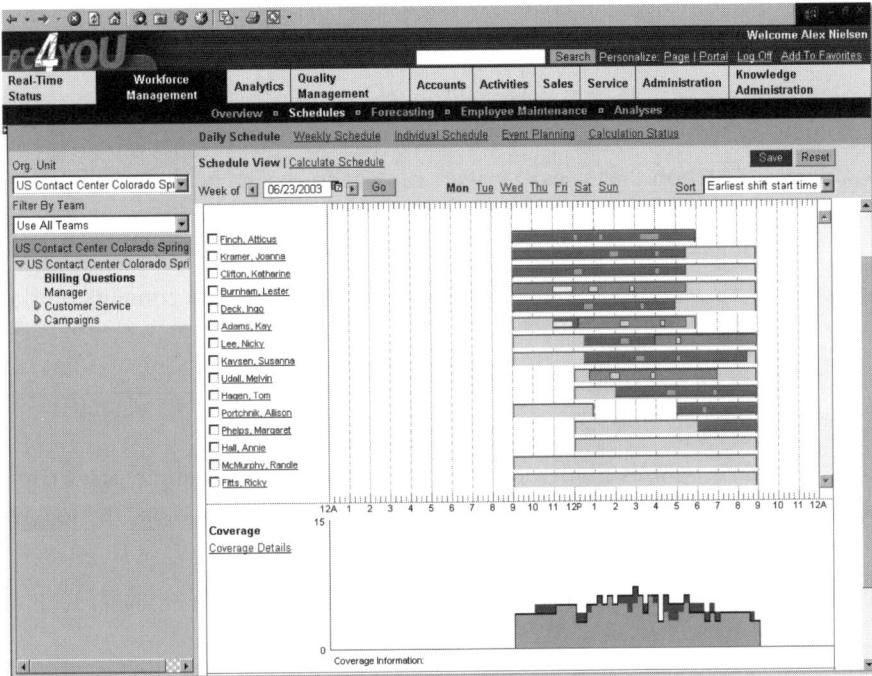

Figure 7.44 Daily Planning of Personnel Resources

Forecasting of personnel requirements occurs using business activities over all channels, taking into account historical workloads, strategic company goals, and local targets and experience. Short-term and long-term forecasts can be adapted or created from scratch if a particular planning time is reached. Because workforce management is an integral part of mySAP CRM, these forecasts or staffing plans can be transferred to other business areas to support, for example, recruitment and budgeting.

As soon as a requirement is forecast, the manager creates an optimized work plan based on different configurable objectives. A work plan can include specific knowledge requirements, personnel requirements, employee preferences, or established methods of practice. These aspects are weighted differently in the planning according to the required complexity.

Incentive and Commission Management

The CRM *Incentive and Commission Management* application rewards employees and partners who have successfully achieved their customer-related goals, having adhered to and implemented the company strategy. mySAP CRM supports different company commission scenarios, although the main focus is on the sales process. This includes the following available functions:

▶ Simulator application that sales personnel can use to determine achievable commission from a particular opportunity or business transaction

▶ Valuation function that sales managers can use to award their sales employees higher commissions for particularly profitable products or for the acquisition of new customers, and therefore control sales activities

▶ Direct access for the sales managers and sales employees to commission statuses

▶ Interface to operational sales transactions

▶ Preconfigured commission applications for standard use cases

mySAP CRM recognizes numerous types of incentives, for example, sales commissions, incentives for sales partners, employee bonuses, and so on. The following workforce management functions are a basis for this:

▶ Exact and automatic calculation of payments for each rule and every type of incentive

▶ Planning tool for incentives that allows flexible modeling, cost simulation, and individual configuration

▶ Administrative functions for daily business (for example, dealing with errors that occur and manually reprocessing commission calculations)

▶ Integration of commission payments in mySAP Financials or payroll from mySAP HR

▶ Utilization of the integration advantages of a complete business suite

With new distribution channels, increasingly more complex sales cycles, and continuing competition to win the best employees, effectively managing commissions and incentives must be considered a strategic element of the sales process for companies in dynamic business environments.

Workforce Planning in Field Service

The *resource planning tool* (see also Section 7.5.6) enables the resource planner to assign service orders to field service employees based on specific conditions (for example, SLAs), geographical considerations, availabilities, and also personal knowledge and equipment requirements. Alternatively, assignment can be performed automatically.

The resource planner receives information about the availability of individual employees, for example, based on integration with time management from mySAP HR. Mobile communication services, such as pagers and SMS, allow the resource planner to communicate current information about the existing schedule for the field service employee and possible emergencies that could occur. Appointments are presented to field service employees in SAP calendar format or, alternatively, by using Microsoft Outlook or Lotus Notes. Field service employees send status details about assignments to resource planners, for example, *accepted*, *rejected, completed, on site*, and so on. The field service employee can also confirm working times, materials used, possible damage codes, traveling times, and expenses.

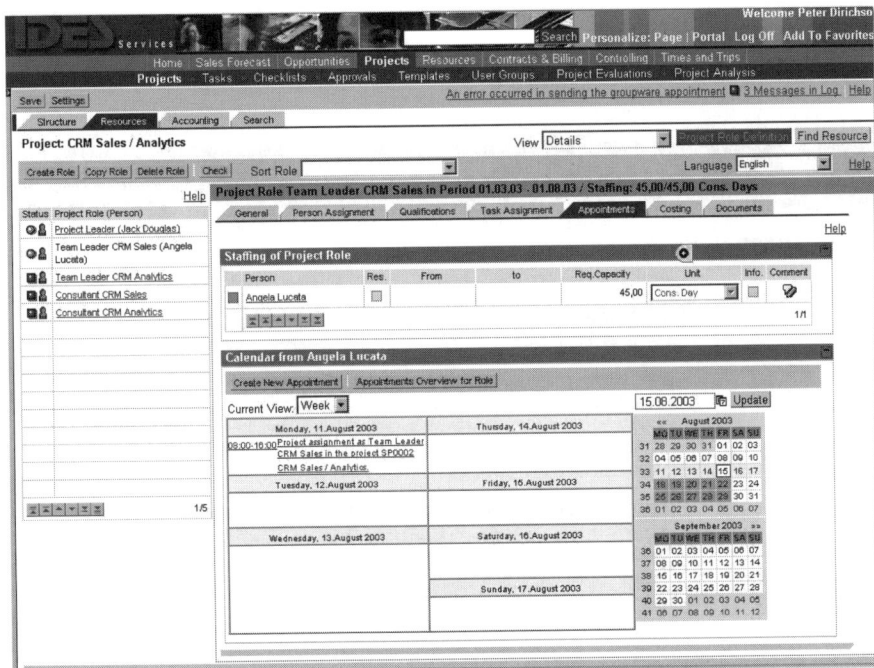

Figure 7.45 Resource Planning for Field Service

Orders and service items can be allocated either automatically, for example, by an Interaction Center agent or through an e-service request, or manually, by a resource planner. This means considering both the customer's preferences (dates requested by the customer and SLAs) and the optimization of the operational service processes. The resource planner gains flexibility by assigning more than one employee from the same team to the individual parts of a service order. Furthermore, different resource planners can access planning data for field service employees who can be scheduled jointly.

Planning Project Employees

Nowadays, work is increasingly planned and carried out in the form of projects, for example, in Professional Services (see also Section 7.5.7). All sorts of resources participate in such projects, including internal employees, contractors, and external companies. The optimal assignment of mapping personnel resources to project tasks—taking into account both employee availability and individual skills—is the task of Project Resource Planning in mySAP CRM.

The tools provided by mySAP CRM for project resource planning can be used in the project planning process to identify required roles and thereby define the requirements for the project members. Tasks can then be assigned to each of these roles, even when the actual person who will be filling the role is not yet known.

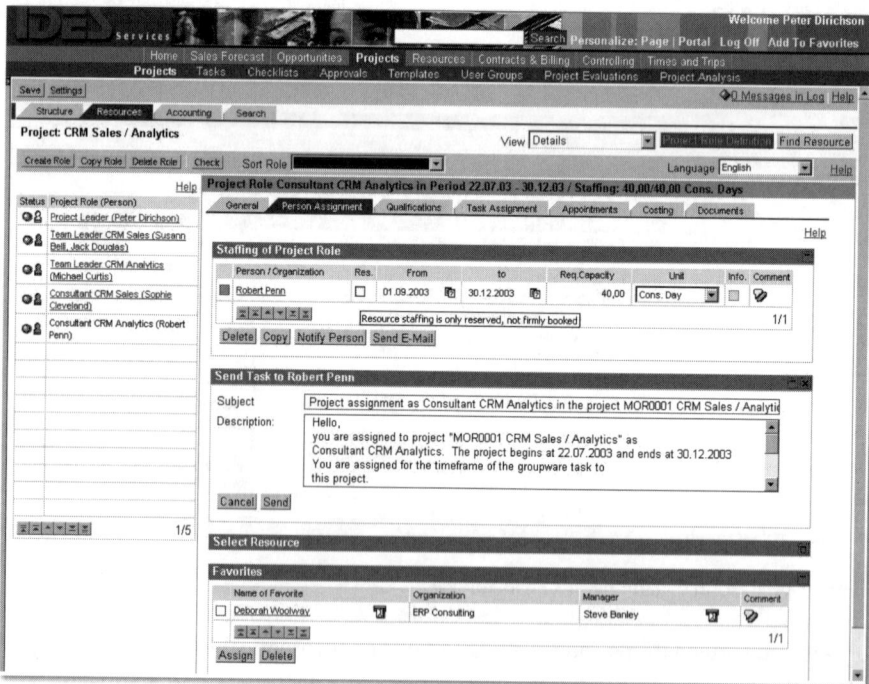

Figure 7.46 Planning Project Resources

The resource planner can also provisionally book personnel resources. Resources are booked definitely only when the final project order is known, either in the form of an assignment according to capacity (for example, three days next week) or as a definite appointment that has already been approved. As soon as a person is scheduled for a project, this assignment can be synchronized using a range of project management and calendar applications, for example, via integration with

Microsoft Outlook or Lotus Notes. Planning according to capacity enables resource planners to send a groupware task to employees already accounted for. Unfilled project roles can also be advertised in a marketplace for project vacancies in the enterprise portal.

mySAP CRM project resource planning can be used to manage employee qualifications better. The global view of resource assignments supports the resource planner with the optimal assignment of employees and tasks and provides the basis for a significant improvement in employee satisfaction. The analysis of ongoing projects enables the early identification of employee qualifications that will be required in the future (pipeline analysis). Integration with mySAP HR, CATS, and mySAP Financials enables the maintenance and monitoring of entire billing cycles and the integration of employee master data.

Workforce Planning for Retail

An option for centralized workforce planning across several branches of a company is one of the key requirements of retail companies. The solution available with mySAP CRM for workforce planning in retail deals with both the requirements of store groups and those of individual branches. This includes the following available functions:

▶ Configuration, grouping, and evaluation of work location characteristics and profiles

▶ Creation of forecasts relating to expected workload based on historical data such as customer figures, sales transactions, or revenue

▶ Entry of specific quantities and figures based on experience for the forecasting of expected workload, taking into account location-specific facts, such as special offers or the receipt of delivered goods

▶ Storage of historical data for specific periods to record the specifics of this period, such as a special clearance sale, and to use the data for forecasts

▶ Calculation of work plans for individual work locations or groups based on forecasts of expected workload

▶ Cross-branch scheduling to enable the utilization of employees from one region in more than one location

The number of advantages gained from the ability to group and maintain different work locations enables retailers to ensure consistent and standardized procedures across all company locations, reduce training requirements in the company branches, and support company-wide reporting using aggregated key figures.

8 On-Site Business Processes—Support for Mobile Users by mySAP CRM

"Companies are mobilizing."
Forrester Research [Prince 2001]

"Ignoring mobile solutions is risky."
Gartner Group [Johnson/Deighton 2003]

8.1 From E-Business to M-Business

An increasing number of users appreciates the benefits of using mobile computers. Every fifth PC sold is now portable; by 2006, this figure will increase to every fourth PC [Gammage 2002]. Many users find that being able to access their email from hotel rooms or work on their computers when commuting by train is indispensable.

The arrival of manageable portable computers has given rise to the development of new application types. M-Commerce (Mobile Commerce) and M-Business (Mobile Business) showed development comparable to that of E-Commerce and E-Business [Kalakota/ Robinson 1999].

While E-Commerce focuses on marketing, sales, and service over the Web, E-Business looks at the broader concept of business, which also includes back-end processes, and encompasses the entire order management process, including delivery and invoicing, in addition to the Web shop application.

The appearance of mobile devices and wireless networks means that mobile trade developed under the M-Commerce umbrella in parallel to E-Commerce. M-Commerce describes business transactions that can be managed "on the move," specifically the execution of purchasing and payment transactions. M-Business takes this concept further and is the mobile equivalent of E-Business. M-Business makes applications and processes available everywhere and in so doing, provides new application options in the areas of supply chain management (SCM), production monitoring, and customer relationship management (CRM) [Kalakota/Robinson 2001].

8.2 Business Benefits Provided by Mobile Applications

While fascination with mobile technology has often exceeded interest in the business benefits of M-Business projects, analysts believe that it is risky to ignore the options provided by mobile applications. The number of mobile users is rising constantly and numerous case studies show areas where mobile solutions have been employed to increase turnover and profitability [see Prince 2001, Johnson/Deighton 2003]. Mobile business applications can also add value in the following areas [Basso 2003, MacMillan/Hart 2002]:

▶ **Fewer interruptions and delays to work processes**
These processes become faster and more efficient. If a warehouse employee identifies a product using a mobile barcode scanner or a sales employee enters the address data for a contact made at a trade fair using his or her PDA using the mobile device to enter and forward data directly means that certain process steps can be eliminated.

▶ **Direct availability of current information**
Mobile field sales representatives also require current information on products, prices, offers, and conditions. Central sales and marketing departments are eager to obtain current data on customers and their buying behavior from their field sales representatives. M-Business opens a communication channel for automatically providing all relevant information to both parties.

▶ **More flexible work processes and working conditions**
Mobile applications enable employees to access commercial applications independently of time and location. The ways in which one works have become increasingly flexible.

▶ **Increased return on investment due to better use of existing systems**
Companies often invest in software applications that their employees can initially use only from stationary PCs. If mobile access options are added to these applications, the return on investment (ROI) increases.

Two typical target groups for M-Business in customer relationship management are sales employees and service technicians in the field.

8.2.1 Sales Employees in the Field Sales Force

Sales employees in the field sales force visit their customers to make them offers on-site or to collect orders. Data entry and document creation is often performed manually and is therefore highly susceptible to error. Errors lead to customer complaints, lost orders, and increased administration. Mobile computers—from PDAs to laptops—that can be customized to meet the training needs and personal requirements of the field sales representative can prove invaluable here.

Sales employees from the field sales force can use mobile devices to obtain information on cancelled dates, new products, or sales campaigns en route. If the device contains a GPS (Global Positioning System) module and specifies the current location of the employee, a new visit with a prospect can be scheduled along the route to ensure that the tour is as efficient as possible. The field sales force can enter orders on-site and immediately compare these orders with the delivery options available. Previously, this was possible only in a systematic format at the end of the day. Back-end systems can perform real-time plausibility checks, compare any discounts granted with guidelines and bonus agreements, and inform customers of other sales opportunities during the sales call.

Ratiopharm Customer Example

The Ratiopharm pharmaceutical company has provided its 500 sales employees with the laptop solution from mySAP CRM. This means that the difficult process of data integration—with customer information that was frequently incomplete—is becoming a thing of the past. Ratiopharm obtains current information on customers and contact persons from mySAP CRM, which is connected with an external address pool. This also simplifies date agreements, correspondence, expert selection, and tour planning. Ratiopharm was able to increase the total number of customer contacts by 17%, and increase turnover with its most important customers by 46%. Ratiopharm was able to amortize its investment in mySAP CRM within 16 months [Millar 2002].

8.2.2 Service Technicians in the Field Sales Force

Service technicians are responsible for the maintenance and repair of devices, machines, and manufacturing installations. If they are to perform their tasks efficiently, they must be familiar with the components to be maintained or repaired, and know when and how quickly service tasks are to be completed according to the service contract.

Mobile service solutions mean that this information can be queried from the customer site at any stage. All information at the customer site—the identity of the customer, the equipment, and the description of the problem—is available. Once these tasks have been completed, the service technician need enter only the working hours and the required materials for invoice creation and history. Data on hours and materials is forwarded to Human Resources and Materials Management directly. Companies can trace the progress of work, check the execution, and monitor all escalations. Both technicians and customer service providers are kept informed at all times and can therefore offer optimum service.

> **Sydkraft AB Customer Example**
>
> Sydkraft AB, the leading utility company in Sweden, has introduced the service solution for handhelds that is available in mySAP CRM. All current customer information is always available to the field sales force. Data and confirmations can be made on-site. Costs for dispatchers and work planners were reduced by 25%, and work process flows were accelerated by 50% [Henneboel 2002].

8.3 Criteria for Use of Mobile Applications

Implementation of mobile applications in a company must be justified by a specific business benefit and not simply by technical enthusiasm. An M-Business project is successful not simply because M-Business is currently in vogue and a chrome PDA is an attractive accessory. Technical questions come to the fore quickly in M-Business. Many different devices, such as cell phones, PDAs, laptops, and tablet PCs, are available. Different operating systems and transfer technologies make choosing mobile applications even more complex. Protocols such as WLAN (Wireless LAN), WAP (Wireless Application Protocol), or Bluetooth exemplify this dilemma. The fundamental decision as to whether the mobile device requires a continuous online connection should be made.

In M-Business projects, you must adhere to the following criteria when using mobile applications (compare with [Prince 2001, Clark 2003]):

▶ **Business processes**
A careful analysis of which business processes are suitable for M-Business is required. The issue of whether it is necessary to make a specific business process available as a mobile application and the feasibility of doing so requires clarification. You must carefully evaluate cost versus benefit.

▶ **Platforms and devices**
The mobile device selected must be a good fit for the business process and all of its requirements. The capabilities of cell phones are limited, while laptops and tablet PCs can provide a service that is similar to that provided by PCs. PDAs have the advantage of being comparatively inexpensive and simple to maintain. It is important to remember that the mobile device must be both accepted and used by the end users.

▶ **Transfer technology**
Many mobile applications are now based on procedures that synchronize data at specific points. This means that users can execute independent programs on the end device without an online connection to the server. A field service technician can, for example, download software, emails, and business data, such as

customers, products, and documents, to his or her mobile terminal and then process this from this terminal. Once the field sales representative has established an online connection to the central server, data that is entered on the road can be synchronized with the central data.

Wireless transfer technologies are an alternative that can be used to work online permanently. This type of mobile application will become increasingly important in the future; however, these solutions are currently very expensive and no suitable transfer technology that handles all areas is available. Technology candidates are WLAN and UMTS.

8.4 Mobile Applications in mySAP CRM (Field Applications)

Mobile applications have been part of the mySAP CRM solution since it was first launched. They are combined under the SAP CRM Field Applications name, and provide sales and service employees with a means of accessing core functionality in mySAP CRM directly from the customer site (see Figure 8.1). This means that mobile users can work just as productively, effectively, and efficiently as employees with a direct connection to the CRM server at the head office.

SAP CRM Field Applications include mobile solutions for the following device types:

▶ Laptop
▶ Tablet PC
▶ Handheld

While mobile CRM solutions for laptops and tablet PCs are independent applications with their own databases, handheld solutions are closely linked to the central server and download only the respective worklist required from this server on a temporary basis. They don't have their own databases. Both types of solution cover the different usage requirements from real situations. The selection decision must be made on the basis of specific project requirements.

A sales and service variant of the SAP CRM Field Applications is available. Marketing functions and industry-specific enhancements are added to applications. The following section provides an overview of the mobile solutions in mySAP CRM and focuses on which solution is best suited to each use.

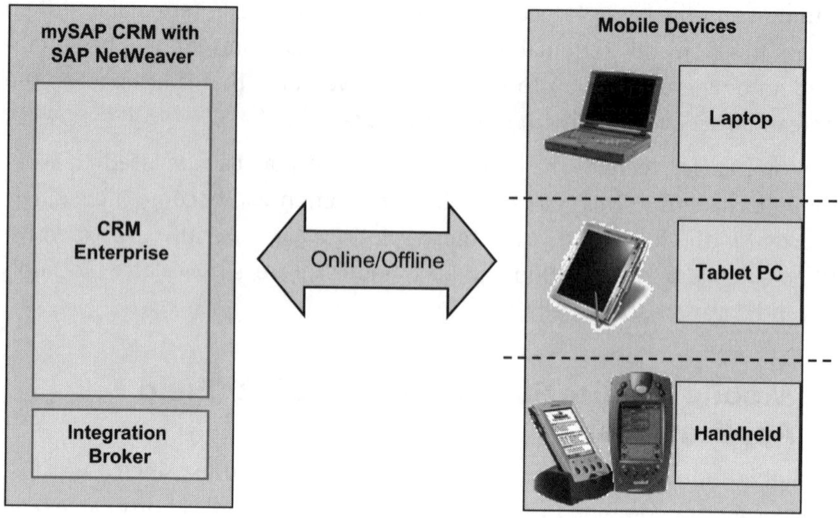

Figure 8.1 Mobile Applications for Customer Relationship Management

8.4.1 Solutions for Laptops

Laptops currently offer the same service as PCs. They are expensive in comparison to handhelds, but have a significantly broader range of functionality. The laptop solutions in mySAP CRM therefore provide the field sales force with the same sales and service applications as those available to office-based personnel.

Laptop applications are available in the following versions:

▶ Mobile Sales

▶ Mobile Service

▶ Mobile Service (R/3 Edition)

All three solutions use the same technical platform and have access to the same components (such as management of current and potential customers, data on contact persons, product data, calendar). This close connection enables companies to use and promote synergies between the sales and service areas.

Laptop solutions from mySAP CRM are independent applications with their own database on the laptop. Synchronization services from CRM Middleware perform the communication and data exchange between these applications and the CRM server (refer to Section 15.3.1). Field sales representatives need to connect to the CRM server on a temporary basis by telephone or via the data network where they synchronize the data. To minimize data transfer times, the system transfers only those data fields that have changed since the last comparison.

Distribution of data between mobile laptops takes place according to pre-defined subscription rules. For example, a field sales representative receives information only on customers in his or her sales area. The sales representative also receives all data that is dependent on these customers, such as their orders or associated quotations.

Laptop solutions in mySAP CRM are characterized by the following attributes:

▶ Intuitive, browser-based user interface. Tools are available for showing and hiding data fields, changing texts, or creating new applications.

▶ Incorporation of additional applications, such as groupware solutions like MS Outlook or Lotus Notes. Data from mobile applications can also be converted to MS Word documents, for example, during customer invoicing.

▶ The *SAP Internet Pricing and Configurator* configuration component can be installed on the laptop to perform product configuration and complex pricing procedures. This means that the same pricing and product configuration rules are available to field sales representatives as office-based personnel (see Section 9.4.3).

▶ The applications for time and travel management ensure that field sales representatives adhere to company policy with regard to business trips. Mobile users can enter, check, and update travel information, enter the corresponding documents, and record hours.

▶ Memory options for the laptop enable mobile field sales representatives to carry larger volumes of relevant information with them. The Mobile Sales and Mobile Service applications both have an Infocenter, which provides mobile users with direct access to time-critical documents and important information. This can include service reports, repair procedures, and service instructions for a service employee. A sales employee can obtain marketing brochures and presentations. The Infocenter also uses a subscription-based model. This means that users register for topics and obtain the corresponding documents during the next synchronization process. CRM Content Management is completely integrated in the Infocenter.

Mobile Sales

Mobile Sales makes the sales functionality from mySAP CRM (see Section 7.3) available in a mobile form and provides employees with access to all relevant data on-site, such as data on opportunities, offers, orders, contracts, availability, open orders, and sales histories. Orders created at the customer site are loaded into the CRM system automatically once an online connection has been established.

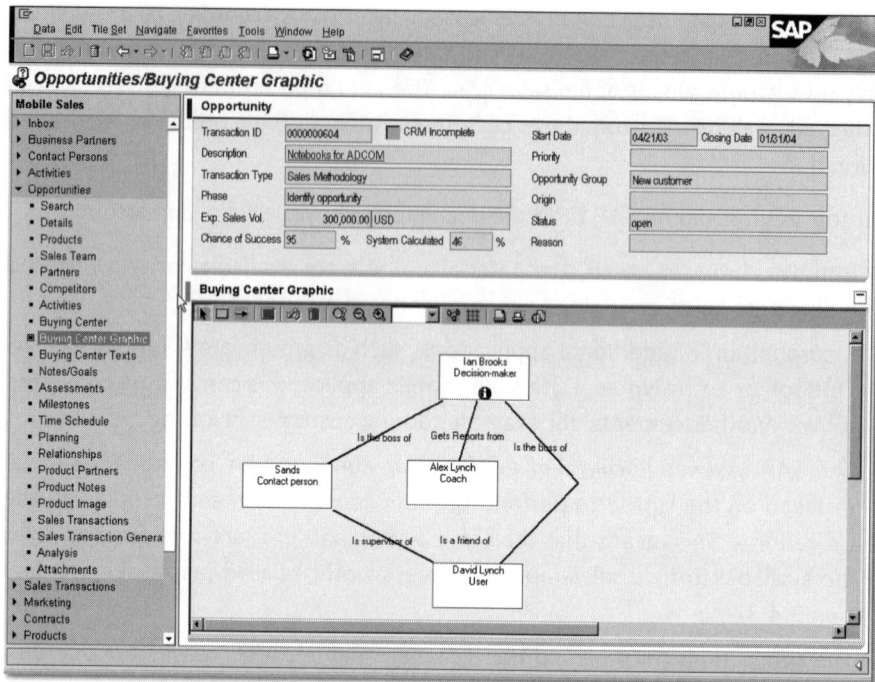

Figure 8.2 User Interface for the Mobile Sales Application

Mobile Sales covers the following core functions, which correspond to the central sales application described in Section 7.3.

▶ Account and contact management

▶ Product information on your own products and those from competitors

▶ Activity management

▶ Opportunity management

▶ Sales methodology

▶ Quotation and sales order management

▶ Campaign management

▶ Trade promotion management

▶ Demand planning and forecasting

▶ Infocenter (marketing encyclopedia)

▶ Evaluations on the basis of local data and offline availability of central data analyses, especially reports from SAP Business Information Warehouse (SAP BW)

Mobile Service

Service departments are constantly dealing with a number of problems: Information on service orders is not available on time, delivery of replacement parts for an open order is delayed, hours and costs are not entered correctly, invoicing and receivables collection is delayed by accounting errors, and so on.

By resolving these problems when service orders are signed, the accuracy of invoices, payment flow, and resource allocation is significantly improved. Mobile users can use the functions in Mobile Service for service confirmation to define time and materials expenditure for service dates directly using their mobile communication devices. Direct entry of financial information on-site means that invoices for service orders can be entered faster and more accurately, revenues can be recognized promptly, and costs can be lowered.

Core functions in Mobile Sales that correspond to those in the central sales application (see Section 7.4) are as follows:

▶ Service order and service request management

▶ Service contract management

▶ Installation management

▶ Resource planning and optimization

▶ Knowledge Management

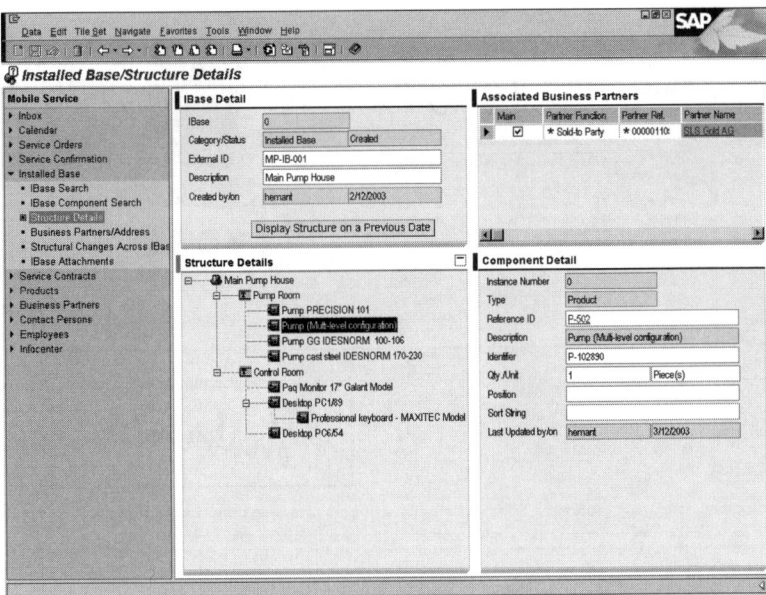

Figure 8.3 Installation Management (Mobile Service)

Mobile Service (R/3 Edition)

Companies who want to obtain the full benefit from their existing investment in the SAP R/3 *Customer Service* component can use Mobile Service (R/3 Edition). Companies can continue to use their current SAP R/3 system while profiting from the benefits and functions of the mobile solution. The mobile service application connects the field sales or service employee with the function and processes in the SAP R/3 Customer Service module using CRM Middleware (see Section 15.3.1). Since the mobile solution is based on CRM Middleware, field sales representatives can also use the sales and marketing functions in mySAP CRM.

8.4.2 Solutions for Tablet PCs

Tablet PCs are the latest type of mobile device supported by SAP. They combine the powerful functions of the laptop with the easy handling of a PDA. The user can enter data manually by writing directly on the screen using a sensor pen. Language entry is also supported. The tablet PC is technically based on the MS Windows XP Tablet PC Edition, which is specifically developed for that kind of device [Arend 2003].

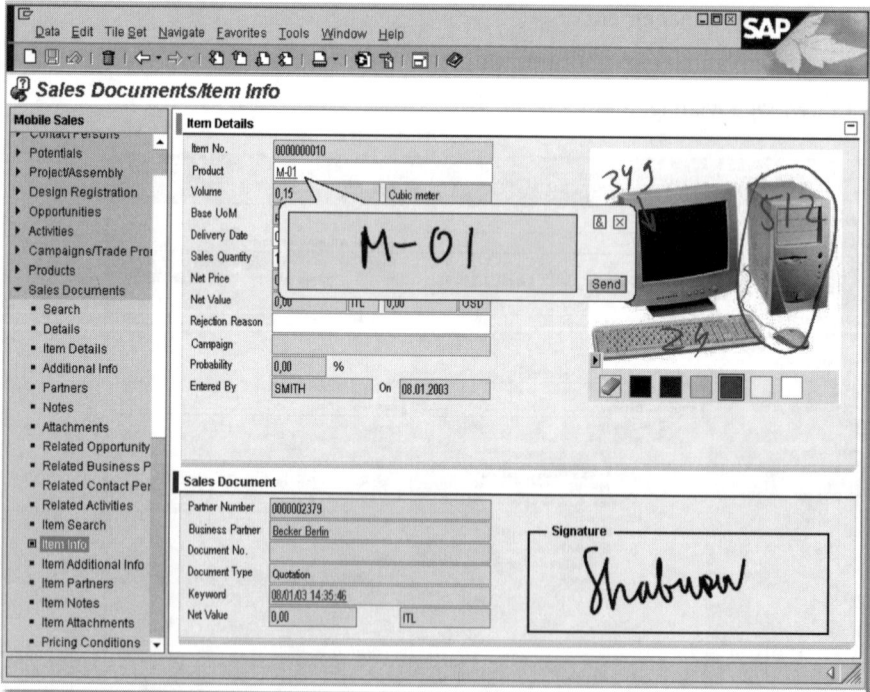

Figure 8.4 User Interface for a Tablet PC with Mobile Sales

Mobile laptop applications have been enhanced for the use of tablet PCs. Users can also take advantage of the following options:

▶ Navigate and enter data using the sensor pen that comes with the Tablet PC. mySAP CRM recognizes the handwriting of a user automatically and inserts the handwritten entry in the entry field as coded text.

▶ Append handwritten notes to business data and transactions. Manual enhancements can be made to graphics, such as product representations.

▶ Enter and save signatures. Users can confirm customer orders by comparing signatures; i.e., the electronic signature can be displayed on the printout.

8.4.3 Solutions for Handhelds

Handhelds are small lightweight devices that can be stored in a jacket pocket. They are cheaper and easier to maintain than laptops; however, their performance is limited. The screen is usually the size of a compact mirror, which means that you can display a limited amount of data. You can navigate and enter data with a pen that you can write with directly on the screen. Pen-controlled navigation is fast and intuitive, while device-specific entry fonts make data entry more difficult. Therefore, handhelds are better suited for displaying modular chunks of data than they are for entering large amounts of information. Selection fields should be available to facilitate entry.

Handhelds are used as the extended mobile arm of the application in mySAP CRM. Mobile users download the information that they require for their daily activities. Limited memory options mean that a handheld device is less suitable for processing large amounts of data.

Handheld applications in mySAP CRM are available in the following variants: *Mobile Sales for Handhelds*, *Mobile Sales for Handhelds (R/3 Edition)*, and *Mobile Service for Handhelds*. They are particularly well suited for less complex sales and service processes.

Mobile Sales for Handhelds

Mobile Sales for Handhelds offer sales functions for simple business processes. Core functions in Mobile Sales for Handhelds include:

▶ Search, display, and enter customer data

▶ Product search and display in the catalog

▶ Display and create opportunities

▶ Display and create customer quotations and orders

▶ Query price information

▶ Compose emails

▶ Display and edit tasks and activities; create follow-up activities

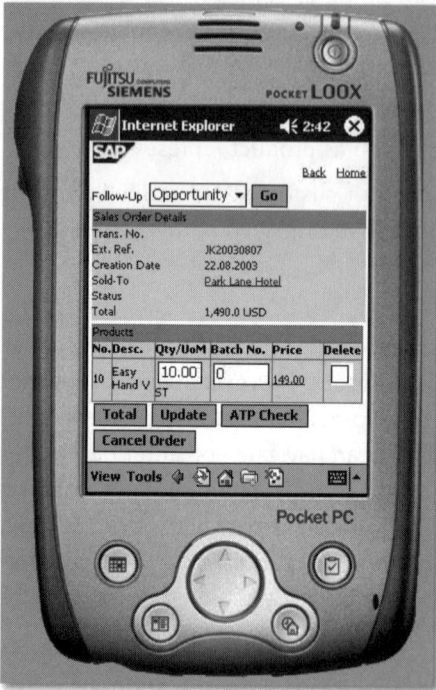

Figure 8.5 Customer Order Screen (Mobile Sales for Handhelds)

Mobile Sales for Handhelds (R/3 Edition)

To provide sales departments in companies that are using SAP R/3 without mySAP CRM with fast and direct access to mobile customer relationship management, the Handheld Sales solution is also available in an R/3 Edition. Mobile devices communicate directly with the SAP R/3 system in this solution. Core functions in Mobile Sales for Handhelds (R/3 Edition) include customer management, customer order management, and display of products and product-specific information.

Mobile Service for Handhelds

The Mobile Service for Handhelds solution contains the following core functionality for use in the service area:

▶ Search, display, and enter customer data

▶ Product search and display in the catalog

- ▶ Display and create service orders
- ▶ Service confirmation
- ▶ Create complaints
- ▶ Compose emails
- ▶ Manage personal tasks
- ▶ Integration with resource planning (see Section 7.5.6)

8.4.4 Mobile Applications in Industries

The field sales force has traditionally played a central role in certain industries, such as the pharmaceutical or consumer goods industry. Some of these industries have very specific requirements of mobile applications (compare with [Buck-Emden/Böder 2004]).

Specific sales promotion measures (trade promotions) are performed in the consumer goods industry to increase market value, market awareness, sales volumes, and market shares, but also to implement new products and product ranges. Producers organize advertising campaigns with the retail trade that are frequently associated with temporary price discounts. The Mobile Sales application in mySAP CRM supports this process and provides field sales employees with functions that they can use to define campaign planning on-site with dealers.

Pharmaceutical companies require information on products and charges so that they can trace samples of medicines that their sales representatives give out when they visit doctors. The use of tablet PCs means that doctors can confirm receipt of the samples via an electronic signature. Mobile Sales also has functions for managing the samples of medication issued.

Many industries offer customers the opportunity to purchase goods directly on-site (direct store delivery). The sales employee takes goods from the warehouse in the morning, drives to various customers, and sells them these goods. The sales employee returns to the warehouse at the end of the day, delivers the returned goods (unsold products, returns, empty containers), and submits any payments made. The mobile laptop solution in mySAP CRM can be used to define related data such as driver ID, vehicle identification, or starting mileage, and to monitor goods, cash, and activities.

8.4.5 Case Study: Activity Management for Mobile Sales Employees with mySAP CRM

> The PC4YOU company has provided its sales employees with laptops so that they have access to all customer information at on-site meetings. Sales employees manage their calendar and activity lists on laptops and update their task blocks on a regular basis by synchronizing them with the CRM system.

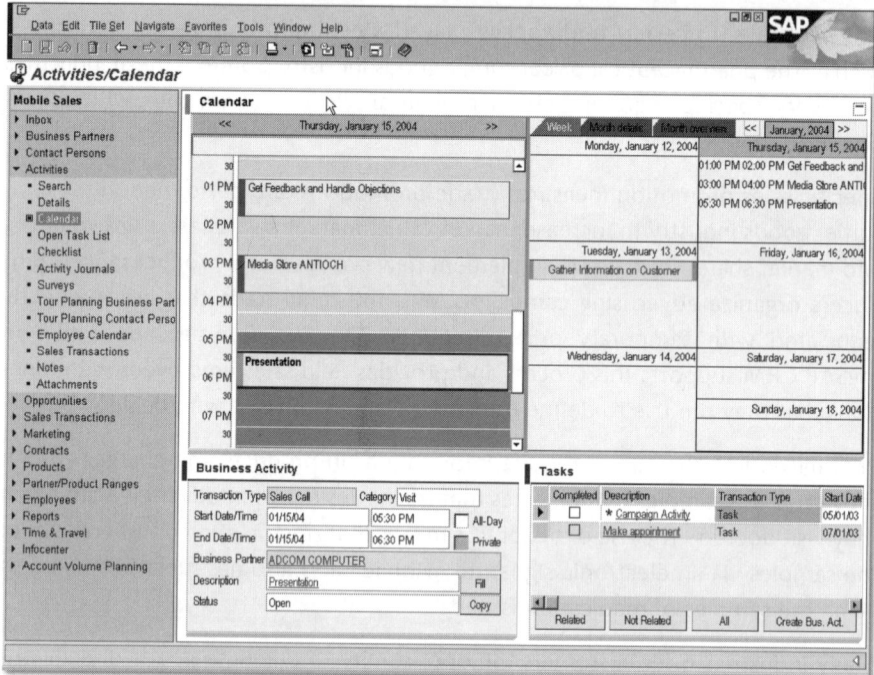

Figure 8.6 Calendar and Task Lists for Sales Employees at PC4YOU

> Once sales employee Scott Green has synchronized his laptop shortly before going home, he checks the tasks and appointments scheduled for the following day. He learns that he has to fill in for a colleague who is sick and was due to visit a customer at the Media Store the next day. Media Store is usually managed exclusively by the colleague who is sick. Scott uses this opportunity to obtain information on the Media Store by reading the business partner information recorded for this customer. He identifies his contact at the Media Store and discovers that he can contact the branch manager directly.

Once Scott has established that this sales call is scheduled to take place between 12:00 and 1:00 p.m. and is therefore during his lunch break, he checks the business hours of the Media Store and arranges to call two hours later.

Scott visits the Media Store the next day. His checklist reminds him that he must record the products he has discussed with the branch manager and any problems that occur in his sales call report. Scott checks the range of PC4YOU products at the branch, including notebooks of the Notebook Professional 15 and Notebook Professional 17 types, and Ergo Screen, and enters the results of his discussion with the branch manager directly in the sales call report. At the end of his visit, Scott informs the branch manager about the forthcoming marketing campaign to be conducted by PC4YOU. When Scott synchronizes his laptop that evening, data in the sales call report is transferred to SAP BW where it is available for reporting purposes.

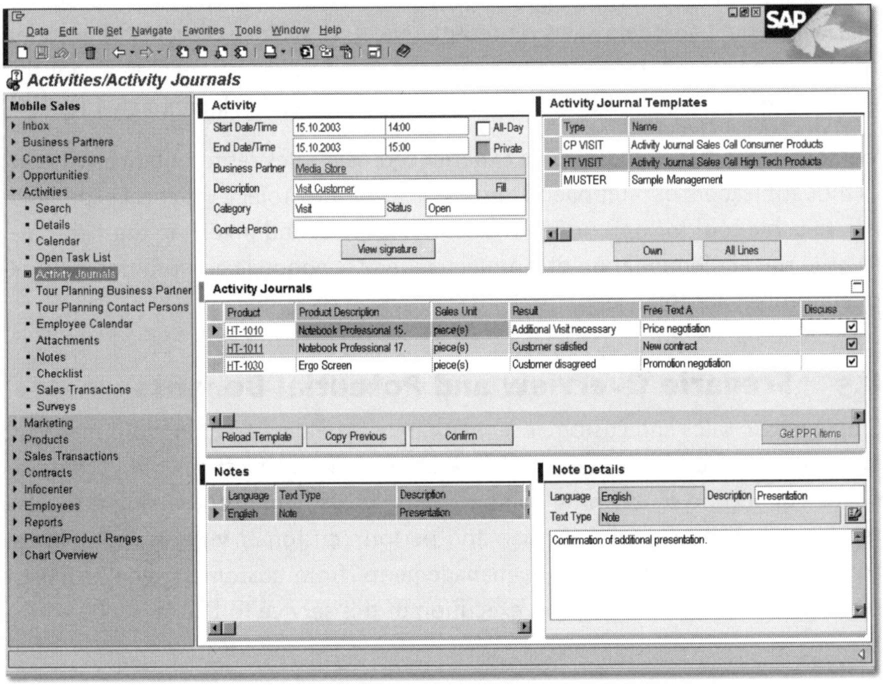

Figure 8.7 Confirmation of Products Checked and Discussed in the Sales Call Report

8.4.6 Recommendations for Successful CRM Projects in Mobile Applications

A step-by-step approach is recommended to avoid overwhelming users with new applications during the implementation of mobile CRM applications. Good places to start are the *Activity Management* and *Account Management* scenarios, which are fixed components in almost all implementation projects for mobile CRM applications. A detailed view of customer master data and efficient date management form the basis for all field sales activities. They are enhanced in additional steps by industry- and company-specific processes, such as creation of quotations, order acceptance, issuing of sample products in the pharmaceutical industry, and so on.

Mobile applications must provide field sales representatives with tangible benefits for their work, such as time savings when managing customer calls, the prospect of increased individual turnover, and faster access to current information. When selecting the mobile business processes to be implemented, we recommend that you balance management's requirement for accurate reporting with processes that will benefit the field sales representative. This avoids problems of accountability in the sales force. The CRM system should never be seen as a tool that patrols and controls the field sales force, even if it does track their activities.

We recommend that you involve experienced field sales representatives who act as thought leaders or multipliers from the start of the project. Practical experience is a valuable tool for optimizing business processes, and involving the field sales force in the implementation of a project generates goodwill and promotes subsequent project acceptance.

8.5 Scenario Overview and Potential Benefits

Employees in sales and customer service can use the data and functions in mobile business scenarios from mySAP CRM that are relevant to their role without an online connection to a central computer. The focus here is on helping field sales representatives to successfully plan and perform customer visits and simplify all activities associated with service management—from customers who request a service to resource planning and execution of this service to billing.

Cross-Industry Scenarios		Short Description	Potential Benefits		
			Revenue	Profitability	Customer Satisfaction
Mobile Sales	Opportunity Management	Accompany the sales cycle from the identification of sales opportunities to successful completion Mobile devices provide a standard view of assigned transactions, history, dates, updates, and responsible decision-makers	✓✓		
	Quotation and Sales Order Management	Support for the entire order process from the inquiry and quotation to the order, including product configuration, availability check, pricing, and integration with order processing Update the laptop dataset from the field sales force employees using customer data and product information from the central CRM system and save order data that was entered from a mobile device in a specific format for handheld devices (Mobile Sales for Handhelds)	✓✓		
	Campaign Management	Add options for campaign planning, definition, and execution by mobile users to the campaign management functions	✓✓	✓	✓
	Territory Management	Sales structuring and sales organization as a result of division into sales territories using freely selectable criteria, such as size, distance, or revenues Territory-related definition of sales targets and assignment of sales employees to territories for mobile devices		✓✓	

Cross-Industry Scenarios		Short Description	Potential Benefits		
			Revenue	Profitability	Customer Satisfaction
	Activity Management	Plan, execute, and manage sales activities and organize daily activities for the field sales force employees so they can close sales more quickly, also in a format for handhelds (*Mobile Sales for Handhelds*)		✓✓	✓
	Account and Contact Management	Provide customer, prospect, and partner data for mobile devices Perform interaction history, profile evaluation, activity tracking, and analysis of successful or critical business relationships		✓	✓✓
Mobile Service	Service Order Management	Support a range of service processes, including inquiries and quotations, order creation, spare parts planning, employee resource planning, and fulfillment, for field sales employees with laptops Option of comparison with the central CRM system with online and offline working options, also in the specific format for handheld devices for real-time access of changes of assignment (*Mobile Service for Handhelds*)		✓✓	✓

Cross-Industry Scenarios		Short Description	Potential Benefits		
			Revenue	Profitability	Customer Satisfaction
	Service Order Management (R/3 Edition)	Service order management with SAP R/3 customer service technicians can access updated laptop data, enter service requests, orders, and confirmations offline, and upload data to the SAP R/3 system		✓✓	✓
	Complaints Management for Handhelds	Management of complaints processes from the acceptance of a complaint and technical analysis to service provision, credit memo creation, and returns processing Complaint entry and qualification on-site using catalog keys and subsequent data return to the system for complaint processing		✓	✓✓

A specialist scenario is available for the consumer goods industry.

Industry-Specific Scenarios		Short Description	Potential Benefits		
			Revenue	Profitability	Customer Satisfaction
Mobile Sales	Trade Promotion Management in Consumer Goods	Plan, execute, and evaluate sales promotion measures (trade promotions) in the field	✓✓		

9 E-Commerce with mySAP CRM—The Internet as a Sales and Interaction Channel

Although the dotcom euphoria has now subsided, the Internet is still an important channel for communication between suppliers, customers, and sales partners in practically all industries—be they in the form of a pure information portal, a fully functioning Web shop or, a service portal in which customers can serve themselves, any time of day or night. E-commerce is therefore, without doubt, a central element of customer relationship management at the operative, analytical, and cross-company level.

Today, the central questions that enterprises must ask themselves—if they want to create and maintain customer relationships over the Internet—can basically be formulated as follows:

▶ How can the Internet be used as an efficient sales and interaction channel?

▶ How can a supplier make it easier for its customers to enter into long-term business relationships with it and carry out business transactions easily and effectively?

▶ How can a Web solution be provided that is fully integrated in existing business processes and systems?

▶ How can existing IT investments—such as those in the ERP area—be used for a Web solution?

▶ How can the service offering to customers be improved?

▶ How can the Internet help to reduce sales and service costs?

9.1 Electronic Commerce Beyond the Electronic Shopping Basket

If a company wants to use the Internet for strategic interaction with the customer, it must consider all customer-related processes as a whole. The Internet as a technical option can only become a strategic and profitable opportunity if the customer is offered real added value, if media discontinuity is avoided, islands of information are merged, sales and service processes are integrated and optimized from end to end, and valuable customer information is mined and used intelligently.

Projects that are only technology-driven and focus solely on the Web shop, without seeing e-commerce as a chance to tailor business processes more effectively to customer requirements run the risk of wasting the invested funds and resources, because customers expect an e-business solution to provide not only user-friendly purchasing transactions, but also efficient and reliable order fulfillment and service processes. Many e-commerce solutions have real shortcomings here, and often cause dissatisfaction among Internet customers. The reasons for this include complicated purchasing transactions, incorrect or incomplete information about prices, products and their availability, goods that are delivered too late or even not at all, invoices that don't match the delivery, and a general lack of information during pre- and post-sale service.

The problem is usually due to the low level of integration between the Web site and the existing IT landscape or the exclusion of the Web site from the company's CRM strategy. In practice, a wide gap between promise and reality in e-commerce often exists. However, the advantages of the Internet as a comprehensive "electronic customer care concept" are clear:

▶ Unlimited global market presence round-the-clock

▶ Accelerated sales processes due to automated procedures

▶ Reduction in transaction costs due to cross-enterprise sales processes

▶ Reduction in support and personnel costs due to fewer telephone orders and inquiries

▶ Targeted, direct customer communication based on extensive customer information

▶ High level of customer satisfaction and loyalty because of optimized customer service

▶ Increased sales due to targeting and attaining new customer groups and the utilization of cross-selling and up-selling potential

To be successful, e-commerce solutions must offer customers real benefit. It is not enough to simply present products on the Internet with colorful pictures and an electronic shopping basket. Rather, competitive advantage is gained beyond the shopping basket. Customer benefits, which measure the effectiveness of an e-business solution, can be determined on the basis of the requirements and the wishes the buyers have regarding the purchasing or procurement process. They include:

▶ Intuitive user interface and interaction

▶ Fast searches and user-friendly navigation

▶ Extensive product information and personalized content

▶ Appropriate, customer-specific offers that will lead to tailored products (keyword: mass customization)

- ▶ Up-to-date and accurate price information and reliable information about availability
- ▶ Straightforward, user-friendly ordering
- ▶ Fast order fulfillment and reliable, on-time delivery
- ▶ Accurate billing and simple payment process
- ▶ Clear information on order status and invoices
- ▶ Immediate support for problems, complaints, and returns
- ▶ Self-service that offers real customer benefit

Suppliers that want to use the Internet for strategic interaction with the customer can use these pointers to determine factors for success that may seem trivial but are in fact critical. In the world of e-business, those companies that can discover and act on the needs and wishes of their customers more individually, efficiently, quickly, and cost-effectively are the companies that will gain a competitive advantage on the market over the long term.

9.2 Strategic Competitive Advantage through Electronic Commerce

The starting points for achieving a strategic competitive advantage in the area of e-commerce can be divided into four areas:

- ▶ Complete integration of the sales process in a value-added process that covers both supplier and customer
- ▶ Inclusion of the Internet in the company's CRM strategy
- ▶ Personalized interaction with customers
- ▶ Acquisition of business intelligence in order to learn more about the customers' requirements and behavior and thus, ultimately better serve them

These four areas are described in detail below.

9.2.1 Integration of the Sales Process in the Value Chain

The aim of an e-commerce solution is to create benefit for both the supplier and the customer. Such mutual benefit can only be achieved if both parties are integrated in the sales or service process in such a way that added value is achieved on both sides. In the case of B2B (see Section 9.3.2), automation must be so advanced that the boundaries between the providing company and the customer are practically removed. This solution requires a total integration of the supplier's sales and logistics processes in the customer's procurement processes.

An e-commerce solution for Internet-based sales processes is therefore aimed at both the needs and wishes of customers and the sales requirements of the supplier, and can typically be divided into the following individual steps:

▶ Product search

▶ Product selection and configuration

▶ Order

▶ Order fulfillment/delivery

▶ Payment

▶ After-sales services

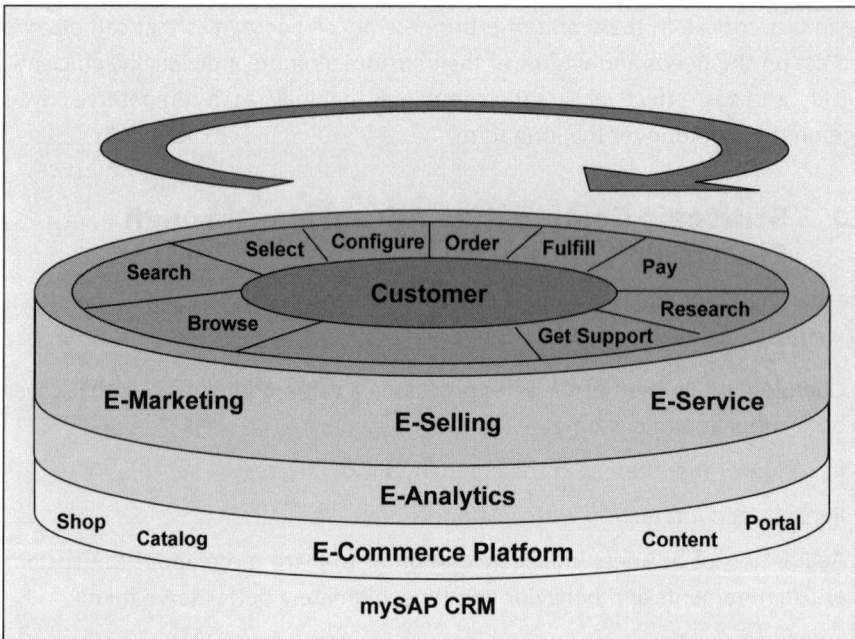

Figure 9.1 Integrated Processes of the mySAP CRM E-Commerce Platform

Product Search

From the customer's perspective, easy navigation through the product range (product catalog), user-friendly search functions to find a specific product, and customer-specific offers are the most important factors in the search transaction. On the part of the supplier, this requires flexible catalog management, powerful search engines, and effective one-to-one marketing functionalities (see Section 9.4.1).

Product Selection and Configuration

In order to provide the customer with the best possible support in searching for individual products, a company should provide options tailored to the specific customer. In addition to selecting products from the catalog, possibilities could include the selection of products from customer-specific product offers, from order templates created by the customer, and from quotations received and previous orders. In addition, the customer may want to configure the product to meet his or her particular requirements. Reliable price information is important in all cases. Here, price determination and configuration should be based on the conditions and rules that are used in the system. This is the only way to ensure that the variant configured by the customer can in fact be produced in that way, and that the prices displayed on the Internet correlate with the subsequent invoice amount.

Order

If a customer wants to order a particular product over the Internet, the transaction is usually handled with a shopping basket function (virtual shopping basket). The product the customer wants to buy is placed in the basket, and can then be ordered. The use of order templates or the direct entry of order numbers simplify the ordering process. Before sending the order, customers often ask to be informed of a reliable delivery date. An availability check in the vendor's system can provide this information in real time. The customer expects an order confirmation directly after the order has been placed.

Order Fulfillment/Delivery

A key factor in ensuring customer satisfaction is the smooth processing of the order placed over the Internet, right up to the delivery of the ordered goods to the customer. For this to be possible, seamless process integration between the Web shop and the executing back-end applications is required. In business practice, many e-commerce solutions certainly lack this end-to-end automation. This results in media fragmentation, unnecessary delays, incorrect deliveries, and high processing costs. A valuable customer service that promotes customer satisfaction on the one hand and increases potential savings on the other is the online display of the order status, which enables customers to find out where their order is in the fulfillment or delivery process at any time. This service cannot be provided without back-end integration.

Payment

In the ordering phase, the customer can choose between various payment methods offered by the retailer, for example, credit card or cash on delivery (COD).

When the payment transaction is processed, integration with the back-end system is imperative once more to ensure that any discounts are considered, invoice amounts are calculated correctly, payment receipts are posted correctly, and reminders are sent out on time, where necessary. *Electronic bill presentment & payment* systems go one step further by fully digitalizing the billing and payment process. These systems permit customers to display their invoices and invoice status over the Internet at any time, and directly trigger payment.

After-Sales Services

In the area of after-sales service, there are many different ways of providing the customer with useful self-services once the purchase has been made. These after-sales services could include returns processing for goods that are damaged or were delivered incorrectly, or products that a customer decides that he or she doesn't want after all. After-sales services is also a venue where customers can submit maintenance and repair orders to, over the Internet, and direct FAQ (frequently asked questions) sections or knowledge databases with information on setting up and using the products, and so on.

9.2.2 Inclusion of the Internet in the Company's CRM Strategy

The Internet is an important channel for interaction that allows a high degree of personalized interaction with customers, despite automation. A good e-commerce strategy does not focus solely on the Internet as a sales channel alone; it also incorporates further channels for interacting with the customer (for example, field sales, retail outlets) and takes a holistic approach to the systematic pre-sales, sales, and after-sales cycles. In many cases, e-commerce is also a multi-channel strategy and comprises the areas of *marketing, sales,* and *service*. Here, it is necessary to ensure that the various channels of contact are synchronized, therefore, regardless of which medium the customer uses to contact the company, the information that he or she receives does not contradict information provided by other means of contact with the supplier.

9.2.3 Personalization of Interaction with Customers

One important way of gaining a competitive edge is to use the Internet as a tool for customer relationship management by personalizing the content of product offers. The direct interaction with the customer corresponds to the fundamental idea of individualized, dialogue-oriented marketing, and enables customers to be personally addressed in ways that go far beyond conventional marketing and classical advertising through mass media. Addressing customers in a personalized way enables companies to tackle the market more effectively. Personalization can take a number of different forms:

- Customer-specific catalogs
- Customer-specific prices and conditions
- Customer requirements fulfilling product configuration (*mass customization*)
- Personal product recommendations
- Personalized user interfaces

Many innovative companies are already using systems that enable them to link up different types of information in order to create personalized offers. For example, data from clickstream analyses and data from investigations exploring the effect of marketing activities are included in the analyses. In addition, variables on demographics, previous buying behavior, and customer preferences are factored into the analyses.

The creation of informative customer profiles—which contain characteristics about the customers' buying behavior (for example, gender, age, income, hobbies, product preferences, usage habits, and previous purchases)—is a basic prerequisite for successful, personalized customer relationship management. Target groups (for example, "men between 30 and 40 with net earnings over $5000 per month, who play sports in their spare time") are defined based on the customer profiles. Specific marketing measures, such as the recommendation of certain products, can now be targeted at individual users, based on their individual requirements and needs.

9.2.4 Gaining Business Intelligence

Customer relationship management is planned less on the basis of general market research information, and more on the basis of individual customer data. A supplier can only provide better customer services if it analyzes the wishes and requirements of its customers in detail. This plays a particularly important role in e-commerce, because on the Internet, the competition is often just a mouse click away.

For this reason, a supplier must monitor its Web site systematically to examine both technical and business aspects. In particular, this monitoring includes capturing information on buying behavior and interaction behavior during a business relationship, in order to compare this behavior with the customer's other characteristics that are relevant to buying behavior, for example, in other sales channels, and therefore obtain a complete picture of the particular customer.

Besides simple clickstream analyses (*hits and visits*) and classical sales statistics (including a comparison of channels), gaining business intelligence requires that complex issues be evaluated with the help of a data warehouse, for example, the attractiveness of product range and online catalog, customer loyalty or retention, and the determination of conversion rates, which describe the ratio of visitors to users for a Web site (for example, look-and-buy ratio).

9.3 Selected E-Commerce Scenarios

The e-commerce solution offered by mySAP CRM supports different scenarios for mapping cross-company business processes. Both single-step and multi-step business processes can be executed over the Internet. The following sections describe the basic characteristics of various business scenarios.

9.3.1 Business-to-Consumer (B2C)

In the business-to-consumer (B2C) area, the focus is on sales to the end user or consumer. Here, the supplier's ordering and sales processes, and a large, and sometimes changing number of potential customers, are important factors. The Internet supplements the existing, traditional sales channels, or in some cases is the only sales channel. In B2C, transactions are characterized by spontaneity, a low to medium transaction volume, and a relatively low level of loyalty between the transaction partners.

One factor that is instrumental in determining the business success of the individual companies is knowledge of the user or customer structure. Only those suppliers that present their products and services on the Internet in an appropriate way for the target group can provide convincing offers. For example, in conventional sales channels, the business atmosphere (type and equipment of the shop) and customer orientation have a considerable effect on the customers' willingness to buy and their subjective assessment of quality. Because the online sales channel cannot create a physical store atmosphere that stimulates buying behavior, it is necessary to offer the customer a similarly satisfying purchase in other ways.

A few structural features are particularly important in creating a stimulating buying atmosphere; they also help to foster a long-term relationship between supplier and customer in B2C. These features include multimedia product catalog, the layout and branding of the Web site, one-to-one marketing (that is, personalized product recommendations, see Section 9.4.1), cross-selling and up-selling offers, order lists, special offers, and support for various, secure payment methods (invoice, COD, credit card, and so on). However, in order to consolidate customer relations in the B2C area, it is also very important to ensure that order fulfillment and distribution logistics are reliable. From a strategic point of view, it may be necessary to consider how the online services can be integrated with conventional sales channels (store network, retail, and field sales).

9.3.2 Business-to-Business (B2B)

Business-to-business (B2B) has to do with the electronic business transactions between companies (suppliers, manufacturers, and retailers). In contrast to B2C, the transaction partners in B2B usually have long-standing business relationships, and consequently, there are close ties between supplier and buyer. The transactions are usually medium to high volume. Therefore, in B2B, negotiating conditions and contracts is more important than it is in B2C. While customer behavior in B2C is usually characterized by product catalog searches, commercial customers often have a clear idea of the products they want to buy. The type and method of navigation therefore differs from transaction partner to transaction partner.

In order to consider the specific requirements in relationships between business partners, the following structural parameters are at the forefront in B2B:

▶ Possibility of customer-specific range and price structure

▶ Order templates and quick-entry screens

▶ Connections to the customer's purchasing systems

In B2B, the integration, completeness, and transparency of the business processes is particularly important—from product selection, the availability check and price calculation, order fulfillment, and production and delivery to different addresses to billing.

If the B2B scenario involves the connection of dealers over the Internet, a few additional factors must be noted. These factors are due on the one hand to the role of the dealer as "go-between," and on the other, to the often close relationships between manufacturers and dealers. Dealers sometimes have extremely high demands regarding the catalog contents and status information about open order and invoice items. It should be possible to change or even cancel orders that have been placed over the Internet. It is also advisable to have a Web-based method of handling returns. In addition, framework contracts, annual agreements, and price protection clauses, which are often referred to in orders, play an important role.

The option of one-stop business (see Section 4.2) is particularly attractive if the business processes are supported by systems on the supplier and customer side. In this case, the opportunities offered by connecting a shop solution to the e-procurement software can be fully exploited.

9.3.3 Business-to-Business Mall (B2B mall)

The Business-to-Business mall (B2B mall) area is a further development of the classic B2B scenario, in which several suppliers offer their products over a shared storefront (a *Virtual Showroom* that is a display of goods on the Web). This can include different areas of a diversified company or, different companies offering customers user-friendly *one-step buying,* following the principle of *one face to the customer.*

The participating suppliers display their products to their customers over the Internet via a product catalog, the attractiveness of which can be further enhanced by the inclusion of multimedia elements (pictures, sound, video). This enables companies to present their offers within a company-specific product catalog (*corporate branding*) or, a shared product catalog (*multi-supplier catalog*).

The special features of a B2B mall include:

▶ User-friendly, cross-catalog search functions
▶ Central availability check and status determination
  (order and invoice status)
▶ Customer-specific pricing and product layout across all suppliers
▶ Central shopping basket that holds the selected products from all catalogs, and calculates and displays the total price

However, the items in the shopping basket must be filtered for the individual suppliers within the mall. It is therefore necessary to split the overall order into several, supplier-specific suborders (*order split*). The suborders are posted to the back-end systems of the relevant companies, where they are available for further logistics processing. As a result, integration options for the back-end infrastructures are absolutely essential to ensure seamless integration of the existing IT landscape in the sales processes. Connections to the customer procurement systems round off the purchasing process and enable *one-step business* to be achieved.

9.3.4 Distributor & Reseller Network (Channel Commerce)

While the scenarios described above are one-step sales processes, the *distributor & reseller network* relates to multi-step, that is, indirect, sales processes. Here, the supplier adopts the role of a *channel master;* controlling both the direct and indirect sales channel over the Internet. In connection with collaborative business processes such as these, in which manufacturers and sellers or distributors jointly sell products over the Internet, we speak of channel commerce and channel management (see Chapter 11).

An example of a "collaborative selling" scenario (online sales through partners) is a computer manufacturer that sells its products to its customers directly and indirectly through a dealer in its Internet sales channel. The manufacturer—as channel master or brand owner—can take over the central management of the multime-dia product catalog in a distributor & reseller network. The individual dealers can then offer further, supplementary services and possibly also additional products that are exclusive to the dealer. Therefore, the manufacturer and its dealers present a shared *storefront* and uniform branding to the end user or customer (consumer or business customer).

In this network, synergies result in considerable cost savings. Products, their descriptions, and multimedia files only have to be maintained once. In addition, the customer is always provided with a uniform, up-to-date product range in the product catalog. The customer is also able to carry out product configuration and the availability check directly at the manufacturer or for various dealers. Problems with outdated product lists, configuration options, and the availability of conventional, multi-step sales processes are therefore a thing of the past.

9.4   E-Commerce with mySAP CRM

mySAP CRM contains a comprehensive e-commerce solution that covers the whole range from pre-sales to sales to after-sales processes, and extends across the areas of marketing, sales, and service:

▶ E-marketing
  ▶ One-to-one marketing
  ▶ Catalog and content management
▶ E-selling
  ▶ Purchase order and order processing
  ▶ Internet auctions
▶ E-service
  ▶ Web self-services
  ▶ Interactive customer support
▶ E-analytics
▶ Web design

Figure 9.2 shows the individual modules of the mySAP CRM e-commerce solution.

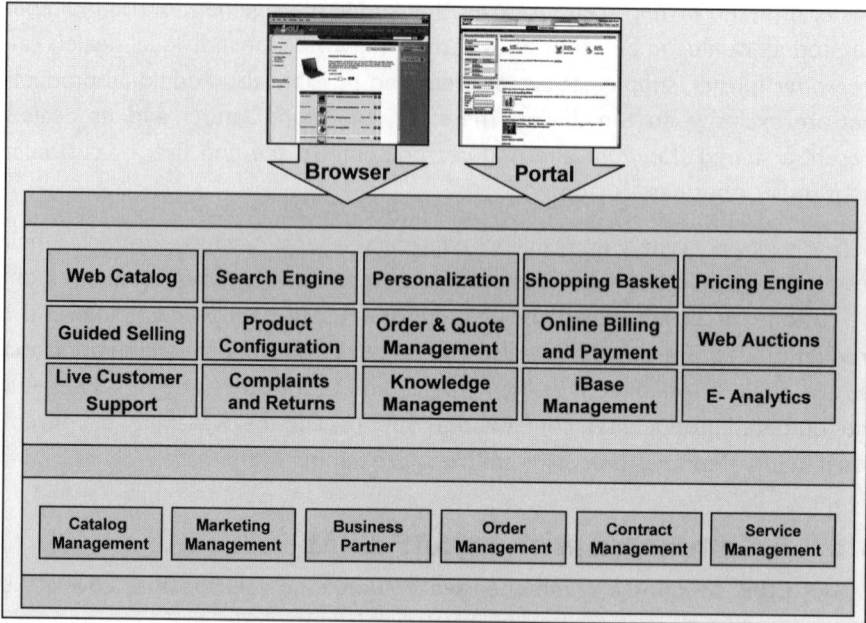

Figure 9.2 Modules of the mySAP CRM E-Commerce Solution

9.4.1 One-to-One Marketing

The e-commerce solution of mySAP CRM has numerous marketing functionalities that enable the Internet to be used as a powerful one-to-one marketing tool. According to Peppers und Rogers [Peppers 1993], one-to-one marketing is based on four principles:

▶ **Identify**
Identify customers

▶ **Differentiate**
Differentiate customers on the basis of their values and needs

▶ **Interact**
Conduct dialogue with the customer

▶ **Customize**
Tailor the content of interaction to the customer

These principles and the resulting mySAP CRM offerings are outlined briefly below.

Identify and Differentiate: Defining Customer Profiles and Target Groups

Meaningful customer profiles, which can be created and maintained in mySAP CRM, form the basis for successful one-to-one marketing. They consist of buying-relevant customer characteristics and key figures (for example, interests, age, income, product preferences, behavior pattern on the Internet); for example, individual preferences and additional customer data can be entered in online questionnaires. Customer profiles are the basis for defining target groups for marketing and sales measures.

Interact: Dialogue with the Customer

mySAP CRM offers a wide range of possibilities for interaction and dialogue on the Internet. For example, the existing customer profiles and mySAP CRM *Campaign Management* enable target group-specific or personalized email campaigns to be carried out. Personalized emails can be adapted to specific customers or target groups within the subject line, form of address, and actual text right through to possible attachments. It is also possible to integrate personalized links to the Web shop. If a customer clicks on one of these links, he or she is greeted by name and the product proposals stored for the customer or target group are displayed.

With the help of the *Personalization Engine*, rules can also be defined that determine the conditions under which a customer is shown specific information or product offers during the Web site interaction. This enables a dynamic personalization of the Web pages, and therefore, a high degree of personal interaction with the customer.

In addition, the customer also has opportunities to initiate a dialogue. In the Web shop, chat functionalities can be offered, which the customer can use to communicate with a service center employee using the keyboard after a telephone callback. Lastly, SAP's e-commerce solution enables customers to configure products interactively according to their own individual requirements.

Customize: Personalized Product Recommendations and Target Group-Specific Best Seller Lists

The most important task of one-to-one marketing is undoubtedly to proactively recommend certain products or services to the customer. In this way, mySAP CRM supports both personalized product recommendations and best seller lists, and cross-selling and up-selling suggestions:

▶ **Personalized product recommendations**

Personalized product recommendations are product lists that were compiled for particular customer profiles. They contain, for example, new products that could be of particular interest to customers with a certain profile, based on considerations or analyses (for example, cross-selling analyses).

▶ **Target group-specific best seller lists**

Target group-specific best seller lists are an important special case. They are based on evaluations of the products sold within a target group. The idea behind this is that a product that is often bought by customers with a certain profile could be of particular interest to customers with the same profile who have perhaps not bought the product yet. The best seller lists can also be used to offer business customers the service of displaying the products they buy most often in a separate list in the Web shop.

▶ **Personalized cross-selling suggestions**

Personalized cross-selling suggestions make it possible for a company to recommend products that are a complement to the products already selected, for example, imaging software in combination with a scanner. In contrast, personalized up-selling suggestions recommend products that have advantages over the selected products for the customer in question, for example, a scanner with a higher resolution. The goal of both strategies is to generate higher sales for the supplier.

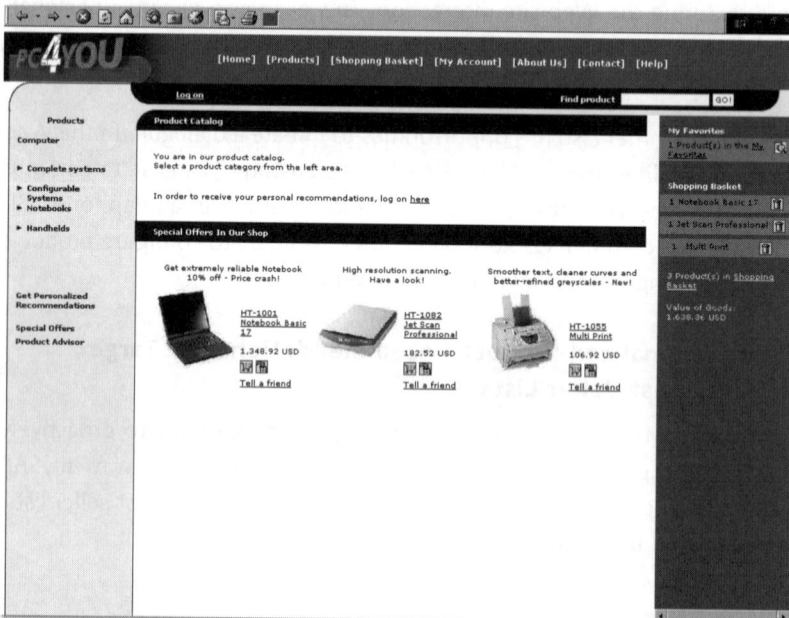

Figure 9.3 Personalized Product Recommendations in the B2C Scenario

9.4.2 Catalog Management and Product Selection

On the Internet, products are usually found and selected using a product catalog. The way in which the product catalog is structured and adapted to fit the buyers' needs plays an important role in the success of a Web shop. In mySAP CRM, products can also be selected from personalized product recommendations, best seller lists, order templates, previous orders or quotations and also—in the B2B scenario—directly by entering an article number in the shopping basket. Here, it doesn't matter how a product is selected—the product information always comes from the same product catalog.

Tasks of the Product Catalog

The Web shop solution from mySAP CRM offers an electronic product catalog and provides customers and prospects with all the necessary information about products, prices, and availability. The advantages of the Web product catalog over conventional printed catalogs are lower production costs; easier, more cost-effective distribution; a more attractive, multimedia product presentation; powerful search features; and more up-to-date product information.

The B2B scenario also supports the interface with *SAP Enterprise Buyer Professional (SAP EBP)*, an electronic procurement application, so that the Web catalog can be directly accessed. You can also send the contents of the catalog to the customer or make them available to other applications using XML export. During export, complete catalogs or specific catalog views tailored to individual customers can be exported in a number of different formats.

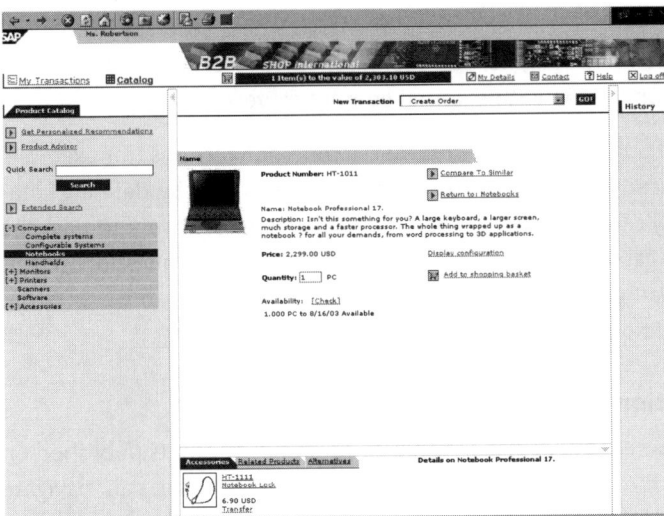

Figure 9.4 Product Details in the B2B Scenario

Catalog and Content Management

The layout of the product catalog and the definition of the content are determined in the Catalog Management module of mySAP CRM. Depending on the application scenario or target group, you can structure the catalog on the basis of either functional or marketing-oriented factors.

The catalog layout is based on freely-definable catalog areas, which can be arranged in any hierarchical structure, according to the specific company requirements. Products or catalog sub-areas can be assigned to each catalog area. The products are selected from the product master in the CRM system, which automatically receives the data from the material master of the SAP R/3 system or another back-end system. Product master records can also be created and changed directly in mySAP CRM. Changes to the material master in the SAP R/3 system are immediately synchronized with the data in the CRM system. In addition, any number of attributes can be defined for each product, which make it easier for the customer to find the required products, and provide additional product information.

The product catalog displays list, scale, and customer-specific prices. The latter are determined by *SAP Internet Pricing and Configurator (SAP IPC)* (see Section 9.4.3).

In addition to displaying the master data, the product catalog can display other areas and products in the form of texts, pictures, documents, and multimedia files (audio and video sequences, and so on), a feature that is essential from the marketing perspective. Consequently, the product catalog contains all the information and data that a company wants to provide to its customers. To manage the additional information and documents, Catalog Management accesses the *Knowledge Provider* of the SAP Web Application Server (SAP Web AS), which can also be used to establish a connection with external content servers.

Web catalogs can be published on the Internet in different versions (for example, different languages, currencies, sales organizations, and so on). By defining catalog views, a company can display customer-specific catalogs that only contain the areas of the product catalog that are relevant to the customer in question. In this way, the company can present customer-specific product offers on the Internet without needing additional maintenance effort.

Catalog Presentation on the Internet

Customers use a browser to access the Web catalog and its contents published on the Internet. With the help of the catalog structure, the user can navigate throughout the Web catalog very easily to the desired product. The visual layout of the Web catalog and the entire Web shop is freely definable. The Web design is not subject to any particular restrictions. The HTML templates delivered in mySAP CRM can be easily adapted to company-specific design requirements and preferred Web page sequences.

Search Functions in the Web Catalog

Besides browsing in the catalog and searching for products through the hierarchy, a customer can use a powerful search engine to call up the required product directly. Here, a number of different search criteria can be combined, and price limits can be defined. As a result, the search for products is very fast, and contributes to customer satisfaction.

One particularly user-friendly feature is the specification of product characteristics in selection boxes that contain attributes that are freely selected by the supplier. From the list of product features, a customer selects the characteristic values that correspond to his or her requirements, and the system then displays all products that match this selection.

In addition, third-party solutions such as intelligent product consultants (for example, eConsultant), Avatare (virtual, personal representatives), and so on, can be integrated in the Web catalog to simplify the customer's search for particular products or to identify customer preferences and thus provide support for product selection.

In the B2B scenario, companies can use contracts to display contract-specific data and prices for the products in the Web catalog. When the customer logs on to the Web shop, the system determines the relevant contracts. However, the customer can also access his or her contracts directly in the Web shop, and use these contracts to select and order products. In this case, the system automatically generates a contract release order.

Guided Selling

The guided selling function in mySAP CRM makes it easier for customers to find the products and services that best suit their individual requirements. Through an interactive set of questions and answers, the product selection is restricted (or in some cases extended) step by step, so that at the end of the process, the customer can be provided with realistic suggestions for products that match the answers given. In this way, the customer can quickly and intuitively receive a suitable offer without complex search algorithms. This offer could be made in the form of an actual product proposal, a selection of product alternatives (several different PCs), or a complete product package (PC with periphery, accessories, and service package), for example.

9.4.3 Purchase Order and Order Processing

Products are purchased with the mySAP CRM e-commerce solution using a virtual shopping basket. The shopping basket is the central administration tool for the ordering process, and fulfills a number of important functions.

The customer selects the required products with a simple mouse click, which automatically transfers them to the shopping basket. This is possible not just in the product catalog, but also on all other Web shop pages that display the product (detailed product view, product configuration window, best seller list, product recommendations, order templates, offers, orders). In the shopping basket, prices and price elements (such as shipping costs or tax) are displayed, along with accessories, cross-selling and up-selling articles and delivery dates. In the shopping basket, customers can also enter order quantities, configure products, enter a requested delivery date, add comments to the order, and change the delivery address, if required. It is also possible to enter the article numbers directly in the shopping basket—even in the article numbering format used by the customer. The system assigns the number correctly in the background.

Once in the shopping basket, the items can be ordered directly. In addition, the shopping basket can be fully or partially cleared, and changed or deleted.

Customers also can save the contents of the shopping basket temporarily if they so choose. Therefore, the purchase transaction can be interrupted at any time: the shopping basket can be stored under any name, and then called up again at a later point in time so that the order transaction can be continued.

The most important order functions of the e-commerce solution are described in more detail below.

Ordering with Order Template

With the e-commerce solution of mySAP CRM, customers can create their own order templates. Consequently, products that are ordered regularly can be put on a fixed order list, for which only the required quantity must be entered. The order templates are available in a template list. Alternatively, existing quotations and orders can also be used as order templates.

Efficient Fast Order Entry

In addition to catalog selection, business customers can be offered fast order entry. Here, the product number and required quantity are all that need to be entered in the shopping basket in order to fill it and create an order. Customer-specific article numbers and manufacturer product numbers can be used in fast order entry. The CRM system ensures the correct assignment between manufacturer and customer product numbers. Therefore, professional buyers who remember article numbers that are frequently ordered can process purchase orders efficiently.

Ordering with Reference to Contracts

In trading between business partners, it is common practice to finalize agreements in the form of contracts (see Section 7.3.10). These contracts contain the quantity and/or price at which a product is sold to a contract party within a specified period. Products with contracts that both parties have agreed to are specially flagged by mySAP CRM in the catalog. Customers can select these products and create an order with reference to the contract, that is, they trigger a contract release order at the agreed upon conditions. The information on the remaining quantity is updated and made available in the Web shop.

Achieving Higher Turnover with Cross-Selling and Up-Selling

One particularly interesting function of the mySAP CRM e-commerce solution from a marketing and sales point of view is the automatic product proposal (see Section 7.2.8). As soon as a customer has selected a product, alternative, higher-value products (up-selling) and/or additional products, such as accessories or supplementary services (cross-selling), are displayed. These links between the products must be maintained in the product master. If the user clicks on a product proposal, it is transferred to the shopping basket, and in the case of up-selling, replaces the product that was already selected. The goal of these measures is to encourage the customer to choose the higher-value product or additional products in order to generate higher sales (see Section 7.2.8).

Correct and Consistent Pricing

On the Internet, the choosing and displaying of the correct prices is frequently a serious problem. Often, the price on the invoice does not agree with the price offered in the Web shop.

For pricing, mySAP CRM utilizes the *SAP Internet Pricing and Configurator (SAP IPC)*. The SAP IPC uses the same conditions and pricing rules as does the SAP R/3 back-end system, which ensures that the prices in the front end and the back end are always consistent. As the price and condition models are always maintained centrally in either the SAP R/3 or CRM system, duplicate work is not required.

The standard condition types from SAP R/3, such as individual prices, discounts, or scale conditions, are automatically considered during the time the online sales price is determined for the shopping basket. The B2B scenario displays the customer-specific product prices with the support of SAP IPC. Net price, gross price, shipping costs, and taxes are displayed separately. This applies to both the individual order items and the total price of the order. SAP IPC supports several currencies and units of measure.

Configuration of Tailored Products (Configure-to-Order)

The Internet poses a particular challenge for companies that make configurable products. In particular, it is necessary to identify the different product variants, dependencies, and restrictions in a customer inquiry, and to determine the correct offer price, which is dependent on the components and options selected by the customer.

In addition to pricing, SAP IPC supports the interactive configuration of products (see Section 7.3.9). If the customer selects a configurable product, SAP IPC guides him or her through the configuration process. The permitted options are displayed—where necessary, with a detailed description, images, and any extra costs or deductions—and can simply be selected by the customer. SAP IPC constantly checks that the configuration is consistent, and updates the price online.

SAP IPC utilizes the configuration models of SAP R/3. Consequently, the powerful SAP R/3 variant configurator is also available on the Internet. Separate product modeling is not required. If customers order products configured to their requirements, the confirmation data is transferred to the order for further processing.

Availability Check and Binding Delivery Dates

The e-commerce solution of mySAP CRM provides customers with reliable information on product availability and delivery dates in real time. For each order item in the shopping basket—including configured products—an availability check, known as an *"ATP" (available-to-promise) check*, is carried out in SAP R/3 or *SAP Advanced Planner and Optimizer (SAP APO)*. Determination of the delivery date is not just based on average delivery times; it is also calculated on the basis of the current warehouse stocks and production capacities in all plants and factors the lead times for picking and shipping. In addition, customers can specify requested delivery dates; in the B2B scenario, they can even specify separate dates for the individual items. This information is considered during the availability check and delivery scheduling.

In addition, integration with SAP APO enables a rule-based ATP check to be activated that makes it possible to ascertain the availability of products in several locations and to suggest alternative products if the selected product is not available.

The importance of an accurate availability check and reliable delivery dates should not be underestimated. The information plays a decisive role in improving customer satisfaction. This is particularly important for the business-to-business area, in which orders are often only placed on the condition that a particular delivery date is met.

Flexible and Secure Payment Methods

With mySAP CRM, companies can also benefit from automatic handling of payments over the Internet. Customers can use different methods of payment, for example, by credit card, in which case the transaction is authorized immediately online. It is also possible to pay by COD or by invoice, whereby billing can take place automatically in the SAP R/3 back-end system (if this exists). Connection to the back-end system also ensures that discounts are taken into consideration, invoice amounts are calculated correctly, and reminders are sent on time. If a company does not use an SAP R/3 back-end system, or uses several SAP R/3 systems, billing can also be carried out centrally by mySAP CRM (see also Section 7.4.6). The latest protection mechanisms ensure the highest degree of security for the transfer of sensitive data.

Ordering at the Click of a Mouse

As soon as the products have been selected, the required quantities and payment method entered, and the prices and delivery dates determined by the system, the contents of the shopping basket can be ordered at the click of a mouse. If necessary, the customer can enter a special delivery address for each individual item in the B2B scenario and select the delivery type. In addition, the customer can add written comments or notes to the order. In the B2B scenario, a customer can enter a separate order text for each item. In this way, nonstandard orders can also be processed.

With mySAP CRM, customers can receive a quotation before they place the order. Then, they can create an order at a later date with reference to the quotation, or copy individual items to an order.

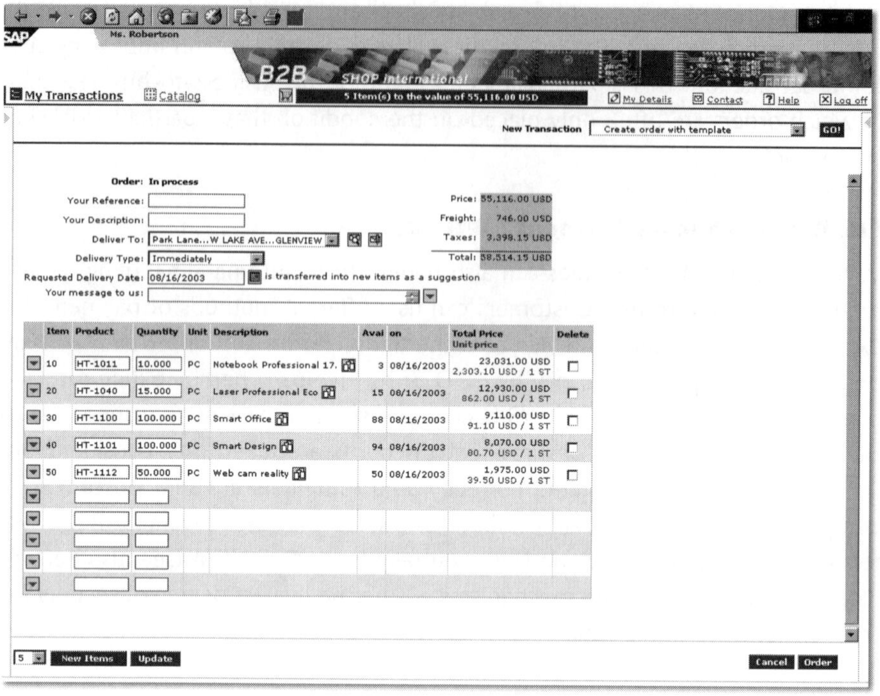

Figure 9.5 Ordering in the B2B Scenario

Automatic Order Confirmation

As soon as an order has been placed, the customer sees the generated order number on the Internet, and receives an order confirmation by email. This automatic order confirmation also applies to quotations that customers have created over the Internet.

Order Fulfillment

Thanks to the integration of e-commerce with the other mySAP CRM applications and the back-end system, automatic processing of the incoming Internet orders is ensured right through to delivery and billing. This guarantees the reliable fulfillment of all orders and increases customer satisfaction and loyalty. The integrated automation from order acquisition on the Internet front end to order fulfillment accelerates the overall sales process and reduces transaction costs.

9.4.4 Additional Sales with Internet Auctions

A Web Auction solution for Internet auctions can be added to mySAP CRM. This solution manages all processes for auctioning goods and services. This is of particular interest for companies that want to achieve the best possible price for surplus goods, discontinued items, or goods with a short shelf life, or test the market for new products.

All phases of an auction are covered by the rule-based Web Auction solution — from the creation and publication of an auction item to the processing of incoming offers, to the comparison of offers and determination of the winner, to order fulfillment. Products that are to be auctioned can be displayed in a separate area of the Web product catalog, for example, in an *auction catalog*; you can also flag the auction objects as such in the regular catalog.

The customer functions include the monitoring of auctions that the customer is participating in or has participated in. The customer can also display the current auction status and all won auctions.

The functions for the company or seller include initiating sales auctions, displaying and changing the current auction status and auction progress, and one-to-one marketing functionalities with the selection of particular target groups for the auctions. Recently, SAP also introduced the option of listing the products on the eBay platform and auctioning them there. With the help of special connectors, the eBay marketplace can be directly connected to mySAP CRM or SAP R/3.

9.4.5 Self-Service for Customers

Transparency Through Online Status Display

The e-commerce solution from mySAP CRM enables customers to display saved order templates, quotations, and orders at any time, independently on the Internet, and to access detailed information on the status of a quotation or order processing for the individual items. Customers obtain a rapid overview of all completed and open quotations and orders, and, if required, can track the progress of the goods via hyperlinks to the transportation and logistics service agents' tracking systems. Depending on the stage the order has reached in the fulfillment process, the customer may be able to cancel or change the order completely or partially (individual items). This self-service option reduces the number of telephone inquiries considerably, which, in turn, reduces the internal sales staff's workload and helps to reduce costs.

Electronic Invoicing

The integration of a comprehensive *electronic bill presentment and payment* functionality (*SAP Biller Direct* from mySAP Financials) enables the electronic transfer, display, and payment of invoices over the Internet. The supplier can avoid the time-consuming and costly printing and sending of invoices, payment reminders, and dunning notices, and at the same time maintains its customer relationships over the electronic invoicing channel. The advantage for the customers is that they can access information not just on the invoice, but also on their overall account situation, including credit memos. To make a payment, a customer selects the invoice, any applicable credit memos, and the desired payment method. Once the payment has been authorized, a payment run is triggered in the back-end system.

Complaints and Returns Processing over the Internet

This self-service function enables customer to trigger and process complaints and returns over the Internet and track their status. Within online complaints and returns management, customers can specify, among other things, whether they prefer a credit memo or a product replacement. All relevant information is displayed, which ensures smooth handling (see also Section 7.5.2).

Solving Customer Problems with FAQs and Solution Databases

mySAP CRM supports customers in independently solving technical problems and other issues related to product use, without the involvement of a service technician. In the Frequently Asked Questions (FAQs) area, customers can find answers to the questions that arise most often. A solution database is available for more specific problems, for which questions can be entered in non-technical language. Customers are therefore in a position to diagnose errors and problems themselves, and in some cases, to solve them as well. Customers can also put together their own personal solution library (mySolutions) (see also Section 7.5.2). Security mechanisms ensure that answers are only available to user groups with the appropriate authorization.

Triggering Service Orders over the Internet

After a purchase has been made, mySAP CRM enables customers to trigger and update service orders themselves, and monitor their current status at any point in time. Additional functions include the automatic check on service entitlement, and, if necessary, the specification of a time period for a service technician visit. Here, parameters such as the service level agreement (SLA), warranty, and product data are taken into account (see also Section 7.5.3).

Online Product Registration and Installed Base Management

With the help of mySAP CRM, customers can register their new products online or enter complex, technical installations and all their relevant data. On the Web site, they can then display an overview of the related SLAs, warranty periods, and conditions at any time. From here, service orders, problem messages, or complaints can also be easily triggered directly over the Internet (see also Section 7.5.5).

9.4.6 Interactive Customer Support (Live Web Collaboration)

Companies install Web shops, at the very least, to reduce sales costs. Nevertheless, there is a lot to be said for maintaining a certain degree of personal contact between customer and supplier. For example, customers may have questions that aren't answered in the Web shop, cannot find their way around the Web shop, or want to use the same sales channel, namely, the *Internet,* to request after-sales services for a product. It therefore makes sense to open up interaction channels for communication between the Internet customers and service staff. For example, contact between the customer and a service employee can be established through the Web shop. If customers have questions while in the Web shop, it is not only advisable but essential to provide them with answers; otherwise, they might turn to the competition.

mySAP CRM offers Internet customers three ways of obtaining direct help on the Web site:

▶ **Email**
The customer can contact the company by classic email. An email form is offered as an option here, so customers don't have to install their own email program.

▶ **Callback**
If the customer has questions or problems that must be dealt with immediately—for example, a problem navigating through the product catalog, a question about prices or order fulfillment—interaction by email is not an appropriate method. In order to establish immediate communication with the supplier, the customer can request a *callback* by pressing a button on the Web site. This request is immediately routed to a service employee in the call center, who calls the customer back. Exact rules, for example, based on the customer status or the service employee's experience, can be stored in the Web shop to establish contact between the Internet customer and service staff. In the callback request, customers can also specify whether they would prefer to be contacted by phone or the *voice-over IP method* (Internet telephony). As the customer is currently in the Web shop, the questions can be answered immediately via the voice-over IP method.

▶ **Chat**
Alternatively, the customer can request the chat option. This is particularly useful if the customer doesn't have the hardware required for voice-over IP or a second telephone line. The chat option also allows you to send the customer URLs or files.

9.4.7 Business Intelligence through Powerful Web Analyses

There is more to e-commerce than simply setting up a Web site and hoping that as many people as possible visit it every day. The personalization and optimization of the Web site are also extremely important factors when it comes to helping visitors find their way and reacting effectively to customer requests.

How can the success of these measures be determined? Direct customer contact over the Internet is difficult, and customers rarely respond to inquiries. However, by recording customer activities in the Web shop and subsequently analyzing this data, you can learn how visitors behave in the Web shop. You can then use this information to improve the site and enhance the shopping experience for each individual visitor.

Standard tools can be used to analyze the Web server log files. These tools contain technical information such as browser versions, number of hits, page impressions and visitor sessions. The server load can also be measured and evaluated. These tools, however, often reach their limits when they're required to analyze dynamically generated Web pages, which are very common in Web shops. Yet, it is precisely this analysis that is needed to determine customer activities in the Web shop, not just from the technical perspective, but from the business perspective as well.

With mySAP CRM, customer actions or "events" can be recorded in the Web shop. This means that for every visitor session in the Web shop, you can deduce which articles the visitor looked at, which articles were placed in or removed from the shopping basket, how the number of articles in the shopping basket changed, and whether the order was placed. This data can be directly loaded into SAP Business Information Warehouse (SAP BW) and immediately evaluated with the help of predefined analyses. In addition, thanks to the seamless integration of the components, the data from the visitor sessions can be analyzed in combination with data from mySAP CRM, SAP R/3, and other systems, such as business partner and product information, and the sales history. The results of these evaluations provide Web shop operators with a complete picture of customers, products, and the state of the Web shop at any time, so that improvements can be initiated immediately, if required.

In addition to the usual evaluations on the technical status of the Web site (*site statistics*)—for example, an analysis of links that don't work, or of download volumes, site loading time, error status and so on—mySAP CRM provides reporting options in the following areas:

- ▶ **Customer behavior**
    - ▶ User data (analysis based on user-specific characteristics)
    - ▶ Clickstream (evaluation of user clicks in chronological order)
    - ▶ Top n external referrer (evaluation of the most common sites from which the visitor accessed the Web shop)
    - ▶ Event statistics (overview of the events triggered in the Web shop)
    - ▶ Visitor session (evaluation of all information for a visitor session in the Web shop)
    - ▶ Visit frequency (evaluation of how often an individual user visits the site)
- ▶ **Sales statistics**
    - ▶ Conversion rate (proportion of visitors who actually placed an order)
    - ▶ Articles viewed, selected, and bought by customers in the Web shop
    - ▶ Top-ten articles (analysis of the ten articles most frequently viewed, put in the shopping basket, removed from the shopping basket, or purchased)
    - ▶ Shopping basket values (for example, per customer or average and total value of the shopping baskets at a particular point in time)
    - ▶ Overview of the articles in the shopping baskets at a particular point in time

Based on the collected, aggregated, and analyzed data, the marketing and sales departments of a company are in a position to understand the makeup of customer groups, or to determine which products are in highest demand for a particular group. This information can then be used to effectively develop specific marketing strategies and campaigns.

In contrast, the product management department is more interested in information on the products themselves. In this area, the analyses can provide data on the most frequently and infrequently ordered combinations for configurable products, for example, which enables the company to make decisions about new developments for product groups.

Finally, the analysis of visitors' navigator and search behavior in the Web shop enables the company to quickly locate weak points in the Web design or Web site information quickly, and to take corrective measures.

By recording customer-specific and product-related data in the Web shop and subsequently analyze this data in the Data Warehouse, mySAP CRM ensures that the large volume of useful data that is generated every day in the Web shop is not simply lost. In mySAP CRM, various data is first structured and then analyzed, in order to create an accurate picture of customers' buying habits and their preferences regarding products, services, and content. This knowledge enables decision-makers to perform sales analyses, predict trends in demand, optimize marketing initiatives, and tailor the Web site to meet the precise needs of the customer.

9.4.8 Functional Web Design

To sell products successfully in a Web shop, the Internet site must be attractive and functional; it must reflect the corporate design and branding; and its features must be tailored exactly to the target group.

Users view Web shop solutions via an Internet browser. The user decides whether to enter the Web shop, buy goods, and place follow-up orders at an early stage. In this respect, the user interface layout, or Web shop design, is a determining factor. It cannot be assumed that all users have the same requirements. They come from very different demographic areas, with different prior knowledge, individual goals, and disparate needs. If users cannot navigate around the Web shop, and the functions aren't clear, trust and acceptance are quickly lost, and ultimately, it is unlikely that a purchase will be made.

In addition to increasing user satisfaction, well-organized Web shop solutions, which can be easily understood, have the clear advantage of increased productivity. If a user makes fewer errors, for example, fewer incomplete or incorrect orders, the costs for the shop operator are reduced.

For these reasons, mySAP CRM enables the appearance and the interactive behavior or the shop to be adapted to the provider's needs. The choice of J2EE technology (Java 2 platform, Enterprise Edition) means that the program logic is separated from the user interface. The modification options for both components are based on Java as the programming language and HTML as the layout language. Modifications to the workshop design can affect the general layout, the colors and graphics used, the fonts and so on, however, they don't affect the application logic.

mySAP CRM already provides draft designs for B2B and B2C scenarios, which were developed by leading Web design experts and are continuously subject to usability tests. *Ready-to-run templates* support the complete range of functions and contain attractive graphics, well-defined colors and fonts, and so on. The templates provided can be easily used immediately. They are based on the *best practice* processes of various industries and are characterized by a high degree of flexibility for adjustment to customer-specific requirements.

9.4.9 Implementation Options for E-Commerce with mySAP CRM

In order to meet the differing requirements of companies, four different options are available for the implementation of the e-commerce solution of mySAP CRM:

▶ **E-Commerce with SAP R/3 (SAP Internet Sales, R/3 Edition)**

Before implementing a complete CRM solution, many companies want a simple e-selling solution that enables them to extend their core sales processes to the Internet without considerable effort, and simultaneously, achieve a fast return on investment.

With SAP Internet Sales (R/3 Edition), SAP R/3 customers now have an e-commerce platform that enables them to establish the World Wide Web (WWW) quickly as a profitable sales channel without having to implement a complete CRM solution. SAP Internet Sales (R/3 Edition) supports complete order-to-cash processes with easy-to-use, interactive order functions for business customers and consumers. As a result, companies can leverage their existing IT investments in SAP R/3 and have an easy introduction to mySAP CRM. Planned upgrade scenarios enable additional, far-reaching CRM scenarios to be added to SAP Internet Sales (R/3 Edition) at low cost at a later time.

▶ **E-Commerce with CRM**

E-commerce with CRM is the standard option for an e-commerce implementation. Compared to SAP Internet Sales R/3 Edition, this option offers extended functionality, particularly in the areas of marketing, personalization, and self-service, and also supports further interaction channels such as the call center and mobile sales.

▶ **E-Commerce in the Portal (Customer and Partner Portal)**

With SAP Enterprise Portal, the mySAP CRM e-commerce solution can also be used as a Web-based customer or partner portal. The customer/partner portal provides customers, sales partners, and service partners with central access to all sales and service relevant transactions. A personalized homepage gives customers and partners important, personalized information and messages, and allows direct access to a wide variety of ordering, payment, and self service functions.

▶ **E-Commerce with Sales Partners (Channel Commerce)**

Many organizations are looking for ways to offer their customers better service and generate additional sales by integrating their sales partners (distributors, dealers, resellers, brokers, and agents) in their e-commerce strategy.

With the channel commerce functions from mySAP CRM, companies can provide their sales partners with an e-commerce platform for the sale of their products to end customers. Consequently, joint sales processes are possible across enterprise boundaries. Manufacturers and dealers have a joint, uniform

Internet presence. Customers can use the shared Internet site to order products and services directly from the entire dealer network with a single order; they can even order from several dealers, providing the products are available there. The shared CRM platform also enables collaboration between the company and its sales partner for the maintenance of customer relationships.

9.4.10 Successful E-Commerce Projects with mySAP CRM

Better Customer Service at Lower Cost: The Online Business Center at Canada Post

Canada Post is one of the most technically advanced postal companies in the world. The Canadian company has over 30 million private customers and around one million business customers to whom over 10 billion letters and parcels are delivered each year. Since the late 1990s, Canada Post has been faced with increasing competition, and new Internet technologies were perceived as a threat to existing business. The increasing customer demand for speed, flexibility, and information—in connection with postal services—drove Canada Post to set up its "Business Transformation" project, which involved radical measures to improve the cost structure and the range of new, customer-oriented products and services. mySAP CRM was chosen as the integrated e-business platform to achieve the vision of a fully customer-centric company [Gerbetz 2002]. The focus here was on three central areas of customer relationship management:

▶ **Electronic shipping tools**
  With electronic shipping tools, business customers can place shipping orders independently over the Internet and create shipping documents quickly and easily online. This results in considerable time savings, less paper consumption, and lastly, increases the reliability of shipping processing.

▶ **Internet sales and service**
  Canada Post also decided to provide customers with smooth access to products and services over *www.canadapost.ca*, and to offer a series of self services (package tracking, postage calculation, post office search, account queries, and so on). In addition, employees in the service and shipping departments were able to access detailed customer information (inquiries, complaints, shipping orders, and so on) through a Web browser.

▶ **Contact centers**
  To supplement the "Online Business Center," Canada Post's eight call centers were equipped with mySAP CRM, so that all customer service staff had access to the relevant customer information when handling customer inquiries by telephone, fax, and email.

In 2002, Canada Post was awarded the prestigious Gartner CRM Award of Excellence for its CRM strategy and implementation with mySAP CRM [Gerbetz 2002]. Canada Post received the award for its effective, customer-centric approach and the successful transformation of existing business processes using the Internet as a new interaction channel for its customers.

Personalization in Business-to-Business: Osram Sylvania Brings Information to Light

Osram Sylvania, the North American subsidiary of Osram GmbH, part of the Siemens group, is one of the three largest lighting products in the world.

By using the mySAP CRM e-commerce solution, Osram Sylvania has been able to link up all supplier, customer, and business partner back-end systems with the front-office applications, which all participants can access over the Internet. All of Osram Sylvania's business partners can place orders directly, process payment transactions, and monitor the order fulfillment status online. Both buyer and seller can call up order information such as the order status. Stock monitoring, order issue, and order monitoring are all carried out automatically.

The solution also "takes note" of the customer-specific conditions such as discounts and terms of payment. Osram Sylvania manages around 1.5 million condition records for its customers (customer-specific prices, discount, rebate agreements, and so on). They form the basis for a complex system of rules for pricing. The huge degree of personalization in pricing also has a dynamic element: thousands of changes are made every day. All individual information on the remuneration system must be updated on an ongoing basis in accounting, sales, and on the Web site. SAP's integrated e-business solution ensures that the prices and conditions on the Web site always agree with the billed prices; needless to say, they only have to be centrally maintained once.

Another major challenge is the integration of the extensive technical information and documentation on Osram Sylvania's products into the e-commerce solution. For each product, there is a vast amount of technical data, product data sheets, warning notes, technical drawings, and instructions for use. All this information is important for customers, and can therefore be accessed over the Internet.

Mass Customization: Online Configuration at Fiducia AG

Fiducia Informationszentrale AG is the largest computer service center for German cooperative banks. The company's core activities focus on the dialogue-oriented processing of posting transactions for the participating banks. In addition, it develops its own software solutions, provides implementation, training, and consulting services, and offers centrally controlled delivery of hardware and software to its customers.

Customers can use the Fiducia service portal to order hardware, software, and support services at the click of a mouse. In every case, the customer only sees combinations of hardware and software that are permitted or are relevant for the workplace in question. The customer is guided online to the product configuration that meets his or her requirements and has been approved in that particular combination by Fiducia. Extensive technical documentation is available for each product and component. For configurable products, the current price is determined and availability is checked. Customers can also access the current status of their order transaction at any time later in the order fulfillment process.

The complete integration of front-end and back-end applications creates an end-to-end sales channel and is an important step towards the optimization of business processes across enterprise boundaries.

Thanks to the online solution, Fiducia has not only optimized its ordering processes, it has also ensured that current information is always available. In the past, sales staff had to be informed about all the details of the software and hardware configuration by conventional methods, but now, this information is automatically available to employees and their customers at any time, thanks to the automatic maintenance of product changes.

In addition to improved service and simplified, accelerated information and transaction process, the workload in order management at Fiducia has been permanently reduced. The potential savings achieved through process optimization amount to 95% of the order-specific costs, which means that introduction of the SAP e-commerce solution has reduced the costs per order from 85 to 4 USD. This considerable cost reduction alone has ensured a rapid return on investment.

9.4.11 Use Case: E-Commerce with mySAP CRM

The company PC4YOU has set up a Web shop to offer the Internet as an additional communication and sales channel for its business customers. Chris Robertson is responsible for hardware procurement at an advertising agency and regularly uses the PC4YOU Web shop. Today, she wants to buy PCs for her company there. After the login process, she can see at a glance the status of the purchase transactions she has carried out to date. PC4YOU also presents its latest new products on the first page. Chris finds out about the new Maxitec product line, which boasts ergonomic design and high performance.

As she's on the lookout for a suitable PC model for her advertising agency, she takes a look at the special deals that PC4YOU offers certain business customers. The $1681.60 deal seems like a good value for the R-1003 Maxitec-R 3300 Professional PC.

However, looking more closely, Chris sees that the hard drive size does not meet her expectations. She therefore chooses to configure the PCs online to meet her requirements and chooses Campus PC 2000 as the basic model, which she equips with a larger hard drive with 100 GB memory and 7200 RPM. She also increases the main memory to 256 MB, chooses the fast AMD Thunder Bird processor with 1.4 GHz, and selects the soundcard model Creative SB Audio PCI 64V.

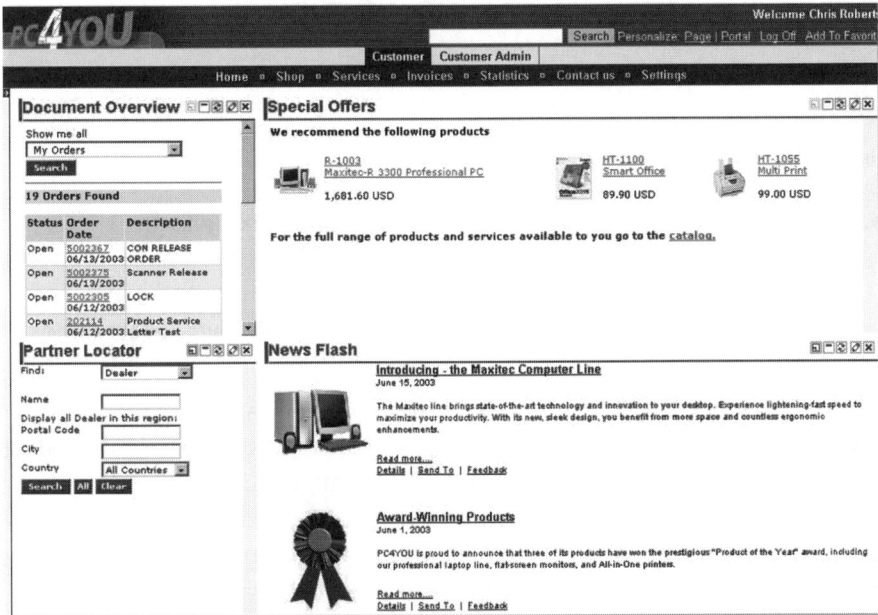

Figure 9.6 Web Shop with Purchasing History, New Products, and Special Offers

As Chris thinks this selection meets the advertising agency's requirements very well, and the overall price of $2643 does not exceed her budget, she places her configured PC Campus 2000 into the shopping basket, confirms the delivery and invoice address, and specifies the payment method. Before she leaves the Web shop, she takes a final look at the order confirmation and sees that all the product details and invoice amount are displayed correctly.

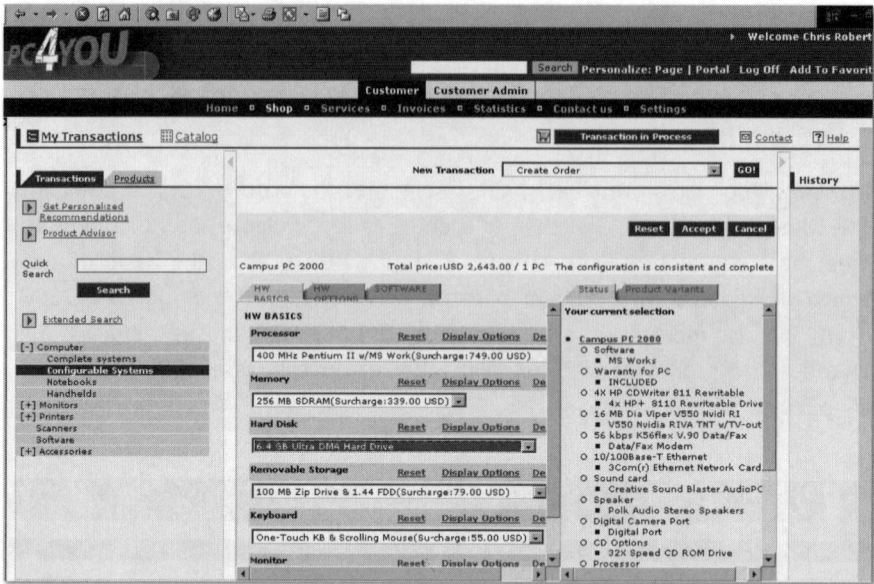

Figure 9.7 Product Configuration in the Web Shop

9.4.12 Recommendations for Successful CRM Projects in E-Commerce

Look at Things from the Customer Viewpoint: "Buying" Determines "Selling"

It may seem banal, but successful e-commerce solutions are those that offer the customer real benefit. This is achieved when the customers' requirements relating to ease of use during purchasing (which includes fast page display), intuitive product selection and ordering, the scope and current relevance of product information, price information, and special offers, speed and reliability of processing, the transparency of downstream processes (for example, the status of the order/delivery), helpful after-sales services, and so on are met. All this relates to the underlying principle of e-commerce, namely that the business processes must be aimed primarily to meet the needs of the buyer (customer), not the needs of the seller. Unfortunately, this goal is all too often eclipsed by efforts to optimize sales processes.

Customer Experience Through Integral Customer Interaction

The Internet is developing from a purely sales channel into an important medium for communication with the customer. The *customer experience*—namely, the perception of the brand, enjoyment, and the use of self services on a supplier's Web site—is becoming more and more important. Web design and corporate design, branding, information, and the option of providing feedback at all stages of the customer life cycle must form a complete unit, and play an important role, not just in the B2C environment. In view of this, it is advisable to involve experts from all areas—that is, marketing and advertising, sales, and customer service—in the implementation of an e-commerce solution so that an integral concept can be drawn up and implemented.

Selecting Implementation Options Taking Account of ROI Factors

In order to achieve the fastest possible return on investment, it is necessary to consider during implementation of the e-commerce solution what effort is expected at what point in time. Many e-commerce projects are characterized by high initial investment, but very slow acceptance and use by the customer base. With its e-commerce platform, mySAP CRM offers a unique opportunity of not just activating individual functions as required, but also implementing the most important functions at relatively little cost in a lean, initial version by using existing SAP R/3 components. The solution can be easily extended at a later date with the implementation of additional mySAP CRM components (for example, for marketing functions) or portal functions (content management).

Integration in the Overall CRM Strategy

An e-commerce strategy should always be incorporated into the overall CRM strategy, and it therefore follows that the e-commerce solution should be integrated in the CRM system. This is the only way to ensure that questions that arise during browsing in the Internet catalog can be answered immediately by call center staff, that the customer can call up—over the Internet—the status of an order placed over the phone, and the sales and service employee has information about the products purchased online.

9.5   Scenario Overview and Potential Benefits

The mySAP CRM e-commerce application is a comprehensive solution for the sale of products and the handling of services over the Internet. It covers all phases of the sales cycle, such as marketing, catalog management, order issuing, payment, order fulfillment, and after-sales service. Many business scenarios that are integrated in the company's regular business processes can be triggered and monitored by the customers themselves. The following cross-industry business scenarios are available:

Cross-industry scenarios	Short Description	Potential benefit		
		Revenue	Profitability	Customer satisfaction
Catalog management and order fulfillment in e-commerce	Organization of products and product information in catalog form for Web shops Personalization options for users with customer-specific views, product recommendations, prices and contracts Order fulfillment functionality of the Sales scenario Optional, direct connection to SAP R/3 (scenario *Catalog Management and Order Fulfillment in E-Commerce Internet Sales, R/3 Edition*)	✓✓	✓	✓
Shop management	Support for Web shop managers for the creation, configuration, processing, and deletion of Web shops for B2B or B2C scenarios Option of product catalog maintenance in SAP R/3 (Scenario version *Shop Management Internet Sales, R/3 Edition*)	✓✓		✓
Contract management in e-commerce	Internet-based agreement of contracts and handling of orders as contract release orders	✓✓		✓
Service request processing	Creation and modification of service and information requests by customers over the Internet Customers can include relevant documents as attachments, specify requested dates, and independently track service activity status		✓✓	✓
Interactive sales	Internet-based processing of complex customer inquiries, quotations, and orders Customers are guided through the configuration process and the system ensures that the specified business rules are observed	✓	✓✓	✓

Cross-industry scenarios	Short Description	Potential benefit		
		Revenue	Profitability	Customer satisfaction
Live Web collaboration	Online support for customers during Web shop visit by means of chat, co-browsing, email, or callback			✓✓
Complaints and returns processing in e-commerce	Management of complaints and returns by customers on the Internet, from the entry and modification of information to status tracking and the triggering of credit memos, product exchanges, or replacement deliveries		✓	✓✓
Solution search	Customer access to the company's knowledge base (solution database) via an intuitive user interface with the formulation of requests in non-technical language Search options based on FAQs, if appropriate, with direct product reference, with step-by-step search refinement, and direct interaction with the supplier		✓	✓✓

10 Customer Interaction Along All Communication Channels—mySAP CRM for the Interaction Center

"The mySAP CRM system will make the lives of the interaction center agents a lot easier. They'll be able to do more for our customers in less time."
Janet Smith, Customer Service Manager, Boots Wellbeing

10.1 Introduction

"The person responsible for handling your query is at lunch. Please call back later." A fateful statement that is heard all too often and can destroy a carefully cultivated customer relationship within seconds. Who is responsible for whom here, customers quite justifiably ask themselves, and they may simply turn to a different service provider—an easy thing to do in this age of electronic trade.

Customers nowadays expect high-quality services that are available around the clock. This can only be achieved by customer relationship management (CRM) that opens all communication channels to the customer, and supports all forms of marketing, sales, and service processes. To gear the whole company towards this new understanding of customer relationship management is the goal of corporate management.

10.1.1 The Call Center in Transition

The call center was traditionally a central place of contact between customers and companies. However, call centers that work only with telephones and supply their agents with very basic data on customers are a thing of the past. They have nothing in common with today's concept of customer relationship management. A company must supply its Interaction Center agents with knowledge and precise, up-to-date information about all its customers. Agents require constant access to this type of information. Data on customer history, buying behavior, and preferences allow agents to interact with customers efficiently and valuably.

In the face of declining customer loyalty in the age of the Internet, companies must make it as easy as possible for their customers to communicate with them. Information about products and services must be easily accessible, transactions quick to complete, the status of delivery processing trackable at all times, and requesting additional services should be intuitive. The Interaction Center is the central instrument in this context for opening up all customer communication channels.

The transition from call center to Interaction Center mirrors the general trend towards optimizing the benefits for the customer using CRM solutions (see Figure 10.1).

Customer value

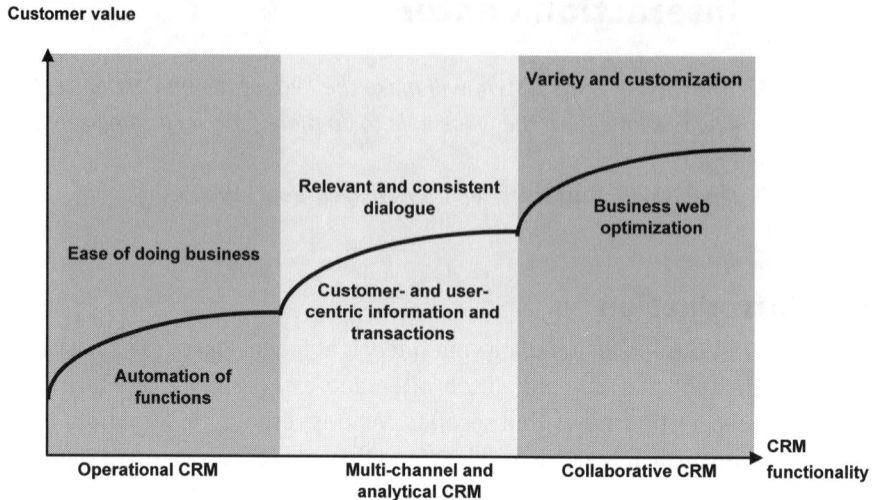

Figure 10.1 Customer Benefits from CRM

Over the last ten years, "process automation" has been a central theme in many companies. Call centers have appeared as a reaction to this trend with the goal of cutting transaction costs. These centers have often been moved out of the actual company. Success was determined only by factors such as duration of calls and personnel fluctuation. Many companies have now recognized that the quality of the call center has a significant influence on customer satisfaction. While customers in the past tolerated the fact that they had to dial a range of different numbers for service requests, sales inquiries, and order management, they nowadays insist that the agent they contact handle all processes and access up-to-date business data. A customer who sends a fax on Monday, writes a letter on Tuesday, sends an email on Wednesday, meets with the board on Thursday, and meets with the sales representative on Friday expects that the agent in the interaction center whom she calls on Saturday knows about all these business activities and agreements. The customer also expects precise information about prices, delivery date, availability of service employees, and the status of order processing.

10.1.2 SAP's Solution

The transition from call center to Interaction Center could not be more radical. The following are some of the difficulties that must be overcome:

▶ The change in the technological basis from the traditional telephone switchboard to Web-based multi-channel systems

▶ The transition from being only the initial point of contact to being responsible for customer service for all business processes

▶ The development from a low-skill to a highly qualified service organization

SAP's Interaction Center provides customers with the technology and instruments necessary to map their business processes. Like all mySAP CRM applications, the component also adapts to fluctuating environmental factors. New technology, enhanced business processes, and innovative business ideas determine the look of the solution.

10.2 Key Elements of the Interaction Center

The mySAP CRM Interaction Center application provides a highly efficient spectrum of functions that greatly simplify the work of the Interaction Center agent. The functions include messages and notes, preformulated dialogs, channel integration, workforce planning, workflow management, and Knowledge Management (KM).

10.2.1 Messages for Agents

The work of Interaction Center agents is extremely diverse, and they themselves often find it stressful. The constant uncertainty as to the demands of the next caller requires a certain type of employee. Just how difficult it is to find and keep such employees is illustrated by various studies on the problem of the high degree of personnel fluctuation in the sector. Reicheld specifies a normal fluctuation rate of 15–25%, for example [Reicheld 1996]. The messages generated in the SAP system by the Alert Modeler help agents orient themselves with respect to the customer. Triggered by particular events such as incoming calls, certain business process rules are processed and the results are formatted for the agents in real time. As a result, many companies can thoroughly check customer status in a split second. Agents see a display that informs them whether all invoices have been paid and deliveries made on time, and whether the customer is a special customer (a premium customer, for example). The fact that the information is provided automatically means that the agent can quickly become familiar with the customer.

10.2.2 Preformulated Interactive Customer Dialogs

The scripting functionality is an integral part of the Interaction Center and supports agents in conducting calls. Preformulated dialogs are stored in the system and help the agent to enter all relevant information about a customer complaint, for example, thus avoiding the need to make additional inquiries later. This makes it possible to find a quick solution even for complex problems.

As well as simple, linear dialogs, the scripting also supports adaptive dialogs that are adjusted to suit the course of the call. Entire dialog trees can be mapped. The scripting functionality also allows the agent to branch immediately from individual customer dialogs to the relevant business transactions.

10.2.3 Channel Integration

mySAP CRM includes a new universal interface for all communication channels (telephone, email, chat, fax, and so on). The interface is based on open Web standards such as XML and SOAP, and is set to replace existing channel interfaces such as SAPphone over the next few years. SAP developed the concept together with leading multi-channel partners such as Genesys, Siemens, and Aspect. Partners can also get the connectors they create certified (see Section 15.3.2).

10.2.4 Workforce Planning

Each Interaction Center depends on the employees who come into contact with the customers. Human resources planning is one of the most important tasks of management. Administrators must draw up work schedules, taking into account seasonal and business factors. The Workforce Management application supports the Interaction Center management in determining the necessary personnel resources (see Section 7.5.13). Figure 10.2 shows the number of anticipated customer contacts and available agents.

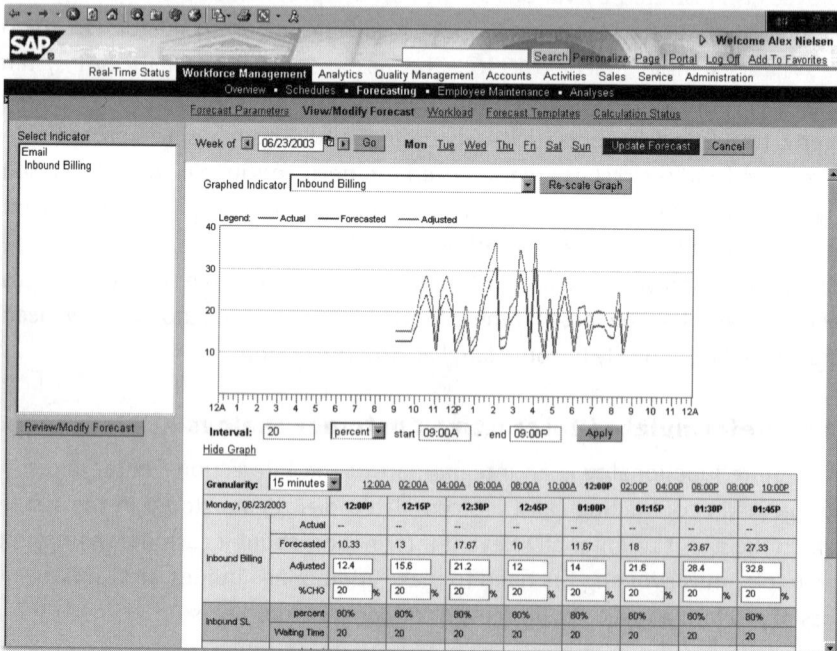

Figure 10.2 Workforce Management for the Interaction Center

Unlike many other workforce planning systems, mySAP CRM Workforce Management enables integration with SAP's human resources systems and with other CRM applications. The forecast volume of contact is not based only on the extrapolation of historical data. Thanks to the link to mySAP CRM's marketing application, future campaigns and their projected success can be included in the projection of the volume of customer contact.

10.2.5 Workflow Management

Almost as old as data processing is the question of the correct storage location for the flow logic that controls the sequence of processes. There are two possible answers: The logic can be represented in programs or in declarative workflows.

This question is central to active customer relationship management, since customer-oriented processes change much more frequently than financial application processes, for example. The questions during the implementation phase of financial applications are primarily to do with the flow logic, whereas the daily business of an interaction center manager includes monitoring the processes in the center and adapting them to current needs. If the service department detects a serious problem, any related customer messages must be processed with high priority and possibly by a separate agent group.

In response to this requirement, SAP provides a new Workflow Modeler, which is designed for the needs of call center managers and their employees. Even complex workflows can be simply presented on a graphical interface. Additional support from consultants is not usually required (see Figure 10.3).

In addition to ease of use, another major factor in workflow management is the ability to control operating costs. An analysis of various customer projects shows that workflows for escalation management or approvals, for example, are implemented very similarly in different companies. SAP takes this into account with standard workflows that are included with the package. Based on the standard templates, company-specific workflows can be set up at little cost and can be continuously adapted to take into account current conditions in the company. mySAP CRM provides functions that allow Interaction Center managers to send automatic emails to area managers as soon as important customers enter high-priority messages, for example. Other standard workflows see to it that new sales requests with a potentially high order value are presented first to the sales manager to be checked. The sales manager can then decide whether the case is passed on to a particularly experienced sales employee or stays with the current sales team.

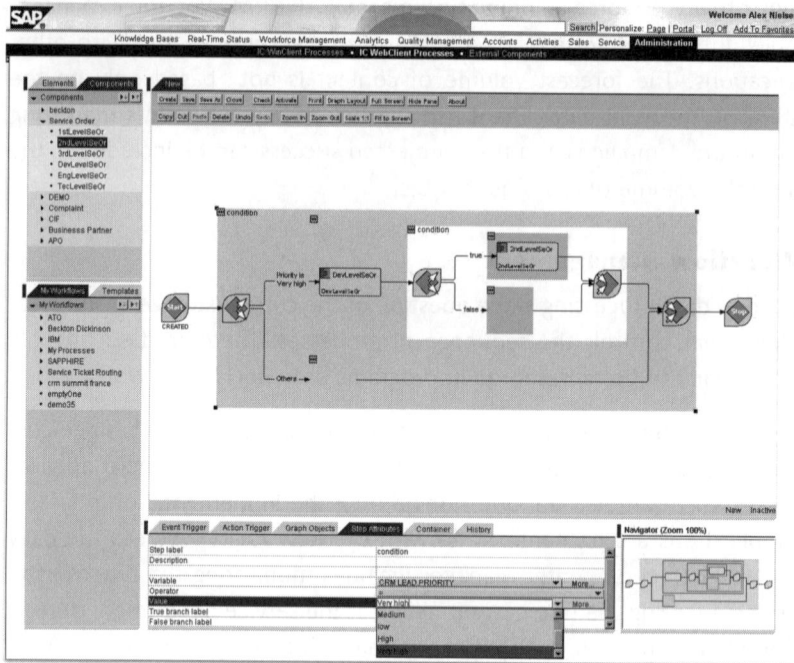

Figure 10.3 Workflow Modeler in Interaction Center

10.2.6 Knowledge Management

The significance of Knowledge Management is discussed in Sections 7.5.4 and 14.5.3. The *Software Agent Framework* is of central importance from the point of view of the Interaction Center (see Figure 10.4).

The Software Agent Framework allows the agent to search a solution database either in free text format or for attributes. The agent chooses the relevant solutions from the ones found, places them in a virtual shopping cart as in a Web shop, and sends them to the customer by email, for example.

One special feature of the Software Agent Framework is that all applications access the same solution infrastructure. The concept has a modular structure. The standard SAP search engine can be exchanged for a third-party product, for example. The user is not committed to a specific solution database at repository level either. The agent can specify in the search dialog whether the inquiry entered should be run against SAP's solution database or an external content management system.

The Software Agent Framework is also used in the context of email response management. An incoming email is forwarded for automatic preprocessing to the *Auto Suggest Repository* of the Software Agent Framework. The framework presents the agent with solution proposals with the required precision of hit. The agent checks the quality of the proposals and forwards the relevant notes to the customer.

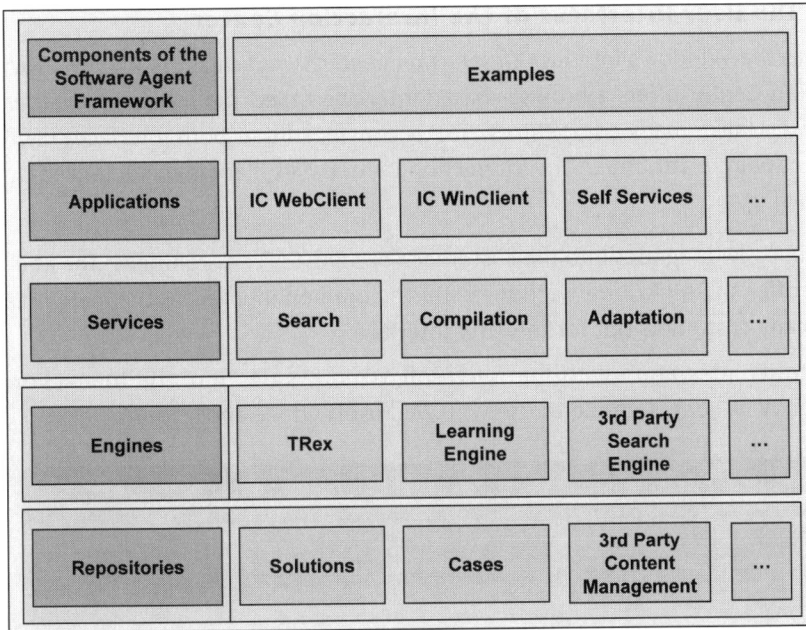

Figure 10.4 Architecture of the Software Agent Framework

Figure 10.5 Auto Suggest Repository

10.2.7 The User Interfaces of the Interaction Center

As well as the Windows interface (*Interaction Center WinClient*), the mySAP CRM Interaction Center offers a browser-based interface called the *Interaction Center WebClient*. Unlike many competitors, SAP is convinced that both interfaces have significant unique attributes. The Interaction Center WinClient is characterized by the following:

▶ It seamlessly integrates into the customer's existing SAP environment. The ability to offer all SAP R/3 transactions within a common interface is the main reason many customers opt for this user interface.

▶ Due to its integration with the Microsoft Windows desktop, the Interaction Center WinClient is simple to use with Microsoft Office applications.

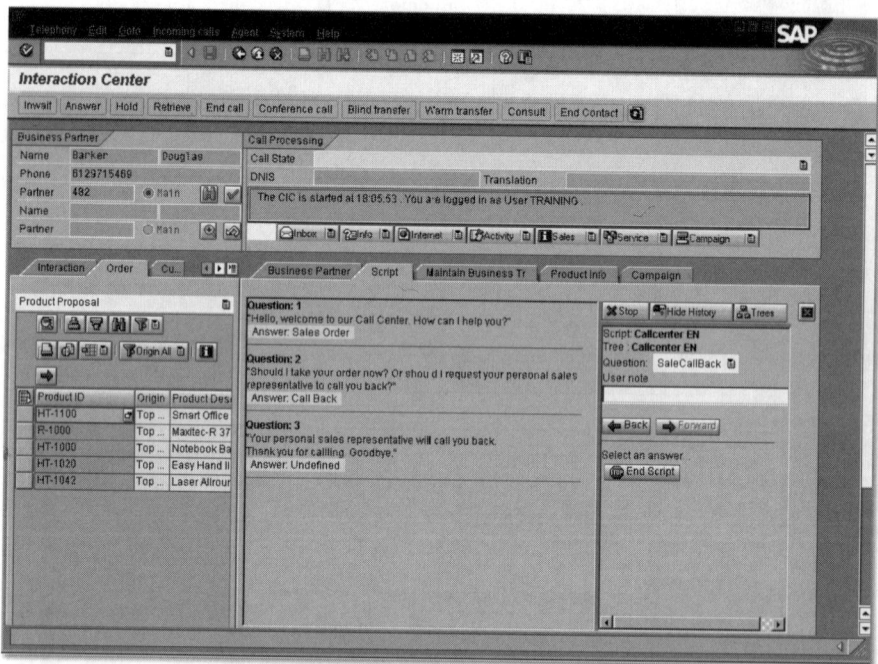

Figure 10.6 Interaction Center WinClient

The Interaction Center WebClient (see Figures 10.7 and 10.8) is characterized by the following attributes:

▶ The interface is intuitive to learn, but still comparable with the familiar Windows interface as far as response time and network load are concerned.

▶ Supported by the services of the SAP Web Application Server (SAP Web AS), SAP has decided to use integrated Java and ABAP components in the Interaction Center WebClient. However, the new Workflow Modeler, for example, is implemented as a Java Applet, and all components that show an extensive data transfer between back end and front end are implemented in ABAP.

SAP also intends to support both interfaces in parallel in the future.

10.3 Central Processes of the Interaction Center in Detail

The central processes in the interaction center are related to telemarketing, telesales, and teleservice. The main elements of these processes are discussed in the following sections.

10.3.1 Telemarketing

One of the core tasks of marketing is to generate sufficient contacts for the sales organization. Campaign management is an important tool in this context. Personalized, customer-specific offers originate on the basis of the target group selection, the identification of appropriate communication channels, and the available products or services. If the marketing management decides on a telephone campaign, call lists are drawn up and passed on to the Interaction Center organization together with predefined scripts. The scripts are used by the agents as personalized templates for their calls, and often contain relevant customer data about preferences, previously bought products, or preferred contact times, for example. They enable the agents to conduct very personalized calls.

The call center manager assigns the call lists to the individual agents or agent groups. They see the calls that are assigned to them in their worklist. The progress of the active campaign can be monitored any time using the *Interaction Center Manager Portal*.

10.3.2 Telesales

Selling products and services by telephone is becoming increasingly popular, both in the business-to-business (B2B) and in the business-to-consumer (B2C) environment. Within order receipt, the agent has access to all instruments that provide information about availability (Available-to-Promise—ATP), pricing procedure, alternative products (up-selling or down-selling), and product accessories (cross-selling).

Longer sales cycles for higher quality goods require that the agent has access to the entire interaction history. All customer-related data and functions for managing contacts and follow-up activities, creating quotations, and converting the quotations to orders can be reached using a single interaction step. By accessing *Incentive and Commission Management*, agents can also see how their sales successes affect their salaries.

10.3.3 Teleservice

In any industry sector, the majority of Interaction Centers are in the service environment. They often take the form of help desks that deal with internal and external complaints or problem messages. The quality of the service processes in the Interaction Center can have a major influence on customer and employee satisfaction. Depending on the complexity of the requests, the service processes are supported by the following functions (see also Section 7.5):

▶ **Activity management**
Confirmations to customers are documented and a check is made to see if they have been observed.

▶ **Case management**
Enhanced activity management with the option of combining different activities into a "case"

▶ **Service orders**
Monitoring of agreements where services and spare parts are used

These different functions allow service processes to be tailored to a company's requirements: anything is possible, from simple activity tracking to complex service scenarios. Many companies in industrial maintenance integrate the mySAP CRM service application with logistics processes in the back-end system, for example. This means that an immediate check can be made to determine whether specific spare parts are in storage. The integration with the human resources systems uses another type of linkage. The company stores the knowledge and skills profiles of its service technicians here. The back-end system manages the shift times of the service technicians and Interaction Center agents.

10.3.4 Interaction Center Analytics

Companies that have already been using customer relationship management systems for years are often dissatisfied with the results Although they have a huge amount of data stored, their knowledge of their customers has not increased. The goal of improving the quality of consultation and decision support has not been achieved. The problem is often that there are not enough analytical instruments for evaluating the collated data and incorporating the insights gained into the operative processes (see also Section 12.2.4).

In the mySAP CRM Interaction Center, many of the analytical tools are combined in the Interaction Center Manager Portal. The Interaction Center management can find all evaluations on channel statistics, capacity of agent groups, and progress of campaigns in the portal.

Analytical applications also simplify the day-to-day work processes of the interaction center agents. At the start of a customer interaction, the system uses the Intelligence Connector to determine key figures such as customer lifetime value. Based on this value, the system proposes certain methods of response if there are complaints. A loyal customer with a high business volume can then be assured by the agent that a faulty piece of equipment will be repaired free of charge. On the other hand, a customer with a low business volume will be offered a quotation for the repair. This is a good example of how mySAP CRM uses the analytical key figure system to strengthen the customer's ties to the company and secure profitability.

10.3.5 Use Case: Problem Solving with the mySAP CRM Interaction Center

The field sales representatives of the computer manufacturer PC4YOU regularly access internal PC4YOU software systems during customer contacts to update presentations and other information material required for customer demonstrations. To prevent the systems from being accessed externally, PC4YOU has implemented a detailed security application where a secure ID card is used to check the identity and dial-in authorization of the sales employees before they are allowed access. The PC4YOU sales employees can contact the company's own Interaction Center if they have problems with the dial-in procedure.

An employee discovers that she has been denied access and calls the Interaction Center. The Interaction Center agent Chris D'Cunha has already identified the employee by her telephone number and transferred the proposed user data to the malfunction report. From the information provided about the employee, the agent is able to limit the inquiry to the problem areas of network and communication, remote access, and secure ID card, and gets a list of solution variants that match the problem description, for example, assigning a new IP address and synchronizing the secure ID card.

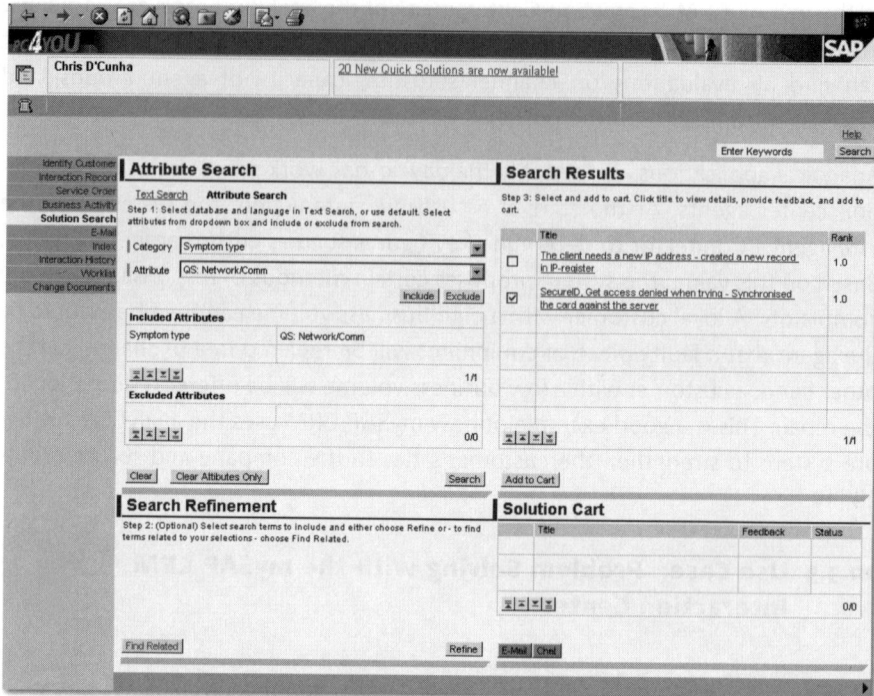

Figure 10.7 Choosing a Possible Solution in the Interaction Center

After looking through the possible solutions and consulting with the caller, Chris discovers that the secure ID needs to be resynchronized. He chooses resynchronization of the card as the solution, and offers to remedy the problem immediately by triggering the resynchronization directly from the interaction center.

The action taken and a description of the solution appear as a note on the malfunction report that is automatically added to the activity list for the problem message. Before the Interaction Center agent closes the message, he can send the sales employee an email confirming that the message has been processed.

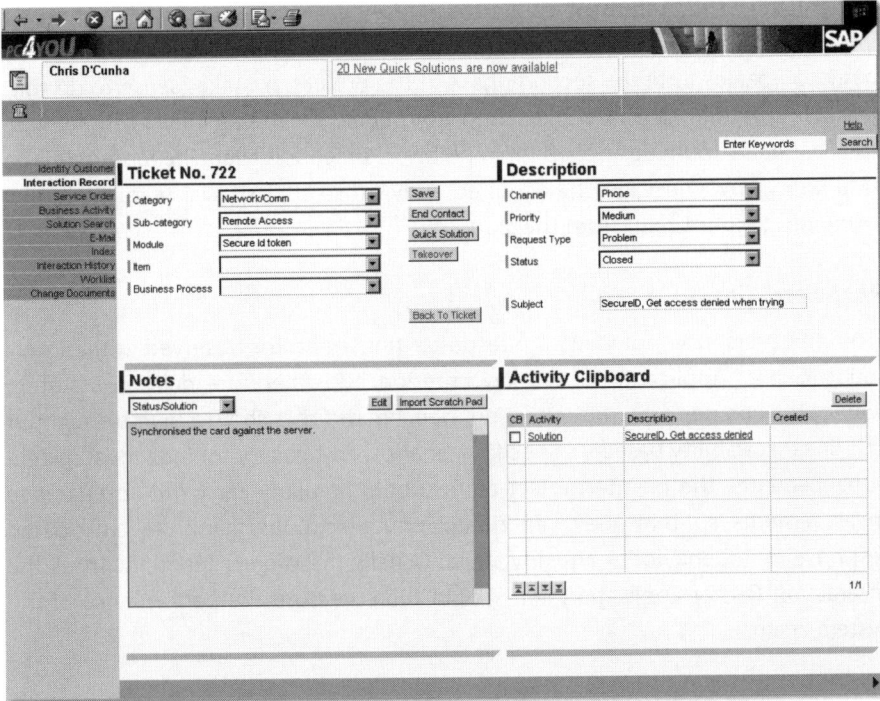

Figure 10.8 Automatic Problem Solving Directly from the Interaction Center

10.3.6 Recommendations for Successful CRM Projects in the Interaction Center

With over 700 successful projects, the Interaction Center is one of the most fre-quently implemented applications in mySAP CRM. One reason for this is the fact that even small-scale Interaction Center implementations quickly provide a noticeably high return on investment (ROI). SAP makes the following recommen-dations for Interaction Center projects.

Set a Manageable Scope for the First Interaction Center Implementation

If possible, the initial phase of the implementation project should not last more than three months. Complex processes can be omitted at this stage. In many cases, simple process chains such as customer identification and activity manage-ment are sufficient as a first step. The short project duration makes it easier to keep up the pace necessary to make the project a success.

The assumptions about ROI can be validated after this initial phase. The project team has gathered the knowledge required to formulate the next steps.

Technical Channel Integration

The integration with telephony infrastructure and email servers is postponed by many companies until the second phase of the project. It makes sense to do this, particularly if the first phase is kept short. A budget for the technical communication channels should be applied for in plenty of time, however. The required technical know-how must also be acquired early on so that special features can be taken into account right from the start.

Response Times

From the users' point of view, the response time behavior observed in the Interaction Center Application is the key criterion. SAP therefore delivers a system with optimized performance. There are benchmarks that show a high throughput and linear scalability based on specific scenarios. Particularly for individual system enhancements, the on-site project team should regularly carry out comparative measurements so that they can detect any deviations from the anticipated response time behavior at an early stage. Usually the project team enhances the Interaction Center application and should then measure the performance of the system again.

Management and Users Work Together

The recommendation to involve all relevant groups in the company applies to every SAP project. This type of collaboration allows the project team to ascertain the requirements of the different user groups early on, and also to keep their demands of the system realistic.

Tetra Pak designed a prototype of the new Interaction Center solution, for example, and presented it in a worldwide road-show since many users and managers initially had no concept of the new system. The chance to get to know this early form of the solution considerably simplified internal discussions.

Other needs could be registered on the basis of the current version. When the users were trained, there were far fewer hurdles to overcome since they were already familiar with the basic system processes.

10.4 Scenario Overview and Potential Benefits

The Interaction Center for communication with customers using various channels (such as telephone, fax, letter, email, and Internet) is a key application of mySAP CRM. It is used as a communication platform to integrate processes between front-end channels and back-office systems. The cross-industry business scenarios of the Interaction Center are summarized below and categorized according to their potential benefits.

Cross-Industry Scenarios	Short Description	Potential Benefits		
		Revenue	Profitability	Customer satisfaction
Lead Qualification with the Interaction Center	Systematic processing of call lists from campaign management. Script-based dialogs for qualification and further development of leads and opportunities.	✓✓	✓	
Opportunity Management in the Interaction Center	Qualification of sales opportunities and their assignment to the responsible sales organizations	✓✓	✓	
Inbound Telesales	Processing of incoming inquiries from customers and other interested persons with quotation and order entry, product information search, and availability check. Also supports agents in generating additional turnover using cross-selling and up-selling strategies.	✓✓	✓	✓
Outbound Telesales	Active sale of products from the Interaction Center by conducting sales campaigns and periodically contacting new customers using call lists and all options provided also by inbound telesales	✓✓	✓	✓
Workforce Management for the Interaction Center	Resource planning for the workforce employed in the Interaction Center by the Interaction Center management		✓✓	✓
Information Help Desk	Supports the Interaction Center agents in answering questions on products and services with scripts for conducting calls and access to solution databases. An IT help desk for internal and external message processing, or an employee interaction center or internal HR help desk for employees.		✓	✓✓

Cross-Industry Scenarios	Short Description	Potential Benefits		
		Revenue	Profitability	Customer satisfaction
Customer Service and Support in the Interaction Center	Answers customer inquiries, resolves technical problems, complaints management, returns processing, exchange activities, entry of service orders, suggesting proposals for additional service products using online access to the solution database and all relevant customer data		✓	✓✓
Complaints Management in the Interaction Center	Entry of product complaints, returns, and services by Interaction Center agents for incoming customer complaints		✓	✓✓

There are separate business scenarios for the special requirements of the automotive and telecommunications industries.

Industry-Specific Scenarios	Short Description	Potential Benefits		
		Revenue	Profitability	Customer satisfaction
Interaction Center for the Automotive Industry	Packaging of information on customers, vehicles, and vehicle parts, and processing of customer inquiries, complaints, maintenance cases, callbacks, and purchasing of accessories for manufacturers and importers	✓	✓	✓✓
Financial Customer Care for the Telecommunications Industry	Management of demands from customers. Processing of customer inquiries such as change of payment method or bank details, enforcing locks or deferrals. Providing all relevant information about customer, account balances, invoices, payments, reminders, and correspondence.		✓✓	✓

Industry-Specific Scenarios	Short Description	Potential Benefits		
		Revenue	Profitability	Customer satisfaction
Interactive Collections for the Telecommunications Industry	Automatic creation of call lists for reminders or collection of due items by telephone, and functions for recording payments, deferrals, or installment plans		✓✓	✓
Dispute Management for the Telecommunications Industry	Entry of customer complaints about invoices and creation of required correspondence. Integration of other processors to resolve the case and grant credit memos.		✓	✓✓

11 Channel Management with mySAP CRM— Controlling Marketing, Sales, and Service Partners Efficiently

11.1 Challenges of Indirect Channels

Many businesses rely on their partners to sell their products. The partners take over responsibility for selling to the end customers and often provide a range of additional services. This is generally known as indirect or multi-tier channel sales. The spectrum ranges from insurance brokers, independent sales agents, wholesalers, retailers, or distributors, to export companies, importers, and service providers, all of whom play a central role in the sales efforts of the brand owner.

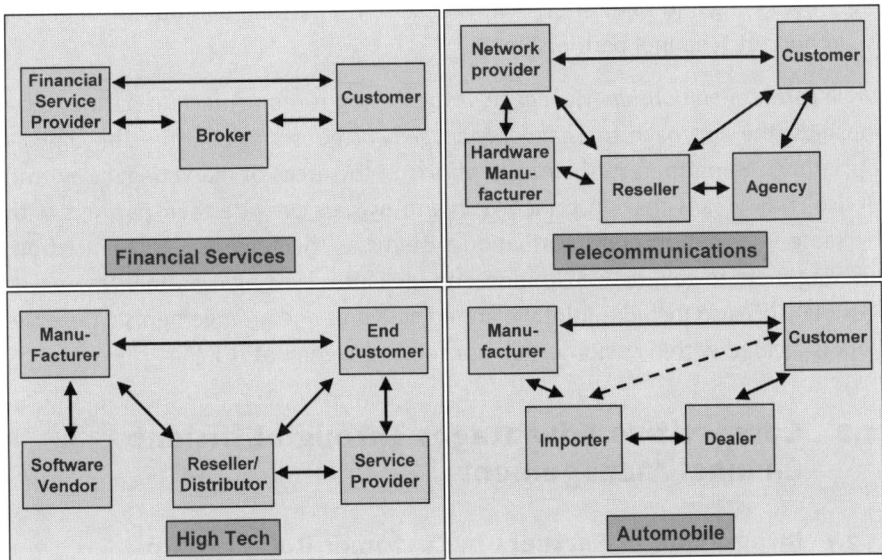

Figure 11.1 Examples of Partner Networks

The percentage of revenues derived from indirect channels has approximately doubled in the last 10 years, with some industries reaching 70% and beyond. Companies like Cisco have already achieved 80%, and some companies operate exclusively using indirect sales. This trend will continue. Gartner analysts predict an overall percentage of 65–85% for indirect channel activities by 2010 [De Sisto 2002].

The importance of channel partners for the success of a company is particularly salient if you consider that ultimately securing distribution and channel partners that provide customer-oriented services is as important as the product and the brand.

Businesses that use multi-tier sales channels are faced with a number of challenges that because partners are independent organizations that are subject to much less immediate control than sales employees and subsidiaries. The relationships to customers depend to a large extent on the partners and are generally formed and maintained outside the brand owner's area of influence.

Therefore, it is crucial for the brand owner not only how sales can be ensured or increased through the multi-tier sales channel, but also how the indirect sales channel is managed. What must a brand owner do, for example, to ensure that the partners correctly represent his brand, identify potential customers early, process leads and opportunities precisely, sell the products competently, provide high-quality customer service, and guarantee a high level of customer satisfaction and a high resale rate? How can the brand owner, if need be, harmonize his own direct marketing and sales efforts with those of his partner, without endangering the important "channel partnership"?

While *Partner Relationship Management* focuses on forming efficient partner relationships, the approach to *Channel Management* goes a step further by actively supporting the partners in their sales efforts in the areas of marketing, sales, and service. This means that, in principle, brand owners provide their partners with the same information and information systems as their own sales organization, enabling them to gain new customers and look after existing customers as well as possible. This also includes jointly planned activities and arrangements where the work is divided within customer relationship management (CRM).

11.2 Competitive Advantages Through Efficient Channel Management

11.2.1 Integration of Partners in Customer Relationship Management

Partners clearly challenge the main principle of customer relationship management: Know your customer and use this knowledge to develop the relationship in the most profitable way.

Partners come between the *brand owner* and the end customer and change the brand owner end customer relationship. They might have the intimate customer knowledge that the brand owner does not and might own the relationship to the end customer more than the brand owner does. On the other hand, the brand owner will always know more about its products and the general market for the products than the partners, who rely on anecdotal experience.

In the case of technical customer service, the partners usually know better how to deal with the end customer (what to say, when to visit the customer site, whom to talk to first), whereas the brand owner often has the best technical expertise to fix a certain problem.

This dichotomy between relationship advantages on the partner side and information advantages on the brand owner side is the main issue that has to be resolved by a channel management solution.

11.2.2 Using Best-of-Breed Partners to Gain Competitive Advantage

Historically, finding the right partners to drive sales was the primary focus of investing in indirect channels. Companies are becoming increasingly aware that partners who excel in the sales arena do not necessarily offer the same level of excellence when servicing the end customer. In addition, what might work for a certain profile of end customer does not necessarily work for another, perhaps more demanding type of customer.

Therefore, more and more companies embrace a best-of-breed strategy for selecting partners. You may want to use a first class logistics provider to offer your customers the best possible levels of fulfillment. For marketing purposes, you rely on an internationally established agency that can provide regionalized yet consistent branding. For the sales process, you might want to use specialized representatives (retail companies or agencies). Service is a different kettle of fish. You concentrate on support and work with regional partners who have regular contact with the end customers and know the local contacts. There is a global call center operation for level 1 and level 2 technical support, and level 3 support is provided by your internal organization. In this way, you can choose the best partner for each and every task in the customer and product lifecycle.

This may look like a compelling scenario, but the challenges lie in coordinating this complex network alongside the business processes. You will realize the ultimate goals of cost reduction, superior customer service, and increased revenues only if the complexity of the endeavor is transparent to the end customer.

11.2.3 Software Support for Better Partner and Customer Relationships

The right software can solve many problems that arise because of the partner's position between the brand owner and the end customer. Above all, passing on information between partners and brand owners can reduce gaps in knowledge so that partners are better informed and can work as professionally and be as well prepared as internal employees. Before the partners make customer contact, they are already aware of earlier inquiries, recent dealings, and open questions that the end customer is likely to have. This knowledge can be used to enhance and deepen the business relationship.

In addition, automated, integrated processes that also include cooperation with partners ensure seamless transfers between the parties involved. Ideally, customers will not notice that their service request is being received in an external call center, from which it is transferred to a global service partner, then sent to a local service bureau, and finally checked by the brand owner's service quality manager.

11.3 mySAP CRM Channel Management

11.3.1 Overview

The *Channel Management* capabilities of mySAP CRM offer companies a comprehensive software solution that enables them to efficiently build relationships to partners, and support them in selling more successfully and serving end customers better. SAP's strengths in the areas of e-commerce (see Chapter 9) and classic CRM with marketing, sales, and service (see Chapter 7) have been expanded and developed to enable partner collaboration. Furthermore, there are completely different functions available in Partner Relationship Management.

mySAP CRM Channel Management covers the following five areas:

- **Partner Management and Analytics** includes functions for managing partner relationships throughout the partner lifecycle.
- **Channel Marketing** is for gaining customers and increasing sales through indirect channels.
- **Channel Sales** helps partners to increase the quantity of their sales and to sell more effectively.
- **Channel Service** ensures a constantly high level of service by providing partners with access to service functions, expert knowledge, and problem-solving help.
- **Channel Commerce** includes sales partners in the brand owner's e-commerce strategy and enables Internet sales between different companies.

Partners can access the Channel Management functions through the partner portal. The employees responsible for the brand owner's indirect channel use the Channel Manager portal:

- **Partner Portal**
  The partner portal supports partners with personalized, simple access to all data and information (products, prices, marketing information, customers, and

so on) relevant to their business. Furthermore, partners receive permanent access to important transaction data such as orders, invoices and claims, as well as statistics and analysis tools.

▶ Channel Manager Portal

The Channel Manager portal gives personalized access to employees working for the brand owner so they can maintain relationships to partners in the most efficient way. This includes partner goal-orientation, planning and execution of collective activities, processing of collaborative business processes, optimization of indirect sales channels, and monitoring and analyzing the marketing, sales, and service capabilities of the partners.

In the following chapters the individual functions provided by mySAP CRM for Channel Management are described in detail.

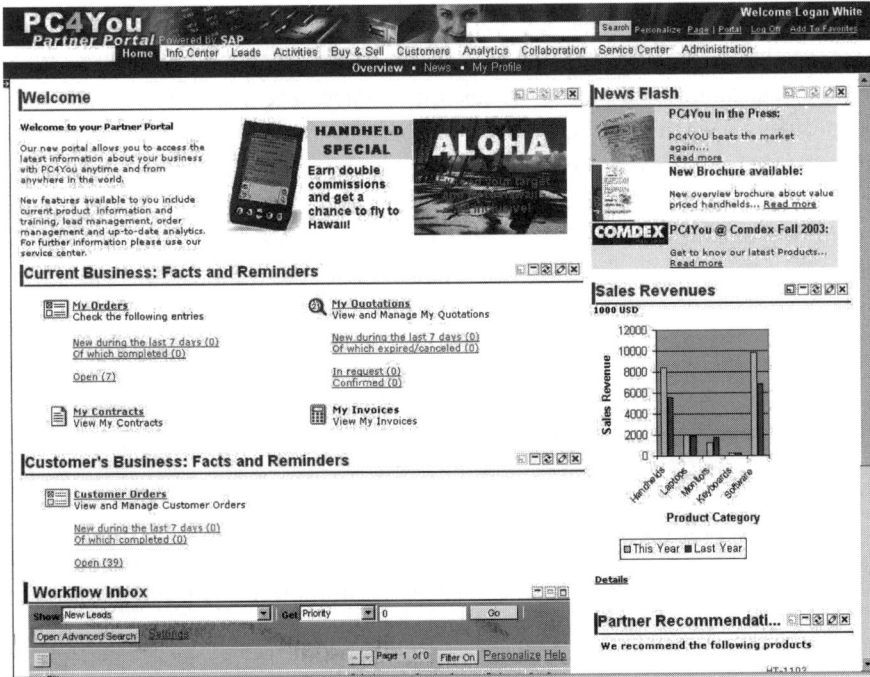

Figure 11.2 Homepage of a Partner Portal

11.3.2 Partner Management and Analytics

The *Partner Management and Analytics* capabilities of mySAP CRM enable companies to manage channel partner relationships more efficiently throughout the partner lifecycle and increase profitability. It contains the following functional areas.

Partner Lifecycle Management

The *Partner Lifecycle Management* capabilities of mySAP CRM enable brand owners to manage their partners throughout the partner lifecycle. They ensure consistent processes with partners from recruitment or applications through approval and ramp-up. This ensures that partners are prepared to efficiently represent the brand owner's products.

Partners are distinguished by their partner profiles. Partner profiles include, for example, partners'addresses, general terms and conditions and accepted payment methods, branches of industry in which they have specialized, product range, qualification, and partner status. Companies need support to create partner profiles for each partner, manage the partner lifecycle, and ensure that the indirect channel is covered and that partner processes are consistent. Often, companies lack a central standardized method for defining partner information and monitoring qualification profiles. Furthermore, many companies do not have an automated way of managing partner applications, registrations, and authorizations.

► *Partner Profiling* enables companies to profile their business partners, who partners are, how they do business, what they sell, where they sell, to whom they sell, what industries they focus on, and what capabilities they have. The profile information also determines how the partner portal is personalized for each type of partner.

► *Partner Registration* enables prospective partners to register online for a partnership by providing Web-based partner registration forms from a corporate Web site. The registration forms are routed to the appropriate internal employees for checking, registration, and ramp-up.

► *Partner Monitoring* provides tools that enable brand owners to monitor partner activities and transactions from a single partner view. Brand owners can review partners' leads, opportunities, orders, and so on.

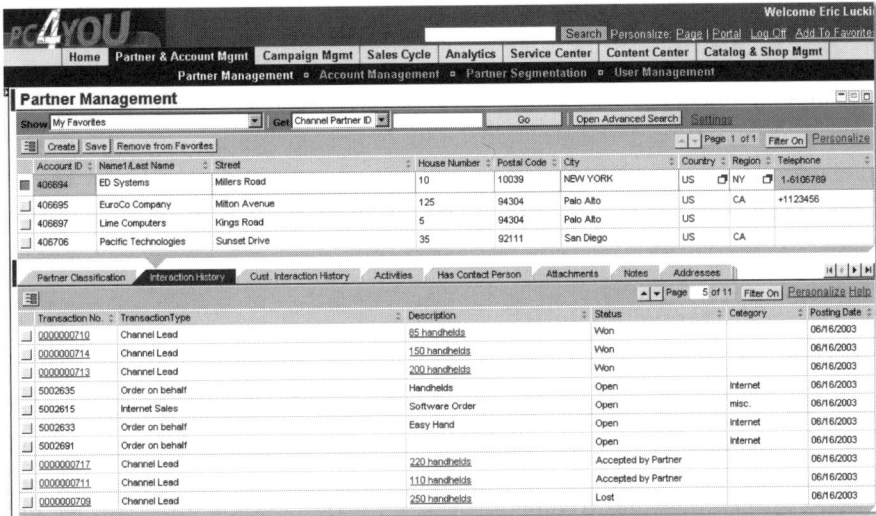

Figure 11.3 Partner Management in the Channel Manager Portal

Partner Planning

Brand owners need a consistent way to plan future indirect channel business and a structured way to manage relationships with channel partners. The mySAP CRM *Partner Planning* capabilities provide tools that enable organizations to plan and manage their sales and channel strategy. Brand owners can set annual goals, objectives, targets, and measurements, as well as track and measure partner progress against those goals.

Partner Segmentation

In order to effectively manage partners, brand owners need a way to segment and target their partner base. Partner information, tools, and processes need to be tailored and targeted based on a partner type (for example, retailer, distributor), partner level, region, and so on. mySAP CRM *Partner Segmentation* enables brand owners to segment partners based on partner type, industry focus, and competencies so they can personalize and target communications, training, marketing efforts, and so on.

Partner Training and Certification

Companies need a way to ensure that partners are effectively educated and prepared to represent their product and services. With the *SAP Learning Solution (e-learning)*, brand owners can provide partners with online access to training courses, curriculum, and registration. They can target courses and information that are most relevant to the right partners. You can track course enrollment, participation, and completion rates for your partners' employees with the SAP Learning Solution.

Furthermore, brand owners can create, target, and manage certification programs for channel partners, and track status and completion at employee level. The numbers of employees certified for products and services can be linked to the partner profile for use in partner analysis, partner segmentation, and lead distribution.

Partner and Channel Analytics

In today's dynamic business environment, brand owners rely on insight into their channel partners—including channel coverage, behavior, trends, and profitability—to effectively manage their partner relationships. The mySAP CRM *Partner and Channel Analytics* capabilities provide a broad range of standard reports and analyses for brand owners to determine partner coverage and gaps, partner and channel performance, revenue and sales statistics, ROI of partner investments, partner gross margins, and partner utilization. This enables brand owners to provide channel partners with reports and analyses relevant to their businesses.

▶ *Sales Analytics* provide sales statistics, top-n lists, and product planning information for brand owners and partners.

▶ *Lead and Opportunity Management Analytics* provide reports for brand owners and partners about lead distribution, success rates, opportunity pipeline, and expected sales value.

▶ *Quotation and Contract Management Analytics* provide reports for brand owners and partners with reports on expected sales values and transition rates of quotations to orders. Furthermore, this function provides brand owners with reports on existing contracts.

11.3.3 Channel Marketing

The *Channel Marketing* capabilities of mySAP CRM enable companies to drive demand for their products through sales and marketing partners. The solution comprises the following areas:

Content Management

Providing appropriate, relevant information and tools to channel partners is critical for maintaining an effective indirect channel. Partners need the right information at the right time in order to effectively sell and service products. Often companies lack the tools to appropriately target and deliver content so that partners are "spammed" with irrelevant information.

Content Management enables brand owners to author, organize, and publish information and tools for their partners. Brand owners can target news about new products, tools, events, and programs for the right partners at the right time. Information is personalized to each partner and employee based on his or her unique business needs. Subscriptions allow partners to subscribe to the content areas of interest to further personalize the content that they receive from the brand owner.

The *Sales and Marketing Library* provides partners with intuitive, searchable and convenient access to a repository of downloadable documents and tools, including marketing documents, presentations, templates, sales tools, product information, price lists, and so on. A search engine enables partners to search for specific content using a wide range of search options and algorithms. Partners have direct access to the information and tools that they need to effectively represent the brand owner's products around the clock.

Catalog Management

Whether purchasing products for themselves, purchasing for end customers or researching products online, partners need simple, intuitive access to all relevant information about a brand owner's products and services. Without such information, partners are unable to provide end customers with accurate product information and pricing.

Catalog Management provides partners with personalized access to up-to-the-minute product information over the Web. This catalog contains product descriptions, specifications, multi-media elements like pictures, pricing, and associated literature. The *Product Catalog Workbench* allows organizations to maintain the catalog hierarchies and product assignments. Tools are available to help organizations manage their catalogs including staging, automatic product assignment, and XML export. Different views of a catalog can be tailored to partners and partner segments to personalize their Web experiences.

Partners can display the catalog in the partner portal and search for products that meet their needs using a powerful search engine. It is also possible to search by product category. Product comparisons in the catalog support customers and partners in making efficient purchasing decisions. Personalized product recommendations supports personalized and generic up-sell/cross-sell of alternate products, related and complementary products, and accessories.

Collateral Management

Brand owners can use mySAP CRM *Collateral Management* to effectively give their partners access to the most current marketing collateral so they can represent their products most effectively.

The collateral catalog provides partners with a complete, hierarchical overview of all available collaterals with descriptions, images, price, availability, related products, and so on. Partners can search the collateral catalog to find the appropriate items and order the desired brochures either for themselves or to be sent directly to the end customers. Electronic versions of the brochures can also be downloaded immediately from the partner portal.

Campaign Management

Demand generation and tracking of marketing investments is critical in a channel environment. Often, companies lack the ability to track channel marketing activities, and don't have visible results and ROI of their channel marketing initiatives. mySAP CRM *Campaign Management* enables brand owners to create and execute targeted, personalized campaigns to drive sales through the channel. Campaign investment and results are tracked and managed centrally (see also Section 7.2.5).

Content Personalization

Whether researching new products, resolving customer issues, or looking for the most current training classes, partners expect the same treatment online as they would receive from an actual contact person. Most companies lack the ability to effectively personalize online information and experiences to provide partners with the best interaction.

The rule-based personalization capabilities of mySAP CRM enable organizations to dynamically personalize partners' Web experiences. Web experiences and content are tailored based on company-defined criteria, for example, type of partner, partner's past purchasing behavior, orders, and predefined buying preferences. The management of personalization standards takes place through a standard editor with user-friendly Web interfaces that are designed for business users.

The portal concept from mySAP CRM also allows role-specific and rule-based personalization. The layout, navigation, and available functions in the channel management portal are tailored and personalized based on the associated role of the user. Adaptable and enhanceable standard roles support the channel personnel in the brand owner organization, as well as personnel in the partner organization. New roles can be defined to accommodate specific personalization requirements.

Lead Management

Lead Management and the matching of demand to partners that are best able to turn leads into sales are critical to the success of any organization with an indirect sales channel. Most companies lack the tools to effectively distribute leads to the right channel partners. Furthermore they have no or very little visibility of the leads once they have been sent.

Lead Management of mySAP CRM provides tools that enable brand owners to capture, route, and manage sales leads to ensure that each lead is directed to the best-fit channel and best-fit partner (see also Section 7.2.7). The following sub-functions are available:

▶ **Lead Generation**
Leads can be captured and created in Channel Management based on uploads of external lists, Web forms for end customers, event-based (for example, from a marketing campaign) creation, or manual creation.

▶ **Lead Qualification**
Leads can be qualified automatically or manually. Automatic lead qualification is based on surveys and associated scoring models. Manual qualification is set based on judgment by the qualifier.

▶ **Lead Dispatching**
Leads can be distributed to partners. The criteria are the partner's location, expertise, customers, and so on.

▶ **Lead Monitoring**
Lead follow-up and conversion rates can be monitored by the brand owner. With this information, brand owners can evaluate the effectiveness and return from individual partners and partner segments.

11.3.4 Channel Sales

mySAP CRM *Channel Sales* provides organizations with the tools to enable partners to sell more of their products, more effectively. Channel Sales consists of the following areas.

Account and Contact Management

In order to successfully manage customer accounts and drive ongoing revenue, both partner and brand owners need full visibility for account information and history. Most companies cannot see their partners' activities with the end customers.

Account and Contact Management enables brand owners to incorporate end customer account information and history into indirect sales processes (see also Section 7.3.4). Both partners and brand owners, according to authorization, can see all customer account information and collaborative activities. This ensures full visibility of the status and customers' circumstances. Partners and brand owners can use search, view, and print functions that are all standard, along with user-friendly interfaces for maintaining customer data and contacts. The customer data sheet provides all essential customer information at a glance.

Activity Management

In a collaborative business environment, it is critical for brand owners and channel partners to be able to track and manage individual and collaborative activities. The *Activity Management* of mySAP CRM provides the tools for brand owners to enable collaborative activity management between their internal team and partners (see Section 7.3.5).

Opportunity Management

In a channel sales environment, it is critical that brand owners and partners have access to and see all the possible customer opportunities. In order to accurately forecast demand and revenue, brand owners rely on their channel partners to obtain information about key opportunities.

Opportunity Management in mySAP CRM gives brand owners and partners a complete overview of all opportunities, including information about an opportunity's history, milestones, progress, and key decision-makers (see also Sections 7.3.6 and 7.3.7). This enables internal sales organizations and one or more partners to work together on any particularly interesting opportunity. In addition, it allows brand owners to gain insight into indirect sales by analyzing leads and opportunities in the partner pipeline.

Pricing and Contract Management

Companies must offer consistent, accurate pricing across all selling channels—including through the indirect channels. Partners and customers need access to accurate, up-to-date pricing, including any special quotes or contracts.

Pricing and Contract Management enables brand owners to manage end customer pricing, partner pricing (including price lists, tiering, contract pricing, discounts, and so on), and rule-based pricing, where pricing is based on the type of customer or partner, product, purchasing volume, or other criteria as defined by the organization (see Sections 7.3.8 and 7.3.10). Customers and partners have real-time access to negotiated and standard prices in the Web shop or partner portal. This enables partners to maintain their own selling prices for end customers.

Interactive Sales and Configuration

Partners need help determining the right mix of products and services to meet the unique business needs of customers, especially for complex, configurable products and options.

Interactive Selling and Configuration provides partners with comprehensive online information to help them choose the products and services that best meet the business needs of their customers. Partners can access multimedia content, guided selling, configuration advice, and real-time pricing to help them provide customers with the right solutions to meet their business needs and technical requirements.

▶ Guided Selling leads partners through a simulated question-and-answer session to help determine which products and services best meet the unique business and technical requirements of their customers.

▶ Interactive Product Configuration, based on SAP's *Internet Pricing and Configurator* provides partners with a comprehensive product configuration solution that ensures the accuracy of complex orders and quotes (see also Section 7.3.9). The product configurator guides partners through the online product configuration process and makes sure that the configuration rules stipulated by the brand owner and permissibility of chosen product options are transferred correctly.

Quotation and Sales Order Management

Partners need support in approving special prices, ordering products, obtaining delivery promises, and tracking their orders throughout the fulfillment process. To ensure superior, uniform service to end customers, companies must deliver simple, personalized, and user-friendly ordering functions to their partners.

The *Quotation and Order Management* capabilities of mySAP CRM enable channel partners to make quotes and order products and services online. The complete fulfillment process is supported, from the point when the order is entered through to shipment and billing (see also Section 7.3.8).

In the partner portal, partners can intuitively and independently research products, inquire about prices, make purchasing decisions, and place orders at any time, from anywhere. Partners have around-the-clock access to real-time order, invoice, shipment, status, and tracking information (for their orders and for customer orders) through the Web shop. Invoices can be checked and paid online.

Multi-Tier Sales Tracking and Forecasting

In a multi-tier sales environment, brand owners struggle to gain insight into actual sales information regarding the end customer—most organizations do not really know what happens to their products after they are sold to their partners (distributors, retailers).

The *Multi-Tier Sales Tracking and Forecasting* capabilities of mySAP CRM enable brand owners to capture and consolidate multi-tier sales information from distributors and retailers to achieve better channel visibility and analyses for indirect sales channels. This allows brand owners to forecast leads and opportunities across all sales channels, including indirect channels. For the first time, they can collaboratively forecast future demand with their channel partners.

Partner Compensation

Compensation is one of the most important motivators for partner loyalty and behavior. Brand owners need a way to create fast and effective compensation plans and communicate these, together with performance information, to their channel partners.

Partner Compensation enables brand owners to design, execute, and administer sales compensation plans for channel partners. Partners can track their current performance, as well as model the potential compensation to their pipelines.

11.3.5 Channel Service

The *Channel Service* capabilities of mySAP CRM provide brand owners with the ability to guarantee end customers consistent and fast service by delivering service and problem solving functions to partners. The function provides partners with the tools and expertise to manage ongoing service relationships with customers. Channel Service includes the following areas:

Partner Knowledge Management

With the right information and tools, partners can resolve customer issues quickly and easily—without involving the brand owner. *Partner Knowledge Management* provides partners with access to the brand owner's solutions database so they can research and resolve customer or product issues. A consolidated repository of symptoms and solutions helps partners to resolve customer issues and inquiries easily without contacting the brand owner (see also Section 7.5.4).

For FAQs and problems, predefined questions can be formulated and linked to solutions. Partners are then able to search a list of FAQs for specific products. In addition, partners can subscribe to service information from the brand owner, including service bulletins, engineering change orders, recall notices, and so on.

Request Management

Partners no longer need to rely on service support employees on the brand owner's side to create and manage service requests for their customers. Instead, partners can create and manage service requests online. Information pertaining to the request may include the name of the end customer, product or installation, requested service, attachments of various document types, and desired appointments for a service visit. mySAP CRM supports complete, integrated service fulfillment processes including planning, recording of time and material used, and billing (see also Section 7.5.3). Service scheduling takes into account the availability of resources with the required profile and skill set. Partners are able to check the progress that has been made on a service request in the partner portal.

Key service request management features include the ability to check entitlements based upon warranty status and existing service contracts.

Live Partner Support

To provide superior partner support, brand owners must provide comprehensive online information that gives partners easy access to a contact person if needed.

The *Live Web Collaboration* capabilities of mySAP CRM allow brand owners to provide immediate assistance to partners across multiple communication channels, including chat, co-browsing, email, and call-back requests. Based on the partners' preferred communications methods, mySAP CRM automatically incorporates all relevant partner information, including portal context, customer profiles, and service histories—and displays it on agents' desktops in real time.

▶ Call Back
Partners can request a call back from a customer service representative within the partner portal. The request is routed to the appropriate representative, who can place a call to the partner by telephone or Web telephony.

▶ Chat
Partners can engage a customer service representative in a one-to-one text chat session for live assistance in the partner portal. The ability of both parties to send messages, files, and links in real time enables fast and effective resolution of partner inquiries and issues.

▶ Co-Browsing
A customer service representative and partner can "meet" in the partner portal, where both parties share control of the same Web session. The customer service representative has access to the same personalized information as the partner.

▶ Email
Partners can engage a customer service representative using email if a real-time response is not required.

Installed Base Management

The *Installed Base Management* function gives partners access to review, manage, update, and analyze the installed base assets of assigned customer accounts. Partners can register recently sold products through the partner portal. Warranty Management provides partners with a current view of the warranty entitlements of end customers. This function enables increased customer service because both brand owner and partners have access to the most up-to-date information on customer installations (see also Section 7.5.5).

Complaints and Return Management

Partners no longer need to rely on service support employees on the brand owner's side to create and manage complaints and returns for their customers. *Complaints and Returns Management* of mySAP CRM enables partners to engage in the complaints and returns processes, both for themselves, and for their end customers. Complaints can refer to a specific end customer, product, or installation. Partners have around-the-clock access to the status of complaints and returns (see also Section 7.5.2).

11.3.6 Channel Commerce

The *Channel Commerce* capabilities of mySAP CRM enable companies to incorporate partners in their eCommerce strategy and enable collaborative selling across organizational boundaries. End customers have access to order products and services across the entire demand network. Channel Commerce comprises the following areas:

Collaborative Showroom

In a collaborative business environment, brand owners need a way to offer their customers a consistent shopping experience, regardless of the way in which products and services are provided. The *Collaborative Showroom* enables brand owners to host a Web shop for collaborative online sales and marketing of products and services. Customers have a single point of access to browse and purchase from across the entire partner network.

Distributed Catalog and Content Management

In an environment where partners are jointly marketing and selling to customers online, brand owners need a way for partners to manage their catalogs and content. *Distributed Catalog and Content Management* enables partners to upload their catalogs and contents for use in collaborative selling to end customers. Partners can make their products, services, pricing, and content available to customers.

Distributed Sales Order Processing

To effectively fulfill customer demand in a collaborative and distributed environment, brand owners need a tool to distribute orders to the appropriate partners. The *Distributed Sales Order Processing* capabilities of mySAP CRM enable brand owners to distribute orders to partners for fulfillment (see also Section 7.4.9).

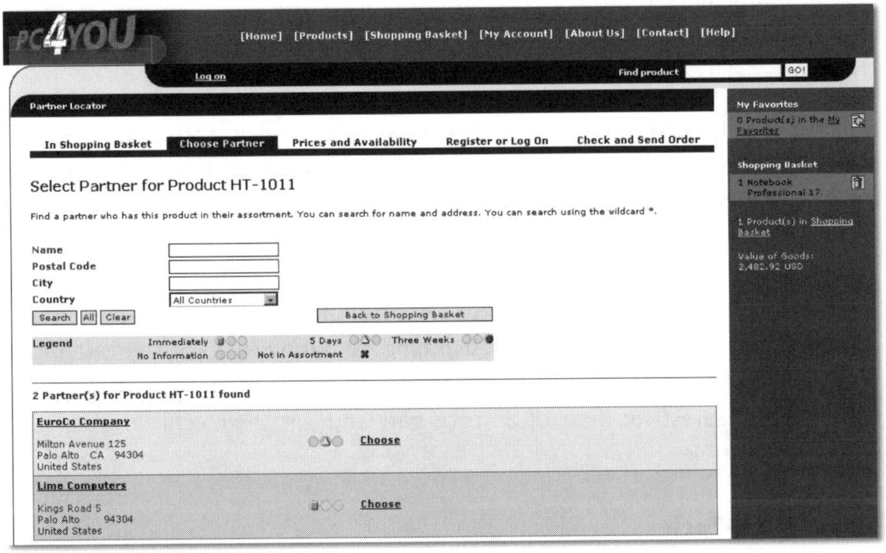

Figure 11.4 Partner Selection in Channel Commerce Scenario

Hosted Order Management

In a distributed business environment, brand owners need a way to support order management processes for channel partners. This is possible with *Hosted Order Management*. This function provides partners with a hosted platform to receive, manage, and fulfill customer orders (that come, for example, from a brand owner's Web shop).

11.4 Industry-Specific Enhancements

11.4.1 Automotive

The automotive business poses a number of special challenges to the management of indirect channels and partners. One reason is that its main product, cars, is at the upper end of the price scale for pre-fabricated goods and therefore has its own "personality."

Vehicles are all individually identifiable, have their own histories and will carry this history with them even if they change owners. *Channel Management for Automotive* of mySAP CRM therefore contains the *Vehicle Management* function that allows brand owners to model these complex relationships and address the resulting data access and visibility requirements. It also enables vehicle-related processes, such as locating a new car from various dealer inventories or ordering it from the manufacturer. Locating and ordering spare parts, and warranty and claim management, are also closely related to the individual vehicle, as is accessory sales.

Another specific area in the automotive industry is the existence of Dealer Management Systems (DMS), the software system that is installed at practically every dealer. Spare parts and vehicle inventories are normally defined in these systems, as well as end customer billing information. An example of such an integration of SAP's *Channel Management for Automotive* with these systems is a spare parts solution implemented at a major European manufacturer. This offers the customers real-time availability of spare parts coming from the dealers' systems (typically DMS inventory systems). Using this channel commerce scenario, customers can identify the nearest location of a spare part and get their vehicle repaired as quickly as possible.

11.4.2 High-Tech

In the high-tech industry, specifically in semiconductors, there is a very special kind of risk-sharing between manufacturers and their partners, distributors, and resellers. Distributors will pay for their inventory, but subsequent price adjustments will be reflected in payments or credits to them (price protection). This reflects the special market dynamics in the semiconductor industry, which sees prices cut in half in a couple of months. In order to efficiently manage this process, the brand owner needs a clear view of the partners' inventory levels.

In addition, due to the substantial influence that resellers can have on the design decisions of Original Equipment Manufacturers (OEMs), it is very important to adequately compensate them for this work. Resellers therefore have to register their initial efforts ("design-in") with an OEM and will be compensated if the established goal is reached, for example, to put a certain number of chips into the OEM product ("design-win"). This special process (called "design registration") ensures that resellers are paid for the actual performance and not based on general assumptions about their effectiveness.

Another very important collaborative process is the negotiation of special pricing for end customers. Especially in very competitive situations the reseller will be required to match the prices of the competitor's reseller ("meet-comp") and therefore sell below reseller price. The brand owner will authorize this special price and then seek reimbursement ("ship and debit").

mySAP CRM addresses all these processes with specific additions to standard CRM functionality. In addition to the operational and analytical side of these collaborative processes, the solution also takes into account that a manual feed of the data is not workable in most cases. Therefore, standardized electronic data interchange (EDI) system-to-system communication channels are provided that can automate the data synchronization between the brand owner and partners.

11.4.3 Telecommunications

For the telecommunications industry, one of the challenges faced when working with partners in the area of mobile phones is the management of the end customer contracts. As these are established between the end customer and the telecom provider, partners act as agents for the provider and have to follow established procedures and policies.

In addition, configuration of products and services can become fairly complex and leads to a lot of potential errors during ordering, contracting, and servicing. Service processes can turn out to be the main driver in deciding the ultimate profit. Therefore, every piece of information enabling the partners to service the end customers more effectively is important for the ultimate goal of indirect channel profitability.

Channel Management for the Telecommunications Industry in mySAP CRM gives partners the right tools to manage contracts and configure even complex products and services online, in real-time, according to the demands of the brand owner.

11.4.4 Use Case: Channel Management with mySAP CRM

Organization PC4YOU distributes its product portfolio to PCs, laptops, and speakers over a network of channel partners with regionally distributed subsidiaries to the end users. PC4YOU places particular importance on end users being looked after competently and therefore regularly checks the sales figures of partner organizations.

Eric Luckins is the channel manager at PC4YOU. He has recently started an email campaign to boost demand for the handheld product line. In May 2003 he evaluated the leads that arose from the campaign. He wants to forward each lead to an appropriate sales channel and assign partner organizations to potential customers to whom they can give the best support. Petra Eder would like to buy 570 handheld devices. Eric therefore decides to give the responsibility for contacting the customer and processing the order to an experienced reseller who is familiar with large sales quantities and has already proven his professionalism. Then he marks the lead as "assigned to a channel partner" and deals with the next prospective customer.

At the end of the month, Eric checks the status of the leads and the sales figures of the channel partners. He sees that the turnover from indirect channel sales has significantly increased from $516.48 in April to $10,369.56 in May. Eric establishes, to his great satisfaction, that the channel partners were able to convert a large percentage of the assigned leads into orders.

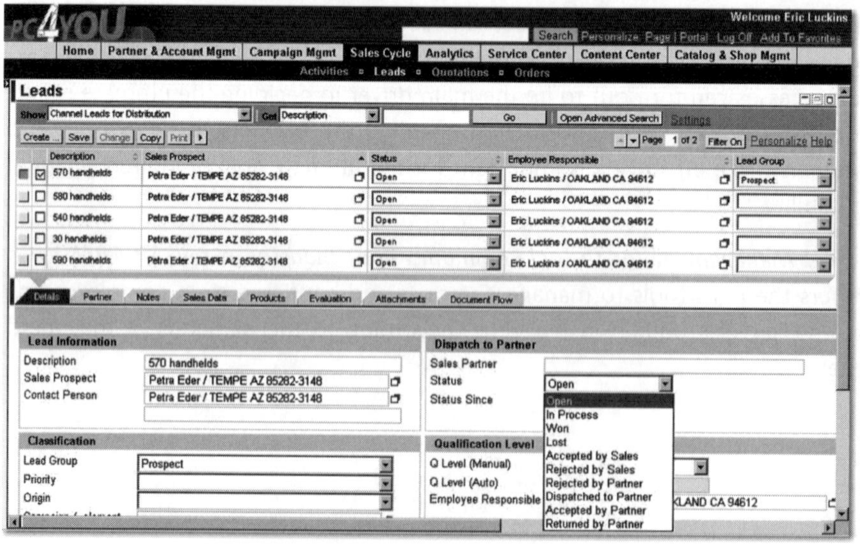

Figure 11.5 Assignment of Leads to Channel Partners

01.2002		$ 956,00
02.2003		$ 258,32
04.2003		$ 516,48
05.2003		$ 10.369,56
Overall Result		**$ 12.100,36**

▽ Chart:

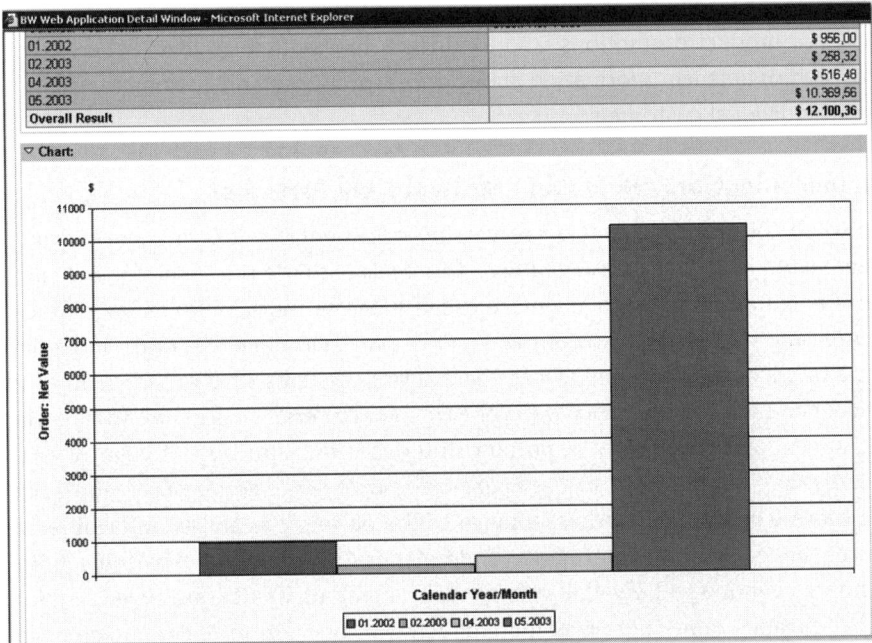

Figure 11.6 Growth in Orders through Channel Partners after Email Campaign

11.4.5 Recommendations for Successful CRM Projects in Channel Management

Basic Principles of Channel Management: Who Are My Partners?

If you sell your products to a retailer or agent and not to the end customer directly, it is essential to know your partners as well as possible: who your partners are, which products they sell, in which regions they operate, the customers or customer groups they sell to, how much turnover they make, the qualifications of their employees, and which additional services they offer. This area is often neglected, but without this basic information, an indirect sales channel cannot be managed well.

Focus on the "Pain Points": Where Do My Partners Most Need Support?

Successful implementation of Channel Management is not so much a question of supporting as many functions as possible using software, as of identifying the core areas and processes critical for business in a particular industry, and concentrating efforts there. Targets could then, for example, be submitting quotes more rapidly, handling the order more efficiently, having a systematic generation and efficient follow-up of leads, collaboratively planning and executing of marketing campaigns or product promotions, and ensuring a constantly high level of service or provision of detailed information about prices, products, and customers, tailored to suit individual customers.

Partner Adoption: "How Can I Motivate My Partners?"

One of the biggest hindrances to successful implementation of a channel management solution lies in *Partner Adoption*. This deals with the problem of many partners being unwilling to actively make use of a partner portal with its information sources and transactions. In contrast to your own sales force, it is much more difficult to encourage partners to use the available systems (this is particularly the case when partners also work with other manufacturers). In addition to financial incentives, usability is very important. Interfaces that are not intuitive or user friendly, or even the need to train partners' employees, can seriously jeopardize the success of a project and acceptance of the partner portal. Last but not least, success depends on the information and functions provided to the partners. If the partners cannot see how the system will benefit them (for example, simpler, faster, cheaper, more, better, or more effective to buy and sell), the implementation project is unlikely to take off. It is important to engage your partners as early and as deeply as possible.

Information Sharing: "Who Sees What"?

One last problem that can prove extremely awkward is the development of a generally accepted concept to manage who can see what in the partner network and how to prevent unauthorized access to data. This is particularly relevant for customer information, if a customer is buying from different partners. This could lead to conflicting interests between the manufacturer and partners (who are mostly in competition with each other). The problem here is not the technical problem or authorizations and access rights (that is dealt with using the software), but the consensus in the partner network with regard to the rules.

11.5 Scenario Overview and Potential Benefits

mySAP CRM offers organizations with channel management a platform to efficiently maintain partner relationships, alert partners to how to sell more of their products, and offer the end customers high-quality service. Cross-industry business scenarios for channel management have different potential focus points.

Cross-Industry Scenarios	Short Description	Potential Benefits		
		Revenue	Profitability	Customer satisfaction
Customer Segmentation with Channel Partners	Post-processing of marketing target groups through individual partners using their individual customer knowledge	✓✓		
Lead Management with Channel Partners	Processing of leads by internal employees and partners Monitoring of project progress	✓✓	✓	
Partner Management	Management of partner relationships throughout the whole cooperation cycle of partner recruitment, registration, planning, segmentation, and training, up to and including certification	✓✓	✓	✓
Catalog and Order Management for Business-on-Behalf	Entry of quotations and orders by the partners in the brand owner's system	✓✓	✓	✓
Collaborative Selling	Provision of a cross-partner order platform with distributed catalog management, collaborative Internet showrooms, and order management for the participating partners	✓✓	✓	✓
Activity Management with Channel Partners	Planning, coordination, and documentation support for joint sales activities	✓	✓✓	
Content Management	Knowledge management and document management for targeted information about sales partners, depending on their profiles	✓	✓✓	✓
Account and Contact Management for Channel Partners	Customer and contact management with common customer knowledge base and other important data	✓	✓	✓✓

There are additional business scenarios available for the needs of the high-tech and telecommunications industries.

Industry-Specific Scenarios	Short Description	Potential Benefits		
		Revenue	Profitability	Customer Satisfaction
Channel Sales Management for the High-Tech Industry	Optimization of collaboration between semiconductor and OEM manufacturers with distributors, contractors, and application engineers	✓✓	✓	✓
Contract Sales in Dealer Portal for Telecommunications	Industry-specific partner portal for activating telephone contracts and telephone cards for mobile telephones	✓✓	✓	✓

12 Decision-Making Support for Employees and Managers—The Analytical Applications of mySAP CRM

12.1 Introduction

Analytical CRM applications primarily support two aspects of customer relationship management. On the one hand, they contribute to individualized personal communication through a comprehensive information base, so that the customer relationship can be systematically improved with each customer interaction performed in the four phases of the customer interaction cycle. On the other hand, analytical CRM applications make the economic consequences of customer interactions and decisions in marketing, sales, and service more transparent, allowing resources to be deployed optimally to attain business objectives.

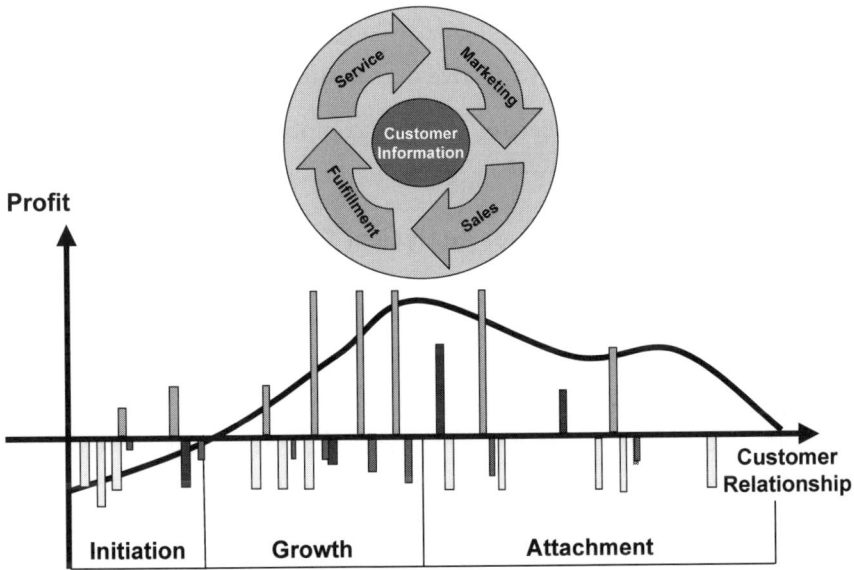

Figure 12.1 Customer Profitability Along the Customer Lfecycle

The return on investment (ROI)of a CRM implementation becomes apparent when a company successfully retains as many valuable customers as possible in a long-lasting partnership. In this way, a CRM implementation must be measured by whether it can optimize the customer value across the entire customer relationship and retain the right customers, and whether turnover with these customers can be increased and their customer lifecycle extended. Analytical CRM applications provide the necessary tools for measuring, predicting, planning, and optimizing, and they supply decision-makers with the right information. Analytical CRM applications help to answer the following types of questions:

- For acquiring new customers:
  - Which types of customers have the potential to drive the future growth of the company?
  - How much money should a company invest in gaining a new customer in a particular customer segment?
- For deepening customer relationships:
  - With which customers can their total spending (customer potential, share of wallet) be increased?
  - What products are normally bought together? Which cross-selling options ought to be considered?
- For lengthening customer relationships:
  - Which customers should be retained as long as possible?
  - Which customers are likely to move over to the competition and why?

The following sections describe the concrete contribution that analytical CRM solutions can make in this context.

12.1.1 Main Challenges for an Analytical CRM Solution

To make interactions and processes with customers as effective and personal as possible, companies need an integrated analysis and planning solution. The following tasks need to be mastered:

- **Central Customer Knowledge Base**
  In nearly all companies, customer information is spread across numerous and often heterogeneous systems. Customer information relevant for decision-making must, therefore, be collected from diverse sources, channels, and communication channels, and combined in a holistic customer knowledge base. A central prerequisite for successfully implementing CRM is, therefore, the coordinated management of customer data (master data, transaction data, and external data). The quality of an analytical CRM solution can be measured by the extent to which it enables a company to integrate all relevant customer information smoothly into a central knowledge base and to keep this knowledge up to date in the course of day-to-day business.

- **Analysis Methods for Measuring and Predicting**
  The true value of a holistic customer knowledge base can be tapped only by deploying a comprehensive system of analysis methods for measuring and predicting. The aim of these methods is both to obtain a deeper understanding of

the customer relationship and to improve the success of all activities in marketing, sales, and service. To this aim, an analytical CRM solution needs to combine a data warehouse for monitoring, analyzing, and distributing information with prediction methods and data mining tools. In customer relationship management, it is not enough to concentrate on the past; it is also a question of looking forward, understanding customer behavior patterns and trends early on, and utilizing these insights.

▶ **Planning Applications**
A great many decisions in marketing, sales, and service cannot be made without a direct reference to target figures. Furthermore, these decisions are largely influenced by plans and budgets. An analytical CRM solution must provide flexible planning applications that are not only embedded in operational processes, but can also simulate the results of "what if" scenarios. For example, the planning of opportunities, campaigns, or promotions should be seamlessly integrated with the creation and simulation of this data. At the same time, CRM plan data must form part of the higher-level sales or enterprise planning that is based on it.

▶ **Operational Use of Analysis Results**
The most important element of an analytical CRM solution, however, is how it allows companies to deploy the analytical results to optimize business processes and customer interactions in their operational systems. This goal is reached only when all employees in marketing, sales, and service are supported in their daily decision-making.

12.1.2 Potential of Analytical CRM Solutions for Adding Value

The introduction of CRM Analytics presents companies with great potential for adding value and offers them the means to improve their business results directly. It allows them to gain a better understanding of customer value and customer needs, ensures that business decisions have a solid foundation, and allows optimization of operational processes.

Better Understanding of Customer Needs and Customer Value

CRM Analytics helps companies to better understand customer needs and preferences and to identify recurring behavior patterns. This lays the foundation for the following possibilities:

▶ Better customer segmentation, optimized approaches to the right customers, and ultimately the deepening of relationships with existing customers through more personal dialog

- Consideration of customer profitability and customer value in all investments in the customer relationship for long-term optimization of the customer portfolio
- Proactive use of cross-selling and up-selling options
- Maximizing customer loyalty by identifying early on valuable customers with a likelihood to churn and retaining these customers
- Gaining new, profitable customers with a similar profile to that of top customers already in the customer portfolio

Improved Coordination and Implementation of Business Decisions

While business objectives, strategies, and departmental targets often fail to be realized in many companies, the implementation of CRM Analytics allows all activities and plans to be geared towards high-level priorities and goals. Without any additional effort, marketing and sales plans flow "bottom up" into higher-level enterprise planning, while business objectives at the company level can be detailed "top down", right down to individual customers. All key figures that are used as control instruments at the process level can be aggregated at area level, linked to any kind of internal or external information, and used for management decisions.

Improved Control and Effectiveness of Operational Processes

CRM Analytics can act as an important catalyst for aligning operational processes in the company with customer wishes. This includes:

- Targeted focusing of resources on important customers and maximizing the profitability of customer relationships. This can be achieved in the following ways, for example:
  - Targeted investments in marketing, sales, and customer service
  - Concentration of attention and services on valuable customers
  - Improvements to the internal processes and efficiency of the company
- Automation and individual design of customer interactions based on solid customer knowledge
- Improved coordination of activities in marketing, sales, and service through forward-looking planning and targets
- Following an enterprise strategy coordinated with marketing, sales, and service

Studies have shown that companies could as much as double their profits just by retaining a small portion of their customers for longer. The Gartner Group estimates that replacing an old customer with a new customer costs up to 10 times more than it does to stop a customer from switching to the competition [Lass-mann/Paris 2000].

12.2 Analyzing and Planning with mySAP CRM

12.2.1 Overview

mySAP CRM contains a complete analysis and planning solution for measuring, predicting, planning, and optimizing customer relationships. It comprises the following components (discussed in detail in the following sections):

► Customer Analytics
► Product Analytics
► Interaction Channel Analytics
► Marketing Analytics
► Sales Analytics
► Service Analytics

Since the analytical applications of mySAP CRM are built on SAP Business Information Warehouse (SAP BW), they are also suitable for heterogeneous system landscapes. SAP BW bundles and consolidates all relevant customer information from a large variety of sources using appropriate data extractors and loading processes for external data. A comprehensive suite of analytical applications draws information from the customer knowledge base for all types of analysis processes, using ready-made business methods and tried and tested business scenarios. These range from simple reporting applications that focus on retrospective analysis and key figure monitoring to forward-looking prediction models that are concerned with future customer behavior patterns. All of this information can be used by classifying procedures or prediction methods (data mining methods), and integration to third-party products is also possible (for example, IBM Intelligent Miner). In this way, past customer behavior can be used to make statements about customers' responses and buying probability and their likelihood to churn.

The planning applications integrated in mySAP CRM are based on SAP Strategic Enterprise Management (SEM) and SAP Business Intelligence (BI). They enable all activities in marketing, sales, and service to be coordinated and managed. The planning applications are characterized by user-friendly interfaces that guide users through processes and flexible customizability for enterprise-specific planning processes.

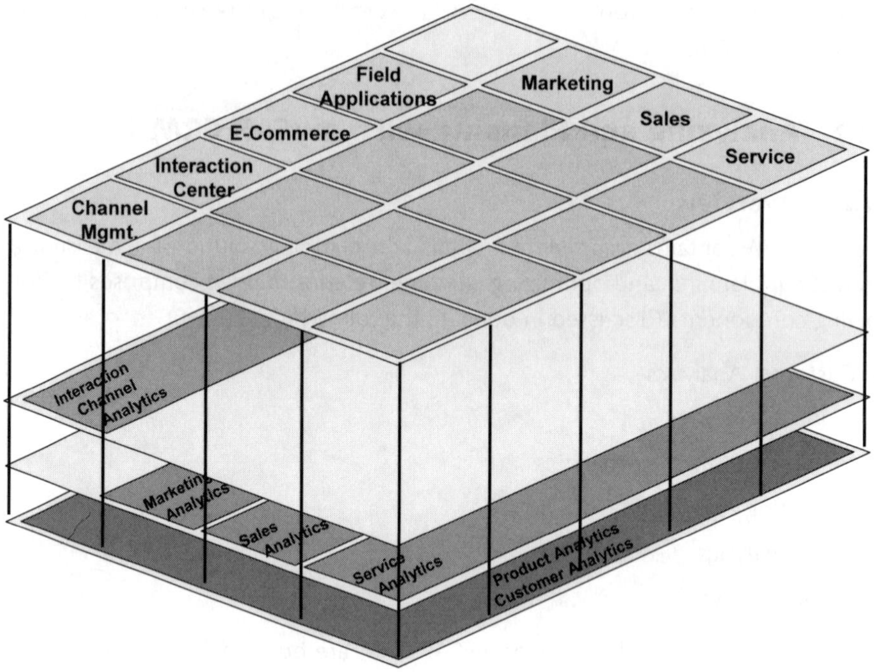

Figure 12.2 Components of mySAP CRM Analytical Applications

Companies can directly apply the analytical business scenarios delivered with mySAP CRM to analyze information gained about customers. It is also possible to enhance these scenarios to meet growing analytical requirements. Data extractors that are also included take care of the automated data exchange between operational and analytical CRM. This doesn't apply just to transaction data, but also to customer interactions, reactions to campaigns, or customer behavior in Web sites, for example. In addition to this integrated data exchange, SAP BW also offers options for loading external data (for example, potential data, market and competitor information) and incorporating this data into the customer knowledge base.

Since analytical and operational CRM share a closely linked system design, analysis results can be evaluated by the end user in the portal as well as integrated into operational processes, forming a feedback loop to marketing, sales, and customer service in a type of closed-loop application.

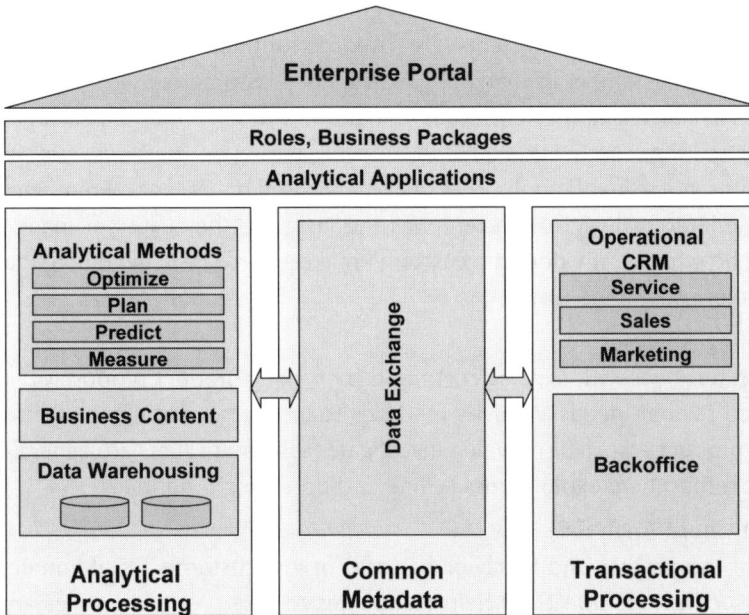

Figure 12.3 Architecture for Integrated Business Scenarios with mySAP CRM

12.2.2 Customer Analytics

A sound analysis of existing customer relationships is the best foundation for developing customer-oriented marketing, sales, and service strategies. Successful companies can anticipate customer needs and even shape and influence them. However, this is possible only with a firm understanding of:

▶ Customer behavior (for example, customer preferences, priorities, activities)

▶ Customer value with respect to customer profitability, customer lifetime value, and anticipated future turnover potential

▶ The composition of a customer portfolio

Analyzing and Modeling Customer Behavior

Various analytical processes embedded in mySAP CRM deal with modeling customer behavior. They provide the company with additional information about who its customers are and what kind of needs they have. Examples of this are:

▶ **Customer Satisfaction and Customer Loyalty Analyses**
These analyses do not just concern using questionnaires to systematically determine customer satisfaction, but also the structured investigation of customer priorities.

- ▶ **Definition of Homogeneous Customer Segments**

  Homogeneous customer segments are used to optimize how a company approaches its customers in marketing, sales, and customer service. Analysis methods such as clustering, customer valuation, and customer classification (customer scoring, see Section 12.2.2), as well as proven methods, such as RFM analysis, are valuable tools. RFM analysis is based on Recency, Frequency, and on Monetary value: How recent was the last time the customer made a purchase, how frequently does the customer make a purchase, how much does the customer usually spend.

- ▶ **Cross-selling Analyses**

  Increase in turnover with existing customers by making product proposals that are tailored to their needs. Analysis methods such as association analysis (for example, product association, which investigates which products are generally bought together) help exploit cross-selling and up-selling potential.

- ▶ **Customer Churn Analyses**

  Analysis of the profiles and behavior patterns of lost customers. Data mining methods such as decision trees help companies to interpret the profiles and churn signals of individual customers, and to use this knowledge proactively for customer retention measures.

These analyses yield key figures, such as the customer satisfaction index, churn rate, and response rate, which can be used to measure the quality of customer relationships and influence them positively.

Example: Churn Analysis

The company PC4YOU is interested in monitoring and analyzing the churn behavior of its customers. As shown in the top right of Figure 12.4, it is interesting to observe the number of customers lost over time and then to determine *customer loss rates*.

Using simple reporting techniques, churn behavior can now be viewed in the context of complaints received or for particular product, sales, or service areas. Using an assumption (such as considering customers as lost if they do not make a purchase over four months), mySAP CRM enables customers to be separated into active and lost customers.

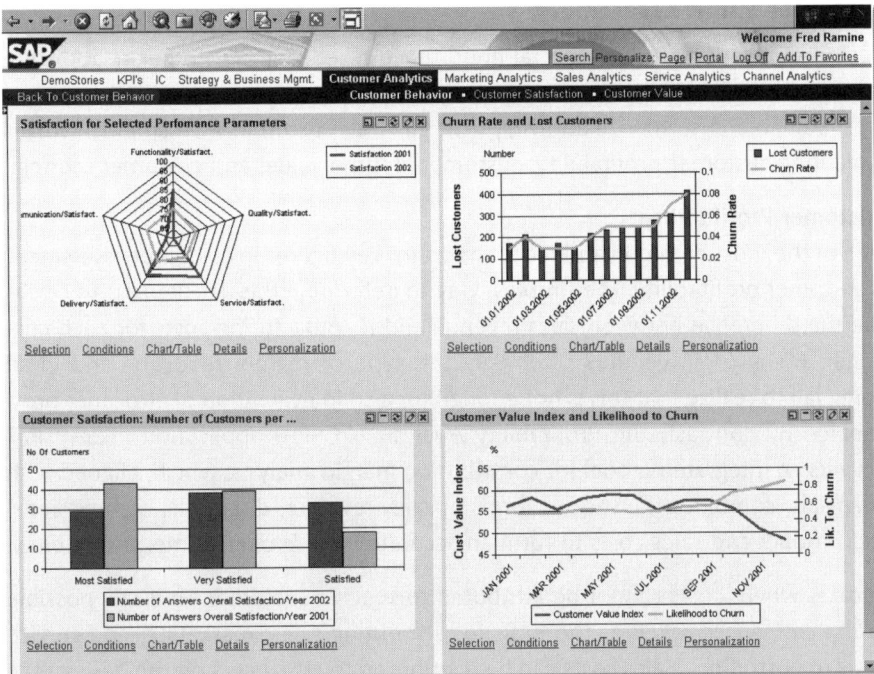

Figure 12.4 Key Figures for Customer Behavior

With observing the number of customers lost, companies are interested in obtaining answers to the following types of questions:

▶ What kind of profiles do lost customers have?

▶ Is it possible to identify particular patterns that recur often?

▶ How valuable were the lost customers for the success of the company?

To investigate possible dependencies, PC4YOU can use decision trees. The results of the decision trees show that customers' likelihood to churn is dependent on the class of product bought and the family situation of the customer.

To channel this information as directly as possible into customer retention measures, PC4YOU uses this procedure to determine the likelihood to churn of its existing active customers. The information gained can now be incorporated into reminder scripting for Interaction Center agents, for example, so that they can tailor their interactions more appropriately to the individual customers, and thereby proactively retain them.

Customer Value Assessment

Customer assessment is of central importance to efficient customer relationship management. It helps companies concentrate limited resources on the best and most valuable customer relationships. In general, customer assessment involves evaluating customer profitability, customer lifetime value, and customer scoring.

Customer Profitability

One of the most common and most important key figures in customer assessment is customer profitability. The simplest way to determine this key figure is to calculate the difference between sales revenue and manufacturing costs for each customer. Many CRM vendors offer only this type of margin reporting and in so doing fail to realize that this is not enough for a solid evaluation of customer profitability. By contrast, the Profitability Analysis (CO-PA) application in SAP R/3 delivers an integrated model for contribution margin analysis, which, aligned with financials, combines the various forms of sales revenue, discounts, commissions, and product and sales costs to form an accurate picture of customer profitability.

In cases where costs cannot be attributed to specific customers, it is still possible to use *cost driver values* as the basis for attributing sales, marketing, and service costs to customers. Sales costs can be distributed to customers on the basis of the number of customer activities performed, for example. This produces a straightforward assignment of customer-related costs (such as costs incurred in customer visits, support, or campaigns). It goes without saying, though, that customer profitability is not a substitute for product profitability, which remains a decisive factor for company success. Figure 12.5 shows what is involved in customer profitability.

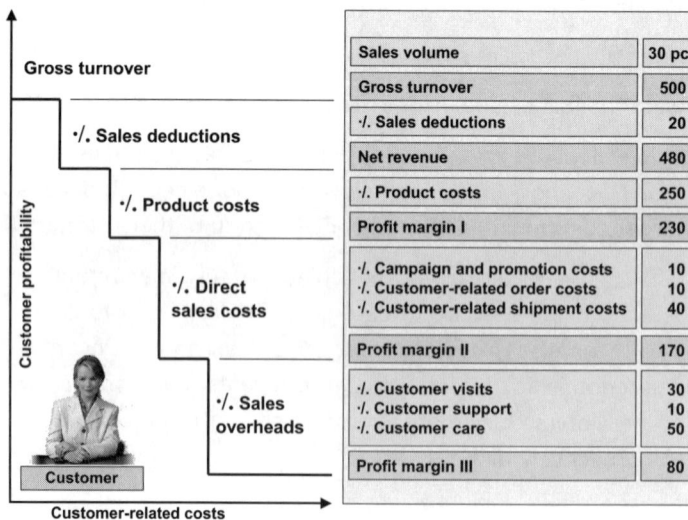

Sales volume	30 pc
Gross turnover	500
·/. Sales deductions	20
Net revenue	480
·/. Product costs	250
Profit margin I	230
·/. Campaign and promotion costs	10
·/. Customer-related order costs	10
·/. Customer-related shipment costs	40
Profit margin II	170
·/. Customer visits	30
·/. Customer support	10
·/. Customer care	50
Profit margin III	80

Figure 12.5 Customer Profitability

Customer Lifetime Value

It is hard to believe, but a company's most important capital does not appear in its financial statement—the list of its active customers! What is more, the financial statement fails to reflect the hardest and most expensive sales transaction: the very first that is made with a new customer.

Once a company has gained the confidence of a customer, the road is then paved for many subsequent purchases. Furthermore, customer recommendation can generate more new customers. Customers should therefore be viewed as investments that need to be valuated, protected, and incorporated into decision-making.

Customer lifetime value refers to the current net value of the profit that a company can make with an average new customer in a specific customer segment over a specified number of years. This is the true value of a customer, and it is this value that should be considered in decisions affecting investments in new customers. Unlike customer profitability, which relates to a calendar period view, the customer lifetime value is based on lifecycles and therefore provides a measure for the maximum amount that a company should invest in seeking to gain a new customer. With the integration to the SAP R/3 back-end, SAP's Customer Lifetime Value solution deploys profitability data that is stored in Profitability Analysis (R/3 CO-PA) and transferred to SAP BW using the extractors included with the solution. On the basis of this data, the Customer Lifetime Value application determines the desired customer retention rates as well as how the customer value has developed over the entire customer relationship. It then delivers the information in integrated form for marketing decisions.

Customer Classification and Customer Scoring

Customer key figures such as contribution to sales or contribution margin can also be used to classify the customer master using ABC classification. In this way, companies can determine, for example, what share of company sales or profit is made with what percentage of their customers. The customer classes generated can be used directly for operational customer handling or they can be the object of detailed customer churn analyses.

In Customer Scoring, various customer-relevant aspects are weighted and deployed in a comprehensive assessment of the individual customers. For example, overall customer attractiveness and satisfaction can be valuated and then combined to form a single valuation key figure for each customer.

With this type of overall valuation of customers, it is not possible to exclude subjective estimations completely. However, Customer Scoring offers the great advantage of enabling quick and efficient customer valuations that can be implemented immediately in the Interaction Center or in the service area, for example, for customer retention measures. Furthermore, such a key figure forms the basis for considerations about what customers make up the customer portfolio.

Optimizing the Customer Portfolio

In analyses for strategic decisions in marketing, sales, and service, it is not usual to run searches for specific characteristics on every single customer. It is far more typical for decisions to be made on the basis of the overall composition of the customer base. The analysis of the customer base with the customer portfolio, an appropriate classification of the customer profiles, is an important tool for optimizing the type of customers that make up the customer base. For example, customers can be divided up into different categories (such as profit-making customers, star customers, question mark customers, and profit-taking customers) on the basis of the key figures *Customer Attractiveness* and *Intensity of the Customer Relationship*. Other key figures, such as the customer score, can be applied for valuating customers or customer groups to assist in the selection of measures for optimizing the customer portfolio by acquiring new customers or securing the customer base.

12.2.3 Example: Customer Valuation and Scoring

More and more companies are discovering the fact that only a relatively small number of customers actually makes a significant contribution to the company result. Consequently, it is essential to make transparent the significance of individual customers to the company by applying suitable methods for ABC classification and scoring, and then to consider this significance in all decision-making regarding customers. Figure 12.6 (top left) shows, for example, that about 10% of customers account for a 30% share of sales and a 45% share of the company revenue.

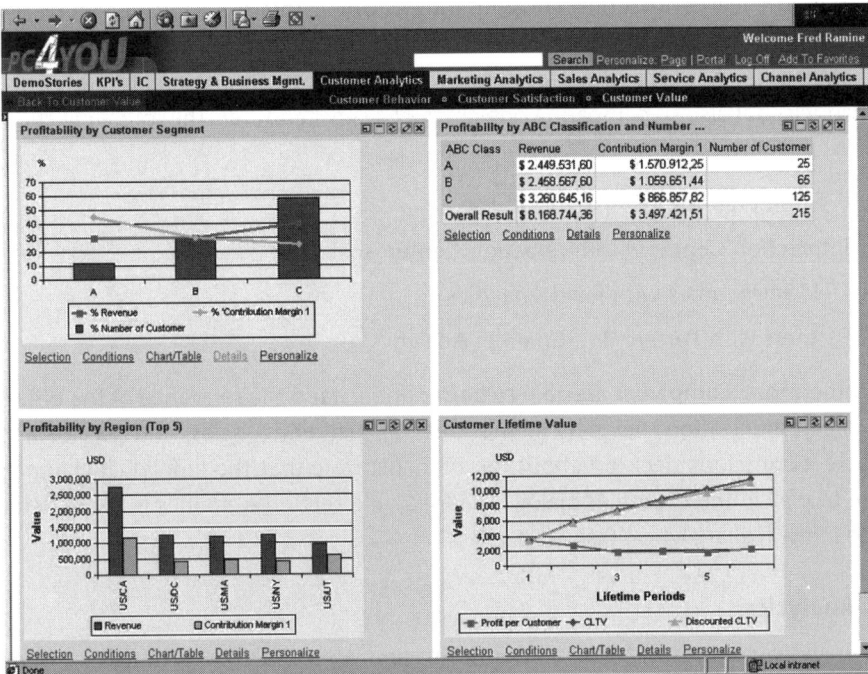

Figure 12.6 Customer Valuation Using CRM Analytics

12.2.4 Product Analytics

The importance attributed to customer orientation and thereby customer-specific analyses should not cause the analysis of the products themselves to be neglected. Companies need to monitor to the same extent product profitability, and the services and complaints associated with products and product groups. Here again, companies benefit from using SAP's Profitability Analysis component, which determines contribution margins in a broad range of dimensions. In the same way as the customer, region, or sales office, the product is considered an analysis level to which revenues and costs can be allocated. Supported by the years of experience SAP has in controlling, companies can analyze product revenues and costs to a detailed level of differentiation.

12.2.5 Interaction Channel Analytics

The choice of communication channel can make the difference between profitable and unprofitable customers. mySAP CRM therefore contains analyses that examine the usage and performance of the different interaction channels such as e-commerce, Interaction Center, field sales force, or channel partner. This is what fundamentally distinguishes the SAP solution from point solutions currently available on the market that only consider the customer from the perspective of a single communication channel. mySAP CRM offers companies not only the option of analyzing key figures and performance relating to the individual communication channels, but also of comparing one channel against another. The following channels are considered:

▶ E-commerce with E-Analytics

▶ Interaction Center with Interaction Center Analytics

▶ Field sales forces with Field Analytics

▶ Partners with Partner and Channel Analytics

Furthermore, companies are able to better understand the relevance of the different communication channels in the areas of marketing, sales, and service and make a conscious decision about the particular role that the individual channels are to play in the customer dialog. The following section examines in more detail the individual analytical task areas.

E-Analytics

E-Analytics comprises Web Site Monitoring and Web Analytics. Whereas *Web Site Monitoring* is more concerned with the technical aspects of the availability and performance of Web servers and Web sites, *Web Analytics* targets analyzing user behavior in the Web shop (see also Sections 9.2.4 and 9.4.7).

Key figures that typically occur in Web Site Monitoring are number of visits, dwell times, number of pages viewed, number of files downloaded and their type, or the pages that led visitors to the Web site. Web Site Monitoring enables companies to quickly remedy weak spots in Web sites and to measure the success of email or banner campaigns.

Web Analytics makes a significantly greater contribution to the analysis of customer behavior. It enables companies to sift out interesting Web events and customer activities (such as downloads, searches, or order transactions). Extensive market-basket analyses can be performed, ranging from visit frequency to first purchase (*conversion rate*), from customer interests to the customer structure.

Interaction Center Analytics

Interaction Center Analytics addresses different areas of decision-making. First, it makes the workload and the rate at which incoming queries are processed transparent. For this, Interaction Center statistics are applied. Typical key figures like connection volumes, average processing time, or abandonment rates are placed in the foreground of the analysis. This information can be used in resource planning, for example, or in the assessment of Interaction Center agents.

Moreover, permanent efforts are made in the Interaction Center to increase efficiency. The effectiveness of the *interactive scripts* (see also Section 10.3.1) and the extent to which they are used is tested continuously and analyzed on a regular basis.

Field Analytics

The most expensive distribution channel is without doubt direct sales. It is therefore indispensable to monitor this communication channel continuously and to direct scarce resources to the most promising sales opportunities. Field Analytics helps management make such decisions.

Partner and Channel Analytics

Partner and Channel Analytics analyzes the performance of indirect sales. At the same time, it allows partners to implement the analysis tools and to use the insights gained to optimize success (see also Section 11.3.2).

12.2.6 Marketing Analytics

The decisive factor for the success of marketing is the quality of the information that is available. Knowledge of personal details about a customer makes it possible to analyze information concerning markets and competition and to optimize the success of marketing initiatives and campaigns early on—right from the planning phase. Economic success can then be valuated during and after the implementation of marketing measures using the actual data posted.

On the one hand, the analytical marketing applications delivered with mySAP CRM enable companies to achieve detailed insights and analysis results, and to use simulations when planning campaigns. On the other hand, the closed-loop applications also allow companies to derive the economic growth that a campaign represents. The following areas are covered by Marketing Analytics in mySAP CRM:

▶ Market and competitor analyses
▶ Marketing budget planning and analysis
▶ Analysis of external lists
▶ Target group optimization
▶ Campaign planning
▶ Marketing optimization and refinement

- Campaign monitoring and success analysis
- Lead analysis

All of the above-listed marketing scenarios are described in Section 7.2.

12.2.7 Sales Analytics

Reliable sales information is practically indispensable for every company. mySAP CRM delivers ready-to-use analysis cockpits that provide all the relevant information for sales tasks and decisions.

Sales employees and their managers need to have not only a clear picture of the current revenue situation and of goal achievement in their areas, but also predictive information concerning the sales pipeline and the future development of revenue. Relevant key figures about customers as well as about the success and reach of past sales activities help manage the activities and decision-making in sales. An essential characteristic of the analytical applications of mySAP CRM is that this information is drawn not just from sales sources but also from Logistics, Accounting, and Human Resources.

Sales Analytics comprises the following areas:

- Sales planning and forecasting
- Funnel and pipeline analysis
- Opportunity planning and analysis
- Analysis of sales activities
- Analyses of Contracts, Offers, Orders, and Billing Documents
- Sales performance analysis

For a description of these business scenarios, see Section 7.3.

12.2.8 Service Analytics

The efficiency of customer service directly influences customer satisfaction and loyalty. To provide customers with professional services, service employees require a broad spectrum of information about the customers, their importance to the company, their contracts, and their history. These information requirements cannot be met just by analyzing the service processes themselves (key figures regarding the service tasks that have been processed, are still to be dealt with, or are still open). Information on customer profiles and customer profitability is just as important as information relating to the product or the employee.

The customer satisfaction and loyalty analysis is of particular significance in this respect. It enables service employees to measure the level of satisfaction among customers, and from there to analyze the customer priorities and factors that substantially influence the level of satisfaction. mySAP CRM provides service employees and management with an extensive range of information sources and key figures that can be deployed for managing services, in planning, and for decision-making.

Service Analytics comprises the following areas of analysis:

▶ Strategic service planning

▶ Quality analysis

▶ Service contract and order analysis

▶ Warranty analysis

▶ Profitability analysis

▶ Sales performance analysis

These business scenarios are described in Section 7.5.

12.3 Analytical Applications for Customer-Oriented Enterprise Management

The close link between customer and company value is borne out by the fact that the market value of a company depends to a large extent on the value of its customer base. Companies therefore need to rethink how they can gain and retain customers in highly competitive markets. Every company must learn how to successfully implement customer-oriented strategies and turn visions into actions without delay. Software-based management systems can assist companies in aligning their strategies with the operational processes.

The *Balanced Scorecard* method developed by Robert Kaplan and David Norton [Kaplan/Norton 1996] enables company strategy to be converted into understandable terms that can be communicated, monitored, and implemented. It provides a comprehensive key figure system for enterprise management that not only generates traditional financial figures, but also incorporates non-monetary figures such as customer satisfaction and the company's ability to innovate. Such figures can be evaluated, for example, by analyzing complaints or returns data or the number of new product developments per given time unit. All measurements are placed in relation to each other so that activities necessary in the short term as well as long-term company strategies, can be derived.

Companies can deploy the *SAP Strategic Enterprise Management* component to convert company goals into concrete strategies for marketing, sales, and customer service, and ultimately into the achievement of operational goals. The implementation of this strategic management system, combined with the analysis functions and key figures delivered with CRM Analytics, creates excellent foundations for deploying customer orientation as a strategy across the company.

12.3.1 Example: Integrated Planning in CRM

The company PC4YOU sets great store by organized success monitoring, predictive planning of company goals, and coordination of all activities and measures. The sales planning functions of mySAP CRM allow for short planning cycles and support the interplay of top-down and bottom-up planning, common practice in most companies (Figure 12.7).

The great advantage offered by the SAP solution is that the planning of company goals is fully integrated with the corresponding detail plans in mySAP CRM. For example, detailed opportunity planning provides the basis for the sales plan, which can be set up by the sales division (bottom-up). Once drawn up, the detail plans then flow into strategic enterprise planning.

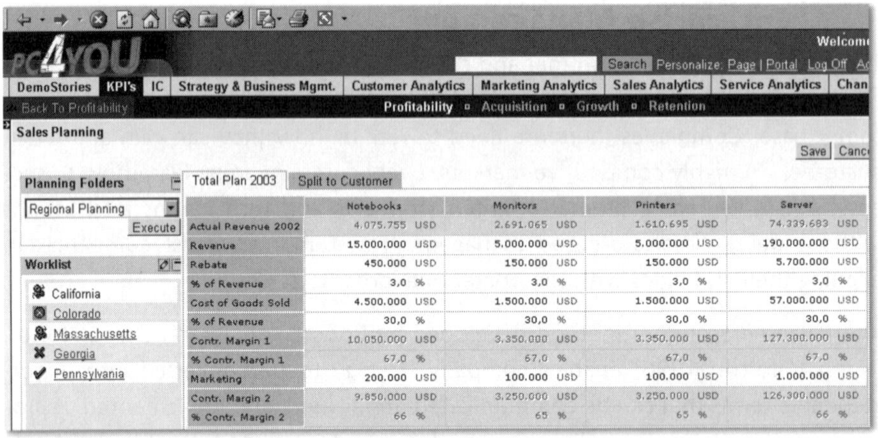

Figure 12.7 Sales Planning

12.3.2 Example: CRM Analytics

The company PC4YOU would like to provide its sales, marketing, and service divisions with extensive customer information as the basis for optimized decision-making. First, to retrospectively valuate the success of sales and marketing, the sales and profitability data of all sales channels at PC4YOU are transferred automatically into the analysis platform, SAP BW.

Employees in sales and marketing use analysis cockpits in a Web portal to access all of the key figures gathered and analyze them.

Fred Ramine is sales manager at PC4YOU. By analyzing the sales and contribution margin of the regional sales areas in the USA, he establishes that the contribution of California to company profitability falls 65% short of the plan values. Using the detail view to examine the shares that the individual product divisions have of the sales and contribution margins, Fred sees that this variance can be traced back to sales in different areas failing to meet the planned targets. With a variance of 68%, the area of e-commerce was furthest from the plan figures, achieving sales of only $42,157,506 instead of the $125,109,712 planned.

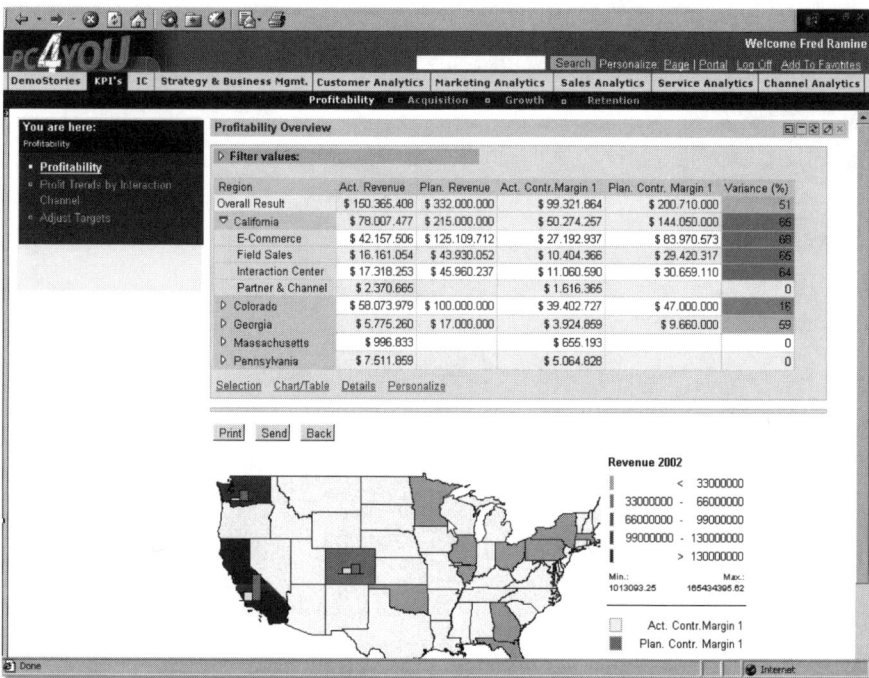

Figure 12.8 Measuring and Monitoring Sales and Contribution Margin Figures

Fred now explores ways of improving the California sales figures and concentrates first on the notebook division. He consults the cross-selling analyses performed in SAP BW, which enable him to establish that approximately 22% of PC4YOU customers buy the notebook Professional 17 in combination with the laser printer Professional Eco (*Support* in Figure 12.9, that is, the overall probability of both products being bought together).

More than 41% of customers who have already decided to buy a notebook add a laser printer to their cart (*Confidence* in Figure 12.9, that is, the dependent probability that a customer who is buying one product also selects a second product).

The high dependency between the two products can be exploited in the future with improved cross-selling by proactively informing prospects in the notebook division about the selling points of the PC4YOU printer during the sales conversation.

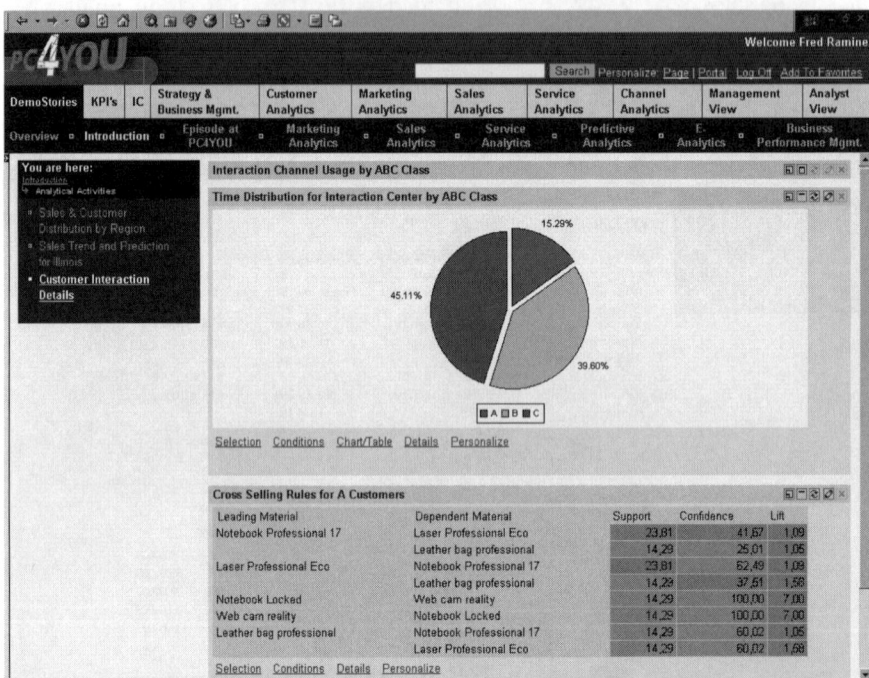

Figure 12.9 Example of Cross-Selling Analysis with SAP's Association Analysis

These cross-selling rules can now be uploaded into the CRM system. Their integration means that they can be used for specific target groups in the Interaction Center or in the Web shop.

Furthermore, Fred can now use this information as part of a targeted cross-selling campaign. For this, he valuates the results of earlier campaigns with regard to their response rates.

The calculated response probabilities tell him that a response rate of 9.3% can be achieved when call center agents call customers in person, and this is considerably greater than the response rate of 5.1% achieved by contacting customers in writing. To obtain these results, SAP uses RFM analysis. In the past, the worst response rates were always achieved with email campaigns. Using the expected costs and revenues, Fred can now distribute the target group of the marketing campaign optimally across the different interaction channels. For this distribution, various aspects—such as capacity restrictions in the Interaction Center or product availability—are taken into account.

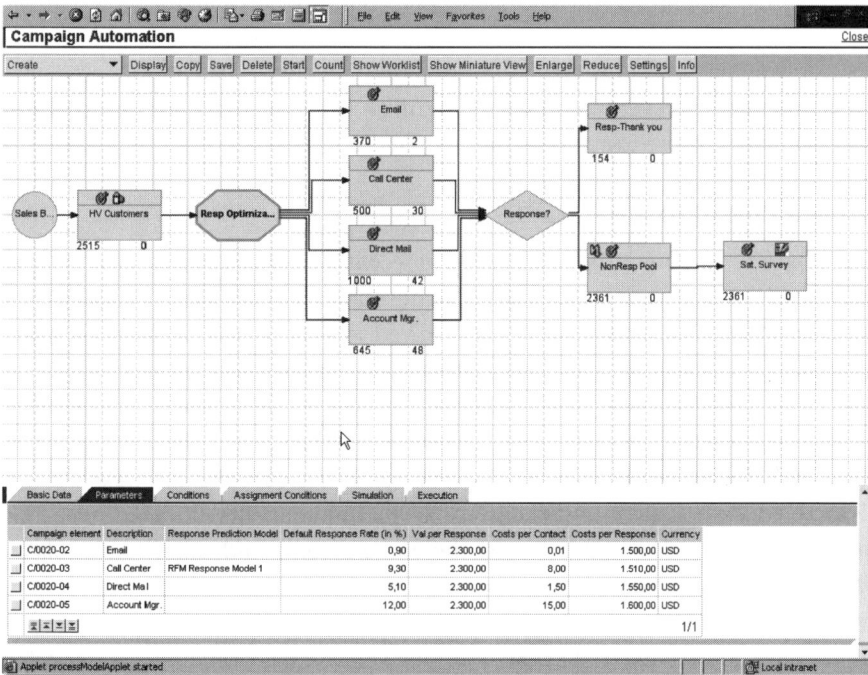

Figure 12.10 Optimizing a Marketing Campaign Using Response Probabilities

12.3.3 Recommendations for Successful CRM Projects in Analytics

Focusing on the Business Problems

Key figures are not determined and analyzed for their own sake, of course, but as a means to an end. The purpose is to help find answers to specific business problems. With this in mind, two possible approaches can be applied for analytical CRM applications, both of which have proven successful in practice.

When a solution comes up against concrete operational problems, the implementation of the scenario should be integrated closely with the process concerned. If systematic analysis forms the main focus and analysis results are not required immediately by operations, then a comprehensive CRM Analytics scenario can be used. When building analytical scenarios, the focus should be on which goal is primarily to be achieved by implementing the scenario.

CRM Analytics Scenarios for Analyzing Data in Areas of Weakness

The first strategy integrated with the process is concerned with analytical support for a few minor aspects. For example, Campaign Monitoring and Campaign Success Analysis analyze campaign management processes. Data collection is concerned first of all with information directly related to marketing campaigns. In this way, only minimal effort is needed to examine campaign data with targeted analyses soon after the event in order to determine the causes of poor results and to gear campaigns more towards market requirements.

Using a Consolidated Data Basis

Although implementing the solution in line with processes helps solve specific problems, this approach is not always the best one. An incomplete data basis prevents concrete problems from being resolved rapidly. This is because campaign monitoring, for example, initially ignores certain interaction channels or dispenses with comprehensive data consolidation. If it is not so much a matter of remedying weaknesses currently in operations, a more comprehensive implementation strategy should be chosen instead. Such a strategy uses a consolidated data basis for all medium-term analysis and decision-making requirements. It includes all communication channels and data across the entire system landscape. Any duplicate data (occurring, for example, due to variances in customer numbers between the systems concerned) first have to be reconciled. In the first instance, this produces an accurate and reliable data basis. Although this initially requires greater effort prior to starting any analyses, the CRM Analytics scenarios of this second strategy provide a better base in the long term for the optimization and further development of customer relationship management.

12.4   Scenario Overview and Potential Benefits

For measuring, predicting, planning, and optimizing customer relationships, the following business scenarios are delivered with mySAP CRM and can be applied in any industry.

Cross-Industry Scenarios	Short Description	Potential Benefits		
		Revenue	Profitability	Customer Satisfaction
Product Analytics	Analysis of the products and product properties preferred by customers as well as the analysis of product profitability	✓✓	✓	
Marketing Analytics	Optimization of the efficiency and effectiveness of marketing measures on the basis of market analyses, ranging from the predictive assessment of marketing programs to the concluding success analysis	✓✓	✓	✓
Sales Analytics	Optimization of the efficiency and effectiveness of sales processes, entailing sales planning, predictive analysis of business trends, and corresponding pipeline analyses, and concluding with success analysis in sales	✓✓	✓	✓
Service Analytics	Planning and controlling service activities and processes, with success analysis	✓✓	✓	✓
Interaction Channel Analytics	Analysis and comparison of the performance of the individual communication channels. Additional analytical functions for each communication channel in the following business scenarios: E-Analytics, Partner and Channel Analytics, Field Analytics, and Interaction Center Analytics	✓	✓✓	
Customer Analytics	Analysis of customer behavior and customer value to optimize and personalize how a company approaches customers	✓	✓✓	✓

13 Implementing mySAP CRM in the Enterprise

"Despite the negative press buzz, most firms say they are pleased with both their CRM business results and app vendor."
Forrester Research [Temkin/Schmitt/Herbert 2003]

13.1 Business View

13.1.1 Experience Gained from CRM Projects

Many a customer relationship management (CRM) project in recent times failed to achieve its ambitious goals. The reasons for this were quite different in nature but normally had less to do with the software implemented than the organizational or strategic deficits in the enterprise itself (see Section 13.2). However, experts believe that these problems are now understood and resolved, meaning that the expectations of CRM projects can be met [Nelson/Marcus 2002]. In February 2003, Forrester Research published the results of an investigation of 111 large American enterprises [Temkin/Schmitt/Herbert 2003]. In answering how they rated their experience with CRM projects, 75% of the respondents claimed to be satisfied with the business success resulting from the projects. The consulting company PricewaterhouseCoopers reports a similarly positive assessment of CRM projects, based on a survey of 402 of the fastest-growing American product and service enterprises [PricewaterhouseCoopers 2003]. According to this survey, 81% of these businesses have implemented customer relationship management projects in the last three years. The majority of the enterprises questioned intends to build on these existing initiatives or even initiate new projects in the future. Precisely those enterprises that have registered a particularly high economic growth in the past are planning to invest in new or enhanced CRM projects in the near future.

A number of SAP customers also reports significant business benefits achieved through implementation of mySAP CRM. For example, Brother International Corp. is expecting investment in its CRM solution to yield a return on investment (ROI) of 129%, determined as the internal rate of return (IRR, see Section 13.1.2). The following enterprises also report on the ROI of their CRM solution: Canada Post (IRR: 26%), Digital Wellbeing (IRR: 72%), IPSOA (IRR: 30%), Ratiopharm (IRR: 63%), Villeroy & Boch (IRR: 30%), Water Corporation (IRR: 35%), and Tyrolit (IRR: 83%). Detailed ROI reports on all named enterprises can be found under [SAP 2003a].

13.1.2 Return on Investment for CRM

Increased cost-consciousness and diminishing IT budgets are causing more and more enterprises to check the economic value of their IT investments in advance using profitability analyses. These analyses assess the profitability of an investment using an ROI key figure that mirrors the relationship between the amount of investment and the economic benefit this investment generates. Generally accepted ROI key figures are:

▶ **Payback Period**
Time required to reach the break even point, in other words, time needed for the invested capital to be regained

▶ **Net Present Value**
Net value that describes the appreciation caused by the investment as a present value of all future cash flows from the investment (depreciated by lowest rate of return available on the capital market) minus the initial investment. A positive net present value means that the investment will generate more money than can be earned with the lowest rate of interest available on the capital market.

▶ **Internal Rate of Return (IRR)**
Corresponds to the interest rate on the market, where the net present value of the investment equals zero. The internal rate of return is often used as a measure for the proper interest rate of an investment.

An overview of ROI calculation for IT investments, more information, and examples can be found in [Computerworld 2003], for example.

While the costs of a CRM investment in practice are relatively simple to measure, it is considerably harder to determine the economic benefit. It is often either difficult to attribute the direct improvement of enterprise processes to the implementation of CRM or these improvements cannot be assessed financially. The following example will show how it is nevertheless possible to measure previously hard to quantify or unquantifiable benefits of CRM investments in monetary terms, using a special method.

Determining the Costs of CRM Projects

The costs incurred during the implementation of an IT project can be structured according to various criteria. Companies often differentiate between one-off and ongoing costs, and between material costs and personnel costs [Kargl 1996]. One-off costs occur mainly through purchasing, implementing, and configuring the application system. Ongoing costs arise through the operation of the application solutions, including all follow-on costs for maintenance, customizing, and functional enhancements. The total cost of software along the entire life and use cycle are described by the TCO (total cost of ownership) value. Figures 13.1 and 13.2 show an overview of the major one-off and ongoing costs that arise during CRM projects. This assumes that a basic IT infrastructure already exists. Investments in networks and plant work, as well as special room layout such as physical access control or air conditioning, are not taken into consideration.

One-off costs
Implementation costs by IT staff
> – Analysis
> – Conception
> – Training
> – Integration
> – Test
> – Documentation

Implementation costs by departmental staff
> – Analysis
> – Conception
> – Training
> – Downtime/changeover period

Implementation costs by consultancy services
> – Analysis
> – Conception
> – Realization/Configuration
> – Modification
> – Data migration
> – Integration/Interfaces
> – Test
> – Training
> – Organizational change
> – Documentation
> – Travel costs

Acquisition costs/investments
> – Software production system
>> • Server licenses
>> • User licenses
>> • Customizing by manufacturer if req.
> – Software development and test system
>> • Server licenses
>> • User licenses
> – Hardware
>> • Purchase
>> • Installation
> – Tools
> – Material

Other project costs
Staff-related overhead costs

Figure 13.1 One-off Costs of CRM Projects [Beringer 2001]

Ongoing costs
Execution of changes after project close
        – Possible follow-up
        – Possible additional training
Software
        – Maintenance (certain percentage of annual licensing volumes)
Hardware
        – Support
        – Maintenance
Expenses according to data volume (for example, management costs)
Electricity
Depreciation of hard- and software
Internal user support
External user support
Proportional system use (including room costs and general data processing overhead costs)
Proportional system maintenance
Release upgrade

Figure 13.2 Ongoing Costs of CRM Projects [Beringer 2001]

If the company is using application service providing (ASP) or hosting models where software or hardware is not purchased but rented from a hosting provider, the cost structure depicted in Figures 13.1 and 13.2 changes. One-off investments made during software implementation are almost completely avoided. Instead of these, rental costs for hardware setup, application use, and other services (for example, data saving and data archiving) occur periodically throughout the duration of the software use.

Determining the Benefits of CRM Projects

If you look at the frequently touted used arguments made for implementing CRM solutions, you can see that these are only qualitative statements about the improvement potential arising from implementation of a CRM application and do not mention any valuation in financial terms. These use arguments include, for example:

▶ Higher customer satisfaction

▶ Close customer ties

▶ More detailed customer information

▶ Improved transparency for customer-centric business processes

▶ Potential for up- and cross-selling

However, without an assessment of its financial value, justifying the business case for a CRM project can prove difficult. In the least desirable situation, no investment is made in a CRM project.

For this reason, quantification of the financial business benefit of a CRM implementation is of great importance. The existing enterprise-specific business processes, which are documented and described, serve as the basis for evaluating the business benefit. Once these processes are known, possible weak points or improvement potential can be identified. To do this, the functions of the CRM application and their effects on the business processes, for example, the reduction of sub-process steps or the acceleration of process execution, are examined. Strategic considerations can also lead to the creation of completely new processes. If the standard solution does not support the desired process modifications, the individual development and enterprise-specific enhancement of the IT solution, which incurs additional costs, must also be considered.

If the planned process modifications are fixed, the benefit of the CRM project can be derived from a comparison of the actual situation and planned processes. This is done by deriving the effects of the changes that can be financially quantified in a step-by-step procedure from the process modifications. This derivation process, known as an effect chain, leads to concrete measuring points and units that allow the qualitative effects to be quantified from the start of the effect chain.

The procedure is explained here using an example: A CRM solution supports direct access to current customer data, thus enabling better target group determination for marketing campaigns. Although the quality of the target group determination cannot be measured in terms of money, the success of the campaign, for example in the form of higher response rates (proportion of the target group that reacts to the campaign by deciding to purchase), can be displayed quantitatively. In this way, the accurate selection of customers for a campaign has an indirect effect on the turnover and profit of a company. At the end of this effect chain are monetary factors, which are in a causal relationship to the start of the chain and its qualitative use categories. The formulation of a suitable effect chain for this case in point could lead to the following result:

1. Access to current customer data

2. Accurate selection of target group for marketing campaigns

3. Increase in response rate

4. Higher turnover

5. Greater operating profit

The step to valuation in monetary units can be made on various levels along the effect chain. In a first variant, the quantification occurs after the third step.

For example, if the costs for a marketing campaign to contact 50,000 prospects run to $25,000 and the response rate can be doubled from 1% to 2% by using the CRM application, the more accurate customer selection means that 1000 prospects will respond instead of 500 prospects, as was the case in the past.

After implementing the CRM solution and due to the doubled response rate, only half as many prospects need to be contacted to reach 500 responses. The campaign costs will therefore amount to approximately half of the original sum, in other words $12,300. The difference of $12,300 can therefore be attributed to the CRM system.

Alternatively, the campaign is valuated after the fourth and fifth steps. The increased quality of the campaign brings with it higher turnover, which can be measured concretely by customer orders. If from 50,000 contacted prospects 1000 instead of 500 people accept an offer and the average turnover per customer increases simultaneously from $60 to $75, the CRM solution generates the company revenue of $74,000 instead of $30,000. With an average profit margin of 40%, growth of ($74,000 − $30,000) × 40% = $17,000 can be calculated.

Which stage of the effect chain is used for calculating the use and which values are used in the calculation is up to the individual enterprise. When choosing a higher stage of the effect chain to use in the ROI prediction, you must remember that there are more assumptions and therefore more instabilities in the calculation, although potential influences on the operating result are easier to recognize.

One of the dangers of IT business analyses is double valuation of effects. With reference to the example above, one could conceive that the use valuated at $12,300 at Step 3 and $17,000 at Step 4 could be added together and attributed to the campaign management of the CRM solution. However, this would be wrong. The higher turnover can be realized only after the campaign with the corresponding costs amounting to $25,000. If you include the use of the first calculation at $12,300, fewer people are contacted, the number of returns decreases, and the increase is not as great. A use category mutually excludes the potential for a second benefit. This is why such double effects must be excluded when forming an effect chain.

If you repeat the definition of effect chains across all potential use effects of a CRM project, you end up with an enterprise-specific profitability model (see Figure 13.3).

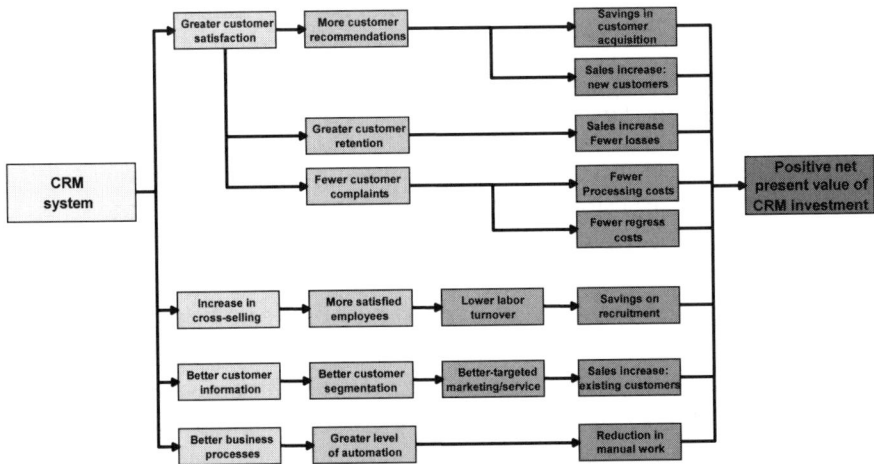

Figure 13.3 Example of a Simplified CRM Effect Chain Model [Beringer 2001]

Concrete Results for Users of mySAP CRM

The procedure described in the previous section was implemented by 35 users of mySAP CRM in Germany, Austria, and Switzerland and the results analyzed [Selchert 2003]. The analysis showed that extremely positive financial results could be obtained by using mySAP CRM. On average, the following ROI key figures were determined: IRR over three years of 55% and over five years nearly 100%, net present value of $7.8 million, and a break-even of almost 22 months.

Considerable productivity gains could be found in the areas of marketing, sales, e-selling, and Interaction Center. In marketing, the improved quality of customer information and additional evaluation possibilities were noticeable. The time required to access customer information was reduced by 30%. In some enterprises, the CRM application enabled employees to access structured customer data for the first time. Marketing analyses and campaigns reached the same result with 15% less time required. Sales, both in the field and the office, was on average 15% more productive. In the area of e-selling, the efficiency gain was mainly in order management, where a portion of the enterprises could achieve an efficiency growth of 40%. In the Interaction Center, the call time of outbound calls was reduced on average by 40%. Finally, some companies observed a rise of 10% in telesales success.

The observed increase potential can mainly be traced to the following improvements:

▶ Increase in turnover with regular customers for a third of the companies by on average more than 5% of the total turnover

▶ Increase in cross- and up-selling with 40% of participants by approximately 10%

▶ In 20% of all cases, there are possibilities of price increases or avoiding price reductions in a generally depressed market environment. Customers accept higher prices because the CRM solution ensures competent customer service that customers don't want to miss.

Half of the companies recorded an average increase of 25% in customer satisfaction and a 20% rise in customer retention. In total, viewed as an average across all companies, this value was still 10%. A quarter of all companies also reported definite time advantages as a result of mySAP CRM: Time-to-market, time-to-volume, and time-to-delivery were also reduced by between 10 and 25%. Moreover, the success of new product introductions increased. In one company, the proportion of new products in the company's top 30 sales generators nearly doubled from 7% to 13%. The delivery-to-promise was also improved in one fifth of the companies by an average of 20%, despite the accelerated processing.

13.1.3 Methods for Fast ROI

At the start of a CRM project, investments are required for hardware and software purchasing, customizing, and user training. Once CRM is being used productively, the use threshold is exceeded because the software is making a positive contribution to enterprise profitability. The quicker the solution is implemented, the longer it is used and the better it can be aligned to changing company requirements over the course of time, which all have a positive effect on the ROI.

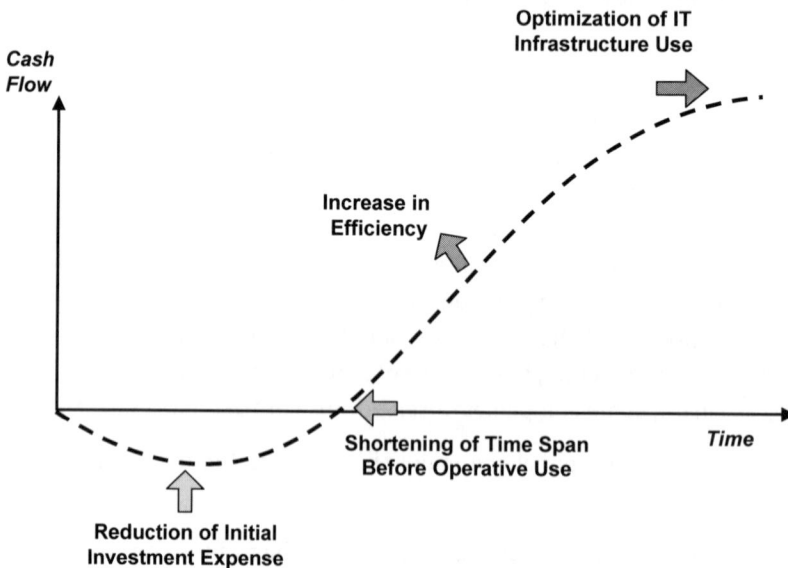

Figure 13.4 Methods for Fast ROI

The alignment to actual business scenarios enables mySAP CRM to be implemented in more than one sub-project, which reduces the initial investment and shortens the time to the start of use. By concentrating on the business scenarios that have the greatest improvement potential and by offering many possibilities for company-specific and employee-specific configuration of these processes, the efficiency of the software solution is increased. Powerful tools enable optimized use of the CRM solution over the entire lifecycle (see Sections 14.8.1 and 15.5).

13.2   Project View

13.2.1   CRM Software Implementation as a Big Bang?

> *"How to eat the CRM elephant? ... Break it up into little bite-sized pieces."* [Deloitte 2002]

Customer relationship management as a corporate philosophy requires a holistic business vision and an implementation strategy that is pursued across the entire company (see Sections 3.6 and 13.2.2). In many cases, this knowledge was used to reach the conclusion that implementation of CRM software had to take place simultaneously in all areas of the company as part of a single, large project. However, this works only in ideal conditions. Risk factors for a big bang of this kind are:

▶ The amount and complexity of processes connected to customer-oriented applications, in both the front and back office, makes the simultaneous changeover of all enterprise areas a risky undertaking. *"When it comes to CRM, Murphy's law is optimistic."* [Deloitte 2003]

▶ Extensive organizational changes in the enterprise frequently meet with resistance from the employees affected and require an intensive and sometimes time-consuming change management process.

▶ In times of shrinking budgets, managers expect success reports within a few months. This is often not possible with large projects.

It goes without saying that customer relationship management is a holistic task spanning the entire enterprise. Therefore, the corporate CRM strategy must also consider the repercussions it will have for the entire company. However, this is not the same as the requirement for a CRM implementation in a single, large, all-encompassing project. The implementation of the CRM strategy in several small steps is by far the better way to reach this objective and has the following advantages:

▶ Focus on those business processes with the greatest potential for improvement and the fastest ROI

▶ Manageable projects and budgets

- ▶ Rapid visible use

- ▶ Improved employee acceptance

- ▶ Possibility to continually validate the implementation strategy with appropriate corrective measures

For example, to begin with, mobile employees can be supported by the CRM solution, and in subsequent sub-projects the critical business processes in the Interaction Center and e-commerce can be improved. SAP Solution Manager supports the execution of these subprojects (see Section 14.8.1). Moreover, it makes sense not to introduce the CRM solution to all customers and markets at the same time but rather to introduce it to particular market segments, for example. This also makes it possible to compare the success of those areas implementing a CRM solution and those without one.

Before starting a larger CRM implementation project it is often helpful to take a closer look at the software solution. To this end, SAP offers the *JumpStart program*, with which companies can test mySAP CRM without risks. The JumpStart program for mySAP CRM contains a three-month, free-of- charge test license for mySAP CRM, as well as consulting services on implementation and subsequent un-installation of the test system. During this test period, additional hardware can be rented at a low price. The packages for mobile sales, e-selling, Interaction Center, and marketing are available for use with the JumpStart program.

13.2.2 Challenges and Success Factors

A study of CRM project experiences carried out by Forrester Research [Temkin/Schmitt/Herbert 2003] among 111 large American companies showed that only 13.5% of the companies saw problems in retrospect regarding the choice of software or software implementation. 22.5% of the companies felt that the greatest challenge was the project phase in which the end user needed to be won over to the project. The Gartner Group also confirms that the software used has only marginal influence on the success or failure of a CRM project [Nelson/Kirby 2001, Hagenmeyer/Nelson 2003]. Main reasons for failure are found in the areas of "implementation strategy" and "organization."

Success Factors in CRM Projects

In SAP's consulting experience, the following success factors have proven critical to CRM implementation projects:

▶ **Use of a CRM-oriented implementation methodology**

The implementation methodology serves as a guideline for the course of the CRM implementation project. It should be founded on practical experience gained from successfully concluded CRM implementation projects.

▶ **Acceptance of CRM software in the company**

Because employees have to adjust to new software and to a new organizational structure, it is important to include the end users in the project and its implementation methodology at an early stage. Otherwise, resistance from the end users can be expected.

▶ **Strategy and planning**

Many companies are under such time pressure to implement their CRM systems that they lose sight of the overall strategy. The congruence of the company, CRM, and IT strategy is decisive and should be the starting point for project planning.

▶ **Support from top management**

Given the far-reaching consequences that implementation of a CRM solution has for a company, support from management is vital. The managers involved should have CRM know-how (*content promoter*) and hold positions in the company that allow them to make and implement decisions (*power promoter*). Management must make clear statements about project goals and implementation, and must take responsibility for the project's success.

▶ **Definition of success metrics**

The project goals and the methods used to gauge success (success metrics) must be fixed by the start of the project. The project must be ended as quickly as possible if the objectives set cannot be reached.

▶ **Cooperation with end users**

Since the systems used can be very complex, collaboration between technicians and users to specify user requirements is necessary. The cooperation should be in the form of continuous teamwork.

▶ **Detailing the project plan**

The project plan for a CRM implementation must describe goals, methods, visions, responsibilities, milestone planning, and resources (employees, budget, and so on) in sufficient detail.

▶ **Expert knowledge**

A good project plan specifies when which person is needed and whether external know-how is required. As the analyses occur with reference to business processes, a responsible person should be appointed for each central process (such as campaign management).

► **Development of a documentation and communication plan**
A communication plan that specifies when to communicate information about which project topic is the basis for the distribution of project information within the company. In addition to this, documentation of the project itself and of the solution functionality is important. A user handbook can make system implementation easier for the end user.

► **Pilot users and system implementation**
Use of a pilot system should begin as early as possible to give the affected users an opportunity to practice using the new technology. This increases the project acceptance and makes results more transparent. The roll-out in the company must also be planned.

► **User training**
Before the system is used productively, user training should occur; it should focus on the system and its benefits for working with business processes. Separate training courses for technical topics (for example, system administration) should be scheduled.

To help companies with implementation of mySAP CRM, SAP has developed powerful tools based on extensive project experience. To support SAP software solutions during their entire lifecycle *SAP Solution Manager* is available (see Section 14.8.1), which makes the implementation, based on business scenarios and the operation of SAP solutions, considerably more comfortable. It offers a proven implementation methodology for use in the project (see Section 13.2.3). Furthermore, SAP has developed preconfigured systems for different CRM scenarios, which allow companies to implement CRM processes quickly and smoothly (see Section 13.2.4).

13.2.3 Methodical Software Implementation

AcceleratedSAP (ASAP) is SAP's generic implementation methodology for fast and efficient implementation of SAP solutions. It is supported by SAP Solution Manager. The characteristics of AcceleratedSAP are:

► Standardization of the implementation of SAP solutions

► Guarantee of successful implementation with consideration of *time, budget, and quality factors*

► Knowledge transfer within SAP as well as to customers, consultants, and so on

To take into account the specific requirements of CRM implementation projects, a special ASAP variant known as *AcceleratedSAP for mySAP CRM* was developed.

Overview

AcceleratedSAP for mySAP CRM (ASAP for mySAP CRM) is SAP's implementation methodology for CRM solutions and projects. It addresses the requirements of CRM and is based on ASAP for SAP R/3 in the main project phases. ASAP for mySAP CRM components (process library and procedure model) are delivered with SAP Solution Manager.

A special implementation methodology addresses the requirements of CRM projects is necessary because a CRM project differs from an SAP R/3 project in a few important aspects:

▶ Differences in technology and system landscape (for example, in mobile sales)
▶ Different user groups
▶ Different influence on internal company organization
▶ Different roles and project structures
▶ Customer requests for non-standard or enhanced functionality are more frequent than those for SAP R/3

Project Plan for Implementation of mySAP CRM

Implementation of the CRM solution is supported by ASAP for mySAP CRM through a special project plan (roadmap) with the following phases:

▶ Feasibility study
▶ Project preparation
▶ Business blueprint
▶ Realization
▶ Final preparation
▶ Go live and support

This project plan is contained in SAP Solution Manager as an *Implementation Roadmap* (see also Section 14.8.1 and Figure 13.5). It offers a collection of documents that show in chronological order which activities need to be performed at what time for a project implementation to succeed.

Feasibility Study

One important aspect in which ASAP for mySAP CRM differs from the standard method is its use of the feasibility study as an important preliminary phase of the CRM implementation project.

This phase takes place when a company has decided to implement a CRM solution and needs to determine to what extent the software covers the customer's functional requirements. In this phase, the customer is supported in defining business and IT strategies as well as in selecting the scenarios and processes relevant from a business perspective. The result of this phase is generally a quotation including a labor and scheduling estimate (rough project planning, date planning, internal and external resource requirements, and so on).

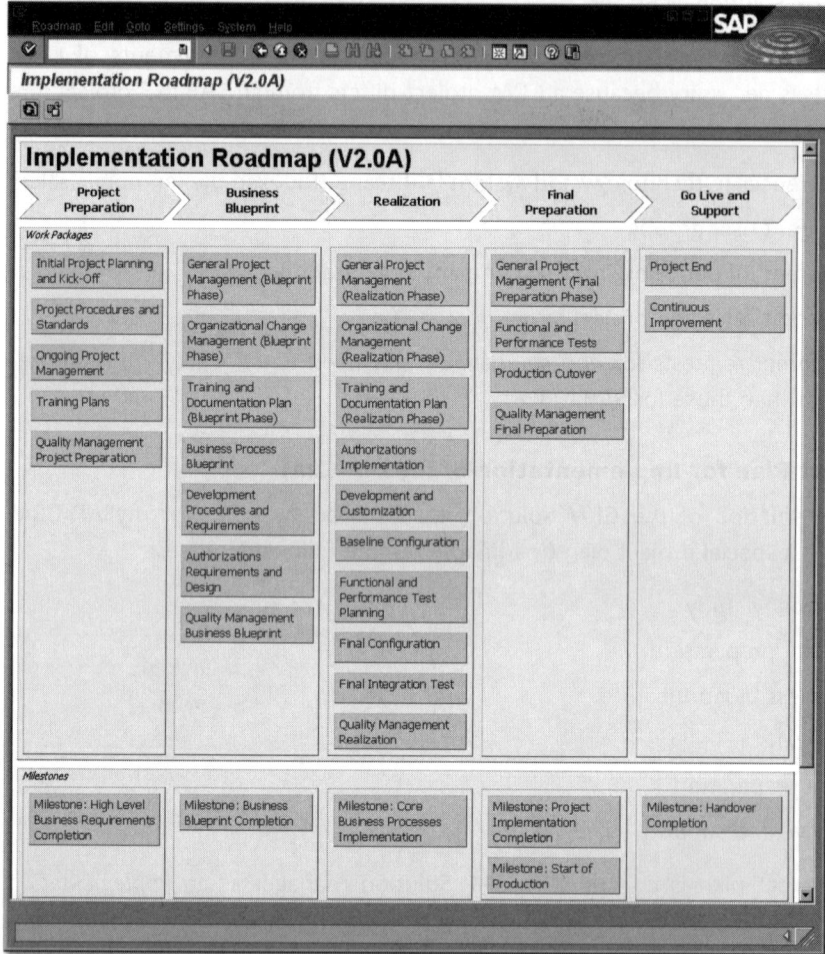

Figure 13.5 Implementation Roadmap in SAP Solution Manager

The goals of the feasibility study are:

▶ To understand the customer's business and requirements

▶ To understand the customer's business processes

▶ To understand the existing system landscape and the extent of customizing of the applications used

- To collect data about the project scope, resources, and costs
- To draw up hardware- and software-specific requirements
- To reach decisions with the relevant decision-makers, i.e., the customer, SAP, and partners

Project Preparation

This phase is used to plan, define, and prepare the CRM implementation project. Although every SAP project differs with respect to objectives, scope, and priorities, the following steps can determine further project success:

- Creation of project charter
- Definition of project objects
- Clarification of implementation scope
- Determination of implementation strategy
- Creation of a general project timeline and order of implementation
- Setup of project structure and committees
- Assignment of personnel resources
- Setup of system landscape (hardware and software components)
- Project kick-off

Completing these steps early on creates a solid foundation for a successful SAP implementation and ensures project efficiency. SAP Solution Manager *supports the project definition* and *definition of system landscape steps in particular*. In addition, SAP Solution Manager contains the basic project data, such as employees and their tasks, timeline and milestones, and necessary hardware systems.

Business Blueprint

The aim of this phase is to document the company's business process requirements, as determined in requirement workflows in a *Business Blueprint*. This forms the basis for a common concept about how the company wants to map its business processes with the CRM system.

The following steps are taken during this phase:

- Refinement of the original project aims and objectives
- Implementation of change management
- Setup of the system environment
- Determination of the basic scope of the solution
- Detailed composition of a project timeline and the course of implementation

SAP Solution Manager can support creation of the business blueprint by evaluating the business processes, describing the desired scenarios and processes in the system, and generating the business blueprint document with the following information:

▶ General information about the business areas in question

▶ Processes that are to be realized

▶ Requirements for master data and organizational units

▶ Required systems and components

Realization

The aim of this phase is to implement the business and process requirements defined in the business blueprint. This is achieved by setting up a pilot system landscape in which the planned business processes can be mapped and tested. The goals of this phase are final implementation of the system, a comprehensive test, and release of the system for productive operation.

SAP Solution Manager enables you to perform a process-oriented system configuration. Jumps to the detailed Implementation Guides (IMGs) of the systems involved allow you to configure the system landscape from one central position. *Customizing Distribution* and *Customizing Scout* are easy-to-use tools for system-wide distribution and comparison of configuration settings. Moreover, SAP Solution Manager supports the organization and documentation of functional tests for each business process (see Figure 13.6).

Final Preparation

The purpose of final preparation is to prepare the results of the realization phase for productive use. This involves tests, user training, and creation of a system management and user support organization. All open issues concerning readiness for going live are resolved. After successfully completing this phase, productive business processes can run in the CRM system.

The test management capability of SAP Solution Manager provides valuable help even in this phase: integration, interface, and, if necessary, load tests can be prepared and documented. The documentation collected in SAP Solution Manager is also used to prepare the user training.

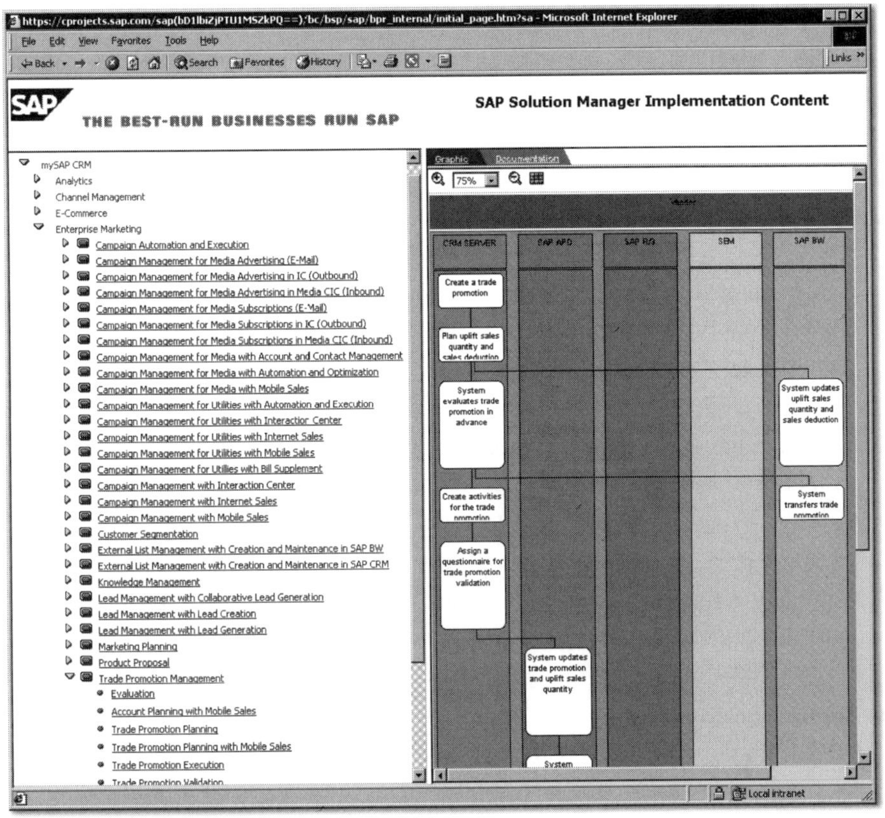

Figure 13.6 System Configuration Using SAP Solution Manager

Go Live and Support

The goal of this phase is to switch from the pre-productive environment to productive operation. Here it is important to offer user support that is not just available in the first critical days of productive operation but on a long-term basis. The support desk integrated in SAP Solution Manager can be used for this.

Users of the CRM solution have their first practical experiences with the solution in the go-live phase. For this reason, there must be a well-organized user support facility that all employees can easily access. This phase is also used to monitor the system transactions and to optimize the system performance as a whole. SAP Solution Manager provides numerous utilities and tools to help with operations (see Section 14.8.1). This phase marks the completion of the project.

Employee Roles in a CRM Implementation Project

The ASAP for mySAP CRM method requires suitable project organization. Furthermore, it is necessary to define responsibilities clearly to ensure that the tasks and process steps from this method are fulfilled optimally. An overview of the typical roles found in a CRM implementation project follows:

▶ **Project lead**

The project lead is responsible for the project results and the operative project management. The project lead anticipates deviations from the project plan and immediately takes corrective measures. The project lead should also understand the system integration of the business processes with the company environment.

He or she has the authority to make decisions concerning the project and its budget, and passes strategic questions on to allow for joint decisions to be made.

Depending on the size and complexity of the implementation project and whether it is necessary, a second project management level can be introduced. In this case, the global project lead would be supported by additional regional project leads.

▶ **Application consultant**

The application consultant is responsible for the configuration of the software for the business processes and fulfillment of the analysis and report requirements. He or she also shares application and configuration knowledge with the business process team leads and other team members. The application consultant is familiar with established business procedures and can use this knowledge to support the application design. The application consultant also functions as an advisor for the project team.

Modifications to the standard software often lead to open questions regarding software change management. The application consultant occupies a key position here by offering valuable advice and information to contribute to the problem's resolution. If legacy data needs to be extracted, close collaboration with the legacy system experts is also necessary.

▶ **Technical consultant**

Together with the project lead and the technical team lead, the technical consultant plans the technical requirements and carries out the corresponding system tasks and customer-specific development. Depending on the scope and complexity of the implementation, this consultant can work in one or more specialized areas, for example, in system, database, network, or operating-system administration, in development of cross-application components, or in ABAP development.

13.2.4 Preconfigured CRM Systems

SAP customers are able to implement and use extensive CRM functionality quickly and smoothly. To this end, *Best Practices for mySAP CRM* are preconfigured CRM systems for various application scenarios with the following objectives:

▶ Creating organizational and technical foundations for fast and trouble-free use of the new CRM solution

▶ Ensuring optimal alignment to customer needs of all business processes mapped in the CRM system

Best Practices for mySAP CRM also offers SAP customers access to the entire knowledge repository that SAP and SAP partners have built up through numerous evaluation and implementation projects.

Components of Best Practices for mySAP CRM

The following components form part of Best Practices for mySAP CRM:

▶ **Easy-to-understand implementation method**
Best Practices for mySAP CRM delivers a clearly structured implementation method based on a phase-by-phase approach. It covers numerous documents and procedures that help to ensure optimal usability.

▶ **Detailed documentation**
The reusable documentation for mySAP CRM is suitable for private study, evaluation, and training project teams and users.

▶ **Complete preconfiguration**
The preconfigured settings make it possible to implement core processes productively in a short time. This involves only minimal implementation effort.

The components of Best Practices for mySAP CRM make it possible to put together an operational prototype from mySAP CRM in the shortest possible time. This is integrated into the customer's existing system landscape. Customer data from existing SAP Enterprise Resource Planning (ERP) systems can simply be transferred to the new CRM system. This CRM prototype is fully documented and can be used as a basis for further customization and thus for the final implementation and operation.

Customers can also use Best Practices for mySAP CRM to enhance an already productive SAP solution with CRM-supported business scenarios, including technical and business aspects. For example, included in the delivery is a largely automated installation process to connect SAP Mobile Sales to the CRM server.

All configuration settings that enable CRM components to communicate with each other are available with SAP Best Practices. Best Practices for mySAP CRM ensures that all required data on products, business partners, and pricing conditions contained in an existing SAP R/3 system can be transferred to the new solution and simultaneously made available to the mobile components.

Up until now, project experience has shown that an operational scenario prototype can be implemented within three to four weeks using Best Practices for mySAP CRM. In this time, installation and configuration of mySAP CRM, integration with an existing SAP R/3 system, and connection to SAP Business Information Warehouse (SAP BW), SAP Strategic Enterprise Management (SAP SEM), and SAP Advanced Planner and Optimizer (SAP APO) are performed. The initial data transfer from the SAP R/3 system is also included. If data from other systems is required, the project runtime increases accordingly. The configuration of each additional scenario takes one to three days, depending on complexity.

Supported Business Scenarios

Best Practices for mySAP CRM provides direct implementation support with the following preconfigured scenarios:

- ▶ Marketing
  - ▶ Campaign Management
  - ▶ Lead Management
  - ▶ Customer Analysis
- ▶ Sales
  - ▶ Sales Planning
- ▶ E-Selling
  - ▶ Order Process: B2B
  - ▶ Order Process: B2C
- ▶ Field Sales
  - ▶ Customer Visit with Order Entry
  - ▶ Opportunity Management
  - ▶ Campaign Execution
- ▶ Interaction Center
  - ▶ Information Help Desk
  - ▶ Interaction Center Service
  - ▶ Inbound Telesales
  - ▶ Outbound Telesales

These scenarios are described in Chapters 7 to 10.

Packaged Solutions

Included with Best Practices are specially designed solutions intended for quick productive use of a CRM business scenario. These are known as *Packaged Solutions* (formerly referred to as *Quickstep*). A Packaged Solution contains the software licenses, the implementation of a CRM scenario within a predetermined project runtime including necessary consulting support, and an optional training offer for end users. This allows enterprises to take their first steps with mySAP CRM without the risks of a big implementation project, and enables them to enhance the solution later on as required. If desired, the business case for such an implementation can be determined using an ROI study contained in the package.

The business scenarios offered as Packaged Solutions are generally the same as those in Best Practices for mySAP CRM. The exact offer varies according to each individual SAP subsidiary.

Special Scenarios for Small and Medium-Sized Businesses

On the basis of SAP Best Practices, numerous SAP partners offer *mySAP All-in-One* solutions tailored to the requirements of medium-sized businesses. The industry-specific preconfigured versions of mySAP CRM also belong to these sector-specific SAP Best Practices offers.

Advantages of Preconfigured Systems for Customers

The advantages of Best Practices for mySAP CRM for the customer can be summarized as follows:

▶ **Typical beginner's mistakes are avoided**
Best Practices for mySAP CRM is a tried and tested product and helps to avoid errors in systems, business processes, or configuration settings that beginners often make. SAP has identified potential sources of error and shows how to sidestep these in Best Practices for mySAP CRM.

▶ **Time and cost savings**
Best Practices for mySAP CRM anticipates general company requirements and necessary project steps. The documentation and configuration are reusable and can be easily customized for individual requirements.

▶ **Expertise**
With integrated, continuous business processes that extract the greatest benefits from mySAP CRM, Best Practices for mySAP CRM delivers everything you need to become an expert. This includes information on the system landscape,

an established implementation approach, documented business processes, configuration, documentation, user roles, test data, and practical examples.

▶ **Trouble-free enhancement of company solutions**
Best Practices for mySAP CRM includes an automated implementation procedure and can be used with other mySAP Business Suite solutions. Even the connection of SAP BW and SAP APO to mySAP CRM can be automated. This coupling can enrich CRM installations with additional functionalities, such as *availability check with reservation*.

▶ **Fast construction of an operational prototype**
With Best Practices for mySAP CRM, it is possible to construct an operational and completely documented prototype within a few days, which can be used as a starting point for further implementation.

13.2.5 Services, Consulting, and Training

mySAP CRM is not just a software solution for customer relationship management. It also includes a comprehensive range of complementary services, consulting offers, and training courses. These include:

SAP Service Marketplace

SAP Service Marketplace (www.service.sap.com) is an Internet platform for collaboration between SAP, customers, and partners. SAP Service Marketplace helps customers to access the full range of SAP service offers using a central access point and user-friendly navigation.

Additional SAP Service Maintenance Offers

In addition to the standard maintenance offer, SAP offers the following support programs, which enable customers to take advantage of their investments in SAP solutions.

▶ **SAP Safeguarding** is a group of proactively executed system checks that determine potential risk factors early on and identify appropriate potential solutions. These checks are used in customer-specific situations as required and are aimed at minimizing total costs.

▶ **SAP Empowering** is a package consisting of services, training, instructions, and documentation, which provides enterprises with the knowledge and skills required to set up a support organization and optimally operate an SAP solution landscape.

▶ **SAP Solution Management Optimization** consists of various services for guaranteeing the optimal operation of an SAP solution landscape. These services concentrate on performance, application integration, data volume, and system administration, and help to prevent and resolve problems.

Consulting

Customers needing support in the areas of business solutions, software implementation, and software operation can use the extensive consulting services offered by SAPConsulting:

▶ **Strategic consulting services**
Coordination of business and IT strategy

▶ **Solution delivery services**
Support for quick and cost-effective software implementation

▶ **Operations services**
Customizing and enhancement of SAP software solutions according to demand

▶ **Lifecycle management services**
Consulting throughout the software lifecycle

Hosting

SAP Hosting provides data center services that companies can use to implement the newest SAP solutions quickly and effectively. The services are optimized to meet the requirements of mySAP Business Suite users and include evaluation hosting, implementation hosting, application hosting, remote application operations, application management, and hosted learning.

Training and Knowledge Transfer

SAP offers a multitude of training offers for implementation and operation of mySAP:

▶ Business know-how

▶ CRM applications

▶ CRM technology

▶ Information on new software versions

The following training methods are offered:

▶ Instructor-led training

   ▶ Classroom training
    Traditional training in the classroom

   ▶ Virtual classroom training
    Training on the Web

► Private study units (e-learning)

  ► SAP Tutor

    Application examples to explain the user interface. Interactive knowledge tests possible.

  ► Web-based training

    Professionally prepared training units that use diverse multimedia; access from the Web possible

  ► E-books

    Textbooks in electronic form; also available on the Web

Further Information

For detailed information on SAP's training offers, please see *www.sap.com/education*. Customers can also order the *Internet Demo and Evaluation System* (IDES), a completely preconfigured mySAP Business Suite for demonstration and training purposes, through *SAP Service Marketplace*. A detailed description of all SAP Service and Support offers can be found in [Oswald 2003].

14 The Integration and Application Platform—SAP NetWeaver

"At SAP, business drives technology."
Shai Agassi, member of the SAP Executive Board, at the
SAP NetWeaver presentation in New York on 16th January 2003

14.1 Technology Development at SAP

SAP has many years of experience, not only as a provider of business applications, but also as a developer of innovative platform technologies. The multilevel Client/Server system architecture introduced in the early 1990s with *SAP R/3* remains a milestone in the history of business application systems to this day [Buck-Emden/Galimow 1996]. Further significant results of SAP technology development were 1998's *EnjoySAP* with the user-oriented optimization of user interfaces and 1999's *SAP Business Framework* for supporting cross-component business processes founded on open Internet standards. In 2001, based on this longstanding experience of practice and development, SAP created a platform for open e-Business solutions with *mySAP Technology* and the *SAP Web Application Server (SAP Web AS)*. As a consequential further development of these technologies into a comprehensive integration- and application platform for the Enterprise Services Architecture (ESA, see Section 5.1), the *SAP NetWeaver* solution is now available, and is described in the following sections.

14.2 Integrated Platform Suites

Today, modern business applications use different infrastructure technologies, such as application servers, portals, integration brokers, multi-channel communication servers, and so on. In the past, companies often acquired these platform technologies from various providers and combined them with great effort in individual implementation projects. In an evermore demanding application- and software world, however, companies are looking for solutions to help them implement and operate their business applications more effectively and increase productivity to develop and adapt applications. Integrated platform solutions (*Application Platform Suites*, APS) sourced from a single manufacturer can fulfill these requirements. The Gartner Group [Natis 2002] sees the following basic elements of such an *APS*:

▶ Application server for company applications
▶ Enterprise portal
▶ Integration technologies for enterprise applications

Also required, for example, are an integrated development framework and tools for system management, which support both system implementation and operation. Process, implementation, and maintenance costs can be reduced significantly by using such a uniform technological application basis.

SAP NetWeaver is SAP's implementation of an application platform suite. The path chosen by SAP—namely, to provide an integrated platform suite from one source—differs significantly from the path taken by other CRM software manufacturers, who try to combine different manufacturers' technologies in the context of a partner strategy. This approach might be interesting for enterprises that already operate a very heterogeneous system and application landscape. However, they would find it difficult to achieve the same degree of integration at a comparable cost when compared to a platform suite sourced from a single manufacturer.

14.3 SAP NetWeaver Overview

Solving integration problems in a suitable cost period and timeframe is not only a technical challenge, but also requires comprehensive knowledge of the business processes to be supported. A purely technical approach to solving complex integration tasks is obviously inadequate and can only rarely portray all business processes. Comprehensive integration solutions therefore must consider the following requirements:

▶ Integration of people (People Integration)

▶ Integration of information (Information Integration)

▶ Integration of business processes (Process Integration)

SAP NetWeaver has been developed to cover completely all the requirement areas named above. Furthermore, *SAP NetWeaver* includes the application platform *SAP Web AS*, support functions for the software lifecycle (*Lifecycle Management*), and the *Composite Application Framework* for *Composite Applications*. This is the new generation of service-based, cross-component applications.

SAP NetWeaver, with its fine-tuned end-to-end integration services across all application levels, makes an emphatic contribution to keeping total costs of installing the mySAP Business Suite as low as possible. With SAP NetWeaver, there is no need to combine different manufacturers' platform products in the customer project. With *SAP Solution Manager,* SAP NetWeaver also provides an extraordinarily efficient tool for implementing, operating, and monitoring all processes, applications, and systems.

Figure 14.1 SAP NetWeaver Integration and Application Platform

The prerequisites for cross-system component integration today are driven by Web services and open technology standards. SAP NetWeaver takes this into account and is therefore based on corresponding Web standards; it can also communicate with other manufacturers' application components. Additionally, SAP NetWeaver works together with *IBM WebSphere* and *Microsoft .NET* development tools so that business applications can be created and extended by using the development environment of all three manufacturers (see Figure 14.2).

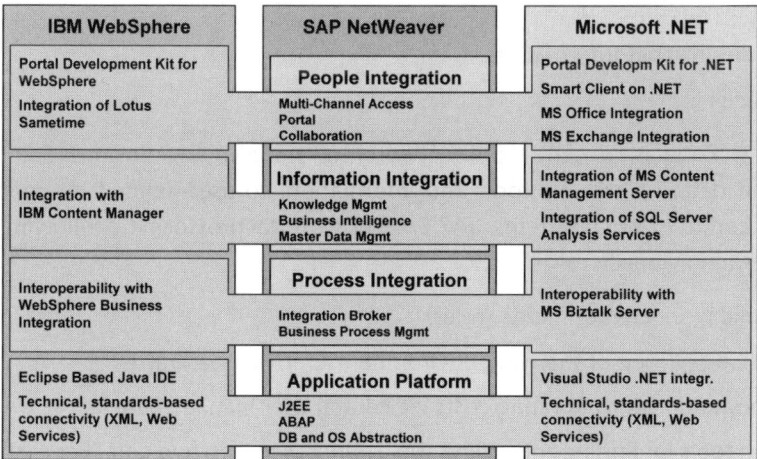

Figure 14.2 Interoperability of SAP NetWeaver with IBM WebSphere and Microsoft.NET

14.4 People Integration

The top level of SAP NetWeaver (Figure 14.1) contains all platform technologies required to give access to employees, partners, and customers inside and outside the enterprise, to the information and applications they need. The key parts of this level include the portal infrastructure, the development- and runtime environment Web Dynpro for browser-based user interfaces, personal collaborative tools, and interfaces for all access channels such as Internet, mobile communications devices, and telephone (Multi-Channel Access). In this context, "Collaboration" is the collective term for the various forms of communication and cooperation between portal users and includes, for example, virtual offices (Collaboration Rooms), Launch Pads for central access to contact person lists (Buddy Lists), favorites, and personal collaborative services (email, document sharing, and so on).

The SAP NetWeaver portal infrastructure and collaborative services are provided by the *SAP Enterprise Portal*. Web Dynpro is part of the *SAP Web AS*. Mobile communication devices are connected through the *SAP Mobile Infrastructure*.

14.4.1 SAP Enterprise Portal

For *SAP Enterprise Portal* users, application and enterprise boundaries are no longer important, that is, as long as the context of business processes and authorization concepts doesn't require it to be so. Any location in the world with an Internet connection can be reached by SAP Enterprise Portal by using a Uniform Resource Locator (URL). Examples of objects that can be addressed are:

▶ Business transactions

▶ Reports and evaluations

▶ Knowledge Warehouse data

▶ Internet and Intranet information

▶ Marketplaces

SAP Enterprise Portal is the central point of entry to various mySAP Business Suite solutions and data, to external tools and information, to user-defined Internet documents, and to external systems. SAP Enterprise Portal provides the following services, listed individually:

▶ Task-specific work environments (roles)

▶ Individual configuring of the work environment (personalization)

▶ Consistency and lower operating costs via central user management

▶ Navigation tools for finding and calling applications, services, and data. For each user, multiple roles with corresponding work environments can be provided.

- *iViews* (integrated Views) as a window to user-defined applications. Users are automatically provided with content according to their roles, needs, and preferences, for example, email, calendar, Webnews, and so on. A portal page is a combination of one or several iViews.

- *Drag & Relate* as a tool for executing business-related tasks simply by moving objects in the browser. For example, in the browser, a user can use the mouse to move an overdue purchase order onto the symbol representing the forwarding agent, which then automatically displays the corresponding delivery information.

- *Single Sign-On* (SSO): Users can access internal and external applications and content without having to log on several times with different passwords. After the one-time logon, the user can access all required services, applications, and data without having to log in again. Single Sign-On in the SAP Enterprise Portal supports two authorization concepts (see also Section 14.8.2):

  - Single Sign-On with user ID and password

  - Single Sign-On with X.509 Client Certificate

- Integration of non-SAP solutions and external content

- Integrated Knowledge Management with functions for retrieving and classifying documents (Retrieval and Classification)

- Access to information from the SAP Enterprise Portal for mobile users too. To do this, the SAP partner BackWeb *ProactivePortal* server extracts information from the SAP Enterprise Portal and sends it to the mobile devices. From there, the user can access this information offline as usual.

Roles

The SAP Enterprise Portal offers content and services tailored to the needs of employees, partners, and customers, as a role-based enterprise portal. A role defines a group of activities, including all associated data, authorizations, and functions a person carries out to reach a desired business target.

Through its role-based architecture, the SAP Enterprise Portal can, for example, provide an area manager with a work environment that looks completely different in some sub-areas than it appears to a product developer. On the other hand, area managers and product developers have the role of employees in the enterprise, and have the same administrative functions, for example, for leave requests implemented as an *Employee Self-Service* (ESS) in *mySAP Human Resources* (mySAP HR). SAP Enterprise Portal addresses this requirement and supports multiple roles for each user.

mySAP CRM supports as standard over 30 different roles that constitute both industry-dependent and industry-independent requirements. The following list is a selection of roles that are currently delivered with mySAP CRM:

Marketing
▶ Campaign Manager
▶ Lead Manager
▶ Lead Qualifier
▶ Trade Marketing Manager

Sales
▶ Sales Manager
▶ Sales Representative
▶ Sales Assistant
▶ Account Manager
▶ Brand Manager
▶ Billing Clerk

Service
▶ Service Manager
▶ Service Representative

Channel Management
▶ Channel Manager
▶ Partner Manager
▶ Partner Management Channel Communicator
▶ Partner Employee
▶ Customer

Interaction Center
▶ Interaction Center Manager
▶ Interaction Center Agent

Administration
▶ CRM Portal Administrator
▶ Knowledge Management Author

Leasing
▶ Leasing Manager
▶ Leasing Administrator

- ▶ Leasing Accountant
- ▶ Leasing Equipment Manager

Media
- ▶ Rights Manager

Pharma
- ▶ Sales Representative Pharma
- ▶ Chargeback Analyst

Public Services
- ▶ Constituent Service Agent

Professional Services
- ▶ Consultant
- ▶ Resource Manager
- ▶ Services Director
- ▶ Project Manager

Utilities
- ▶ Key Account Manager

Automotive
- ▶ Dealer Manager

14.4.2 SAP Mobile Infrastructure

The *SAP Mobile Infrastructure* (SAP MI), as an enhancement of the *SAP Mobile Engine* (SAP ME), forms the technological basis for general mobile SAP applications. It can be used to run business applications on mobile communication devices such as laptops, PDAs, and mobile telephones, and exchange data with user-defined SAP or non-SAP systems. Figure 14.3 shows the possibilities for connecting mobile communication devices to SAP systems.

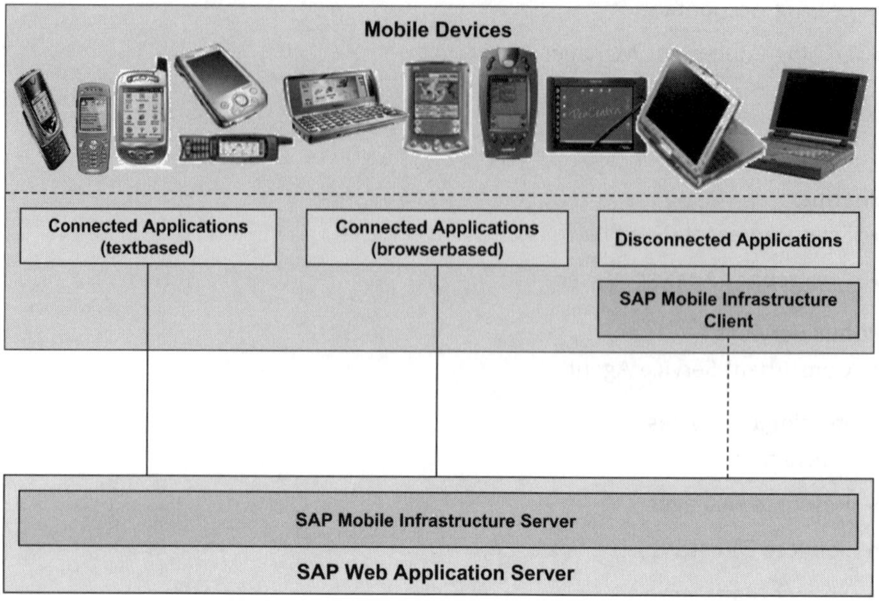

Figure 14.3 Connecting Mobile Communication Devices to SAP Systems by Using the SAP Mobile Infrastructure

The *SAP Mobile Infrastructure* supports the following mobile business scenarios:

▶ **Online—browser-based**

This business scenario provides mobile communication devices with a direct connection to the *SAP Web Application Server*. As in standard Internet connections, the mobile communication device browser can directly access applications in back-end systems by using this Web-based connection through the SAP Mobile Infrastructure. By using standard browsers, no software needs to be installed on the mobile communication devices.

▶ **Online—text-based**

For mobile communication devices that don't support GUIs, the SAP Mobile Infrastructure enables you to connect these devices to back-end applications by using a text-based mode. Text-based communication devices are, for example, *radio frequency devices* such as barcode scanners or picking terminals.

▶ **Offline**

For business processes that run offline on the mobile communication device, the SAP Mobile Infrastructure provides a platform-independent framework that can be used to allow mobile communication devices to work independently and without a direct network connection. The business data saved locally on the mobile communication devices is then synchronized with the back-end system at a later time.

The SAP Mobile Infrastructure consists of a client part, the SAP Mobile Infrastructure Client (SAP MI-Client), and a server, the SAP Mobile Infrastructure Server (SAP MI-Server). For all types of connections, the mobile communication devices access the SAP MI-Server, which is part of the SAP Web AS. The SAP MI-Client is only required for mobile communication devices working offline.

In contrast to the mobile applications supported by the SAP MI, the laptop applications of mySAP CRM, *Mobile Sales* and *Mobile Service,* place very special requirements on data synchronization with the CRM Server (replication, realignment, Territory Management Support, and so on). To fulfill these requirements, these mobile applications are therefore synchronized by the CRM Middleware, which has been specifically optimized for this purpose, and is part of mySAP CRM (see also Section 15.4.2).

14.5 Information Integration

SAP NetWeaver is also an efficient platform for combining and handling all kinds of data and information in an enterprise. This applies both to structured and unstructured information. *Structured information* is master data for products, materials, or business partners, transaction data on business transactions, or data in SAP BW for creating analyses and statistics. *Unstructured information* takes the form of documents, brochures, texts, presentations, or audiovisual data, and is managed by using SAP Knowledge Management tools.

14.5.1 SAP Master Data Management

Managing shared master data presents a great challenge in distributed, heterogeneous application landscapes. The same master data is frequently used, changed, and saved by various applications on different servers, which consequently often leads to inconsistencies in the databases involved. Nevertheless, cross-application business processes require consistent master data nevertheless.

With *SAP Master Data Management (SAP MDM)*, enterprises can consolidate their existing master data and maintain it so that consistent distribution of the data is guaranteed across all application components. You must be careful to display the master data objects in the formats of the application components involved. This includes converting data structures, values, and keys.

Distributed master data can be handled in enterprises in three structural steps. These steps build upon each other; nevertheless, they can also be used as stand-alone master data management scenarios (see also Figure 14.4):

1. **Master Data Consolidation**

   Consolidating distributed master data objects includes finding and recognizing identical and similar master data objects. The same master data in different application components (Clients) with different keys (IDs) is combined via conversion (ID mappings). After consolidation, for example, sales and marketing analyses can be executed enterprise-wide on the basis of harmonized master data by using SAP BW (see below).

2. **Master Data Harmonization**

   Whereas master data consolidation is carried out uniquely as a rule, master data harmonization ensures the continuous and consistent maintenance and distribution of the master data. In this scenario, master data continues to be maintained decentrally in various application components, from where they are forwarded to the Master Data Server (see Figure 14.4). A similar check takes place there, adding new entries in the ID mapping table if necessary. Finally, the changes are distributed to all decentralized application components involved.

3. **Central Master Data Administration**

   A further option for administrating distributed master data is to maintain the data exclusively at a central location. To do this requires a central master data server, the Master Data Server (see Figure 14.4), where the complete object definitions are stored, including the definitions of all dependent objects. This scenario has the advantage that maintenance and distribution of the master data is transparent and is controlled centrally, but presupposes a greater homogeneity of the master data in the entire system group.

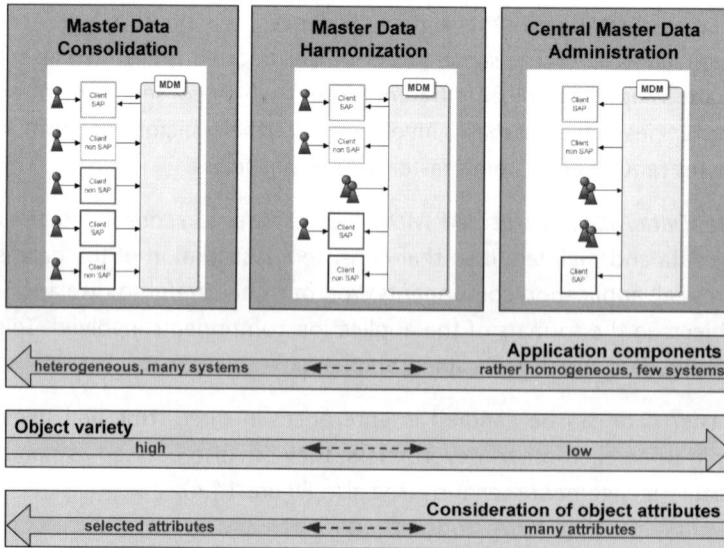

Figure 14.4 SAP Master Data Management Scenarios

SAP Master Data Management (SAP MDM) consists of the following four modules, which together address all requirements of master data administration:

▶ **SAP Exchange Infrastructure (SAP XI)**
As a component of *SAP NetWeaver,* SAP XI enables communication between various application components. SAP MDM uses the SAP XI for data buffering (queueing), message distribution (routing), and for converting structures and values (mapping).

▶ **SAP Content Integrator (SAP CI)**
The Content Integrator assumes master data consolidation tasks (matching and mapping), both for initial as well as for continuous consolidation of data.

▶ **Master Data Server (MDS)**
The Master Data Server is used for enterprisewide central master data distribution. For decentralized maintenance of the master data, the MDS assumes the consolidation, harmonization, and administration (distribution) of the master data to all application components in the system group. To do this, it accesses functionalities of the SAP XI and the SAP CI.

▶ **SAP Master Data Management Adapter (SAP MDM-Adapter)**
SAP Master Data Management communicates with external application components by using the Adapter. This SAP MDM-Adapter converts the data formats of the application components into a central format (Common Data Format), with which SAP MDM works.

Typically, the conversion of data structures and values is executed by the SAP Exchange Infrastructure, whereas the SAP Content Integrator, based on the results of object comparisons, creates conversion tables. For CRM business processes, business partners and products can also be harmonized by using CRM Middleware (see Section 15.4.2).

14.5.2 SAP Business Information Warehouse

SAP Business Information Warehouse (SAP BW) provides decision makers in an enterprise with swift and efficient access to all the information that they require. Hallmarks of SAP BW are:

▶ Coordinated information flow from internal and external information sources

▶ Optimized data storage and processing

▶ Comprehensive evaluation options and end-user-compatible data formatting

SAP BW consists of the following elements:

▶ **Business Content**
Preconfigured reports and analyses and information models (InfoCubes) and tools to extract and format data

▶ **Business Explorer**
User interface for analyzing data and reports stored in the Business Explorer Library

▶ **Business Explorer Analyzer**
In the event that data analysis is required but this is not covered by any standard report in the Business Explorer Library, the Business Explorer Analyzer enables an ad-hoc report to be defined quickly.

▶ **Administrator Workbench**
By using the Administrator Workbench, SAP BW can be implemented, monitored, and customized to fulfill new requirements.

14.5.3 SAP Knowledge Management

SAP Knowledge Management (SAP KM) generally describes the management of unstructured information such as audiovisual data, presentations, and texts in different formats. As part of the SAP Enterprise Portal, SAP KM includes the following functions:

▶ Central access to different information sources (CI)

▶ Tools for creating, publishing, and managing versions of documents

▶ Retrieval and classification of documents
Document indexing, classification, and search and navigation mechanisms

▶ Functions for information-related collaboration among individuals, for example, discussion groups, and mechanisms for processing information

In enterprises, information is often stored in different formats and distributed throughout various storage areas, for example, in file servers, groupware solutions, document storage systems, or ERP systems. In order to be able to access this information uniformly and centrally, SAP Knowledge Management provides interfaces for many current document repositories such as Windows-File-System, Lotus Notes, Microsoft Exchange, IXOS document management, and SAP R/3. Of course, customer- and product-related mySAP CRM information objects are also provided. Interfaces for additional external products can also be developed on a product basis.

14.6 Process Integration

By using SAP NetWeaver's process integration levels, cross-application- and -component business processes can be processed easily, regardless of whether mySAP Business Suite applications or non-SAP applications are involved. To do this, on the one hand, the SAP Exchange Infrastructure provides elementary services such as message distribution (routing) and the format conversion of messages, whereas on the other hand, at a higher level, entire business flows can be configured, monitored, and managed (Business Process Management).

14.6.1 SAP Exchange Infrastructure

The capability to integrate different applications is one of SAP's recipes for success. SAP R/2 and SAP R/3 stood out for being able to integrate standalone business applications locally by using a shared database. The request also to offer corresponding integration options for systems that were distributed in the enterprise or group was accommodated by SAP in 1995 with the *Application-Link-Enabling* (ALE) process [Buck-Emden/Galimow 1996]. ALE enabled technical and business integration of distributed SAP R/3 and third-party systems through explicit message interfaces.

SAP's experience, starting with ALE, is one of the fundamentals today for the *SAP Exchange Infrastructure*, which is based on open Internet technologies and XML message exchange. It is the SAP Exchange Infrastructure's task to enable standard-based, and hence open, process-oriented integration of heterogeneous application components in a distributed system landscape.

The *SAP Exchange Infrastructure* contains the following elements:

▶ **Integration Server**
The Integration Server secures operative collaboration between application components. A core part of the Integration Server is the *Integration Engine*, which performs the following tasks:

  ▶ Queuing
  Interim buffering of messages

  ▶ Mapping
  Conversion of various message formats and representations

  ▶ Routing
  Recipient determination and message distribution (both Publish/Subscribe and Request/Response)

  ▶ Monitoring
  Monitoring of collaborative processes during runtime

Additionally, the Integration Server includes the *Business Process Engine* for handling business processes modeled in BPEL4WS (Business Process Execution Language for Web Services).

▶ **Integration Repository**
The *Integration Repository* saves the entire knowledge of possible collaboration between application components available at the time the system was designed (design time), for example, definitions of interfaces, mappings, or business processes.

▶ **Integration Directory**
The *Integration Directory* includes the knowledge of the collaboration required between the application components available at the time the system was configured. Unlike the Integration Repository, the information in the Integration Directory is specifically designed for the respective installed base.

The SAP Exchange Infrastructure has been developed for open systems integration, which includes mySAP Business Suite applications as well as non-SAP systems. Complementary to this, mySAP CRM provides special integration services for CRM processes in the form of *CRM Middleware*. In particular, CRM Middleware enables extremely close integration of mySAP CRM with the SAP R/3 applications *Sales and Distribution*, *Customer Service*, and *Project Planning* (see Section 15.4.2 and Appendix B).

14.7 Application Platform

The development and runtime environment for all mySAP Business Suite solutions is the *SAP Web Application Server*. It represents the natural enhancement of *mySAP Technology* and therefore provides all its well-known strengths—high performance, far-reaching scalability, and robust operation. The SAP Web AS supports both *Java 2 Enterprise Edition (J2EE)* as well as *Advanced Business Application Programming (ABAP)*.

The SAP Web AS stands out because of the following characteristics:

▶ **Robust operation**
Trouble-free operation of business applications presupposes an application platform with good response times, load-dependent scalability, and high availability of all components. Depending on the degree of availability required, some component redundancy is inevitable. If an instance of the SAP Web AS breaks down, for example, all server inquiries are forwarded automatically to another instance. Fail-safe computer clusters ensure a high degree of availability of the SAP Web Application Server central database.

- ▶ **Scalability**

  Scalability is the ability to guarantee convenient response times, even for an increasing number of applications and end users. Scalable business solutions grow with business requirements and user access. In the world of scalability, load distribution to multiple systems plays a central role. The SAP Web AS uses software-based distribution of server access to distributed server instances, taking the current load on the relevant systems into consideration.

- ▶ **Openness**

  The SAP Web Application Server is based on widespread Internet and Web service standards. HyperText Transfer Protocol (HTTP) and its more secure variant HTTPS, as well as Internet document standards such as HyperText Markup Language (HTML) and eXtensible Markup Language (XML), are supported by the SAP Web Application Server. The same applies for Web service standards such as Simple Object Access Protocol (SOAP), Web Service Description Language (WDDL), Universal Description, Discovery and Integration (UDDI), and the recently adopted Web Service Choreography Interface (WSCI). Additionally, the SAP Web Application Server fully meets the J2EE specification.

- ▶ **Platform independence**

  The SAP Web Application Server provides a capable extraction level for databases as well as for operating systems, so that business applications need only be developed once and can run without the time-consuming customization that is often needed in different system landscapes, including open-source platforms.

Presentation Services

The SAP Web Application Server presentation services support the creation of user interfaces for Web applications by using *Web Dynpro* technology and server-side scripting with *Business Server Pages (BSPs)* or *Java Server Pages (JSPs)* and pre-defined user interface elements (Tag Library). The user interfaces created in this way can, for example, be included as iViews in portal pages in the SAP Enterprise Portal (see Section 14.4.1).

With Web Dynpro, the options offered by browser-based user interfaces were substantially enhanced to fulfill business requirements for input help, multilingual capability, user-friendly error handling, and input checking in the front end, for example. Web Dynpro is based on an extended server-side scripting programming model and uses uniform, intuitive specified patterns for designing user interfaces. Code can be generated from Web Dynpro's XML-based interface descriptions for various runtime environments.

JSPs and BSPs are languages embedded in HTML for server-side scripting. Java Server Pages extend Java Servlet technology. As a link between presentation and business logic, they allow the provision of dynamic Web pages for browser users. Business Server Pages is an ABAP-based scripting language.

Java Server Pages and Business Server Pages, in comparison to simple HTML, provide much more powerful programming models for Web user interfaces. For example, by including a single BSP tag in the HTML code, you can create a date input field in the browser during runtime that can validate user input. For JSPs and BSPs, besides such simple elements as the date input field, more complex display elements such as trees or sortable tables are also available.

The iViews in the People-Centric User Interface of mySAP CRM are based on *Business Server Pages* (see Section 15.2).

Database Services

Business application requirements placed on the persistence layer of the SAP Web Application Server have to do with the efficient and effective storage and handling of large amounts of data. These requirements include:

▶ High-performance database access (including data buffering, caching)

▶ Transaction support

▶ Secure storage of data

The database interface of the SAP Web AS, which is available for Java and ABAP applications, is based on OpenSQL and offers a high-performance abstraction layer in comparison to manufacturer-specific SQL implementations. Furthermore, the database interface supports technical functions such as caching SQL statements, buffering data, and tracing database access.

14.8   Lifecycle Management

SAP NetWeaver's Lifecycle Management includes all services that support the software lifecycle—from implementation to operation to customizing and extending software solutions:

▶ The implementation phase consists of hardware sizing as well as installing and configuring the software, including data migration and comprehensive tests.

▶ In daily operation, a high degree of performance and availability must be ensured for the entire system landscape. Furthermore, security and globalization services are required to operate larger global software solutions (see Sections 14.8.2 and 14.8.3).

▶ Software solutions change and improve continually, so that tools for customizing and making extensions have to be provided, for example, for software upgrades, managing software customizing (Software Change Management), or scaling hardware.

The central tool to implement and operate mySAP Business Suite solutions is the *SAP Solution Manager*. This tool and the security and globalization services are described in the following section.

14.8.1 SAP Solution Manager

The *SAP Solution Manager* is a standalone system that is provided to all customers free of charge. It combines all information and tools required for implementing and operating mySAP Business Suite solutions. As a uniform central tool that can be used for all SAP applications, it helps to simplify processes, reduce training costs, and shorten the duration of projects.

One of the important hallmarks of the SAP Solution Manager is its business content. For mySAP CRM, for example, 90 business scenarios with a total of over 270 processes are delivered with the SAP Solution Manager. Business documentation describes in detail the use and sequence of each single business scenario. Installation, configuration, and upgrade guides give step-by-step help in the technical and functional implementation of the solution.

Implementation Support

The SAP Solution Manager offers targeted help in all phases of implementing SAP software solutions. To do this, it employs the *AcceleratedSAP* method *(ASAP)* for planning and executing SAP implementation projects (see Section 13.2.3). Among other things, the SAP Solution Manager provides the following tools and content for the implementation phase:

▶ Process library for selecting the business processes to be implemented and assigning the process steps to the respective systems

▶ Graphical structuring of the system landscape at various levels of detail, whereby system data is in part read automatically

▶ Customizing tools for the individual attributes of the solution and for cross-system comparison of Customizing settings (*Customizing Distribution* and *Customizing Scout*)

▶ *Business Configuration Sets (BC Sets)*, a technology for combining Customizing settings flexibly and reusing them, for example, to supply subsidiaries with the same configured systems

▶ Management of the technical implementation of SAP software solutions

- ▶ Securing the runability of all central business processes. This also contains access to the SAP Service GoingLive Check (tried-and-trusted procedure for successful production startup)
- ▶ *Test-Workbench* for defining, automating, and managing test cases
- ▶ Role-based access to all SAP Solution Manager functions, for example, for project leaders or application consultants

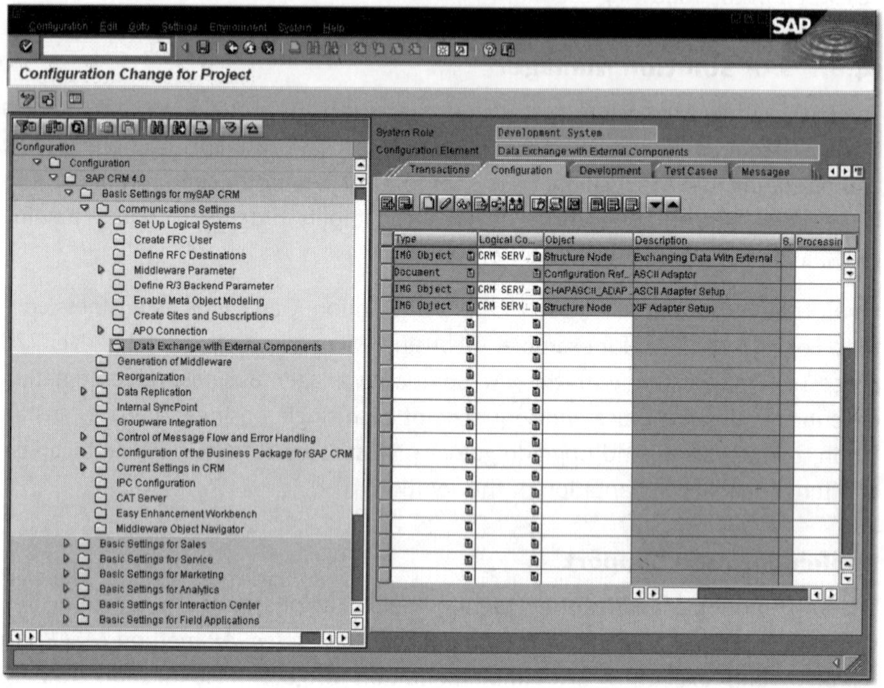

Figure 14.5 Implementation of mySAP CRM with the SAP Solution Manager

When software implementation is complete, all project-relevant information is saved in the *SAP Solution Manager*. Besides the project description, the entire documentation created during the project is also saved there. This ensures that all important information on the project is available if required later for a system upgrade or for problems that might arise.

Operational Support

In productive operation, the SAP Solution Manager is the central instance for monitoring the implemented integrated solution. In this function, it not only provides monitoring services, but also functions as the central interface for SAP Support. Moreover, the SAP Solution Manager offers the infrastructure for setting up an enterprise-internal Support Desk, for example, by also including the mySAP CRM Solution Database (see Section 7.5.2).

In detail, the SAP Solution Manager provides the following services for the operational phase:

▶ Monitoring of all central business processes and safeguarding of their ability to run (business process monitoring)

▶ Observation of the entire system and application landscape, including the interfaces to third-party systems (system and interfaces monitoring)

▶ Access to SAP Service Marketplace support and maintenance services

▶ Use of SAP Notes with current information and error corrections

▶ *Notes Assistant* for automatic implementation of SAP Notes

▶ Desktop sharing by using Microsoft NetMeeting

▶ Remote Support by SAP employees

There is a comprehensive description of all *SAP Solution Manager* services in [Oswald 2003].

14.8.2 Security Services

SAP NetWeaver offers an integrated security infrastructure with the following elements and characteristics:

Secure User Authentication and Single Sign-On

The secure determination of user identities, user authentication, and Single Sign-On for avoiding repeated logons when using multiple application systems are supported by certificates, tickets, and connection options for products from third parties.

▶ **Single Sign-On**
Using the Single Sign-On procedure, users log on just once to a central location. All applications and systems that are called afterwards can get the user's identity from this central location.

▶ **Certificates**
Digital certificates contain identity and public key information for encryption and digital signatures. They are issued by a central certification authority, with which the user must first register. SAP supports the use of X.509-compatible certificates and recommends them for critical applications. The *SAP Trust Center Service* provides SAP customers with digital certificates free of charge.

▶ **Tickets**

Tickets are cookies secured by a digital signature, which forward the logon information to the respective application called. Tickets do not use a public key infrastructure and should be supplemented with additional security mechanisms if necessary.

Secure Communication Between Client and Server Components

For HTTPS connections (secure HTTP) between single system components, SAP NetWeaver supports the Secure Socket Layer (SSL) standard. For connections that do not use the HTTP protocol, there is the Secure Network Communication (SNC). This proven technology has been available since 1996 and can be used for server-to-server connections between SAP systems. Secure Network Communication was developed in accordance with the General Security Services-Application Programming Interface (GSS-API) standard and can be used not only for encryption, but also for SSO with partner products. GSS-API is an application interface for the secure transfer of data between systems and was designed by the Common Authentication Technologies (CAT) group of the Internet Engineering Task Force (IETF).

External access to internal systems can be controlled by using firewalls, which block single communications channels (ports) as necessary. Furthermore, it is possible to check inbound and outbound traffic in the firewall, for example, for viruses or sensitive information. Additionally, in internal communications too, extremely sensitive systems should be protected by *demilitarized zones*, implemented by switching through a series of firewalls.

Secure Processing of Business Transactions

To ensure the security of business transactions, SAP NetWeaver provides digital signatures. These signatures are appended to the business documents to be exchanged and guarantee their authenticity, integrity, and liability (non-deniability, non-repudiation). Furthermore, cryptographic procedures can be used to encrypt the content of business documents.

Audit Framework

For legal reasons, enterprises are obliged to prove the correctness of business processes and the security of the application components in the enterprise. Generally, this is done by auditors who carry out *audits*. An audit is defined as the tracing and joint logging of technical or business events in the application components so that they can be reproduced later. Within single SAP application components, audits can be carried out by SAP's *Audit Information System (AIS)*, for example.

For audits of business processes that span application components from various manufacturers, or for collaborative business scenarios across enterprise boundaries, an audit framework is required to extract and combine the relevant data from the various components by using interfaces with fixed definitions. In a project with customers, SAP is currently determining the requirements for such an audit framework.

14.8.3 Globalization Services

Global business applications must satisfy not only country-specific requirements (languages, laws, regulations, currencies, time zones, and so on), but also enable the interaction of cross-country processes. Important aspects of the globalization of business solutions are:

▶ Languages

Different languages must be supported on different levels. Usually, during logon, end users specify the languages for user interfaces, screens, menus, error mesages, and documentation. The business partners determine the language of the business documents, for example, sales orders, invoices, supply contracts, or business correspondence. Furthermore, the law specifies the language for official documents such as tax and customs declarations.

Additional prerequisites for multilingual business solutions are efficient translation tools for user interfaces, business documents, configurations, and business data. Furthermore, under certain circumstances, several different character sets may need to be supported at the same time. The technical prerequisites for using different character sets are fulfilled by code pages or Unicode. Unicode is extremely important as an international standard for coding languages because it can be used to show all the world's character sets in one system at the same time.

Additionally, when using different languages at the same time, it must be possible to maintain master data multilingually in all application components involved.

▶ Country versions

The success of a global business solution largely depends on how closely local characteristic features can be considered. These features include, for example, tax calculations, invoicing and payment customs, following laws and regulations, order processing, taking inflation rates into account, wage- and salary lists, or displaying time and date specifications.

▶ Currencies

In global business processes, the support of multiple currencies is essential. To establish and ensure this support, it is important that different currencies can be used equally. So, for example, a multinational enterprise can conduct business in America with U.S. Dollars, a French subsidiary can invoice in Euros, whereas Thai business processes are conducted using Baht. To consolidate turnover enterprisewide, any particular currency can be selected. To convert currency, multiple exchange rates must be supported, for purchasing or selling a currency, for example.

▶ **Time zones**
In global business transactions that span different time zones, the employees involved, business partners, and application systems work in different time zones. This can lead to problems, for example, to post being dispatched late or batch processes not being carried out. Batch processes in particular, which not only include logistic functionalities such as availability checks or product planning, but also financial accounting, depend on local time zones. The various applications must therefore either work in a uniform time zone, for example, in a Universal Time Coordinated (UTC) time zone, or be converted so that they adhere to the local time zone.

▶ **Address management**
Address formats differ from country to country. There may even be different address formats in one and the same country. For example, in Japan, addresses for domestic letters are written in Kanji. For correspondence outside Japan, an international character set is used. The different address formats must automatically be factored by the application components.

SAP NetWeaver addresses all technical aspects that are placed on global applications by the aforementioned requirements. Furthermore, mySAP Business Suite applications implement solution-specific globalization services, functions, and characteristics.

14.9 Composite Application Framework

If you analyze options for improving productivity and flexibility in developing business applications, then, currently, the approaches to service-oriented development of applications *(Service-Oriented Development of Applications, SODA)* that have arisen in connection with Web services and modern integrated platform solutions *(Application Platform Suites)* are particularly promising (compare with, for example, [Buck-Emden/Böder 2003a]). The basic principle of a service-oriented application architecture *(Service-Oriented Architecture, SOA)* is that development of innovative applications no longer starts from scratch. On the contrary, application services provided by existing, proven-quality application components, for example, as Web services, can be given special user interfaces or be included in completely new applications (Composite Applications). In this way, the development, customizing, and customer-oriented user interface design becomes markedly quicker, more flexible, and less expensive. This kind of software development lends itself particularly to supporting process-oriented applications that use various service functions from different applications. The Composite Applications developed in this way are not necessarily restricted to traditional transaction processing on the basis of a relational database, but can also integrate functions such as team collaboration, content management, and business analytics [Buck-Emden/Zencke 2003].

Composite Applications address the following challenges, among others:

▶ **Integration of heterogeneous system landscapes**
Composite Applications work with services and business objects from diverse SAP and non-SAP applications, even with different release statuses if necessary. This requires an abstraction layer between the business objects, services, and processes of the Composite Applications and the service applications.

▶ **Consistency across all Composite Applications**
To achieve the highest consistency of all Composite Applications, modeling and generation tools, patterns for user interfaces and subapplications, and reusable predefined object models are required.

▶ **Easy configurability**
Composite Applications should be quick and easy to customize to meet the requirements of enterprises or single employees. To do this, for example, tools are required that allow ad-hoc changes to business processes.

Composite Applications represent a core concept of the Enterprise Services Architecture (see Section 5.1). As part of SAP NetWeaver, the *Composite Application Framework (CAF)* offers a model-driven environment for developing and executing Composite Applications. The following levels make up the CAF (see Figure 14.6):

▶ *User interface level* with SAP Enterprise Portal, Web Dynpro, reusable patterns for user interfaces, and so on

▶ *Process control level* with process templates, guided procedures, ad-hoc workflow, universal worklist, and so on

▶ *Service level* for modeling and using new and extended application services via the Webservice infrastructure of the SAP Web Application Server

▶ *Object level* with the options to model and generate business objects, and access the associated data sources

Composite Application Framework

UI Modeler	Metadata	UI Framework	
Web Dynpro	UI	UI Components	UI Pattern
Pattern Config.		Web Dynpro Runtime	

Process Modeler		Process Framework	
Guided Procedures	Processes Workflows	Guided Procedures	Universal Worklist
Templates		Ad hoc Workflow Runtime	

Service Modeler		Service Framework	
Services	Services	Composite Services	External Services
Templates		BO Services	Generic Services

Object Modeler		Object Framework	
Business Objects	Objects	Business Objects	Lifecycle Methods
Templates		Data Access Framework	

UDDI / WSDL

XMI / JMI   SAP XI   SAP KM   SAP BW   DB

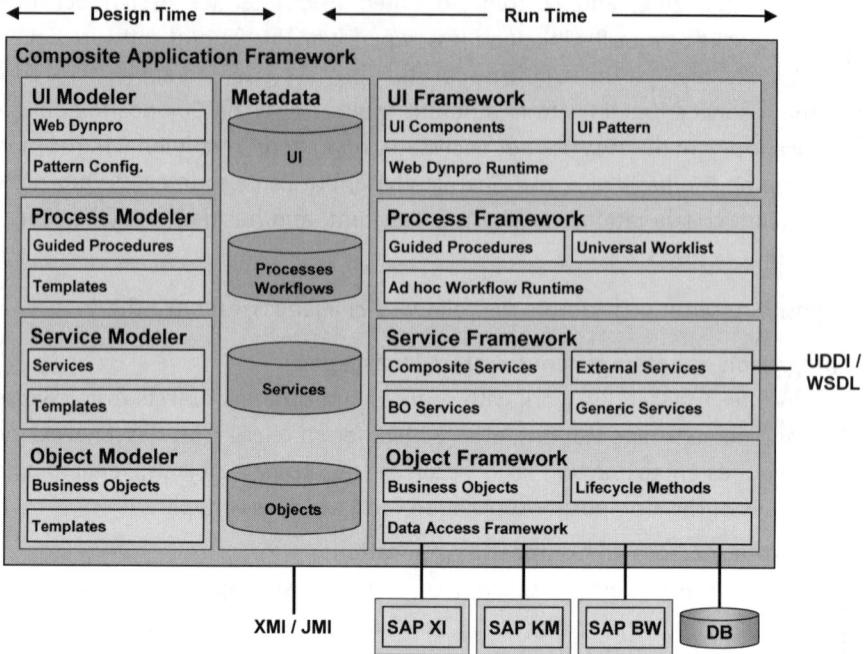

Figure 14.6 Composite Application Framework Overview

For more information on the concept and on converting composite applications, see [Woods 2003], for example.

15 Architecture and Technology of mySAP CRM

"Technology infrastructure is necessary, but not sufficient...
Technology is an enabler."
Don Peppers [Peppers 2002]

15.1 Overview

mySAP CRM is a leading software solution for customer relationship management, not only functionally, but also technically. Early on, mySAP CRM realized concepts that are now in an enhanced and generalized form in all areas of SAP NetWeaver. Additionally, mySAP CRM uses supplementary technical services that address specific CRM requirements in the area of integrating SAP R/3 and synchronizing mobile CRM applications. Figure 15.1 shows the overall context.

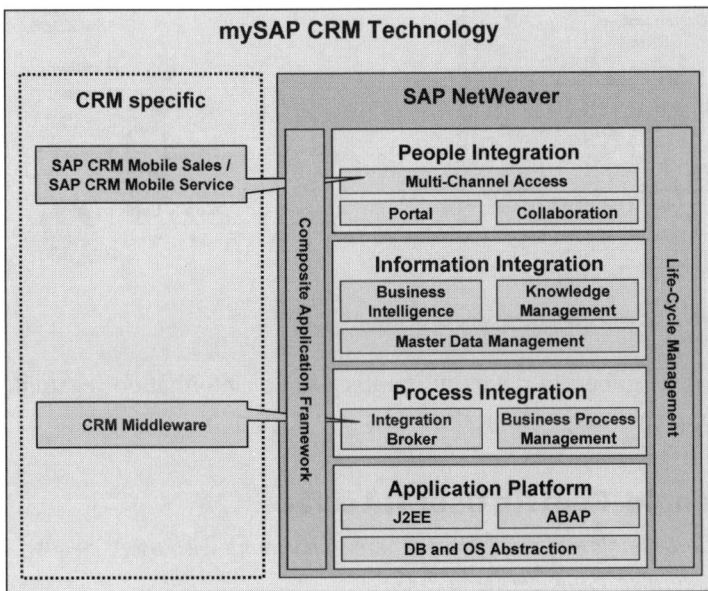

Figure 15.1 mySAP CRM on the Basis of SAP NetWeaver

First, when installing mySAP CRM, the focus is on the CRM Server as the basic software component. The CRM Server includes central CRM applications such as Marketing, Sales, and Service, and the technical components of the integrated CRM Middleware (see Section 15.4). Because the CRM Server runs on the SAP NetWeaver application platform, the SAP Web Application Server (SAP Web AS), these same tools are available for implementing, operating, and extending mySAP CRM just as they are for all other solutions of the mySAP Business-Suite (see Section 15.5). For example, the CRM Server can be coupled with Enterprise Resource Planning (ERP) systems, Supplier Relationship Management systems, or groupware servers, according to functionality and integration requirements. Furthermore, manifold technical communication channels are supported, for example, Internet, telephone, and mobile communication devices (see Section 15.3). Figure 15.2 gives an overview of the CRM Server and how it is embedded in the complete system landscape.

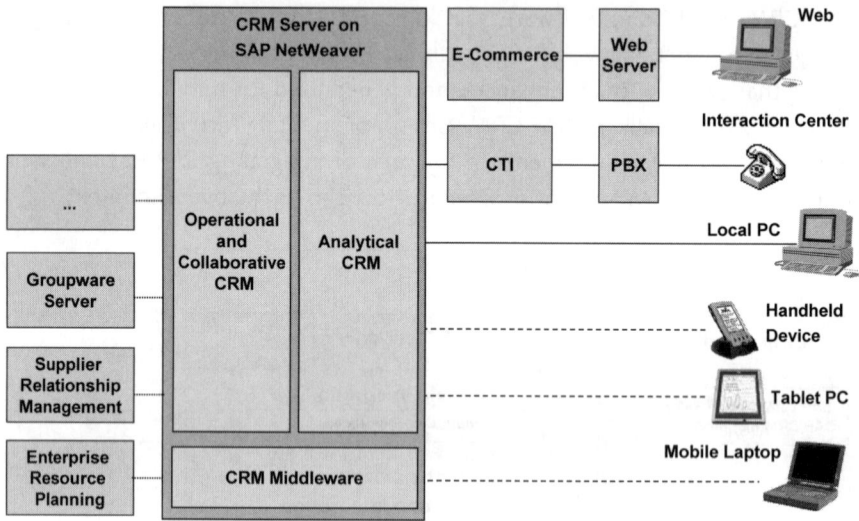

Figure 15.2 CRM Server as a Central Component of mySAP CRM

SAP NetWeaver is described in detail in Chapter 14. For information regarding mySAP CRM's supplementary technical services, see Appendix A.

15.2 The People-Centric User Interface

"Successful technologies are those that are in harmony with user's needs."
Ben Shneiderman [Shneidermann 2002]

Acceptance by an enterprise's employees is integral to the success of CRM implementation projects (see Sections 4.3.2 and 13.2.2). Software that is intuitive and easy to learn plays a key role in this acceptance. To fulfill this requirement, a new graphical user interface was developed for mySAP CRM as the first level of the Web Dynpro (see Section 14.7), the "People-Centric User Interface" [Buck-Emden/Böder 2003]. This user interface is based on the SAP Enterprise Portal and

BSP Scripting (see Section 14.7) and is displayed in a typical Web browser. mySAP CRM functions can therefore be accessed easily by using the Internet and Intranet.

Development of the People-Centric User Interface was based on the method of Contextual Design developed by Karen Holtzblatt and Hugh Beyer, whereby the first step is to determine, in interviews with users, how the workflows look from the user's viewpoint [Holtzblatt/Beyer 1998]. Once these workflows have been visualized in models, the actual design process begins, whereby the user interface is designed by using prototypes and usability reviews. Therefore, the basis for the interface design is not the technical options, but the actual work processes in the enterprise, or the way in which people work, that is, the user context [Brendle/Buck-Emden/Bach 2002].

The following requirements for designing the People-Centric User Interface for mySAP CRM have been identified on the basis of user studies:

▶ Individualized, task-oriented access to applications and information from various sources

▶ Uniform user interface structure to ensure quick orientation for casual users as well

▶ Interactive design that supports employees' actual workflows

▶ Simple, intuitive navigation for quick orientation and for targeted control of the application

The requirements are implemented by using interactive designs based on reusable patterns and a role-based menu.

15.2.1 Pattern-Based Interactive Design

When designing user interfaces, a fundamental distinction must be made between graphical design and interactive design.

Graphical design is concerned with the interface layout. Using standardized format templates (Stylesheets), it determines which colors, fonts, and sizes are used in the interface. Usually, the graphical design of a software application is modified on location to match the layout that the enterprise already uses. Layout modifications of this kind are done by using a *Stylesheet Editor that* is delivered, for example, with the SAP Enterprise Portal.

Interactive design, on the other hand, is not focused on colors and fonts, but rather, on how the system can support users in their single work steps and workflow, and how to structure the user interface accordingly. Interactive design determines the structure of the user interface, which data can be displayed where and when, which interface elements are used for entering data, and how navigation to functions, applications, and information works.

In the People-Centric User Interface of mySAP CRM, interactive design is based on interface modules that are structured according to predefined patterns. A *pattern* is a general term to describe a canonical solution to a special design problem. Combined with the layout of user interfaces, repeating patterns increase consistency and make the system more intuitive and easy to use.

Architecture first took up the idea that proven solutions to design problems can be described by general patterns [Tidwell 1999]. A simple example of an architectural pattern states, for example, that the dining room is next to the kitchen so that there is no need to carry food through the entire house. In a similar vein, pattern solutions can be created for the interactive design of software solutions. SAP has determined from numerous user studies that most users repeatedly execute similar steps when working with the CRM system. These steps include:

▶ Selecting the application category, for example, Lead Management or Activity Management

▶ Checking that the correct application was called

▶ Finding the business object, for example, order, which is to be processed

▶ Selecting the business object

▶ Looking at and modifying the business object header data

▶ Looking at and modifying the business object detailed data

These activities always follow in the same sequence, regardless of whether the user is accepting a service order or is managing his or her personal activities. Therefore, this sequence lent itself to designing a pattern solution to structure the user interface for these basic activities. This is made up of the following elements, which are organized in the screen in descending order (see Section 15.3):

▶ Orientation and navigation area

▶ Search area and search results

▶ Detail areas

Of course, it may be that particular interface patterns are not suitable for all application cases. So, for example, the employees in a Call Center work according to a special procedure. When they call a business partner, they need all relevant information at once and at a glance. The pattern for the user interface of the mySAP CRM Interaction Center application accordingly looks different (see Section 10.2.7).

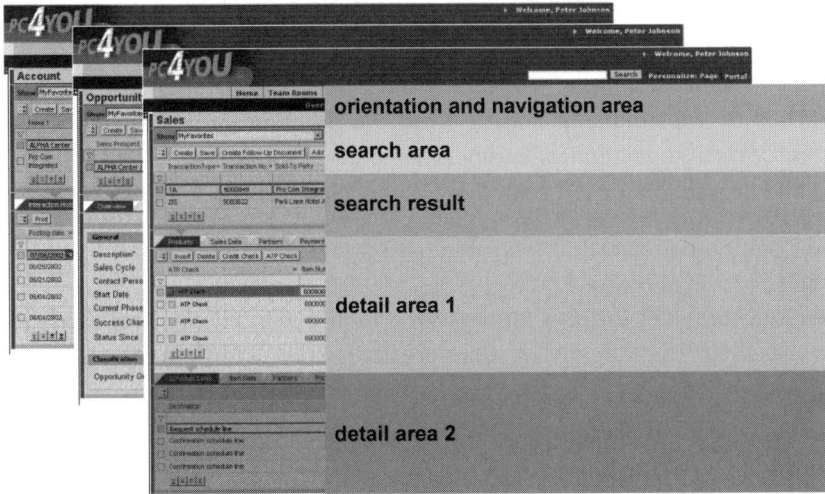

Figure 15.3 Interface Patterns for a Software Solution's Fundamental Tasks

Basic tasks, such as navigation, finding objects, or entering data, are made up of many individual activities. The task "Finding the Business Object," for example, includes selecting search criteria, entering corresponding search terms, and triggering the search. Patterns for the interaction design also need to be designed for these tasks. In this way, patterns occur at various abstraction levels. After designing the master blueprint, the design of the individual screen areas contained in it is developed. The major components of the interface such as the search or detail areas are therefore composed of smaller elements.

Patterns are abstract specifications that are defined concretely for each respective application. mySAP CRM and the People-Centric User Interface are based on SAP Enterprise Portal technology and use BSP Scripting in accordance with the *Model View Controller (MVC) programming model* (see Sections 14.7 and 15.2.3) for creating iViews.

15.2.2 Portal Services for the People-Centric User Interface

The mySAP CRM's People-Centric User Interface uses the SAP Enterprise Portal for role-based system access, for displaying iViews, for navigation and orientation, and for Knowledge Management (see Section 14.4.1). The navigation services also include supporting object links that enable the user to jump directly from one business object to another application transaction.

15.2.3 Interface Implementation Following the Model View Controller Approach

The Model View Controller concept (MVC) is one of the most common approaches to implementing graphic Web interfaces in structured form. It is based on a clear separation of business logic (Model), display of the interface (View) and interaction logic (Controller). The individual elements assume the following tasks:

▶ **Model**
The model provides the data for the user interface without any interest in how it is visualized. The Model's functions are accessed via standardized interfaces.

▶ **View**
The View is the visualization level responsible for the graphic formatting of the user interface (HTML Rendering).

▶ **Controller**
The Controller functions as a link between the Model and the View. It monitors the user's mouse and keyboard input and prompts the View and Model to react accordingly. In this way, data entries are forwarded to the Model for further processing. The results then make their way from the Model to the Controller to the View.

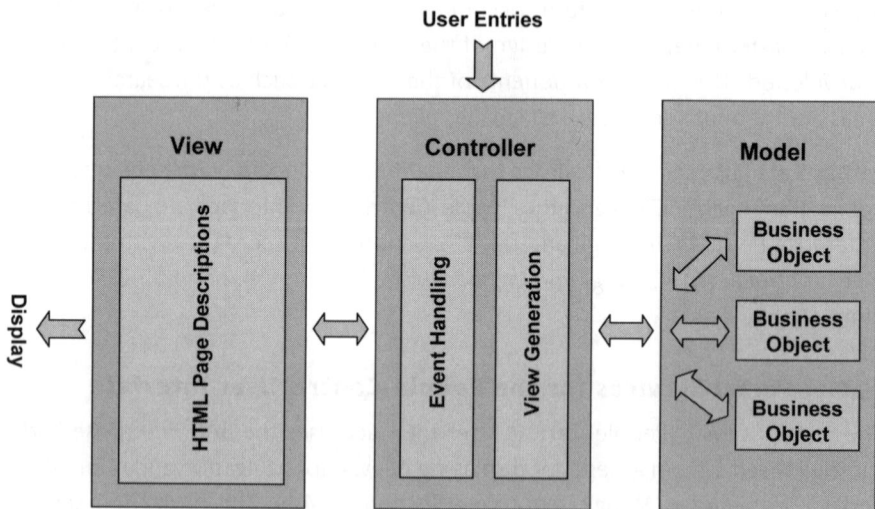

Figure 15.4 Model View Controller Programming Model

To ensure that the specified pattern solutions are also implemented in the interaction design of the applications, the patterns in the mySAP CRM People-Centric User Interface are implemented as part of the View. Each application defines the

View specifically for its needs through configuration tables. These configuration settings specify, for example, the sequence of buttons in the toolbar, but not the position of the toolbar. This has already been specified by the pattern.

15.2.4 Interface Configuration and Personalization

In very rare cases, a single interface design for all users from different enterprises can be used across all industries. In practice, the depicted business processes differ from enterprise to enterprise. It is therefore important that the user interface demonstrates the necessary flexibility to be matched to different requirements.

mySAP CRM's pattern-based user interface consists of fixed, single modules such as navigation bars, toolbars, data fields, or register tabs, and can be defined specifically by enterprise and/or employee via the following means:

▶ Configuration

▶ Personalization

▶ Object Extensions

Configuration enables all users to add, move, or delete interface modules, whereas personalization means the individual matching of such modules [Cooper 1995]. Object extensions, on the other hand, permit the addition of new modules to existing business objects, which can then also be displayed on the screen.

Configuration

Both single roles and the entire application can be adjusted. Therefore, the layout is normally matched to the enterprise's corporate identity. The standard roles delivered by SAP can be adapted specifically for the enterprise. Furthermore, it is possible to design completely new roles.

To configure the People-Centric User Interface, SAP provides various tools, for example, the graphic *CRM Designer* enables most common adjustments to be made by using the mouse. These include:

▶ Positioning of data fields

▶ Showing and hiding data fields

▶ Determining the characteristics of data fields for example, mandatory or optional display fields

▶ Showing and hiding toolbar functions

▶ Showing and hiding register tab titles

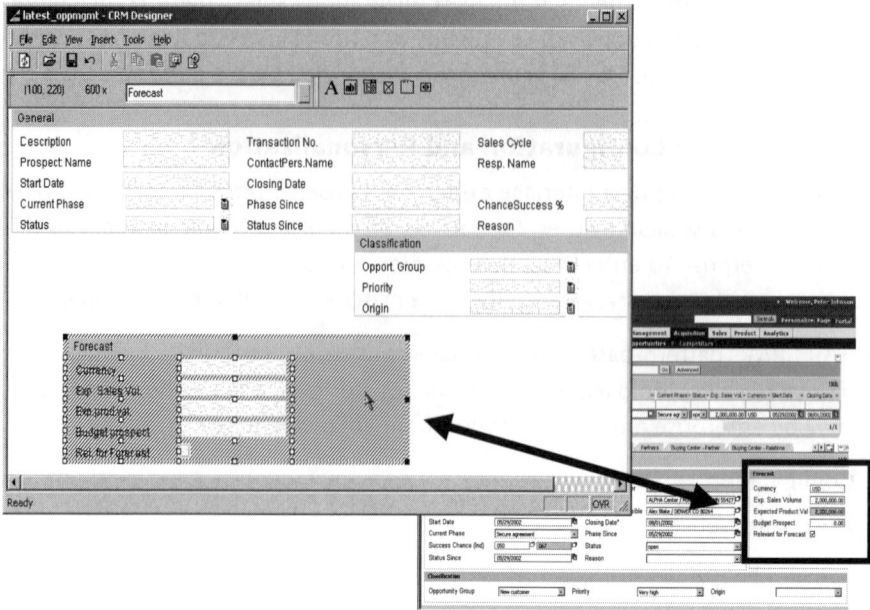

Figure 15.5 CRM Designer in Action

Users adapt markedly quicker to a software solution when the application speaks "their language," that is, using terminology they are familiar with. To translate text, use the *Text Replacement Tool* to match field names and user interface labels to enterprise-internal ones. Listed one-by-one, the Text Replacement Tool provides the following services:

▶ Fixed text substitution for displaying customer- or industry-specific terminology

▶ Context-sensitive text substitution

▶ Tools for translating substituted texts

▶ Options for exporting substituted texts to other systems

▶ Solutions for upgrades

Texts delivered by SAP and the industry-specific matched texts are kept in separate directories. You only need to activate the terminology to be displayed to the user.

Personalization

With the People-Centric User Interface, mySAP CRM offers each user his or her own personalized workspace. mySAP CRM greets each user personally. On the homepage, the user sees the information most important to him or her at a glance.

Employees who log on with the *Sales Employee* role, for example, are shown the current day's activities and their personal alert inbox. When calling a CRM transaction, users first see the business objects they defined earlier as personal favorites.

Furthermore, each single user has various options for personalizing the user interface to meet their individual requirements. These options include defining the structure and content of the initial page, choosing the language, personalizing lists by showing and hiding columns and specifying the column sequence, adjusting the portal window (iViews), and adjusting the style and color of the portal layout.

Object Extensions

Projects often require the extension of business objects, and therefore, special attributes—attributes that aren't part of the standard delivery—are needed. For example, a shoe manufacturer would like to store information on customers' shoe sizes. This kind of extension can be executed in mySAP CRM by defining marketing attributes, or by using the *Easy Enhancement Workbench* (see Sections 15.5.1 and 15.5.2). No programming is necessary in either case.

15.3 Multi-Channel Interaction for mySAP CRM

mySAP CRM supports all popular technical interaction channels such as mobile communication devices, telephone, email, fax, and Internet. The following chapter describes the functions implemented in mySAP CRM to support this interaction.

15.3.1 Mobile CRM Solutions

The mobile solutions offered with mySAP CRM for the sales and service area meet the needs of both the casual and the professional user. Whereas a handheld communication device will typically suffice for casual users, professional field sales representatives will most likely require a laptop or a Tablet PC. Handheld communication devices have little business logic and have no database of their own, and can be considered to be a kind of "long arm" of the central application. Mobile applications for laptops and Tablet PC devices, on the other hand, offer their users highly developed functions with comprehensive business logic and their own local databases. They frequently work offline and synchronize their databases at specific times with those of the CRM Server. In doing so, they place specific requirements on data distribution (replication), because only the data that is really required should be synchronized between central and mobile users, which also accounts for various sales areas, vacation replacements, and so on.

The CRM Middleware integrated in mySAP CRM addresses all the replication requirements of the mobile laptop solutions *Mobile Sales* and *Mobile Service* (see

Section 8.4.1). The following options are available for distributing and synchronizing offline databases:

▶ **Unfiltered replication**
In unfiltered replication, all business objects of a specific type are sent to all recipients (see section 15.4.2) who have previously subscribed to this business object type.

▶ **Intelligent replication**
In intelligent replication, specific selection criteria can be defined so that a recipient only gets selected business objects of a specific type, for example, only customers from a specific country.

▶ **Dependent replication**
In dependent replication, dependencies between business objects can be taken into account during replication. For example, a mobile laptop user can get all customers in his or her sales region and all associated (dependent) activities too. To do this, CRM Middleware supports multiple dependency levels, ranging from very simple dependencies—in which each object can follow just one other object—to freely-definable dependencies between any business objects. No programming is necessary for defining replication and the dependencies of business objects.

Besides replication, CRM Middleware automatically redistributes data (Realignment). If, for example, a customer's address changes so that a field sales representative is no longer responsible for this customer, CRM Middleware automatically removes this customer from the field sales representative's local database and replicates this data to a colleague. Furthermore, CRM Middleware includes special services for managing territories (Territory Management) and substitution rules, for example, vacation replacements.

15.3.2 Interaction Center

The Interaction Center of mySAP CRM supports different communication channels and technologies, such as telephone, email, fax, letter, Short Message Service (SMS), paging, Web Chat, Call-Me-Back, co-browsing, and voice-over-IP (VoIP). Provided that an enterprise enables all channels, the customer can choose which medium he or she will use to make contact.

The Interaction Center user interface allows customer inquiries to be processed quickly, because, on the one hand, all the necessary information about the customer is displayed on one screen page, and on the other hand, the system leads the agent through all the necessary process steps.

Agents can use the Interaction Center of mySAP CRM either through the SAP GUI-based *WinClient* or, through the browser-based *WebClient* (see Section 10.2.7).

Agents who use the Interaction Center WinClient can be supplied with customer contacts in four different ways:

▶ First, it is possible to connect telephone systems (Private Branch Exchange, PBX) via SAPphone with the aid of suitable connectors. Email servers such as Microsoft Exchange and Lotus Domino are connected via SAPconnect via using the Simple Mail Transfer Protocol (SMTP) (see Figure 15.6). In the latter case, the agents access a group inbox that provides the worklist for a user-definable agent group and contains, for example, emails, faxes, and scanned letters (integration of faxes and letters is also supported by SAPconnect) according to the settings made.

The connectors required to connect telephone systems to SAPphone have to convert the CTI software (Computer Telephony Integration) communication protocols of the telephone system manufacturer into the SAP Remote Function Call (RFC) and TAPI (Telephony Application Programming Interface) protocols used by SAPphone.

▶ Second, the *Multi-Channel Interface* of the Interaction Center, as an alternative interface to SAPphone and SAPconnect, allows customer contacts to be delivered to specific agents according to previously defined routing rules (see Figure 15.6), regardless of whether by telephone, email, chat, or paging. This means that agents no longer need to select contacts manually, but are assigned to them automatically. To do this, agents typically work on just one contact channel. The different contact channels are connected technically by using connectors, for example, SAPphone.

▶ Third, integrating the Gplus Adapter from the company Genesys Telecommunications Laboratories into the Interaction Center represents a special solution for realizing a *Universal Queue* that enables routing of inbound contacts from different communication channels to suitable and available agents (see Figure 15.6). In this way, agents can be supplied directly with contacts from various channels. In addition to the contact channels available, co-browsing is also supported.

▶ With the development of the Interaction Center WebClient, a new generation of communication interfaces was also created. The open, *Integrated Communication Interface (ICI)* can be certified and is based on SAP NetWeaver's *Business Communication Broker (BCB)* and therefore, forms a standard interface for integrating communication management solutions, which, in turn, can connect any number of communication channels (see Figure 15.7). To do this, the ICI communicates with third parties' communication management software via Internet standards such as Simple Object Access Protocol (SOAP) and Extensible Markup Language (XML).

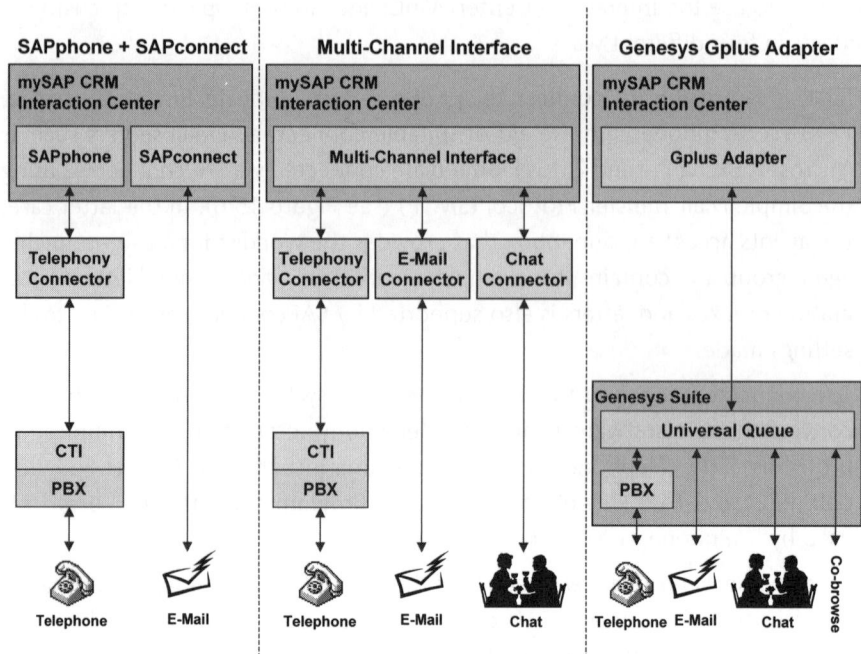

Figure 15.6 Multi-Channel Interface for the Interaction Center WinClient

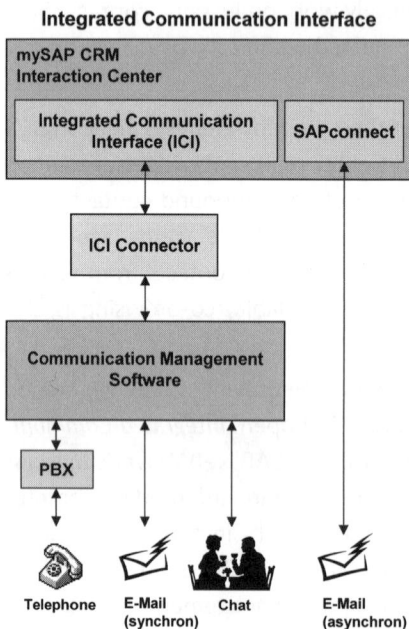

Figure 15.7 Multi-Channel Architecture for the Interaction Center WinClient

15.3.3 Internet

mySAP CRM's e-commerce processes (see Section 9.4) use the Internet as a technical communication channel. Figure 15.8 shows an example of the architecture of the e-selling solution divided up into the logical blocks *Business Execution, Business Service*, and *Internet*. The ability to assign single software components to dedicated servers enables the integrated solution to achieve optimal performance.

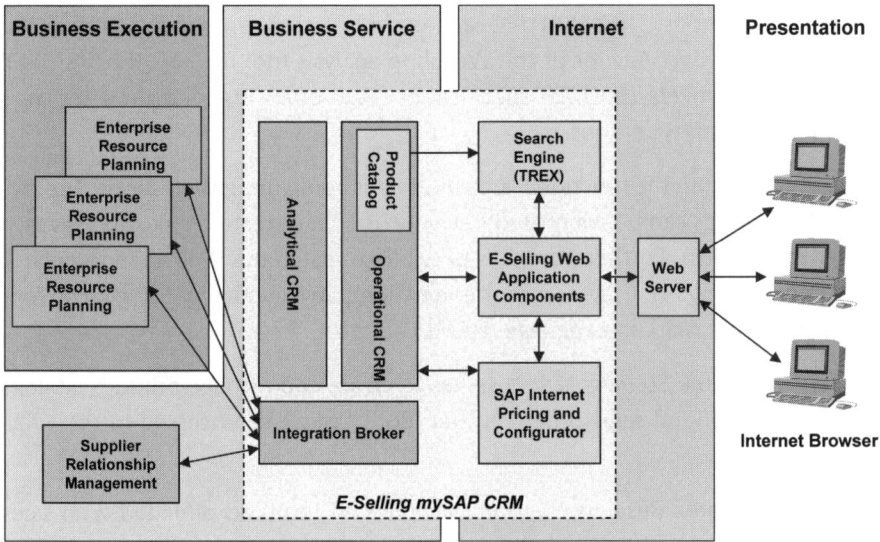

Figure 15.8 Architecture of the E-Commerce Application E-Selling

The functional area *Internet* provides the front-end functionality for the mySAP CRM e-commerce application and includes the following components:

▶ **Web Server**
The Web server connects the Web browser with the e-selling application. A special plug-in in the Web server enables communication with the SAP J2EE Engine. To guarantee quick access and short response times, the Web server automatically receives all static product catalog data from the CRM Server.

▶ **E-Selling Web Application Components**
Java applications that run in the SAP J2EE Engine as part of the e-commerce solution.

▶ **Retrieval and Classification (TREX)**
TREX is a search engine that is used by the e-commerce solution for finding products quickly in Web product catalogs.

► **SAP Internet Pricing and Configurator (SAP IPC)**

The platform-independent Java application *SAP Internet Pricing and Configurator (IPC)* supports not only customer-specific pricing but also interactive product configuration. Internet customers can use this functionality without directly having to access a connected SAP R/3 back-end system or the CRM Server.

► **SAP J2EE-Engine**

The SAP J2EE Engine serves as a runtime environment for the Java components of this functional area and controls communication between the Web server, CRM applications, TREX, SAP IPC, and other optional components such as the *Intelligent Product Advisor* or the Webshop analysis tool *TeaLeaf*. The SAP J2EE Engine fully meets the J2EE specification. It is often installed on a separate server for security reasons.

A major task within the functional area *Internet* is configuring Web shops. The layout of Web shops can be composed freely by using Java technologies such as Java Server Pages (JSPs). Furthermore, it is possible to match the Web shop templates delivered with mySAP CRM to user-defined company layouts by using a conventional Hypertext Markup Language (HTML) editor.

The functional area *Business Service* serves to create and manage product catalogs and process inbound sales orders further. Both tasks are processed in the CRM Server.

The functional area *Business Execution* includes all the tasks affiliated with sales order processing and is typically implemented in one or several ERP systems. If a SAP R/3 system is used in the back-end, business partners, products, and sales orders can be exchanged in real time on the basis of its close integration with mySAP CRM.

15.4 Message-Based Component Integration

To reach the target of comprehensive business process integration, mySAP CRM must cooperate closely with other application components. Message-based integration services are the basis for this, and are provided by CRM Middleware (see Appendix B) optimized for the purpose of connecting SAP R/3 back-end systems and by the SAP Exchange Infrastructure (see Section 14.6.1) for open integration.

15.4.1 Fundamental Tasks

To enable deep integration of business processes across all software components involved, the following fundamental integration aspects must be carried out:

Definition of Business Processes

Before integration solutions can be considered, you must specify the business processes that need to be supported. Only then can the flow of business objects via the single application components be described, for example, in the form of Component Views (see Section 6.2.2). In order to define the business processes, you must have a very thorough knowledge of the application scenario and the application components.

Definition of Shared Business Documents

All application components involved in a business process must have the same technical and business understanding of business objects such as customers, products, or orders. Technically, these objects are typically exchanged on the basis of the XML standard. Unfortunately, there are no common standards for the business viewpoint, and thus, for the semantic content of the objects. For example, nowhere is it specified that a customer object has a field name for the first name, a name field for the family name, an address for receiving goods, an address for sending invoices, and so on. The problem of varying semantic formats can be solved either by bilateral format mapping (Mappings) or, by defining shared business documents to which objects of the single application components that are to be exchanged can be mapped.

An everyday example of bilateral mapping is that four Members of the European Parliament (MEPs) from different countries need twelve different interpreters, on the assumption that one interpreter is necessary for each language pair in each direction. This means n × (n – 1) interpreters for n MEPs. The definition of shared business objects in this example corresponds to the involvement of precisely two interpreters for the country of origin of each MEP whose mother tongue must be translated into English and back.

This means that the MEPs generally cope with eight, or 2n, interpreters. The greater the number of languages to be covered, the better the latter alternative becomes. CRM Middleware works with shared business objects (Business Documents, BDocs) on the basis of this reduced number of mappings to be defined.

Initial and Operative Data Exchange

If the shared business documents have been defined with the associated mappings, it must be determined how the initial data transfer (Initial Load) is to take place and how operative modifications to business objects (Delta Load) are to be handled.

When installing an application component for the first time, it is necessary to first load required business data from other components into the system. Because this initial load typically translates to large quantities of data, this type of data exchange must be very efficient. mySAP CRM supports this data exchange with a scalable *Initial Load*, which can combine many business objects in a message to improve performance.

In operation, modified business data must continually be exchanged in real time between the various application components (*Delta Load*). Both mySAP CRM and connected SAP R/3 back-end systems work according to a "Store-and-Forward" mechanism that ensures that change messages are sent while updating business objects to all components involved (see Section 15.4.2). To improve performance, change messages often contain only a key and the changed values (net data).

Distribution of Customizing Data

To be able to exchange business objects between application components, Customizing data such as units of measure, currencies, country names, and so on, must be consistent. For example, if validation typically takes place in the target component, it checks whether the received object also agrees with the business rules stored there. So, for example, customer objects are checked to verify whether the country in the customer address exists. *Check tables*, which belong to the Customizing data and contain all permitted values, are the basis for this kind of verification. To ensure that all application components execute the same validation process, the Customizing data in all components must be semantically identical. If this is not the case, changes to business objects are accepted by one component, but rejected by another, which leads to inconsistent data.

Within the mySAP Business Suite, Customizing data is distributed and harmonized by using *Customizing Distribution* and *Customizing Scout*, two SAP Solution Manager tools (see Section 14.8.1).

15.4.2 Integration Services in CRM Middleware

CRM Middleware provides integration services specifically for the close coupling of mySAP CRM and SAP R/3 back-end systems, as well as for connecting mobile clients (see Section 15.3.1).

As an integral part of the mySAP CRM solution, CRM Middleware is installed on the CRM Server together with the CRM applications. This has the advantage of not requiring a separate integration server or user-defined installation for mySAP CRM and SAP R/3 consolidation scenarios.

CRM Middleware consists of the following core elements:

▶ Central services for controlling the message flow and synchronization of mobile clients (Replication)

▶ *R/3 Plug-In*, which is installed on the SAP R/3 back-end system for communicating with the CRM Server. The R/3 Plug-In sends change messages to the CRM Middleware R/3 Adapter, event-triggered and in real time. The R/3 Adapter converts the format to the corresponding CRM business objects and starts the message flow for further processing (see below).

Note: Installation of the R/3 Plug-In is without modifications, that is, releases can continue to be upgraded in SAP R/3 systems with an installed R/3 Plug-In. Various R/3 Plug-Ins are available for different SAP R/3 and SAP CRM releases. This enables completely independent release upgrades of SAP R/3 and SAP CRM.

▶ *Communication Station* for converting mobile client DCOM- or SOAP calls into CRM Server RFC calls

▶ *Connection Handler*, which must be installed in each mobile client for communicating with the CRM Server. The Connection Handler is part of the installation of mySAP CRM Mobile Sales and Mobile Service applications.

▶ *MapBox*, which executes complex mappings for multiple back-end scenarios (see Section 15.7.6) and for integrating with groupware solutions (see Section 15.7.4) on the basis of Extensible Stylesheet Language Transformations (XSLT). MapBox is part of CRM Middleware, but is also available in the context of the SAP Exchange Infrastructure.

▶ *Groupware Connector*, which executes the technical format conversion for the groupware server when executing groupware solutions

Sites and Adapters

The CRM Middleware message services can be used by any systems (*sites*) —by a mobile laptop only temporarily connected to the CRM Server, to the permanently connected back-end system, i.e., SAP R/3. Prerequisites are corresponding adapters to convert and forward inbound messages. The following site types are supported:

▶ **SAP R/3**
Data is exchanged by using the R/3 Adapter in the CRM Server and the R/3 Plug-In in the SAP R/3 system.

▶ **SAP Business Information Warehouse**
Data is exchanged between the SAP Business Information Warehouse (SAP BW) and the CRM Server via the BW Adapter. Any number of other sites can exchange messages with SAP BW via the CRM Middleware flow control (see below).

▶ **Groupware-Adapter**
Groupware solutions consist of servers and clients, for example, *Microsoft Exchange Server* with *Outlook Clients*, and *Lotus Domino Server* with *Lotus Notes Clients*. Groupware servers can be connected directly to the *CRM Middleware* by using the Groupware Adapter. In this way, users of groupware clients have direct access to mySAP CRM data (see Section 15.7.4) without having to install additional software.

▶ **Non-SAP Applications**
The *External Interface Adapter* offers interfaces based on XML and IDocs to communicate with non-SAP systems. Furthermore, special formats—such as RosettaNet, xCBL, EDIFACT, ANSI X.12, and ODETTE—are supported via corresponding subsystems.

▶ **Mobile Clients**
Mobile clients are typically connected only temporarily with the CRM Server. If data is to be replicated to mobile clients, it is buffered in the interim in the consolidated database (*Consolidated Database*, CDB) (see Section 15.6.4). If a mobile client is connected to the CRM Server, data is transferred from the consolidated database to the client and, if necessary, vice versa.

Flow Control and BDocs

CRM Middleware flow control takes messages that contain business objects, for example, orders, business partners, or activities, from the sending system and forwards them to the receiver (*sites*). Business objects within the CRM Middleware are transported as *shared business objects* (BDocs, see Section 15.4.1) in the form of BDoc messages.

Each BDoc message belongs to a BDoc type, which specifies its semantics. BDoc type descriptions don't contain any implementation details. BDoc messages can therefore be represented technically in different ways, for example, as ActiveX Data Objects (ADO) Record Sets on laptops, as internal tables on the CRM Server, or in an XML format for non-SAP systems.

BDoc types are divided into the following classes:

▶ *Messaging BDoc types* for exchanging messages between CRM Server applications and other stationary applications. When replicating Messaging BDoc types, neither object dependencies nor data distribution (realignment) are considered. These replication types aren't necessary for connecting back-end systems.

▶ *Synchronization BDoc types* for exchanging messages between CRM Server applications and mobile clients. In contrast to the Messaging BDoc types, all replication types, including object dependencies and data distribution (realignment), are available for Synchronization Bdoc types. This makes it possible for mobile field sales representatives to keep only the business objects that they really require on their computers, thus reducing the amount of data to be exchanged and the time needed for synchronization.

▶ Furthermore, there are *Mobile Application BDoc types* that use the local applications Mobile Sales and Mobile Service on the mobile clients for optimized database access.

BDoc types are defined by using the *BDoc Modeler* and are stored and managed in the *BDoc Repository*. By using the *BDoc Modeler,* one or several Synchronization BDoc types can be assigned to a Messaging BDoc type. CRM Middleware conversion services handle the necessary mapping.

Data Exchange with Back-End Systems

CRM Middleware supports data exchange with back-end systems by using the following services (see also Appendix B):

▶ Initial data exchange (Initial Load) between the CRM Server and SAP R/3, as well as non-SAP systems

▶ Delta data exchange (Delta Load) between the CRM Server and SAP R/3, or non-SAP systems

Both Initial Load and Delta Load work with Unicode, therefore, several languages can be used concurrently in the different systems.

▶ Data exchange between CRM Server and SAP R/3

Close integration with the R/3 applications *Sales and Distribution*, *Customer Service,* and *Project Planning* requires many business objects to be taken into account (see Appendix B). These include:

  ▶ Business partner and business partner hierarchies

  ▶ Products (also configurable and structured products)

  ▶ Objects for condition techniques

  ▶ Orders (Sales and Service) and billing documents

▶ Data exchange between CRM Server and non-SAP systems on the basis of XML messages. The following business objects are supported:

- Business partners, hierarchies, relationships (exchange in both directions)
- Orders, activities (exchange in both directions)
- Products (import into the CRM Server)
- Conditions (import into the CRM Server)
- Invoices (export from the CRM Server)

▶ File-based initial data transfer from non-SAP systems to the CRM Server
  - By using the SAP Data Transfer Workbench with the External Interface Adapter IDoc interface
  - When providing the non-SAP data as an ASCII file

Monitoring Services

The *Middleware Cockpit* offers central functions for monitoring business processes and technical components.

Monitoring of business processes includes:

▶ Cross-component message tracking, for example, tracking a sales order from a mobile client to the SAP R/3 back-end system

▶ Examination of single process steps for a message

▶ Monitoring and tracking object relationships

▶ Representation of object dependencies

The Middleware Cockpit shows:

▶ Buffers (Queues)

▶ Adapters

▶ Message exchange with mobile clients

▶ Performance

Additionally, the CRM Middleware is connected with the SAP Solution Manager *Computing Center Management System* (CCMS) (see Section 14.8.1) for active notification in the event of errors (Alert Monitoring).

15.5 Configuration and Extension

Supplementary to mySAP CRM's comprehensive functionality, many projects also require adaptation to special customer needs. Whereas other software manufacturers' CRM solutions can often realize special requests only in design projects, mySAP CRM offers comprehensive options for making customer adjustments via configuration settings (Customizing) without having to make changes in the program code. Examples are defining transaction categories, item categories, pricing, and marketing attributes. If these options are insufficient, the *Easy Enhancement Workbench* can be used to make cross-component extensions without requiring programming effort for business partners and transactions. Adjustments can be made to mobile sales and mobile service applications by using the *SAP Mobile Application Studio*—a development environment for laptop and Tablet PC applications. For business extensions that cannot be realized by these mechanisms, SAP NetWeaver offers development environments for the programming languages Java and ABAP.

15.5.1 Configuration Settings

In Customizing, mySAP CRM offers the same comprehensive standard configuration options as do the other solutions in the mySAP Business Suite. The following section refers to only several important Customizing options.

Business Transactions and Transaction Types

A transaction type specifies how a business transaction (for example, customer- or service order) is to be processed in a specific business context. For example, the transaction type specifies which business partners, messages, and texts are to be managed or created. Transaction types can be defined, as in SAP R/3, via configuration settings (Customizing), both simply and without programming.

Business transactions contain the following information:

▶ **Transaction header**
Among others, the transaction header contains the business partners involved.

▶ **Item**
The objects that the business transaction refers to are specified on the item level, for example, products or services.

▶ **Schedule line**
Quantities and times to be considered are on the schedule line level; for example, requested dates in Sales.

The properties and characteristics of a transaction item are specified by item categories, which control how an item is processed. For example, you can specify whether an item is relevant for billing, or whether pricing should be active. Accordingly, item types are defined via configuration settings and are assigned to transaction categories.

The interaction of the transaction categories and item categories enables important functions in transaction processing—such as availability and credit checks, partner determination, product substitution, organizational data determination, or order status management—to be controlled. These concepts are presented in the following section, using Pricing as an example.

Pricing

One of the most important functions in transaction processing is determining conditions. These conditions include prices, surcharges and discounts, and taxes. To determine conditions, you must have access to the following information and components:

▶ **Condition records**
  Here, for example, the following are specified:

  ▶ Type of condition (for example, price, surcharge and discount)
  ▶ Validity area
  ▶ Condition rate
  ▶ Calculation type
  ▶ Scale information

  This data can be maintained in SAP R/3 and from there, it can be distributed to the CRM Server and on to the mobile clients. Additionally, it is possible to maintain supplementary conditions in the CRM Server. The conditions of the *Trade Promotion Management (TPM)* can also be transported by the CRM Server to connected SAP R/3 back-end systems.

▶ **Pricing rules**
  The rules for Pricing are defined in configuration tables. For example, you can specify that prices depend on product groups or organizational data. The pricing rules, like the condition records, can be loaded from the SAP R/3 back-end system into the CRM Server or, be maintained in the CRM Server.

▶ **SAP Internet Pricing and Configurator (SAP IPC)**
  Pricing is used by various CRM applications. To ensure a uniform price for all applications, a platform-independent runtime environment was developed for pricing, i.e., the *SAP Internet Pricing and Configurator (SAP IPC)*. The SAP IPC is used by the CRM applications, the E-Selling application (see Section 15.3.3), and the mobile CRM applications for pricing. Since the condition records and pricing rules are distributed accordingly, consistent pricing is guaranteed.

Marketing Attributes

Marketing attributes extend the CRM Business Partner object by additional attributes required for target group segmentation in marketing campaigns. For example, the marketing attribute "Hobby," which is not intended as standard, can be added to the business partner. From a technical viewpoint, marketing attributes deal with additional fields, which are generated additionally for the CRM Business Partner data model without any programming effort required. These extensions are then also available to mobile clients and the SAP BW. The marketing attributes are Customizing data that can be distributed to other systems by using the *Transport Management System* (see below).

15.5.2 Extension Tools

The *Easy Enhancement Workbench* is a Wizard-based tool to extend business partners and transactions by additional fields without programming effort. For CRM Business Partners, you can even add complete tables. All necessary structures, tables, and coding are generated. All changes occur in the customer namespace and therefore are not modifications! The extensions are automatically visible in the People-Centric User Interface, the SAP GUI user interface, the Mobile Sales and Mobile Service applications, and in the SAP Business Information Warehouse.

To match the mobile CRM applications Mobile Sales and Mobile Service to enterprise-specific requirements, SAP provides the *SAP Mobile Application Studio* as an object-oriented, visual development environment. Besides design tools, additional tools are available, for example, for version and change management, and software logistics.

You can use the extension mechanisms described above to execute most CRM projects successfully. If, however, these extensions aren't adequate, the SAP Web Application Server has additional extension options. By using *Business Add-Ins (BAdIs)*, you can add business logic without making modifications to the locations designed for it. Furthermore, you can also modify SAP coding. However, this can lead to conflicts with new developments and further developments by SAP. Customers' own developments are implemented in user-defined namespaces so that the new developments don't collide with SAP outbound deliveries.

15.6 Running my SAP CRM

mySAP CRM in operation supports all the operation modes that you would be familiar with from the mySAP Business Suite, such as international and multiple-client operation. All SAP Solution Manager tools (see Section 14.8.1) are available, as well as supplementary services for CRM Middleware.

15.6.1 International Operation

If mySAP CRM is to be used internationally, country-specific special features must be supported, namely different languages, country versions, currencies, and time zones. It is also necessary that local attributes of different countries run in parallel in a system and that currencies and time zones can be converted. The technical basis for this is supplied by SAP NetWeaver (see Section 14.8.3). Because mySAP CRM supports Unicode, different character sets can be used simultaneously and master data can be maintained multilingually.

15.6.2 Multiple-Client Operation

A client is—both organizationally and from the viewpoint of data systems—a closed unit under commercial law, within an SAP installed base and with its own master, transaction, and configuration data [Buck-Emden/Galimow 1996].

Multiple-client operation means that multiple independent clients run in parallel within an SAP installed base. A client cannot access another client's data. As a rule, enterprises use different clients for test, simulation, and production environments. *Application Service Providers (ASPs)* also use the client concept to enable multiple customers to use SAP solutions without having them need to install their own hardware and software.

Multiple-client operation is also possible for mySAP CRM. In each client, all mySAP CRM applications are available, whereby each client saves his or her business and configuration data separately from other clients.

15.6.3 Data Archiving

During archiving, data that has been processed fully from the business viewpoint—and is therefore no longer required for immediate access—is removed from the database and is copied onto less expensive storage media. Regular archiving of data contributes to reducing total cost for the following reasons:

▶ Simplified database maintenance

▶ Quicker data storage (Backup) and recovery (Recovery)

▶ Improved database performance (Performance)

▶ Reduced hardware requirements

▶ Reduced administration effort

The connected application components are informed by CRM Middleware about archiving of the business data stored in the CRM Server. In the mobile clients, this leads to the deletion of the corresponding data from the local database. If an SAP R/3 system is connected, archiving there occurs independently from the archiving that occurs in the CRM Server. For more information on data archiving, see [Stefani 2002].

Data archiving requires good coordination between user and IT departments. Whereas only the IT departments are actually interested in backup and recovery solutions (see Section 15.6.4), data archiving also directly affects the user departments. For them, functionality is important if archived documents need to be accessed at some point.

15.6.4 Backup and Recovery

In contrast to data archiving, in which business data is removed from the database and copied onto less expensive storage media, backup and recovery solutions assist data security. Here, parts of or even complete database contents are saved on additional storage media, which can be used as a backup copy for data recovery in the event of a database breakdown. mySAP CRM poses particular challenges to backup and recovery, because of the CRM Server interconnection with various other application servers, and because of its inclusion of mobile applications.

Because the CRM Server and the connected systems exchange data in real time, consistency of the distributed data is usually ensured. However, if an older backup must be loaded into one of the affected systems due to a database breakdown, then all changes in this system (since the most recent backup) are lost. This means that the data in the entire network is no longer consistent. In this case, CRM Middleware provides a tool, the *Data Integrity Manager*, which can track data inconsistencies between the CRM Server and the connected systems via comparing data. This makes it possible to compare business objects with each other as a whole, as well as on the field level. Business objects that show differences or don't even exist in one of the systems can be resynchronized by using the Data Integrity Manager.

Mobile scenarios pose the second challenge to backup and recovery. In order to work offline, mobile laptops must have local databases. To make backups centrally, CRM Middleware stores all mobile data in its own area of the central CRM database—the Consolidated Database (CDB). Data is stored in the CDB in consolidated form, that is, for example, if a customer "Mike Winter" is distributed on a hundred mobile clients because a hundred field sales representatives are responsible for customers whose names begin with "L–Z," this customer is stored only once in the Consolidated Database. As part of the CRM database, the Consolidated Database is stored together with the remaining CRM data. By using distribution rules, the local database for each individual mobile client can be reconstructed and extracted from the Consolidated Database. For this purpose, CRM Middleware provides a handy tool, the *Rollout Manager*.

15.6.5 Operation with Multiple Applications on One Database

Distributed system landscapes, in which various applications run on different servers that each have their own database, have their advantages when it comes to flexibility, availability, and scalability of each single system. However, these same distributed system landscapes also place increased demands on system administration and hardware. In order to address these disadvantages, you can install multiple SAP components such as SAP Customer Relationship Management (SAP CRM), SAP Advanced Planner and Optimizer (SAP APO), SAP Business Information Warehouse (SAP BW), SAP Strategic Enterprise Management (SAP SEM), and SAP R/3 together, so that they use a shared database instance. In this context, this is also called Multiple-Component-in-One-Database (MCOD). Figure 15.9 shows the different options for installing SAP CRM and other SAP components.

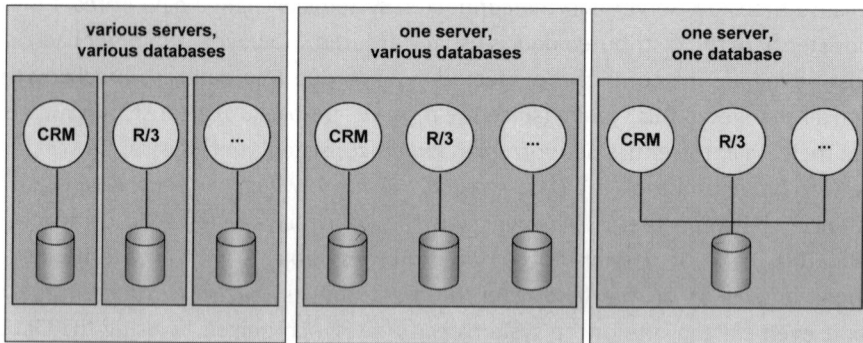

| various servers, various databases | one server, various databases | one server, one database |

CRM   R/3   ...   CRM   R/3   ...   CRM   R/3   ...

Figure 15.9 Installation Options for SAP Components

The MCOD concept also results in advantages when synchronizing the system after a database breakdown, because data consistency is guaranteed by the shared backup of all systems in one database instance. By using a failover solution, which activates a second instance running in parallel if the central database instance breaks down, total availability of the distributed SAP landscape can be improved.

15.7 System Landscape Options with mySAP CRM

Depending on the application case, mySAP CRM is embedded in the operational application landscape in quite different ways. Customers typically encounter the following integration scenarios:

▶ Isolated CRM solution (standalone)
▶ Integration with an SAP R/3 system

- Additional use by industry solutions
- Combination with groupware solutions
- Connection to third-party ERP systems
- Multiple-systems landscapes
- Collaborative CRM solutions

All the aforementioned integration scenarios are presented in brief in the following sections.

15.7.1 Isolated CRM Solution (Standalone)

In the simplest case, mySAP CRM can be implemented without being integrated with other application components. This kind of scenario is interesting, for example, for insurance companies with whom insurance policies are finalized through the different interaction channels. Because no products are delivered for insurance policies, and no logistics functionality is therefore needed, you can, in part, dispense with the connection to back-end systems.

Figure 15.10 shows the standalone integration scenario schematically, based on the SAP NetWeaver platform. mySAP CRM uses the SAP Web Application Server as a server platform (Application Platform). To analyze complex data, mySAP CRM uses the Business Intelligence functionality of SAP NetWeaver. Users access mySAP CRM via the People-Centric User Interface based on the SAP Enterprise Portal.

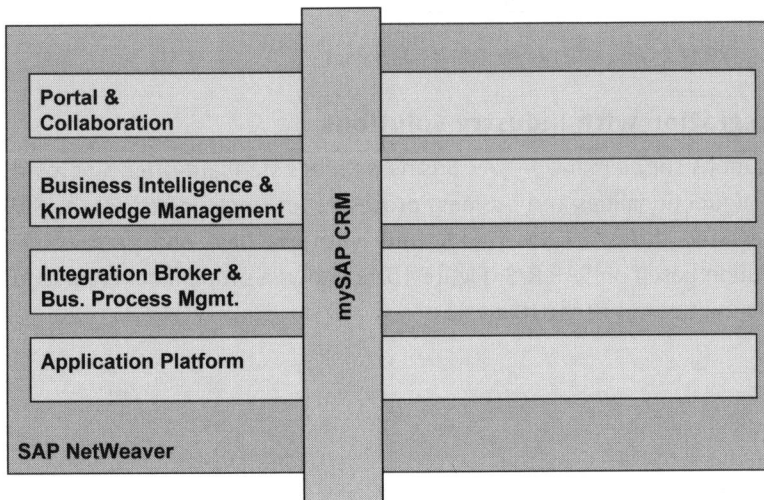

Figure 15.10 mySAP CRM as a Standalone Implementation

15.7.2 Integration with an SAP R/3 Back-End System

Integrating back-end systems is desirable in most implementations of mySAP CRM, for tasks such as sales order processing, invoicing, and so on. This presumes that master data, that is, business partners and products, as well as Customizing data, that is, system settings for sales organizations, and so on, can be exchange between CRM- and back-end applications.

Figure 15.11 shows this scenario schematically. Like mySAP CRM, SAP R/3 is also based on the SAP Web Application Server. CRM Middleware organizes the data exchanged between them.

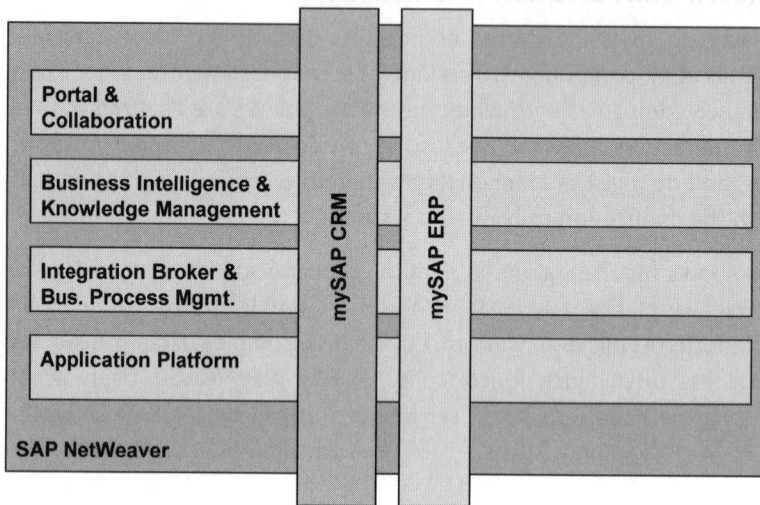

Figure 15.11 mySAP CRM with SAP R/3 Back-End Integration

15.7.3 Integration with Industry Solutions

Industry solutions supplement mySAP Business Suite's standard offer by providing additional functionalities and business processes for single industries. mySAP CRM is integrated through CRM Middleware with the back-end parts of this industry solution based on SAP R/3. Figure 15.12 shows a simplified system landscape for the utilities industry (Utilities).

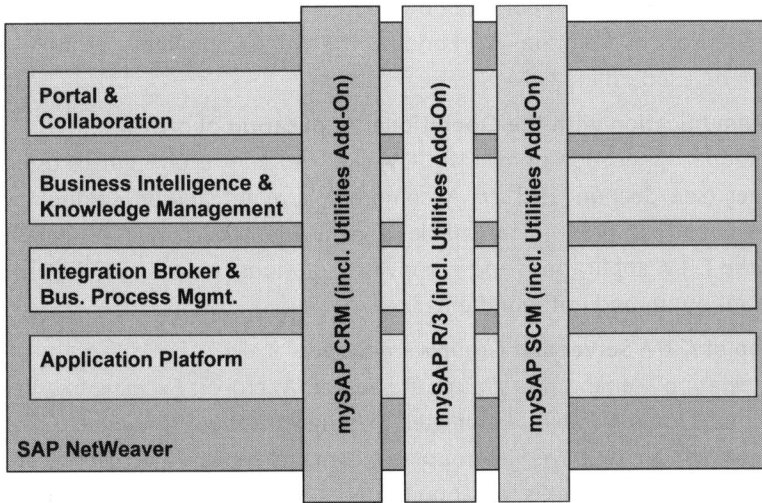

Figure 15.12 The Utilities Industry as an Example of Integration with Industry Solutions

15.7.4 Groupware Integration

The purpose of groupware solutions is ultimately to support teams for shared tasks, or for projects. The typical functionality of groupware solutions includes communication by email, provision and management of team calendars, management of contact persons and tasks, and shared processing of documents. Known examples of groupware solutions are Microsoft Outlook/Exchange and Lotus Notes/Domino. From the technical viewpoint, groupware solutions typically consist of a groupware server, for example, Microsoft Exchange or Lotus Domino, as well as a groupware client, for example, Microsoft Outlook or Lotus Notes. Groupware clients can work either online or offline.

mySAP CRM provides the following integration options with groupware solutions:

► **Integration of Microsoft Outlook and Lotus Notes with the Mobile-Sales and Mobile-Service Applications of mySAP CRM**
Activities (Activities) of mobile CRM applications and tasks (Tasks, Appointments) of the groupware solutions Microsoft Outlook and Lotus Notes can be exchanged in both directions. Furthermore, it is possible to access unread emails from the inboxes of the mobile applications Mobile Sales and Mobile Service using hyperlinks. Vice versa, emails can also be sent from mobile applications.

Furthermore, user-specific reports can be created in SAP BW and replicated to mobile end users as Solution Workbooks. The MS Excel sheets contained therein can be used offline.

▶ **Email Communication with the Operational Application of mySAP CRM**
The operational application of mySAP CRM can read and receive emails using SAPconnect (see Section 15.3.2). A comprehensive integration solution is being developed at present to enable a convenient exchange of emails between the CRM applications and groupware solutions, as well as mass processing of inbound- and outbound email.

▶ **Integration of CRM Server and Groupware-Server**
In this integration scenario, the groupware Server (Microsoft Exchange Server 2000 or Lotus Domino 5.0x) is connected directly with the CRM Server. CRM Business Partners are displayed in groupware contacts and CRM activitities are displayed in groupware tasks or appointments (Tasks and Appointments). These objects are exchanged in both directions. In this way, groupware clients can access CRM data via the groupware Server without installing additional software (see Figure 15.13).

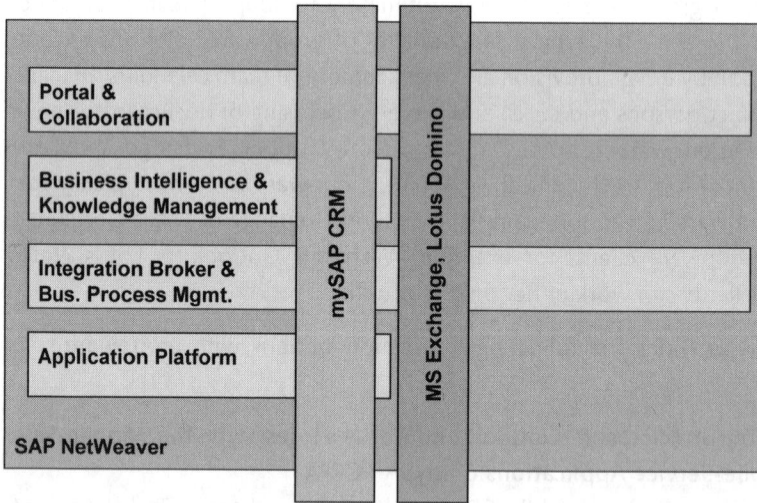

Figure 15.13 mySAP CRM Integrated with Groupware Solutions

From the technical viewpoint, CRM business objects in this scenario are transferred by CRM Middleware as XML documents to the MapBox (see Section 15.4.2). There, an XSLT Engine maps the documents to iCalender (for tasks and appointments) or vCard objects (for business partners). The vCard and iCalender objects are then forwarded to a groupware Connector that converts these objects technically into the format of the corresponding groupware Server (Microsoft Exchange, Lotus Domino) and updates it there. In the opposite direction, from the groupware Server to CRM Middleware, it runs precisely the other way.

15.7.5 Integration with Third-Party ERP Systems

When connecting non-SAP systems to mySAP CRM, two levels must be considered: Integration on the business process level and integration on the level of the user interface.

As soon as the cross-system business processes are defined, it can be determined which business objects have to be exchanged between which systems. This information allows the technical and semantic interfaces for the corresponding business objects to be specified. CRM Middleware supports, for example, interfaces to OneWorld (J. D. Edwards) and Oracle Applications.

In order to give users uniform access to all applications that they use, integration of the interfaces is often desirable. The SAP Enterprise Portal provides a technology that not only displays mySAP CRM's People-Centric User Interface, but can also display user interfaces from other applications, that is, from third parties.

Figure 15.14 shows schematically the integration of mySAP CRM with non-SAP systems. Process integration with non-SAP systems can take place through CRM Middleware or the SAP Exchange Infrastructure.

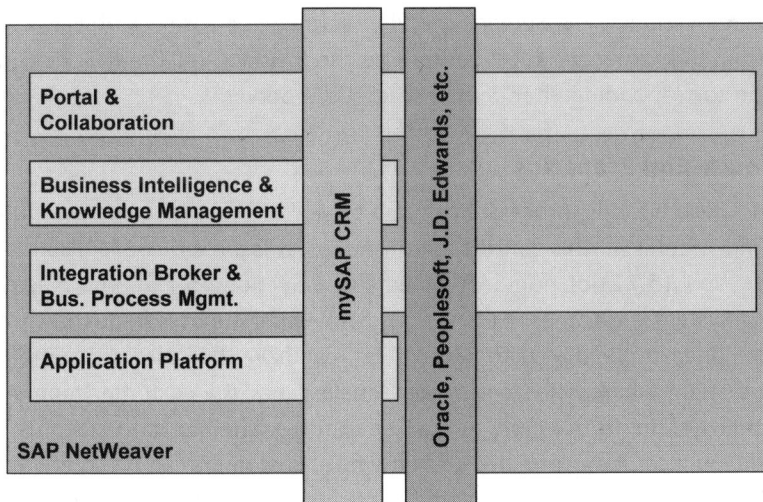

Figure 15.14 Integration with Non-SAP Systems

15.7.6 Multiple-System Landscapes

For larger CRM installations, it may be necessary, for example, to operate multiple CRM Servers and/or back-end systems in a network for organizational reasons. These are called Multiple-CRM or Multiple-Back-End scenarios. In the Multiple CRM case, a back-end system is coupled with multiple CRM Servers. Vice versa, in a multiple back-end scenario, a CRM Server is coupled with multiple back-end systems.

Multiple-CRM and multiple back-end scenarios presume comprehensive knowledge of the cross-system business processes as well as of the business objects to be exchanged between the systems. Because this kind of scenario has very different characteristics according to each customer situation, the respective customer requirements are defined in Workshops and are executed in consultancy projects. Currently, installed multiple-systems landscapes use CRM Middleware and Map-Box services.

Multiple-CRM Scenarios

There are various reasons for integrating multiple CRM Servers with an R/3 back-end system, such as organizationally separating IT departments, distributing systems worldwide, using extremely different CRM functionalities, or implementing a new CRM version in parallel.

For multiple-CRM scenarios too, the CRM Server communicates with the SAP R/3 back-end via R/3 Adapters and R/3 Plug-Ins. To control the separate flow of business data to the various CRM Servers, the filter settings for business objects can be loaded from the respective CRM Server into the R/3 Plug-In. The R/3 Plug-In then uses the corresponding filter data for each CRM Server.

Multiple-Back-End Scenarios

With mySAP CRM, business processes can also be realized that range across multiple back-end systems. In this context, back-end systems are either SAP R/3 systems (see Section 15.7.2) or non-SAP systems (see Section 15.7.5). The master data in such a system landscapes in the various back-end systems is frequently not harmonized. For example, the customer "Müller" can have the customer number 100 in one system, whereas the customer "Mueller" has the customer number 200 in another system. In this case, it must be clarified whether both customers are identical, and if so, it must be decided how both customers can be combined in the CRM Server. Finding and combining duplicates are typical tasks in managing non-harmonized, distributed master data (see also Section 14.5.1).

Multiple-back-end scenarios place requirements on integration technology that exceed requirements for integration with a single back-end system:

▶ **Structure mapping**

Generally, various back-end systems have different data structures for their business objects. If these objects are exchanged between different back-end systems, there isn't always a one-to-one correspondence of the fields in the source and target formats. A simple "resorting" of the fields is not sufficient. It may become necessary to divide up single fields into several, or, vice versa, to merge several fields into one. The situation becomes even more difficult if the semantics of the business objects differ too strongly. If, for example, the business object "Business Partner" has more pertinent data in one system than it does in another system, mapping in one direction can be achieved by omitting fields, whereas, on the other hand, mapping in the opposite direction, called *data refinement*, becomes much more difficult. Mapping requirements of this kind can be solved by using the MapBox (see Section 15.4.2).

▶ **Harmonization and consolidation**

The greatest challenge in multiple-back-end scenarios is, however, harmonization of master data and Customizing data. For non-harmonized master data, the keys for business objects, hence the customer or product numbers, are always unique in one system only, but not across system boundaries. As previously described, duplicates must be recognized and combined when consolidating non-harmonized master data. Before this task can be performed, various solutions must be evaluated on the project level (see also Section 14.5.1).

Besides harmonizing master data, different Customizing settings in the back-end systems also must be considered. If, for example, one back-end system is set to the language "German," and another system is set to "English," then, the form of address for business partners must be adjusted accordingly so that "Frau" is translated to "Mrs." and "Herr" is translated to "Mr.". Mapping definitions of this kind can also be modeled by using the MapBox.

After the master and Customizing data in multiple-back-end scenarios has been harmonized, business processes can be defined in which CRM sales orders can be forwarded to various back-end systems for further processing (see Figure 15.15). Processes of this kind are called *Extended Order Management (EOM)* scenarios (see Section 7.4.9). The special feature of EOM scenarios is that not only complete sales orders can be processed in different back-end systems. It is even possible to divide up sales orders at the item level into multiple partial orders and then forward them to different back-end systems for further processing. Nevertheless, delivery and invoicing take place centrally.

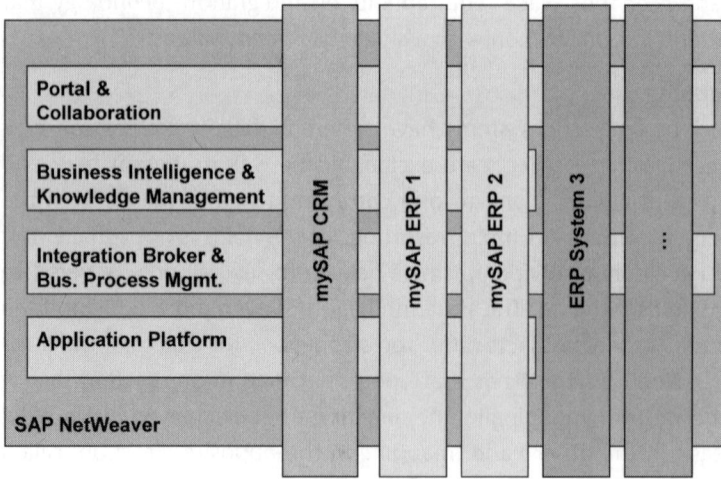

Figure 15.15 Multiple-Back-End Scenarios

15.7.7 Cross-Enterprise CRM Scenarios

E-Business industry standards such as *RosettaNet* or *EDI over Internet* form the technical basis for Business-to-Business (B2B) scenarios. Using these industry standards, mySAP CRM can participate in B2B processes with partner companies, buyers, or sellers. Equally, both Extended Order Management, taking different vendors into account (see Section 7.4.9), and Channel Management (see Chapter 11) fulfill all the technical requirements that have arisen from cross-enterprise collaboration (see Figure 15.16).

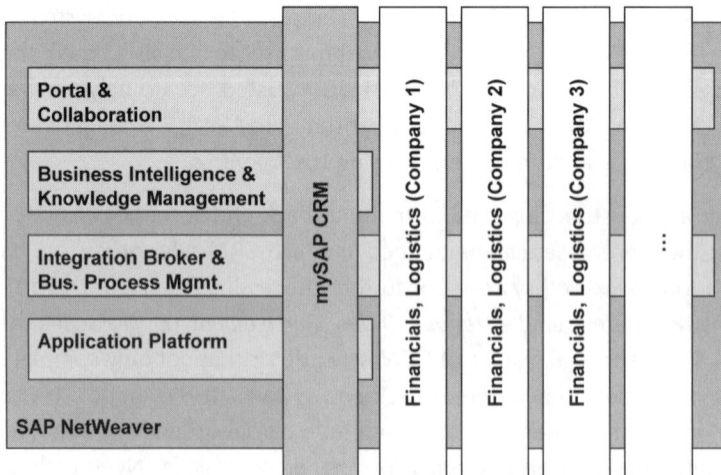

Figure 15.16 Cross-Enterprise CRM

A Technical Component View of mySAP CRM

A.1 Software Components of mySAP CRM

In Chapter 6, we identified the functional key capabilities of mySAP CRM, to which the following business application areas and communication channels belong:

▶ Marketing (MK)

▶ Sales (SL)

▶ Service (SV)

▶ Field Applications (FA)

▶ E-Commerce (EC)

▶ Interaction Center (IC)

▶ Channel Management (CH)

We should also mention the key capability *analytics* here, however, its functionality is an integral part of the key capabilities above and will not be discussed separately in the component overview that follows.

The mySAP Business Suite solutions (for example, mySAP CRM) are based as required on one or more of the large SAP application components such as SAP CRM, SAP BW, and SAP APO, for example. Each of these application components includes one or more technical software components, which can be installed separately.

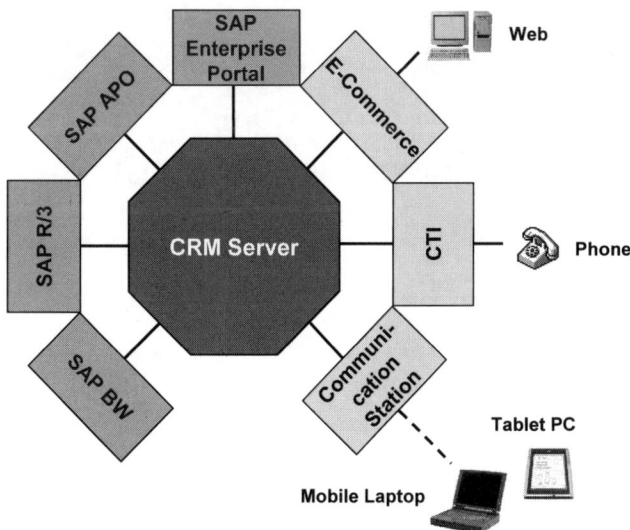

Figure A.1 System Landscape of mySAP CRM

The technical components required to implement the key capabilities are summarized in the following overview of SAP CRM 4.0. *X* means that software components can be used within the key capabilities.

The central component in each mySAP CRM system landscape is the CRM Server. Based on SAP Web Application Server (SAP Web AS), it provides the core functionality for all key capabilities as well as technical services (see also Chapter 15). Depending on the CRM business scenario to be implemented, the CRM server must be enhanced by additional components as shown in the following tables. You can find detailed information on installing CRM business scenarios in the Installation Guides, which you can access using SAP Solution Manager (see Chapter 14) or SAP Service Marketplace (*service.sap.com*).

Installable Software Components for mySAP CRM (Provided by SAP)	Key Capability						
	MK	SL	SV	FA	EC	IC	CH
Broadcast Messaging Server						X	
Communication Station				X			
Computer Telephony Integration (CTI)						X	
cProjects Add-On for CRM			X				
CRM Application Tool Server (CAT)	X						
CRM Server	X	X	X	X	X	X	X
Dynamic Auction and Bidding Engine (DAB)					X		X
Groupware Connector		X	X				
Interaction Center (IC) Scheduling						X	
Interaction Center WebClient (IC WebClient)						X	
CRM Intelligence Connector	X						
MapBox		X	X				
Mobile Client Recovery Manager				X			
Mobile Client Software				X			
Mobile Development Workstation				X			
SAP Advanced Planner and Optimizer (SAP APO)	X	X	X	X	X	X	X
SAP Business Connector					X		

Table A.1 Assignment of Software Components to Key Capabilities of mySAP CRM

Installable Software Components for mySAP CRM (Provided by SAP)	Key Capability						
	MK	SL	SV	FA	EC	IC	CH
SAP Business Information Warehouse (SAP BW)	X	X	X	X	X	X	X
SAP Content Server						X	
SAP CRM Internet Customer Self-Service (ICSS)					X		X
SAP Enterprise Portal	X	X	X	X	X	X	X
SAP E-Selling Web Application Components					X		X
SAP Internet Pricing and Configurator (SAP IPC)	X	X	X	X	X	X	X
SAP J2EE Engine	X				X	X	X
SAP Java Connector	X	X	X				
SAP R/3	X	X	X	X	X	X	X
SAP Strategic Enterprise Management (SAP SEM) Add-On	X						
SAP WFM Add-On				X			
CRM Software Agent Framework (SAF)						X	
Text Retrieval and Information Extraction (TREX)					X	X	X
SAP Workflow Modeler						X	

Table A.1 Assignment of Software Components to Key Capabilities of mySAP CRM (cont.)

The following software components from third-party vendors are integrated seamlessly with the mySAP CRM solution and offer useful additional functions.

Installable Software Components for mySAP CRM (Provided by Third-party Vendors)	Key Capability						
	MK	SL	SV	FA	EC	IC	CH
BackWeb ProactivePortal Server				X			
Computer Telephony Integration (CTI)						X	
TeaLeaf					X		
UBIS IPA					X		X

Table A.2 Assignment of Third-party Software Components to Key capabilities of mySAP CRM mySAP CRM

A.2 R/3 Edition for Internet Sales and Mobile Users

For a quick introduction to e-commerce, SAP offers SAP Internet Sales (R/3 Edition), a solution that is particularly suitable for smaller workloads. In this version, the Web shop accesses the SAP R/3 system data directly instead of accessing the CRM server. Apart from the SAP R/3 system, the following software components are also required:

▶ SAP J2EE Engine

▶ SAP Internet Sales Web Application components

▶ R/3 Plug-In

▶ TREX (optional)

▶ SAP IPC (optional)

SAP Internet Sales R/3 Edition is a lean solution particularly suited to expanding the sales functionality of an existing SAP R/3 system to the Internet.

There are also R/3 versions for the mobile applications of mySAP CRM: Mobile Sales for Handhelds (R/3 Edition) and Mobile Service (R/3 Edition). For these solutions, the following components are required:

Component	Mobile Sales for Handhelds (SAP R/3 Edition)	Mobile Service (SAP R/3 Edition)
SAP R/3	X	X
Mobile Client Software	X	X
Communication Station		X
Mobile Client Recovery Manager		X
Mobile Development Workstation		X

Table A.3 Software Components for Mobile SAP R/3 Solutions

A.3 Short Description of Software Components

BackWeb ProactivePortal Server

BackWeb ProactivePortal is a third-party component that can be used to make information from the portal knowledge management, which is also available to mobile users on their laptops or tablet PCs. BackWeb ProactivePortal allows the user to subscribe to various different topics. The contents of these topics are then available to the mobile user in the Infocenter. Several formats are supported, for example, audio, video, program files, HTML documents, and so on.

Broadcast Messaging Server

With the Broadcast Messaging Server, messages can be sent to all interaction center agents. The Broadcast Messaging Server is a Java application that can be operated either as a standalone solution or as a servlet. The client is a Java applet.

Communication Station

The Communication Station is based on SAP COM+ Connector (or SAP .NET Connector) and transforms DCOM calls (Distributed Component Object Model) from the mobile devices (laptop, tablet PC) to RFC calls to the CRM server. In unicode scenarios, XML/SOAP messages are used instead of DCOM calls.

Computer Telephony Integration (CTI)

The goal of CTI is to make the telephone into an integral part of computer-supported business processes. As described in Section 15.3.2, there are four different ways to connect the telephone communication channel:

▶ SAPphone (for IC WinClient)

▶ Integrated communication interface (for IC WebClient)

▶ SAP Multi-Channel Interface (for IC WinClient)

▶ Genesys Gplus adapter (for IC WinClient)

The required software components for these options are listed in the following tables:

SAPphone		
Component	Vendor	Purpose
SAPphone Telephony Server	SAP component	Only required for communication management software that TAPI supports
Communication Management Software	Third-party vendor (vendor with SAP certificate for direct connection, for example, Siemens, Nortel Networks, and so on, or vendors that support SAP connection with TAPI	Switch between telephone installation (PBX) and software

Table A.4 Software Components for CTI Using SAPphone

Integrated Communication Interface		
Component	Vendor	Purpose
Business Communication Broker	SAP component	J2EE component for providing communication services using the integrated communication interface
Communication Management Software (including ICI Connector)	Third-party vendors (Vendors with SAP certificate, for example Cycos, Genesys Telecommunications Laboratories, AMC Technology)	Switch between communication channels and software applications using integrated communication interface

Table A.5 Software components for CTI using Integrated Communications Interface

Multi-Channel Interface		
Component	Vendor	Purpose
SAP Multi-Channel Interface Server	SAP component	Provision of interface, combining communication channels
Telephony Connector	AMC Technology component	Switch between communication management software from third party vendors
Additional connectors	AMC Technology component	Available for email, chat, interactive voice response (IVR), paging
Communication Management Software	Third-party vendor, for example, Avaya, Aspect, Cisco, Intel	Switch between telephone installation (PBX) and software

Table A.6 Software components for CTI Using Multi-Channel Interface

Genesys Gplus Adapter		
Component	Vendor	Purpose
Genesys Gplus Adapter	Genesys Telecommunications Laboratories component	ActiveX control for SAP GUI for Windows Enables the agent to control the communication channels
Genesys Suite (Communication Management Software)	Genesys Telecommunications Laboratories component	Switch between communication channels and software

Table A.7 Software Components for CTI with Genesys Gplus Adapter

cProjects Add-On for CRM

cProjects is an add-on for the CRM server that supports project management and project planning for professional services.

CRM Application Tool Server (CAT server)

The CAT server generates forms for electronic surveys that can be used when generating leads or evaluating opportunities.

CRM Server

The CRM server is the central, logical SAP system within a CRM system landscape. It is technically based on the SAP Web Application Server and supports the following applications:

▶ CRM Enterprise applications

  ▶ Sales

  ▶ Service

  ▶ Marketing

  ▶ E-commerce

  ▶ Interaction Center

  ▶ Channel Management

▶ CRM middleware for CRM-specific demands for the synchronization of mobile clients and for application integration (see Section 15.4.2)

Dynamic Auction and Bidding Engine (DAB)

The Java application *DAB* supports various dynamic price determination processes, such as auctions and bids.

Groupware Connector

The Groupware Connector is required to connect a groupware server with the CRM server using the MapBox. Connectors for the MS Exchange Server and IBM Lotus Domino are also available.

IC Scheduling

IC Scheduling provides interaction center managers with tools to help them effectively distribute the workload to the available call center agents. IC Scheduling includes:

▶ Workforce Management Scheduling Application Server

▶ Workforce Management Scheduling Calculation Services

The component SAP BW is also needed.

IC WebClient

The Interaction Center WebClient (IC WebClient) allows users to access the Interaction Center using an Internet browser. IC WebClient is a J2EE application.

Intelligence Connector

The Intelligence Connector is a Java application that offers functions for real-time analysis of data.

MapBox

The MapBox maps data objects from different systems and with a different internal display (values, structures, keys) based on XML/ XSLT. For example, the MapBox is used to convert business partners from the CRM system into contacts of a groupware application.

Mobile Client Recovery Manager

The Mobile Client Recovery Manager is a tool that can be used by the central support team in a company to exchange defective or broken mobile devices.

Mobile Client Software

The Mobile Client Software varies according to whether laptops, tablet PCs, or handhelds are used as mobile devices.

Handhelds require the client part of the SAP Mobile Engine. The Mobile Engine is based on Java and is therefore platform-independent. It is used in mySAP CRM with mobile sales and mobile service scenarios for handheld devices.

The mobile sales or mobile service application for laptops is installed on the laptop and the tablet PC, because it also has support functions for the tablet PCs. For price determination and for the configuration of products, SAP Internet Pricing and Configurator (SAP IPC) can also be used on laptops or tablet PCs.

Mobile Development Workstation

The Mobile Development Workstation offers the following administration and development tools for mobile laptop and tablet PC applications:

▶ SAP Mobile Application Studio

▶ Mobile Repository Server

▶ Mobile Admin Workstation

SAP Mobile Application Studio is a development environment for customizing the CRM applications Mobile Sales and Mobile Service to company-specific requirements. GUI tools and process design are also available. Versioning and a transport system make it easy to keep track of changes. Data types are stored in the mobile repository.

For the administration of authorizations on the mobile clients, the Mobile Admin Workstation is available.

SAP Advanced Planner and Optimizer

SAP Advanced Planner and Optimizer (SAP APO) is a comprehensive solution for planning and optimizing all processes along the supply chain. SAP APO is part of mySAP SCM (Supply Chain Management). The following application areas belong to SAP APO:

▶ Demand chain planning

▶ Supply chain planning

▶ Production planning and scheduling

▶ Order promising and global ATP (Available-to-Promise)

▶ Transportation planning and vehicle scheduling

▶ Supply chain collaboration

▶ Supply chain control

To solve various planning and sequence problems, SAP APO implements optimization algorithms such as *mixed integer linear programming* and *constraint programming genetic algorithm* (compare [Stadtler/Kilger 2000]). When executing these processes it should be borne in mind that creating all factors relevant for the optimization can lead to gigabytes of information, even for small supply chains. Since the information for the optimization process needs to be stored completely in the main memory, SAP has developed a specially configured main memory database for planning and optimizing tasks, the liveCache. mySAP CRM uses SAP APO for the availability check (Available-to-Promise, ATP).

SAP Business Connector

SAP Business Connector (SAP BC) is a Java-based middleware product for the integration of SAP solutions with external applications based on open XML interfaces. Using XML/HTML, quotations, orders, contracts, shipping notifications, invoices, or catalog data can be exchanged, for example.

SAP Business Information Warehouse

SAP Business Information Warehouse (SAP BW) gives decision-makers in the company a uniform view on company data as well as integrated and consistent data for analyses. In this way SAP BW supports the operative and strategic decision-making in the company. SAP BW contains, among others, the following elements:

▶ ETL tools (extraction, transformation, load), to bring together data from various sources in SAP BW and to format it for further analysis

- ▶ Comprehensive evaluation options and end-user-compatible data formatting
- ▶ Business Content in the form of pre-configured reports and analyses, as well as information models (InfoCubes) and tools for extracting and formatting data

SAP BW is a component of SAP NetWeaver and is the basis for the analytical functions of mySAP CRM.

SAP Content Server

SAP Content Server supports the administration of large amounts of documents, for example, from the product catalog of the e-commerce scenarios. Smaller amounts of documentation can also be maintained on the CRM Server itself.

SAP CRM Internet Customer Self-Service (ICSS)

SAP CRM ICSS is a J2EE component that provides self-service functionality over the Internet.

SAP Enterprise Portal

SAP Enterprise Portal provides all users with a role-based, central point of access to all necessary applications, services, and information (see Section 14.4.1).

SAP E-Selling Web Application Components

Java applications that run on the SAP J2EE Engine for the e-commerce and channel management scenario.

SAP Internet Pricing and Configurator (IPC)

SAP IPC is a tool for interactive product configuration and automatic price determination on the Internet, in the Interaction Center, or on the mobile laptops of field employees (see Section 9.4.3).

Thanks to its open architecture, SAP IPC can be combined with any product catalog and shopping cart system.

SAP IPC consists of the sales configuration engine and the sales pricing engine, which are both implemented in Java and can therefore run on different platforms.

SAP J2EE Engine

In addition to ABAP, SAP Web AS also supports Java with the SAP J2EE Engine. The SAP J2EE Engine application server is compatible with Sun J2EE (Java-2 Platform, Enterprise Edition).

SAP Java Connector

SAP Java Connector makes it possible to call CRM Enterprise applications from a Java application using RFC (remote function call). SAP Java Connector is also part of SAP J2EE Engine.

SAP R/3

mySAP CRM can be run with SAP's own OLTP (online transaction processing) system SAP R/3 or with external back-end systems. The use of several parallel back-end systems is also possible. A prerequisite for this is that the unification of heterogeneous data and key structures is guaranteed (see also Section 15.6.7).

SAP Strategic Enterprise Management (SEM)

SAP SEM supports the company management when making strategic decisions. The functions of SAP SEM include performance measurement, strategy management, planning, simulation, budgeting, rolling forecasts, consolidation, and shareholder relationship management. SAP SEM is installed as an SEM Add-On to enhance SAP BW.

SAP Workforce Management Add-On

For resource planning of mobile service employees, either Workforce Management Core in SAP APO can be used or SAP Workforce Management Add-On can be installed on the CRM server.

CRM Software Agent Framework (SAF)

CRM SAF is a J2EE application that Interaction Center agents can use in their search for solutions.

TeaLeaf

TeaLeaf is a tool for analyzing the behavior of users on the Internet. TeaLeaf makes it possible to record and save all of a user's interaction steps comprehensively. The evaluation of the data obtained (trend recognition, dependencies, behavioral patterns, and so on) is tightly integrated with SAP Business Information Warehouse.

Text Retrieval and Information Extraction (TREX)

TREX provides the following services:

▶ **Index Management Service (IMS)**
  Tool for indexing random documents: Relevant information from documents is extracted (text mining) and used to index the documents with the help of classification processes. Search machines that match the SAP IMS server API specification (for example, TREX search engine) can use the IMS index to search for documents.

▶ **TREX Search Engine**
  Search machine that offers all standard functions for text search. It supports the SAP IMS server API specification. TREX is used to index product catalogs in e-commerce and therefore enables a fast and easy product search on the Web. Another important area of use is knowledge management, which makes relevant information available to portal users depending on their role.

UBIS Intelligent Product Adviser

UBIS Intelligent Product Adviser is an optional component from a third-party vendor that provides tailored product advice for Web shoppers.

SAP Workflow Modeler

SAP Workflow Modeler is a J2EE tool for configuring workflows. A GUI enables administrators to create or change workflows quickly and easily.

B Data Exchange Between CRM and Back-End Systems

To enable cross-system business processes between CRM and back-end systems, the following objects must be exchanged:

▶ Customizing data

▶ Master data

▶ Conditions

▶ Transaction data

Before object changes are exchanged in daily operations (delta load), an initial data exchange is required from the back-end system to the CRM Server (initial load). Certain dependencies between the individual objects must be taken into account.

The data exchange solution for SAP CRM and SAP R/3 is comprehensive and "out-of-the-box." As of SAP CRM 4.0, Customizing data can be passed on using the Customizing Distribution component in the SAP Solution Manager. Master data, conditions, and transaction data are transported using the CRM Middleware.

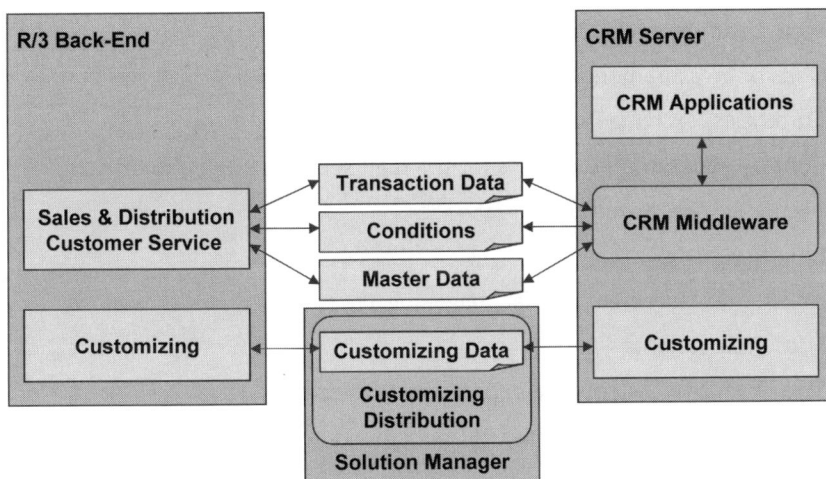

Figure B.1 Overview of Data Exchange Between the CRM Server and SAP R/3

The following sections describe the various business objects that are exchanged between the CRM server and the SAP R/3 back-end system in the same order as the initial data exchange, that is, starting with customizing data, continuing with master data and condition data, and concluding with transaction data. For additional technical information on the data exchange between the CRM server and SAP R/3 on the basis of the CRM middleware, see the "Technical Details" section of this appendix.

B.1 Customizing Data

Before master data, such as business partners and products, can be exchanged between the CRM server and SAP R/3, elementary data, such as units of measurement, must be consistent in both systems. This type of information is exchanged using the Customizing Distribution component in the SAP Solution Manager. In the standard delivery, the following customizing data can be loaded from the SAP R/3 back-end system to the CRM server:

▶ Basis tables for CRM
  ▶ Name formats
  ▶ Academic titles
  ▶ Forms of address
  ▶ Name prefixes and affixes, titles of nobility
  ▶ Regional zones for customers
  ▶ Countries
  ▶ Form of address texts
  ▶ Units of measurement
  ▶ Currencies, exchange rates, and exchange rate types
  ▶ Country codes and exceptions for the digit sequence (telephone, fax)
  ▶ Tax codes, tax-related provincial codes
  ▶ Country IDs
  ▶ Units of measurement and language-specific spelling
  ▶ Fiscal year variants
  ▶ Screen variants for country-dependent address screens
  ▶ Description of pager services (central address management)
  ▶ Address routines
  ▶ Reserved names for Customizing tables and objects
  ▶ Summer time regulations
  ▶ Time zones, time zone regulations

- ▶ Business partners
  - ▶ Marital status ID
  - ▶ Function of contact person
  - ▶ Department numbers of contact persons
  - ▶ Transaction form
  - ▶ VIP indicator for contact persons
  - ▶ Authorities of contact persons
- ▶ Products
  - ▶ Data for material number conversion
  - ▶ Product types (material groups, material types, product hierarchies)
  - ▶ Sales-related product status
- ▶ Service catalogs
  - ▶ Inspection catalog with codes and code groups
- ▶ Customizing service master
  - ▶ Service category
- ▶ Bank master data
  - ▶ Bank master, post office bank branches
- ▶ Sales pricing
  - ▶ Terms of payment
  - ▶ Customers with customer groups and terms of payment
  - ▶ Conditions including groups of customer classes and price list types
  - ▶ Pricing procedures: debitor, transaction
- ▶ Variable conditions for *SAP Internet Pricing and Configurator* (SAP IPC)
  - ▶ Variant conditions
- ▶ Sales
  - ▶ Industry sectors
  - ▶ Sales districts
  - ▶ Customer groups
- ▶ Sales and shipping
  - ▶ International commercial terms (incoterms)
  - ▶ Delivery priorities
  - ▶ Shipping conditions

- ▶ Information about the organizational units
  - ▶ Sales divisions
  - ▶ Sales areas
  - ▶ Distribution channels
- ▶ Payment plan
  - ▶ Customer payment guarantee procedure
  - ▶ Billing plan type, date category of billing plan type
  - ▶ Payment card type and category
  - ▶ Results of payment card checks
  - ▶ Lock reason for payment cards
- ▶ Service order and order confirmation types
  - ▶ Service order types
  - ▶ Message types
- ▶ Sales product item
  - ▶ Sales volume rebate groups
  - ▶ Material groups
  - ▶ Commission groups

B.2 Master Data

Master data is data that stays the same over a fairly long period of time. Master data contains information that is required repeatedly and always in the same way. Typical examples of master data in SAP R/3 are the customer master and the material master.

The following sections describe the master data that can be exchanged between the CRM server and SAP R/3.

B.2.1 Business Partners

SAP R/3 distinguishes between the customer master (R/3 table: KNA1) and the vendor master (R/3 table: LFA1). Employees are managed in the human resources application and users in the user master. However, the CRM server and SAP R/3 industry solutions maintain their business partners as an attribute of the SAP business partner (table: BUT001).

In addition to the business partner master data, relationships between individual business partners are managed, for example, "is contact person for" or "is customer representative." These relationships exist between R/3 customers and also among SAP business partners. If the relationships are exchanged between SAP R/3 and the CRM server, the relationship tables in the relevant systems must be converted. SAP R/3 also provides customer hierarchies for the customer master. In the CRM server, the customer master is mapped using group hierarchies.

The initial data exchange from business partners usually occurs in three steps:

1. Load business partners. Both the R/3 customers (R/3 adapter object: CUSTOMER_MAIN) and the SAP business partners (R/3 adapter object: BUPA_MAIN) can be transferred initially to the CRM Server.

2. Once the business partners are known in the new system, the relationships between the business partners can be transported to the CRM Server, both for R/3 customers (R/3 adapter object: CUSTOMER_REL) and for SAP business partners (R/3 adapter object: BUPA_REL).

3. The customer hierarchies are then imported from SAP R/3 to the CRM server (optional). The customer hierarchies are translated into the CRM group hierarchy "R3-CRM." Customer hierarchy data must be exchanged if pricing is to take place in CRM. Pricing is carried out in CRM on the basis of group hierarchies. Since special conversion tables are set up during the first data exchange, a distinction must be made between initial data exchange (R/3 adapter object: DNL_BUPA_KNVH) and delta data exchange (R/3 adapter object: BUPA_KNVH).

B.2.2 R/3 Plants

CRM applications can carry out Available-to-Promise (ATP) checks in a connected SAP Supply Chain Management (SCM) system. To do this, the CRM applications must be familiar with the plants from SAP R/3. The plants (R/3 table: T001W) are loaded to the CRM server (R/3 adapter object: DNL_PLANT) where they are then available as business partners belonging to the "location" category.

B.2.3   Products

The R/3 material masters are also transferred initially to the CRM server (R/3 adapter object: MATERIAL). Subsequent changes to the material master are exchanged by a delta load in two directions between the CRM server and SAP R/3. The R/3 material master data can be mapped in the CRM server as products belonging to the "material" category. In addition to the R/3 material master, structured products from *SAP for Retail* can also be loaded to the CRM server (R/3 adapter object: BOM).

Configurable products can be maintained in SAP R/3. So CRM applications can access these types of products, the product configuration master data is also transferred to the CRM server (R/3 adapter object: SCE).

Finally, the R/3 customer material numbers can also be transferred to the CRM Server (R/3 adapter object: CUST_MAT_INFO). This is necessary if a search for products by customer material number is required when sales orders are created in CRM.

B.2.4 Service

For the CRM service applications, the R/3 service master data is sent from SAP R/3 to the CRM server (R/3 adapter object: SERVICE_MASTER), where it is available as a product (or products) belonging to the "Service" category. You can also transfer CRM products of the "service" or "material" category in the reverse direction, i.e., from the CRM server to SAP R/3. A delta load of the service master data can be performed in both directions.

B.3 Condition Data

The data required by SAP CRM for the condition technique comprises both customizing data and master data. The condition data therefore has a special role.

The initial data exchange of condition data takes place in three steps:

1. The customizing data is first transferred together with meta information to the CRM server.
2. The meta information generates the condition objects, such as tables, structures, views, and reports. These objects are generated immediately after the customizing data is loaded.
3. The newly generated condition tables in the CRM server are then filled by transferring the condition master data.

Of the meta information available in SAP R/3, only the data that is also required by the CRM applications is loaded to the CRM server, and filtered according to applications and uses.

The following applications are supported in CRM for the condition technique:

▶ Sales

▶ Purchasing

▶ Tax

The CRM applications are familiar with the following uses of the condition tables:

- ▶ Pricing
- ▶ N—Free goods discount
- ▶ E—Rebate
- ▶ D—Material determination
- ▶ 3—Campaign determination

The customizing data for the condition technique is defined in an R/3 adapter object (DNL_CUST_CNDALL) and includes the following information:

- ▶ Condition types (R/3 tables: T685, T685A, T685T, and T685Z)
- ▶ Processing status for conditions (R/3 tables: T686E, T686F)
- ▶ Maintenance control for distributed systems (R/3 table: MNTCNT)
- ▶ Meta information from the condition tables (R/3 tables T681, TMC1, TMC1D, TMC1K, and TMC1T)
- ▶ Access sequences to determine condition records (R/3 tables: T682, T682I, T682T, T682V, and T682Z)
- ▶ Price calculation and free goods determination schemes, and product and campaign determination (R/3 tables: T683, T683S, T683T, and T683U)
- ▶ Condition exclusion groups (R/3 tables: T684, T684G, T684S, and T684T)

Access sequences, schemes, and condition exclusion groups are available for the applications and uses that are mentioned above and supported by CRM.

There is a certain dependency between the condition types and the condition tables. The schemes reference the condition types, which, in turn, refer to the access sequences. The access sequences refer to the generated condition tables. The access sequence tables and the condition tables are client-independent.

As previously mentioned, the R/3 adapter object DNL_CUST_CNDALL contains all the customizing data for the initial data exchange. There are other R/3 adapter objects available for synchronizing individual objects (DNL_CUST_*). Substitution reasons, rebate agreement types, and the "group of allowed condition types/tables" for the usage "Rebate" can be loaded into the CRM server.

The condition master data supports all R/3 conditions. Because the condition master data refers to the customers and the products, the master data must first be loaded into the CRM server.

B.4 Transaction Data

Transaction data is transaction-related data that is not permanent and is assigned to certain master data. The most important transaction data in CRM includes sales orders, service orders, time and material confirmations (in service), and billing documents.

B.4.1 Sales Orders

Sales orders from SAP R/3 can be transferred initially to the CRM server (R/3 adapter object: SALESDOCUMENT) and mapped to CRM business transactions. Real-time delta loads are available in both directions for sales orders and CRM business transactions.

B.4.2 Service Documents

CRM service documents are mapped to CRM business transactions with additional service items (replacement material and time confirmation). These service documents, like all other sales orders, can be exchanged with SAP R/3 (R/3 adapter object: SALESDOCUMENT).

B.4.3 Billing Documents

CRM billing is an application for invoice creation and is tailored to CRM business processes. It works on the assumption that all business partners, products, and prices are available in the CRM server. CRM billing accepts business transactions or R/3 delivery data as entries. Billing documents are then generated and can be passed on to accounting applications such as SAP R/3 FI and SAP R/3 FI-CA.

Delivery data can be sent for billing from the R/3 delivery to the CRM server (R/3 adapter object: LEDELIVERY). Once the billing documents have been created, the billing document data can be sent back to SAP R/3 (R/3 adapter object: BEA-BILLDLV) to adjust the status and document flow of the delivery. Besides CRM billing for products, service, and financing, there are also special forms for *SAP for Media*, *SAP for Telecommunications*, and *SAP for Utilities*.

B.5 Data Exchange for Industry Solutions

In addition to the business data already described, industry-specific master data and transaction data can also be exchanged between the CRM server and the SAP R/3 industry solutions. The following sections provide examples of this type of data exchange.

B.5.1 Media (SAP for Media)

The management and exploitation of intellectual property (Intellectual Property Management, IPM) is *the* critical success factor in the media industry. With Intellectual Property Management, SAP for Media provides a comprehensive instrument that covers the entire value chain—from acquisition and creation of intellectual property and development of new media products, to selling of licenses and rights, to processing of inbound and outbound license payments. SAP for Media uses CRM functions to maintain business relationships with rights owners, licensors and licensees, actors, or authors of intellectual property. Royalties accounting is also supported. "Royalties" are the license revenues and outgoing royalties that are produced from the sale or acquisition of licenses.

The two billing applications IPMI (IPM Incoming Royalty Billing) and IPMO (IPM Outgoing Royalty Accounting) create invoices for acquisitions and sales contracts for royalties. The invoices can be exchanged with SAP R/3.

The acquisition and sales contracts are based on revenues from products sales and payment information that is loaded from SAP R/3 to the SAP Server (R/3 adapter objects: IPMBEAPRDSLS and IPMBEAFIPAYMENT).

The transfer of the sales contracts from the CRM server to the SAP R/3 Accrual Engine (ACE) is done using sales orders (R/3 adapter object: SALESDOCUMENT). The Accrual Engine determines the revenues and posts them in Financial Accounting (FI). The result is then transferred to the CRM application IPMO (IPM Outgoing Royalty Accounting) (R/3 adapter object: IPMBEAACECONF).

B.5.2 Telecommunications (SAP for Telecommunications)

The industry solution *SAP for Telecommunications* provides functional enhancements and adjustments taking account of the requirements of the telecommunications industry. Billing documents for services can be created using the billing application TCIB. The documents can then be exchanged with the back-end system of the industry solution. Convergent invoicing is possible, that is, invoicing that combines accounting data from different sources in one standardized billing document.

B.5.3 Utilities and Waste Disposal Industry (SAP for Utilities)

SAP for Utilities was specially developed for the requirements of gas, water, electricity, and waste disposal companies of all sizes. The following objects can be exchanged between the CRM system and the Utilities back-end system:

▶ Business partner contacts (R/3 adapter object: SI_BCONTACT)

▶ Connection objects, premises (R/3 adapter object: SI_CONNOBJ)

- Contracts (R/3 adapter object: SI_CONTRACT)
- Points of delivery (R/3 adapter object: SI_POD)

B.6 Technical Details

B.6.1 Data Exchange Between the R/3 Back-End System and the CRM Server

The CRM middleware is delivered with many adapters that enable the connection of the CRM server to other systems, for example, SAP R/3, SAP BW, mobile CRM applications, groupware solutions, and other non-SAP systems.

The R/3 adapter ensures the semantic integration between the CRM server and SAP R/3. The following types of data exchange are supported by the R/3 adapter:

- **Initial load**
  Once the CRM server has been installed, the CRM applications require customizing data and business data from an existing SAP R/3 back-end system. The challenge for this type of data exchange is the high volume of data that is transferred between the systems. The CRM middleware provides an extremely scalable initial load solution that allows for a fast exchange of mass data.

- **Delta load**
  In a productive landscape, modified business data must be loaded continuously in real time from the CRM server to SAP R/3 and vice versa. This guarantees data consistency within the system landscape. Both the CRM server and SAP R/3 work according to a "store and forward" mechanism, in which change messages can also be sent to other systems when business objects are posted.

In order to exchange business data between the CRM server and SAP R/3, the R/3 adapter of the CRM server must communicate with a plug-in on the back-end side. When business objects are sent from R/3 to the CRM server, the contents of the relevant R/3 database tables are mapped to a BAPI transport structure (BAPIMTCS). The contents of the R/3 database tables are retrieved from the applications if there is a delta load, and extracted directly from the R/3 database tables for an initial load. Before the business objects are sent to the CRM server, filters can be applied. The contents of the inbound BAPI transport structure are mapped to a business document (BDoc) message in the CRM server and a message flow is started. Figure B.2 illustrates the process flow.

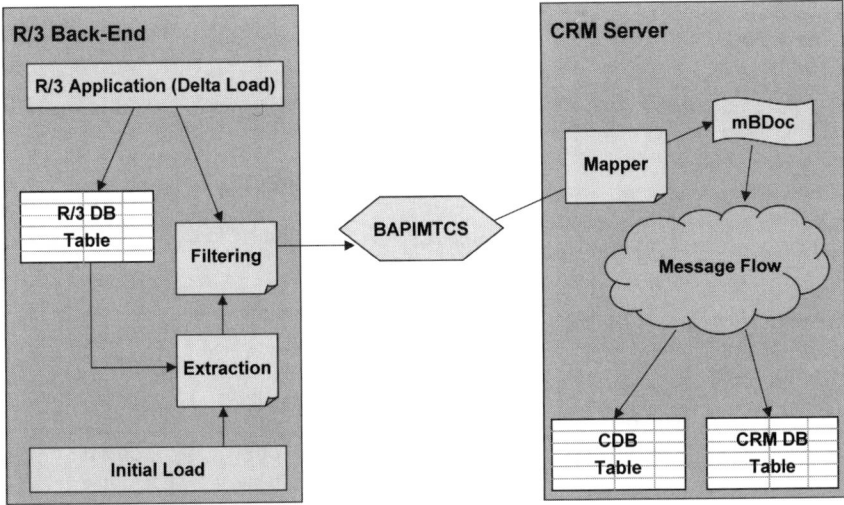

Figure B.2 Data Exchange from SAP R/3 to CRM Server

If business objects are to be sent from the CRM server to the SAP R/3 back-end, the business document (BDoc) messages are mapped to the BAPI transport structure and sent to the SAP R/3 back-end system. A proxy BAPI function module is then called, which, in turn, calls standard application interfaces (BAPIs) for posting. The data flow from the CRM server to the SAP back-end system can be filtered using subscriptions and publications within the replication model of the CRM middleware. Figure B.3 illustrates the process flow.

All definitions for data exchange are stored in the adapter object repository on the CRM server. The R/3 adapter objects are also stored there, as are all other adapter objects. They contain all the information required for the data exchange of business objects with SAP R/3 back-end systems, for example, the relevant R/3 database tables, business document (BDoc) types, extractor, proxy BAPI and mapping function modules, and filter settings.

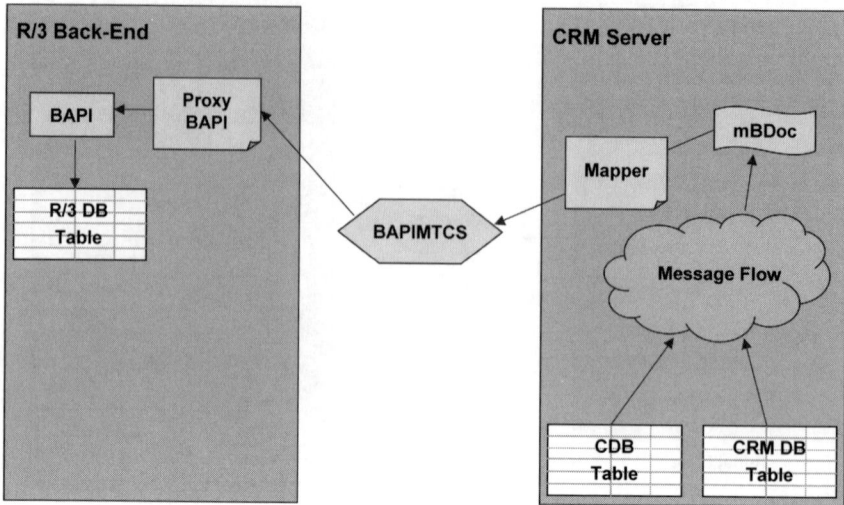

Figure B.3 Data Exchange from CRM Server to SAP R/3

C   Literature

[AlphaBrand 2001] AlphaBrand Strategies, *Best Practice Principles for Market Leadership*, White Paper, Colorado Springs, 2001

[Arend 2003] Thomas Arend, *A Rousing Debut*, in SAPinfo, No. 103, March 2003

[Basso 2003] Monica Basso, *Key Issues Set the Agenda in Wireless and Mobile*, Gartner Group, Research Note LE-19–1628, January 16, 2003

[Beringer 2001] Daniel Beringer, *Development of Efficiency-Analysis-Models for IT-Solutions in Customer Relationship Management*, Degree Dissertation, Private University of Applied Sciences, Göttingen, Germany, 2001

[Blattberg/Getz/Thomas 2001] Robert C. Blattberg, Gary Getz, Jacquelyn S. Thomas, *Customer Equity*, Harvard Business School Press, Boston, Massachusetts, 2001

[Blumstein/Wardley 2003] Robert Blumstein, Mary Wardley, *Worldwide Marketing and Sales Automation Applications Software Forecast, 2003–2007: A New Look at 2002*, IDC, Study No. 29387, 2003

[Brandenburger/Nalebuff 1996] A. M. Brandenburger, B. J. Nalebuff, *Co-Opetition*, Doubleday, New York, 1996

[Brendle/Buck-Emden/Bach 2002] Rainer Brendle, Rüdiger Buck-Emden, Thomas Bach, *People-Centric User Interface for mySAP CRM*, in: SAPinfo, Nr. 99, October 2002

[Brinkmann/Zeilinger 2001] Sandra Brinkmann, Axel Zeilinger, *SAP R/3 Financial Accounting*, Addison-Wesley, Harlow, UK, 2001

[Bruhn/Homburg 2003] Manfred Bruhn, Christian Homburg (Hrsg.), *Handbuch Kundenbindungsmanagement*, 4. Auflage, Gabler, Wiesbaden, Germany, 1999

[Buck-Emden 2002] Rüdiger Buck-Emden (Ed.), *mySAP CRM—Solution for Success*, SAP PRESS, Bonn, Germany, 2002

[Buck-Emden 2002a] Rüdiger Buck-Emden, *Customer Relationship Management*, in: Thomas Schildhauer (Hrsg.): *Lexikon Electronic Business*, Oldenbourg Verlag, München, Germany, 2002

[Buck-Emden 2002b] Rüdiger Buck-Emden, *CRM-Softwarelösungen*, in: Thomas Schildhauer (Hrsg.): *Lexikon Electronic Business*, Oldenbourg Verlag, München, Germany, 2002

[Buck-Emden/Böder 2003] Rüdiger Buck-Emden, Jochen Böder, *The People-Centric User Interface of mySAP CRM—The Book for Developers and Technical Consultants*, SAP AG, 2003

[Buck-Emden/Böder 2003a] Rüdiger Buck-Emden, Jochen Böder, *Integrierte Geschäftsanwendungen—Serviceorientierte Architektur als zukunftsweisendes Modell*, in: Informatik Spektrum, Vol. 26, Nr. 5, Oktober 2003

[Buck-Emden/Böder 2004] Rüdiger Buck-Emden, Jochen Böder (Hrsg.), *Customer Relationship Management with SAP Industry Solutions*, SAP PRESS, Bonn, Germany, projected for 2004

[Buck-Emden/Galimow 1996] Rüdiger Buck-Emden, Jürgen Galimow, *The SAP R/3 System—A Client/Server Technology*, Addison-Wesley, Harlow, UK, 1996

[Buck-Emden/Saddei 2003] Rüdiger Buck-Emden, Dietmar Saddei, *Informations-technologische Perspektiven von CRM*, in: Manfred Bruhn, Christian Homburg (Hrsg.): *Handbuch Kundenbindungsmanagement*, 4. Auflage, Gabler, Wiesbaden, Germany, 2003

[Buck-Emden/Zencke 2003] Rüdiger Buck-Emden, Peter Zencke, *mySAP CRM and SAP NetWeaver –A Powerful Combination*, in: SAPinfo, No. 106, June 2003

[Clark 2000] Sam Clark, *Putting Marketing Wheels on the Customer Life Cycle*, META Group, Delta, ADS 886, July 20, 2000

[Clark 2003] B. Clark, *Mobile Workers Need Well-Matched Architectures*, Gartner Group, Research Note DF-18–0043, February 21, 2003

[Computerworld 2003] Computerworld, *Knowledge Center ROI*, in: Computerworld, Vol. 37, No. 7, February 17, 2003

[Cooper 1995] Alan Cooper, *About Face. The Essentials of User Interface Design*, IDG Books Worldwide, Foster City, 1995

[Curry 2000] Jay Curry, *The Customer Marketing Method*, Free Press, 2000

[DaimlerChrysler 2003] *DaimlerChrysler Annual Report 2002, Stuttgart, Germany, 2003*

[Davenport/Short 1990] T. H. Davenport, J. E. Short, *The New Industrial Engineering: Imformation Technology and Business Process Design*, Sloan Management Review, Vol. 31, No. 4, 1990

[Deloitte 2002] Deloitte Consulting, *How to Eat the CRM Elephant*, Straight Talk Series, Book No. 2, 2001

[DeSisto 2002] R. DeSisto, *Partner Relationship Management—Optimizing the Demand Network*, Gartner Group, Management Update IGG-05222002–04, May 22, 2002

[Drucker 2001] Peter F. Drucker, *The Essential Drucker*, Harper-Collins, New York, 2001

[Dudenhöffer/Krüger 2003] Ferdinand Dudenhöffer, Marcus Krüger, *Der ADAC-AutoMarxX im Juni 2003*, Center of Automotive Research, Fachhochschule Gelsenkirchen, 2003

[Dyché 2002] Jill Dyché, *The CRM Handbook—A Business Guide to Customer Relationship Management*, Addison-Wesley, Boston, 2002

[Eckert 2003] Claudia Eckert, *IT-Sicherheit*, 2. Auflage, Oldenbourg-Verlag, München, 2003

[Gammage 2002] Brian Gammage, *The Changing Spectrum of Mobile PC Usage*, Gartner Group, Article Top View AV-18–4898, October 30, 2002

[Gerbetz 2002] Ken Gerbetz, Beth Ferber, Linda Plazonja, Robert Scalea, *Canada Post Powers Business Transformation with mySAP CRM*, The ROI Report, Vol. 6, No. 1, June 2002

[Grönroos 1989] C. Grönroos, *A Relationship Approach to Marketing: The Need for a New Paradigm*, Swedish School of Economics and Business Administration, Helsinki, 1989

[Hack 2000] S. Hack, *Collaborative Business Scenarios—Wertschöpfung in der Internetökonomie*, in: A.-W. Scheer (Hrsg.): E-Business—Wer geht? Wer bleibt? Wer kommt? 21. Saarbrücker Arbeitstagung 2000 für Industrie, Dienstleistung und Verwaltung, Physica-Verlag, Heidelberg, 2000

[Hagemeyer/Nelson 2003] D. Hagemeyer, S. Nelson, *Management Update: CRM Success Lies in Strategy and Implementation, Not Software*, Gartner Group, Research Note IGG-03122003–01, March 12, 2003

[Henneboel 2002] Georg Henneboel, *Upwardly Mobile—Mobile Solutions for Managing Technical Assets*, in: SAPinfo, No. 96, July 2002

[Holtzblatt/Beyer 1998] Karen Holtzblatt, Hugh Beyer, *Contextual Design. Defining Customer-Centered Systems*, Morgan Kaufmann Publishers, San Francisco, 1998

[Homburg 2000] Christian Homburg, *Customer Relationship Management*, Arbeitspapier M52, Universität Mannheim, 2000

[Homburg/Bruhn 2003] Christian Homburg, Manfred Bruhn, *Eine Einführung in die theoretischen und praktischen Problemstellungen*, in: [Bruhn/Homburg 2003]

[Johnson/Deighton 2003] G. Johnson, N. Deighton, *Key Issues for Mobile Business in 2003*, Gartner Group, Research Note K-18–7119, January 6, 2003

[Kagermann/Keller 2001] Henning Kagermann, Gerhard Keller, *mySAP.com Industry Solutions*,, SAP PRESS, Bonn, Germany, 2001

[Kalakota/Robinson 1999] Ravi Kalakota, Marcia Robinson, *e-Busines—Roadmap for Success*, Addison Wesley Longman, Reading, Massachusetts, 1999

[Kalakota/Robinson 2001] Ravi Kalakota, Marcia Robinson, *M-Business: The Race to Mobility*, McGraw-Hill, 2001

[Kaplan/Norton 1996] Robert S. Kaplan, David P. Norton, *The Balanced Scorecard: Translating Strategy into Action*, Harvard Business School Press, Boston, 1996

[Kargl 1996] H. Kargl, *Controlling im DV-Bereich*, 3. Auflage, Oldenbourg-Verlag, München/Wien, 1996

[Kreindler/Lutz 2002] Philip Kreindler, Alain Lutz, *Die Crux bei der Einführung von CRM-Systemen*, in: Neue Zürcher Zeitung Online, 24.09.2002

[Kumar 2001] Anil Kumar et al., *Beyond CRM—Realizing the Customer Value Promise*, McKinsey & Company, 2001

[Lassmann/Paris 2000] Jay Lassmann, David Paris, *CRM in the Call Center and Contact Center*, Gartner Group, Tutorial DPRO-93666, November 21, 2000

[Lübke/Ringling 2004] Christian Lübke, Sven Ringling, *SAP HR: Personnel Planning and Development*, SAP PRESS, Bonn, Germany, 2004

[MacMillan/Hart 2002] D. MacMillan, T. Hart, *Key Issues for Mobile Services and Markets*, Gartner Group, Research Note K-18–9886, December 30, 2002

[Marcus 2003] Claudio Marcus, *The Future of Technology-Enabled Marketing*, Gartner Group, CRM Summit Spring 2003, Chicago, 3–5 March 2003

[McKenna 1995] Regis McKenna, *Real-Time Marketing*, in: Harvard Business Review, Jul/Aug 1995, Vol. 23, No. 4

[Mercedes-Benz 2003] *http://www.mercedes-benz.com/d/innovation/fmobil/default.htm*, Status 28th July 2003

[META 1999] META Group, IMT Strategies, *Customer Relationship Management Study*, Sep 22, 1999

[Millar 2002] Bill Millar, Chris Helm, Joseph Daly, Lisa Larsson, Philippe Payard, *Deregulation & Commoditization: The Customer Holds the Key*, in: CRM ROI Review, Vol. 2, No. 1 (09/2002), Peppers and Rogers Group, 2002

[Morris 2000] Henry Morris, *Analytic Applications Market Forecast and Analysis, 2000–2004*, IDC Report 23498, December 2000

[Natis 2002] Yefim Natis, *Application Platform Suites: The Shape of Things to Come*, Gartner Group, Research Note AV-18–6261, October 31, 2002

[Nelson 2000] S. Nelson, *Customer Service is the Most Important CRM Function*, Gartner Group, Research Note SPA-11–7680, Nov 9, 2000

[Nelson/Comport 2003] S. Nelson, J. Comport, *The Evolution of CRM Requires Redefinition*, Research Note M-19–0045, March 21, 2003

[Nelson/Eisenfeld 2002] S. Nelson, B. Eisenfeld, *Salvaging a Failed CRM Initiative*, Gartner Group, Research Note SPA-15–4007, February 13, 2002

[Nelson/Kirkby 2001] S. Nelson, J. Kirkby, *Seven Reasons Why CRM Fails*, Gartner Group, Research Note COM-13–7628, August 20, 2001

[Nelson/Marcus 2002] S. Nelson, C. Marcus, *CRM in 2003: Light at the End of the Tunnel*, Gartner Group, Research Note COM-18–6862, December 5, 2002

[Newell 1997] Frederick Newell, *The New Rules of Marketing: How to Use One-to-One Relationship Marketing to Be the Leader in Your Industry*, Irwin Professional Publishing, 1997

[Newell 2001] Frederick Newell, *Loyalty Rules! How Today's Leaders Build Lasting Relationships*, HBS Press Book, 2001

[O'Halloran 2001] J. Patrick O'Halloran, Todd R. Wagner, Theodore Ansusinha, Richard Lawrence, Kevin N. Quiring, *Insight Driven Marketing—Using Customer Insights to Build Brand Loyalty and Increase Marketing ROI*, Accenture Executive Summary, 2001

[Oswald 2003] Gerhard Oswald (Ed.), *SAP Service and Support*, SAP PRESS, Bonn, Germany, 2003

[Peppers 2002] Don Peppers, *Customer Relationship Management: The Importance of Competitive Strategy*, SAP Global Customer Advisory Board, November 21, 2002, Philadelphia

[Peppers/Rogers 1993] Don Peppers, Martha Rogers, *The One to One Future: Building Relationships One Customer at a Time*, Doubleday, New York 1993

[Peppers/Rogers 1997] Don Peppers, Martha Rogers, *Enterprise One to One—Tools for Competing in the Interactive Age*, Doubleday, New York, 1997

[Peppers/Rogers 1999] Don Peppers, Martha Rogers, *The One to One Manager*, Doubleday, New York, 1999

[PeppersRogersGroup 2002] Peppers and Rogers Group, *The Role of Personalization and Privacy in Streamlining Government*, White Paper, 2002

[Pine 1993] Joseph B. Pine, *Mass Customization: The New Frontier in Business Competition*, Harvard Business School Press, Boston, Massachusetts, 1993

[Porter 1986] M. Porter, *Competitive Advantage*, Harvard Business School Press, Boston, MA, 1986

[PricewaterhouseCoopers 2003] PricewaterhouseCoopers, *Trendsetter Barometer*, January 7, 2003

[Prince 2001] Frank Prince, Charles Rutstein, Christian Buss, *The Real Cost of Mobility*, Forrester Report, May 2001

[Radcliffe 2001] John Radcliffe, *Eight Building Blocks of CRM: A Framework for Success*, Gartner Group, Researche Note AV-14–9265, December 13, 2001

[Rageth 1999] Luzi Rageth, *Tante Emma und ihre 10.000 Angestellten*, in: Marketing & Kommunikation, Ausgabe 6/1999

[Rapp 2000] Reinhold Rapp, *Customer Relationship Management*, Campus, Frankfurt/Main, Germany, 2000

[Reicheld 1996] Frederich F. Reichheld, *The Loyalty Effect: The Hidden Force behind Growth, Profits, and Lasting Value*, Harvard Business School Press, Boston, 1996

[SAP 2003] SAP AG, *mySAP CRM Customer Success—ROI Reports*, *http://www.sap.com/solutions/crm/customersuccess/roi.asp*

[Schneiderman/Yih 2001] Nathan Schneiderman, Adrienne Yih, *The Ermerging Face of Customer Relationship Management*, Wedbush Morgan Securities, Industry Report, August 2001

[Selchert 2003] Martin Selchert,*Value Added with mySAP CRM*, University of Applied Sciences Ludwigshafen, Benchmarking Study by Order of SAP, 2003, *http://www.sap.com/solutions/crm/customersuccess/roi.asp*

[Shneiderman 2002] Ben Shneiderman, *Leonardo's Laptop. Human Needs and the New Computing Technologies*, MIT Press, Cambridge, Massachusettes 2002

[Siebel/Malone 1996] Tom Siebel, Michael Malone, *Virtual Selling*, The Free Press, New York, 1996

[Simkovits 1998] Harvy Simkovits, *New Ways To Win Customers*, Mass High Tech Journal, October 5, 1998

[Slywotzky/Morrison 1998] Adrian J. Slywotzky, Dave J. Morrison, *The Profit Zone: How Strategic Business Design Will Lead You to Tomorrow's Profits*, Random House 1998

[Spang 2000] K. Spang, *Customer Relationship Management*, Current Analysis, Market Assessment, Nov 13, 2000

[Stadtler/Kilger 2000] Hartmut Stadtler, Christoph Kilger (Ed.), *Supply Chain Management and Advanced Planning—Concepts, Models, Software and Case Studies*, Springer, Berlin/Heidelberg, 2000

[Stefani 2002] Helmut Stefani, Archiving your SAP Data, SAP PRESS, Bonn, Germany, 2003

[Temkin/Schmitt/Herbert 2003] Bruce D. Temkin, Eric Schmitt, Liz Herbert, *CRM Status: Satisfaction Rate Approaches 75%*, Forrester TechStrategy Research, February 12, 2003

[Thompson/Radcliffe 2003] Ed Thompson, J. Radcliffe, *Enterprise Suites Will Dominate CRM Spending*, Gartner Group, Research Note SPA-19–3009, February 24, 2003

[Tidwell 1999] Jenifer Tidwell, *A Pattern Language for Human-Computer Interface Design*, *www.mit.edu/~jtidwell/ui_patterns_essay.html*, 1999

[Topolinski/Eschinger/Kumar 2002] Thomas Topolinski, Chad Eschinger, Pranav Kumar, *Outlook for the CRM Software Market: Trends and Forecast*, Gartner Group, October 21, 2002

[Treacy/Wiesema 1995] Michael Treacy, Fred Wiersema, *Discipline of Market Leaders*, Perseus Books, Cambridge, Massachusetts, 1995

[Vering 2001] Matthias Vering et al., *The E-Business-Workplace*, Pricewaterhouse-Coopers, 2001

[Woods 2003] Dan Woods, *Packaged Composite Applications*, O'Reilly, Sebastopol, California, 2003

[Woods 2003a] Dan Woods, *Enterprise Service Architecture*, O'Reilly, Sebastopol, California, 2003

[Zencke 2002] Peter Zencke, *Value Optimization in Customer, Partner and Employee Relationships*, SAP Conference on Business Intelligence and Enterprise Portals, January 30—February 1, 2002, Leipzig, Germany

[Zencke 2003] Peter Zencke, *CRM nach dem Hype: Vom Frontoffice zum One-Office*, in: Wirtschaftsinformatik, Band 45, Nr. 2, April 2003

D   The Authors

Achim Appold studied business management and holds an MBA. Since 2003, he has directed the ramp-up for SAP CRM 4.0. Before holding this position, he worked as a senior consultant and regional manager for the SAP CRM Regional Group. Achim Appold honed extensive CRM sales and consulting experience at SAS Institute and Kiefer & Veittinger Information Systems.

Gero Auhagen is product manager for mySAP CRM Channel Management in Palo Alto, California. He began his career in 1983 as a freelance developer for market research and billing. After completing his business management degree, he worked as a consultant for several CRM projects, most recently as a functional architect and team lead of a call center and customer service system for a German financial provider. At SAP AG, Gero Auhagen has held positions in product management in CRM Marketing and CRM Analytics; he also worked in the areas of e-commerce and channel management in Palo Alto.

Daniel Beringer has a degree in business studies and has worked as assistant to board member Dr. Peter Zencke since 2001. As part of his thesis at the University of Göttingen, he concentrated on the profitability analysis of IT projects in the area of customer relationship management.

Jochen Böder studied mathematics, history, and computer science before becoming a consultant in the area of e-commerce for the SAP subsidiaries e-SAP and SAP Portals. He currently works for SAP Product Management in CRM Architecture & Technology. Jochen Böder is co-editor of the book *Customer Relationship Management with Industry Solutions*.

Dr. Rüdiger Buck-Emden has a degree in computer science. He joined SAP in 1990 and has held different management positions in development, product management, and strategic planning, including having worked as an assistant to executive board member Prof. Hasso Plattner. Currently, he is Vice President of CRM Architecture & Technology. Before joining SAP AG, he worked in the Business Systems development area for Nixdorf Computer AG as a manager for network-based application systems. Rüdiger Buck-Emden studied industrial engineering and computer science before getting his doctorate in computer-based information systems at Braunschweig Technical University. He has written many text books and other publications.

Christopher Fastabend joined SAP AG in 1998 as product manager for CRM Marketing. Prior to joining SAP AG, he worked with the CRM specialists Kiefer & Veittinger Information Systems in Mannheim. He holds a bachelor's degree in industrial engineering and an MBA.

Tomas Gumprecht is an IT graduate and works as product manager for CRM Service. He is responsible for international brand positioning, roll-in and roll-out, coordinating market demands with development, and the documentation and translation of service components in mySAP CRM. Tomas Gumprecht joined SAP in 1993 and, in addition to his role in mySAP CRM Product Management, he has worked on the development of software for utilities companies and for service management/maintenance.

Frank Israel is a sales executive for mySAP CRM. Before taking this position, he worked as a consultant for Kiefer & Veittinger Information Systems and for SAP CRM Consulting in the area of capital goods/high-tech.

Dr. Volker Hildebrand is Vice President for eCRM and responsible for product management and strategy in the areas of e-commerce, channel management, and product configuration. Prior to holding this position, he occupied various roles in SAP Product Management, including PM Director for SAPMarkets, Inc. in Palo Alto, California. His career at SAP began in 1998 in sales, where he helped build the sales area for CRM software. Before joining SAP, Volker Hildebrand worked as a business consultant and assistant at the universities in Frankfurt and Kassel. A graduate of economics, he has authored and co-authored several books and numerous articles on CRM and e-commerce.

Fabian Kamm studied business management and holds an MBA. Since 1996, he has worked at Kiefer & Veittinger Information Systems, and then at SAP as a consultant, where he has project lead various CRM projects throughout Europe. Today, Fabian Kamm is a senior consultant, specializing in CRM implementation methods, content, and tools such as SAP Solution Manager.

Stefan Kraus studied business management. From 1992 to 1996, he was a consultant for the implementation of industry-specific software solutions for profitability and sales accounting at many different enterprises. He subsequently joined SAP AG as a product manager and was responsible for profitability analysis. In 2000, Stefan Kraus became the product manager for CRM Analytics.

Dr. Peter Kulka studied computer science and has been with SAP AG since 1999. He worked in product management for CRM Middleware until 2003. Since then, he has worked in the product management area of CRM Architecture & Technology. In this role, Dr. Kulka has focused on topics of integration and SAP NetWeaver, and their importance for mySAP CRM.

Mark Layden is Vice President worldwide for the Workforce Management application of mySAP CRM. He was a founding member of Campbell Software Inc. (Chicago), and a leader in the area of workforce management solutions for the retail and service industries until the company was taken over by SAP. As President of SAP Campbell, he was responsible for integrating the strategies, processes, and development of both companies. Mr. Layden studied economics at Harvard.

Claudia Mairon is product manager for the Channel Management area in mySAP CRM. Prior to holding this position, she worked in strategic product management for e-selling solutions and in product management for mySAP Workplace. In 1998, she joined SAP AG, as a product manager for EnjoySAP. Claudia Mairon studied business management at the University of Mannheim, where, in addition to pursuing her studies, she also became involved with various areas of SAP AG.

Wolfgang Oelschläger is product manager for the mySAP CRM area of Field Applications. In this role, he works with customers and developers to refine product requirements, which then serve as a basis for further planning and development at SAP. Wolfgang Oelschläger is an economics graduate with more than 12 years' experience in consultancy, product management, and business development in sales force automation. After working for the Mannheim-based CRM specialist Kiefer & Veittinger Information Systems, he joined SAP AG in 1998.

Jörg Rosbach joined SAP AG as an ERP consultant for logistics in 1994. In 1997, he moved to international marketing. As corporate marketing manager, first for sales force automation and then for CRM, he has built up marketing for CRM in close collaboration with product management. Since 1999, Jörg Rosbach has been the product manager for CRM Sales. Furthermore, he is responsible for the documentation of the CRM Sales area. He studied at the Technical University of Karlsruhe and the ETH in Zürich, where he concentrated in industrial engineering.

Gabriele Roth has worked in mySAP CRM product management since 2003 in the area of Architecture & Technology. Since joining SAP in 1994, she has gained development experience in various R/3 modules, and from 2000 on, was project lead for cross-application developments and customer projects for the industry solution Public Services. She is a graduate of physics and is currently writing her doctorate on business management.

Dr. Andreas Schuh is Director of Product Management and is responsible for component integration topics such as business scenario descriptions for mySAP CRM. Since joining SAP in 1997, he has held management positions in the areas of product management and business development, and was previously project lead of a strategic SAP customer project.

Dr. Erik Tiden is Vice President for the development of marketing and analytics solutions in mySAP CRM. During his career, he has amassed extensive experience with research, software development, and development management at leading research institutes and technology companies in addition to many years' experience in marketing for high-tech products. He is a graduate of computer science and also holds a degree in physics and mathematics.

Stein Wanvik graduated from the Technical University of Karlsruhe with a degree in economics. He has worked at SAP AG in various business units and positions since 1995. He started his career as a developer; however, since 1998, he has worked as a product manager in the area of product configuration.

Dr. Thomas Weinerth has worked in SAP Product Management for Best Practices for mySAP CRM for two years. Prior to joining SAP AG, he worked at the University of Mannheim as a researcher in the area of CRM. He wrote his doctorate on marketing and organization and holds degrees in business management and psychology.

Dr. Peter Zencke joined SAP in 1984, having earned a doctorate in mathematics and economics. As member of the board of SAP AG since 1993, he manages large parts of the development of SAP R/3, mySAP Business Suite, and industry solutions. Under his leadership, the mySAP CRM solution has attained a leading market position. Currently, his area of responsibility includes the development of SAP application architecture and application platform, the coordination of SAP research activities worldwide, and the SAP Labs development centers. Dr. Zencke has published a number of articles and books on mathematical and software-related topics. He is also co-editor of the book series *SAP Competent* (Springer).

Rainer Zinow studied business management and has held various management positions at SAP AG for more than ten years. His work has included building up the SAP-IBM Competency Center, the international (business) coordination of the SAP training offer, and managing the area of knowledge management. He was also assistant to former board member Dietmar Hopp. He is currently Vice President of the mySAP CRM Interaction Center application.

Index

A

ABAP 55
ABC analysis 139
ABC classification 315
AcceleratedSAP 340, 369
AcceleratedSAP for mySAP CRM 340
Account management 102, 105, 189
Account manager 138
Account planning 102
Accounting 52
Accounting Engine 135
Accounts receivable accounting 159
Action profiles 132
Actions 123
Activities 108, 109, 110
Activity Journal 108
Activity management 107, 109, 114, 218, 220
Activity plan 112
Address Verification System 152
Administration 358
Administrator Workbench 364
After-sales area 68
After-sales cycle 230
After-sales services 228, 230
Agent 165
Agent support 166
Aggregation method 84
Alert inbox 385
Alert modeler 166
Alert monitoring 396
Alerts 154
Analysis 114, 118
Analysis of competition 116
Analytical applications 160
Analytical CRM 38, 40
Analytical CRM applications 305
Analytical report 110
Analytical reporting 161
Analytics 58
Application hosting 351
Application Platform Suites 353, 374
Appointment scheduling 183
Architecture and technology 58
ASAP 340, 369

Assessment 114, 117
Asset accounting 135
Assortment 121
ATP 244, 419
ATP check 147
Attachments 122
Auction catalog 247
Auctions 246
Audit 372
Audit framework 372
Audit Information System 372
Authorization 152
Authorization horizon 153
Auto Suggest Repository 268
Automatic appointment scheduling 170
Automatic classification 135
Automotive 359
Availability check 121, 147, 149, 244
Availability information 149
Availability time 172
Available-to-Promise 147, 244
Avartars 241

B

B2B 31, 41, 151, 227, 233, 239
B2B Mall 233
B2B sales process 41
B2C 31, 41, 125, 151, 232, 233
B2R2C 234
Back-end 37, 42, 243
Back-office 94
Backorder Processing 150
Backup 401
BackWeb ProactivePortal Server 414
BAdI 399
Balanced scorecard 40, 321
BBBOnLine 31
BCB 387
BDocs 394
Best practice processes 252
Best Practices for mySAP CRM 347
Best seller lists 238
Best-of-breed 44
Billing 147, 157, 158, 185

Billing Data 159
Bluetooth 208
Bottom-up 102
Brand owner 235
Brand value 72
Branding 72, 235
Broadcast Messaging Server 415
Business activities 107
Business Add-Ins 399
Business applications 48
Business blueprint 341, 343, 344
Business case 64
Business Communication Broker 387
Business configuration sets 53
Business Content 364, 420
Business Explorer 364
Business Explorer Analyzer 364
Business focus 25
Business intelligence 55, 227, 231, 250
Business maps 57
Business Partner Cockpit 106
Business Partner Management 105
Business process 17, 57
Business process step 57
Business processes 31, 205
Business scenario 57, 64, 348
Business strategy 18
Business success 19
Business transactions 120
Business value 17
Business view 61, 63
Business vision 30
Business workflow 134
Business-to-Business → see B2B
Business-to-Business Mall → see B2B
  Mall
Business-to-Consumer → see B2C
Buying center 114, 115

C
CAD 127, 171
Calendar 108
Call center 33, 102, 249, 253, 380
Call center solutions 43
Call me back 249
Callback 237, 249
Campaign 83

Campaign management 57, 61, 85,
  135, 237
Campaign manager portal 85
Campaign monitoring 94
Campaign planning 85, 93, 319
Cancellation 159
Cancellation rules 132
Card Number 151
Card Verification Value 151
CAS (computer-aided selling) 35
Case 168
Case management 168, 272
Cash on delivery 151, 153
CAT server 417
Catalog management 239, 240
Catalog presentation 240
CATS 183, 203
C-Business Maps 58, 60, 63
CCMS 396
CDB 401
Central Master Data Administration
  362
Certificates 371
Change management 343
Channel commerce 234, 253
Channel management 18, 41, 58, 234,
  358, 411
Channel master 234
Chat 237, 249
Claims management 147, 160
Classification 135
Classroom training 351
Clickstream 251
Clickstream analysis 231, 251
Closed-loop 310
Collaborative Business Maps 60, 63
Collaborative CRM 37, 38
Commission simulation 136
Communication channels 33, 38, 39
Communication Station 393, 415
Company profitability 30, 42
Company-wide collaboration 37
Competitive advantages 33
Complaints 17, 171, 172
Component integration 390
Component view 62
Composite Application Framework
  354, 374

Composite Applications 54, 354
Computer telephony integration 415
Computer-aided design applications 171
Computing Center Management System 396
Configuration 229, 244, 383, 396
Configuration settings 397
Configurator 125, 129
Configure-to-Order 244
Confirmation schedule line 148
Connected CRM 37
Connection Handler 393
Connectors 247, 387
Consolidated Database 401
Consumer analysis 78
Consumer industries 53
Consumer packaged goods 71
Consumer promotions 83
Consumer segmentation 82
Contact channels 33
Contact management 35, 105, 189
Content management 240, 364
Content server 240
Contract accounting 159
Contract and order analysis 191
Contract management 130, 134
Contracts 131
Controller 382
Controlling 160, 183, 186
CO-PA 94
Corporate branding 234
Corporate strategy 30
Correlation 61
Cost effectiveness 164
CPG 71
cProjects Add-On for CRM 417
Credit check 122, 154
Credit management 147, 151, 153
Credit problems 154
CRM → see Customer Relationship Management
CRM Application Tool Server 417
CRM business strategy 31
CRM company strategy 33
CRM content management 211
CRM designer 383
CRM implementation 305, 329, 337

CRM implementation project 31, 37
CRM information technology 33
CRM investments 330
CRM middleware 210, 214, 361, 366, 377, 386, 390, 392, 401
CRM project 18, 37, 143, 329, 334, 338
CRM server 210, 417, 433
CRM software 33
CRM Software Agent Framework 421
CRM software solution 30, 31, 33, 37, 42
CRM software vendor 45
CRM software vendors 42
CRM solutions 42, 147
CRM suite vendor 44
CRM system 143
CRM vendor 38
Cross-Application Time Sheet 183
Cross-selling 63, 91, 150, 238, 242, 243, 306
Cross-selling analyses 312
Cross-selling offers 232
Customer 17, 27, 29
Customer analysis 78
Customer analytics 309, 311
Customer attractiveness 316
Customer behavior 17
Customer cards 27
Customer churn analyses 312
Customer clubs 27
Customer complaints 171
Customer contact 27
Customer data 31
Customer events 85
Customer installation 177
Customer interaction center 43, 335
Customer interaction cycle 49, 67, 305
Customer intimacy 19, 23
Customer lifetime value 40, 314, 315
Customer loyalty 33
Customer needs 27, 31, 169
Customer orientation 19, 24, 30, 38
Customer portal 253
Customer portfolio 316
Customer potential 40
Customer problems 166
Customer profitability 314
Customer questions 165

Customer relationship 25, 28, 67
Customer Relationship Management
    17, 19, 25, 27, 28, 33, 47, 68, 143, 210,
    225
Customer requirements 17, 39
Customer retention 232
Customer retention programs 27
Customer retention rate 40
Customer satisfaction 29
Customer scoring 314, 315
Customer segmentation 82
Customer segments 39
Customer service 163, 164
Customer Service & Support 164, 165
Customer service concepts 28
Customer support 249
Customer value 314
Customer-oriented value 19
Customer-oriented value discipline 20
Customize 236, 237
Customizing 116, 336, 369, 423
Customizing data 392
Customizing distribution 392
Customizing scout 392

D
DAB 417
Data Integrity Manager 401
Data protection 31
Data protection policy 31
Data warehouse 40, 76, 232, 251
Date management 122
Date profiles 131
Date profiles and rules 131
Decision-making factors 17
Deliver-to-Order 127
Delivery group 150
Delivery-to-promise 336
Delta Data Exchange 395
Delta Load 391, 395, 432
Demand chain planning 419
Differentiate 236
Direct marketing 71
Direct Store Delivery 217
Discrete industries 53
Dispute case processing 160
Distributed sales order processing 162
Distribution channels 38

Distributor & reseller networks (B2R2B,
    B2R2C) 234
Document flow 123
Document header 120
Document management systems 55
Documents 123
Down-selling 91
Drag & Relate 357
Drill-down method 84
Drill-up method 84
Dunning 160, 161
Dynamic Auction and Bidding Engine
    417

E
E-analytics 318
Early warning lists 154
Easy enhancement workbench 385,
    399
eBay 247
E-books 352
E-business 130, 205
E-commerce 43, 58, 205, 225, 232, 242,
    253, 317, 338, 389, 411
E-Commerce Web Applications 389
Economies of scale 27
eConsultant 241
EDI over Internet 410
Effect chain 68
E-learning 352
Electronic bill presentment and
    payment 230, 247
Electronic customer care concept 226
E-mail 93, 165, 237, 249
E-marketing 28, 41
Employee development 140
Employee relationship management
    34
Employee roles 346
Employee Self-Service 357
Engage 38
Engagement management 188
Engineering-to-Order 128
Enterprise application suite vendor 44
Enterprise Buyer Professional (EBP)
    239
Enterprise Portal 51, 353

Enterprise Resource Planning → see
   ERP
Enterprise Service Architecture 47
Entitlement check 248
EOM 162
E-procurement 233
ERM 34
ERP 34, 37, 164
ERP area 225
ERP system 164, 183
ESA 47
E-selling 41, 227, 335, 389
E-selling business scenarios 232
E-selling platforms 17
E-selling projects 254
E-selling solutions 27
E-selling strategy 230
E-service 41, 170, 184
ESS 357
ETL 419
ETO 128
Euro-Label 31
Events 250
Extended Order Management 42, 162
Extensible Markup Language 52

F

FAQs 167, 170, 177, 230, 248
Feasibility study 341
FI 52
Fiducia AG 255
Field analytics 318, 319
Field applications 58, 209, 411
Field sales force 206
Field service 164, 180, 200
Final preparation 344
Financial accounting 17
Financial services 53
Financing company perspective 135
Firewall 372
Flow control 394
Follow-on campaign 97
Free goods 121
Frequently asked questions → see
   FAQs
Front office 43
Front-end 37, 243
Fulfill 38

Fulfillment 147
Fulfillment processing 161
Funnel Analysis 138

G

Generic application services 58
GIS 140
GIS format 139
Global Positioning System 206
Globalization 17
Globalization services 373
Go live 341, 345
Go live and support 345
GoingLive Check 370
Goods Issue 156
GPS 206
Groupware 406
Groupware Connector 393, 417
Groupware Integration 405
Groupware-Adapter 394
Guided selling 241

H

Hacker attacks 32
Handheld 209
Handheld device 181
Handling Units 156
Header 120
Help desk 39, 168
Hierarchies 138
Hits 250
HR 52, 140
HTML 241, 252, 368
HTML form 170
Human Resource Management → see
   HR

I

IC Scheduling 417
IC WebClient 418
ICI 387
Identify 236
Implementation 162
Implementation Guide 344
Implementation of mySAP CRM 341
Implementation roadmap 341
IMS 421

Incentive and Commission Management 136, 199, 272
Increase in sales 33
Index Management Service 421
Industries 217
Industry sectors 71
Industry solutions 53, 404
Industry-specific CRM 37, 38
Infocenter 211
InfoCubes 364, 420
Information Integration 354
Information logistics 31
Information society 17
Infoteam Sales Process Consulting AG 112
Initial data exchange 395
Initial Load 391, 395, 432
Input Processing 158
Inside-out approach 27
Installed base 178
Installed base database 167
Installed base management 164, 167, 177, 248
Integrated Communication Interface 387
Integrated Sales Planning 107
Integration 35, 37, 94, 101, 114, 135, 404
Integration broker 55
Integration directory 366
Integration repository 366
Integration server 365
Intelligence Connector 418
Intelligent Miner 309
Intensiy of the Customer Relationship 316
Interact 236
Interaction Center 43, 58, 165, 176, 198, 263, 317, 318, 358, 386, 411
Interaction Center agent 127
Interaction Center Analytics 272, 318
Interaction Center WebClient 387
Interaction Center WinClient 270
Interaction Channel 101, 225
Interaction Channel Analytics 309, 317
Interaction History 107
Interactive design 379
Interactive Intelligent Agent 168

Interfaces 52
Internal rate of return 330
Internal sales processes 140
Internet 29, 225, 230, 234, 249, 389
Internet auction 246
Internet Customer Self-Service 170
Internet sales 162, 414
Invoice 151, 153
Invoicing 158, 247, 248
IRR 330
IT 69
IT investments 225, 330
IT landscape 226
Items 120
iViews 357, 368, 381

J
J2EE 55, 252, 366, 390, 414, 422
J2EE technology 252
JumpStart 338
JumpStart program 338

K
Key accounts 41
Key capabilities 58
Key figures 41
Key performance indicators 40, 81
Knowledge Management 55, 75, 164, 167, 176, 213, 268, 357, 381
Knowledge Provider 240
KPI 40

L
Laptop 181, 208, 209, 385
Lead 89, 105, 109, 320
Lead analysis 96
Lead generation 39
Lead Management 78, 89, 380
Lead manager portal 89
Lead qualification 89
Leasing 133, 358
Leasing contracts 130, 134
Leasing solution 133
Life cycle management services 351
Lifecycle Management 55, 368
Listing 121
Live Web collaboration 249

Logistics 18, 52
Look-and-buy ratio 232
Lotus Notes 188, 211, 364
Loyalty index 40

M

Mail shot provider 62
Mail shots 62
Mailing campaigns 83
Mailings 93
Make-to-Order 127
Management 40
MapBox 393, 418
Market advantage 19
Market analysis 78, 79
Market leader 20
Market leadership 21
Marketing 40, 58, 67, 69, 135, 305, 335, 358, 411
Marketing analytics 309, 319
Marketing applications 39
Marketing calendar 85
Marketing planning 80
Marketing strategies 27
Marketing workflows 80
Marketplaces 52
Mass customization 27, 226, 231, 255
Mass marketing 71
Master Data Consolidation 362
Master Data Harmonization 362
Master Data Server 363
Materials Management 164
M-Business 205
MCOD 402
M-commerce 205
MDS 363
Media 359
Message-based component integration 390
Microsoft Windows XP Tablet PC Edition 214
Middleware Cockpit 396
Minimizing total costs 350
Mobile applications 205, 209
Mobile Client Recovery Manager 418
Mobile Client Software 418
Mobile Clients 394
Mobile Development Workstation 418

Mobile Sales 162, 210, 211, 361
Mobile Sales for Handheld 414
Mobile Sales for Handhelds 215
Mobile Sales for Handhelds (R/3 Edition) 216
Mobile Service 210, 213, 361
Mobile Service (R/3 Edition) 210, 214
Mobile Service for Handhelds 216
Model 382
Model View Controller Approach 382
Model View Controller Concept 382
Monitoring 309, 354, 370, 396
Monitoring Services 396
MS Outlook 188, 211
MS Word 211
Multi channel strategy 230
Multi supplier catalog 234
Multi-channel access 55, 356
Multi-channel functions 85
Multi-channel interaction 385
Multi-channel interface 387
Multi-dimensional planning 102
Multiple back-end scenario 408
Multiple CRM case 408
Multiple-system landscapes 408
MVC 382
mySAP All-in-One 48, 349
mySAP BI 51, 78, 137, 140, 160, 190
mySAP Business Intelligence → see mySAP BI
mySAP Business Suite 47, 49, 53, 58, 64, 365, 392, 404, 411
mySAP CRM 18, 47, 49, 58, 64, 69, 77, 89, 102, 110, 114, 123, 128, 143, 150, 157, 161, 162, 171, 176, 205, 225, 242, 305, 337, 368, 377
mySAP CRM Mobile Service 414
mySAP CRM Sales Methodology 114
mySAP CRM Workforce Management 196
mySAP Enterprise Portal 52
mySAP ERP 52, 162
mySAP FI 51, 159, 164, 203, 247
mySAP Financials → see mySAP FI
mySAP HR 51, 164, 198, 357
mySAP HR Payroll 183
mySAP Human Resource → see mySAP HR

mySAP Marketplace 52
mySAP Mobile Business 51
mySAP PLM 50, 128
mySAP Product Lifecycle Management
→ see mySAP PLM
mySAP SCM 128, 154
mySAP Supply Chain Management →
see mySAP SCM
mySolutions 248

N
Net present value 330
New economy 18, 29
Non-profit organizations 31
Non-SAP systems 122

O
Object extensions 383, 385
OLAP 40
OLAP functions 40
One face to the customer 234
One office 37
One-step business 233
One-step buying 234
One-to-one marketing 28, 228, 232,
236, 247
Online analytical processing 40
Online status request 247
Open interfaces 52
Open item 160
Operational CRM 38, 39
Operational excellence 19, 22, 25
Operations services 351
Operative report 110
Operatives Reporting 161
Opportunities 35, 109, 136, 139, 211
Opportunity 187
Opportunity assessment 114, 117
Opportunity hierarchies 111
Opportunity Management 39, 100,
102, 110, 112, 116, 143, 212
Opportunity pipeline 118
Opportunity plan 114, 117
Opportunity planning 102, 111
Order 229, 245
Order analysis 191
Order confirmation 246
Order fulfillment 229, 242

Order management 67, 118, 180, 182
Order promising 419
Order scenarios 127
Order split 150, 162, 234
Order-to-cash process 253
Organizational culture 30
Organizational data 120
Organizational knowledge 176
Osram Sylvania 255
Outbound calls 335
Outbound delivery 155
Outgoing invoice 160
Output 122
Output processing 159

P
Packaged composite applications 54
Packaged solutions 349
Packing 156
Page impressions 250
Partner and Channel Analytics 319
Partner determination 120
Partner management 18
Partner portal 253
Partner relationship management 34
Payback period 330
Payment card 151, 152
Payment card processing 151
Payment card transactions 151
Payment handling 245
Payment processing 147, 151
Payment transaction 229
Payment types 151
PDA 206, 214
People Integration 354
People-centric CRM 37
People-Centric User Interface 379,
381, 382
Performance analysis 161, 191
Performance measurement system 40
Personalization 90, 230, 383, 384
Personalization Engine 237
Personalized communication 92
Personalized customer contact 27
Personalized customer relationship
management 31
Pharma 359
Picking 156

Pipeline analysis 138, 139
Planning applications 76
Planning levels 102
Planning tasks 102
PLM 17, 52
Point solution vendor 44
Portal 142, 253
Portal Services 381
Potential benefits 163, 194, 259, 326
Pre-sales cycle 230
Prices and conditions 27
Pricing 121, 243, 398
PRM 34
Process industries 53
Process integration 354
Processes 17
Processing Incoming Payment 160
Product analytics 309, 317
Product association rules 91
Product catalog 239
Product configuration 27, 121, 124
Product configurator 125, 127
Product determination 121
Product development 52
Product leadership 19, 21, 25
Product Lifecycle Management → see
    PLM
Product lists 92
Product recommendations 27, 238
Product search 228
Product selection 229, 239
Production planning and scheduling
    419
Professional Services 187, 359
Profitability 18, 28, 33
Profitability analysis 94, 191
Project goal description 115
Project kick-off 343
Project management 188
Project planning 342
Project preparation 343
Project resource planning 188
Project view 337
Prospective buyers 39
Public services 54, 359
Purchase order 242

Q
Qualified sales opportunity 110
Quality analysis 190
Quantity contract 130
Queries 118
Quickstep 349
Quotation and order management 57
Quotation Management 118

R
R/3 Edition 253, 414
R/3 Plug-In 414
Radio Frequency Devices 360
Ready-to-run templates 252
Realization 344
Realtime monitoring 198
Recommendations 162
Recovery 401
Reduction in costs 33
Relationship management 71
Relationship networks 33
Replication 386
Report 161
Reporting 76, 114, 118, 161
Reports 176
Resource planning 180, 181, 201
Resource planning and optimization
    164, 180
Resource planning tool 200
Response time 172
Retrieval and classification 389
Return on investment → see ROI
Roadmap 341
ROI 63, 81, 164, 180, 329, 336, 349
ROI key figures 330, 335
ROI reporting 86
Roles 357
Rollout Manager 401
RosettaNet 410
Routing 365
Rule-based ATP check 244

S
Sales 58, 67, 87, 305, 335, 358, 411
Sales analytics 100, 137, 138, 309, 320
Sales applications 39
Sales assistant 112
Sales contracts 130

Sales cycle 230
Sales force automation 33, 43, 44
Sales Funnel Analysis 138
Sales Methodology 114
Sales order 148, 152
Sales order processing 146, 161, 162
Sales performance analysis 139
Sales pipeline 77
Sales pipeline analysis 138
Sales planning 102
Sales process 200, 227
Sales volume forecast 111
SAP Advanced Planner and Optimizer
    → see SAP APO
SAP APO 122, 244, 348, 419
SAP Biller Direct 247
SAP Business Case Builder 58, 64
SAP Business Connector 419
SAP Business Information Warehouse
    → see SAP BW
SAP Business Maps 57
SAP Business One 48
SAP BW 61, 164, 250, 309, 348, 361,
    363, 394, 419
SAP CI 363
SAP Collaborative Business Maps 58,
    60
SAP Content Integrator 363
SAP Content Server 420
SAP CRM Field Applications 209
SAP CRM Internet Customer Self-
    Service 420
SAP Dispute Management 160
SAP EBP 239
SAP Enterprise Buyer Professional →
    see SAP EBP
SAP Enterprise Portal 356, 413, 420
SAP E-Selling Web Application
    Components 420
SAP Exchange Infrastructure 363, 365,
    390
SAP for Media 431
SAP for Telecommunications 431
SAP Help Portal 57
SAP Hosting 351
SAP Internet Pricing and Configurator
    → see SAP IPC
SAP Internet Sales 253

SAP Internet Sales Web Application
    components 414
SAP IPC 125, 211, 240, 243, 390, 414,
    420, 425
SAP J2EE-Engine 390, 414, 420
SAP Java Connector 420
SAP Knowledge Management 364
SAP Master Data Management 361
SAP Master Data Management
    Adapter 363
SAP MDM 361
SAP MDM-Adapter 363
SAP ME 359
SAP MI 359, 361
SAP Mobile Application Studio 399
SAP Mobile Engine 359
SAP Mobile Infrastructure 359, 361
SAP NetWeaver 48, 52, 353, 354, 356,
    365, 374, 377, 387, 403
SAP product configurator 128
SAP R/3 128, 421
SAP R/3 4.6C 52
SAP R/3 Customer Service 214
SAP R/3 Enterprise 52, 122
SAP Safeguarding 350
SAP Service 350
SAP Service Marketplace 57, 350, 352,
    412
SAP Smart Business Solutions 48
SAP Solution Composer 58
SAP Solution Management Optimi-
    zation 350
SAP Solution Manager 341, 369, 392,
    412
SAP Solution Maps 57
SAP Strategic Enterprise Management
    309, 321, 348, 421
SAP Trade Promotion Management 87
SAP Tutor 352
SAP Web Application Server 55, 240,
    353, 354, 361, 366, 412
SAP Workflow Modeler 422
SAP Workforce Management Add-On
    421
SAP xApps 48, 54
SAP XI 363
Satisfaction index 40
Scenario overview 163, 194, 326

SCM 17, 34, 37, 52, 128, 196, 205
Self-service 41, 165, 247, 253
Service 58, 67, 163, 305, 358, 411
Service analysis 171, 189
Service analytics 189, 190, 309, 320
Service applications 39
Service concept 189
Service confirmation 183
Service contract management 213
Service contracts 130, 172, 173
Service entitlements 172
Service industries 53
Service level agreement 166, 171, 172,
    183, 190, 200, 248
Service Operations Management 164
Service planning 175, 190
Service Planning & Forecasting 164
Service processing 172
Services 173, 175
SFA (sales force automation) 35, 43
Share of wallet 40
Shipment Cost Processing 157
Shipping 147, 154
Shipping documents 155
Shipping Process 154, 155
Ship-to-Order 127
Shop-solution 233
Simple Object Access Protocol 387
Simulated availability check 149
Single Sign-On 357, 371
Site statistics 250
SLA 172, 190
SLA parameters 172
Smart Forms 159
SOAP 387
Software Agent Framework 268
Software components 57
Software solutions 57
Solution Database 168
Solution database 168, 170, 176, 248
Solution delivery services 351
Solution library 248
SRM 34
SSO 357
Stand-alone 403
Status management 124
Storefront 234
Strategic consulting services 351

Strategic service planning 190
Stylesheet editor 379
Stylesheets 379
Subcase 169
Success analysis 94
Supplier Relationship Management →
    see SRM
Supply chain collaboration 419
Supply chain control 419
Supply Chain Management → see
    SCM
Supply chain planning 419
Support 165, 341, 345
Support desk 345
Survey 108
Survey Tool 117
System landscape 31, 411
System status 124

T
Tablet PC 208, 209, 214, 385
TCO 54, 331
TeaLeaf 421
Telecommunication 431
Telemarketing 77
Telesales 92, 162, 335
Telesales activities 39
Territory Determination 104
Territory Hierarchies 103
Territory Management 103, 386
Text management 122
Text Retrieval and Information
    Extraction 421
Tickets 372
Time-to-delivery 336
Time-to-market 336
Time-to-volume 336
TM 52
Top-down 102
Top-down distribution 102
Top-n product lists 92
Total cost of ownership → see TCO
Tracking ID 93
Tracking systems 247
Trade promotion 87, 88, 217
Trade promotion management 39
Trade promotion planning 88
Transact 38

Transaction Data 423
Transport 147, 156
Transportation planning 419
Travel management 52
TREX 389, 414, 421
TREX Search Engine 421
TRUSTe 31

U

UBIS Intelligent Product Adviser 422
UMTS 209
Up-selling 91, 150, 242, 243, 308
Up-selling offers 232
Usability test 252
Use potential 64, 98, 143
User interfaces 27
User status 124
User support 344
User training 344
Utilities 359

V

Validation 87
Value 19
Value contract 131
Value disciplines 20
Value focus points 25
Value optimization 33
Vehicle scheduling 419
View 382
Virtual classroom training 351
Virtual showroom 234

Voice-over IP 249

W

WAP 208
WAP cell phone 181
Warning lists 154
Warranties 174
Web analysis 250
Web analytics 318
Web auction solution 246
Web auctions 246
Web catalog 241
Web requests 170
Web self-services 235
Web server 389
Web shop 225
Web shop design 252
Web site monitoring 318
Web-based training 352
WebFlow 123
Wireless Application Protocol 208
Wireless LAN → see WLAN
WLAN 208, 209
Workflow 105, 123, 124, 134, 154, 422
Workflow Management 105
Workflow procedure 154
Workforce Management 196, 421

X

xApps 54
XML 52, 239, 387
XML schema 170

Tips and tricks for dealing with SAP Business Information Warehouse

450 pp., 2004, US$ 69.95
ISBN 1-59229-017-5

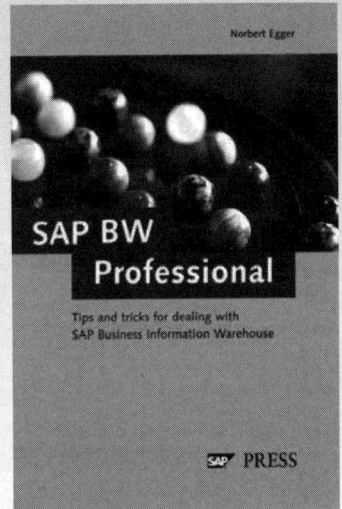

SAP BW Professional

www.sap-press.com

N. Egger

SAP BW Professional

Tips and tricks for dealing with SAP Business Information Warehouse

Learn the ins and outs of SAP Business Information Warehouse (BW), and gain the knowledge to leverage the full potential of this key technology. Whether it's in terms of project management, data modeling or reporting, you'll benefit from volumes of basic and advanced information. All content is presented in an easy-tofollow format, illustrated by proven examples, sample solutions and clear graphics and screen shots.

Take full advantage of Employee Self-Service (ESS).

352 pp., 2003, US$ 59.95
ISBN 1-59229-021-3

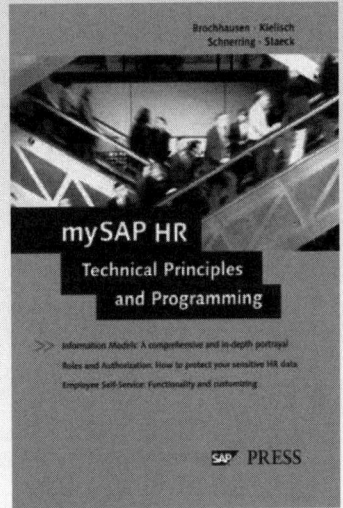

mySAP HR Technical Principles and Programming

www.sap-press.com

E. Brochhausen, J. Kielisch, J. Schnerring, J. Staeck

mySAP HR Technical Principles and Programming

Finally, a technical reference book that gives you an in-depth, firsthand look at the data structures of SAP HR. You can greatly advance your key projects with detailed insights for analyzing and working with this mission critical data, and much more. First, gain a thorough understanding of the concept of information models, through which the master data in HR is structured. Then, learn about the individual information models of personnel administration and time management. Special features of HR role and authorization concepts are clearly defined-from both the functional and technical perspectives.

Authorization concepts for SAP R/3 and Enterprise Portals!

284 pp., 2003, US$ 59.95
ISBN 1-59229-016-7

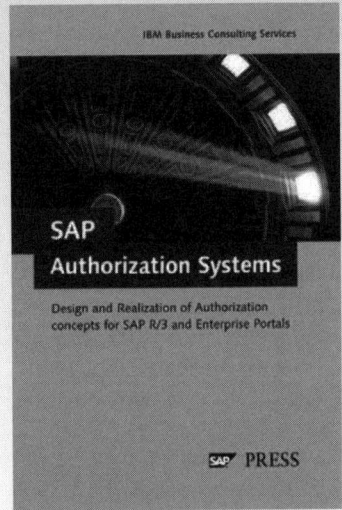

SAP Authorization System

www.sap-press.com

IBM Business Consulting Services GmbH

SAP Authorization System

Design and Implementation of Authorization concepts for SAP R/3 and SAP Enterprise Portals

This practical guide offers you a detailed introduction to all the essential aspects of SAP Authorization management, as well as the necessary organizational and technical structures and tools. Take advantage of a proven Phase Model to help you navigate through all of the stages leading up to the implementation and deployment of an authorization concept, from the procedural steps required to design the concept, to the production phase, and lastly, to the supervision phase. In addition, you'll quickly learn how to set up authorization via the SAP R/3 Profile Generator.

How to get most from your SAP HR systems

552 pp., approx. US$ 69.95
ISBN 1-59229-024-8, April 2004

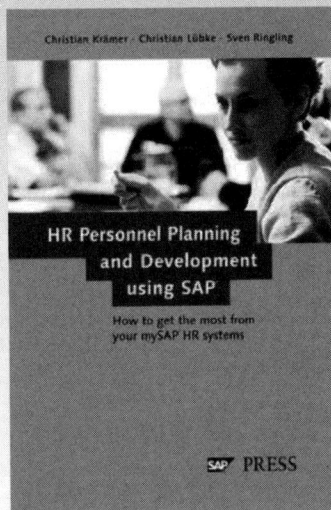

HR Personnel Planning and Development Using SAP

www.sap-press.com

Christian Krämer, Christian Lübke, Sven Ringling

HR Personnel Planning and Development Using SAP

How to get the most from your SAP HR systems

This compelling new reference book gives you a comprehensive view of the most important personnel planning and development functionality within SAP. Whether you need to implement, customize, or optimize your HR systems, the real-world insights this book provides will help you master the concepts essential for effective personnel planning and development. This book will help you leverage the many HR options and processes supported by SAP and gives you practical examples and key metrics to help you measure your success.

Practical solutions to streamline 24/7 operations Service Level Agreements, disaster recovery, security

355 pp., 2004, US$ 79.95
ISBN 1-59229-025-8

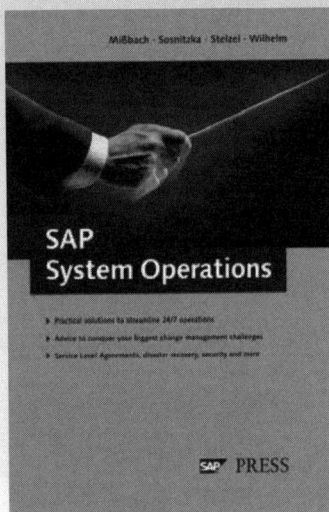

SAP System Operations

M. Missbach, R. Sosnitzka, J. Stelzel, M. Wilhelm

SAP System Operations

With system landscapes becoming increasingly more complex, administering them efficiently is proving equally difficult. This unique new book provides you with concepts and practical solutions that will enable you to optimize your SAP operations. Get in-depth information to set up a viable Standard Operation Environment (SOE) for SAP systems, as well as time-saving tips for certification and validation of your system landscape. Plus, benefit from and customize the numerous examples and case studies extracted from the worldwide operations of many large SAP customers.

Unlock the full potential of your SAP systems!

220 pp., approx. US$ 79.95
ISBN 1-59229-026-4, May 2004

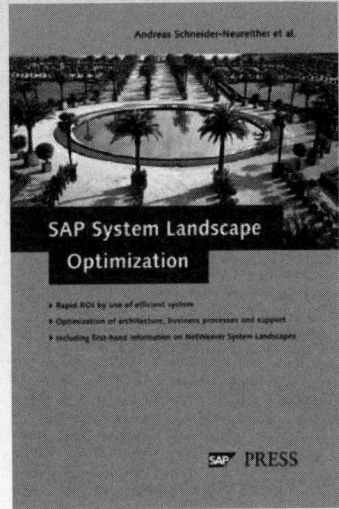

SAP System Landscape
Optimization

▸ Rapid ROI by use of efficient system
▸ Optimization of architecture, business processes and support
▸ Including first-hand information on NetWeaver System Landscapes

Andreas Schneider-Neureither et al.

SAP PRESS

SAP System Landscape Optimization

www.sap-press.com

A. (Ed.) Schneider-Neureither

SAP System Landscape Optimization

This reference book serves as an essential collection of insights, procedures, processes and tools that help you unlock the full potential of your SAP systems. First, hit the ground running with a detailed intro- duction to SAP NetWeaver and the mySAP Business Suite. Then, elevate your mastery of key concepts such as system architecture, security, Change and Transport Mana- gement, to name just a few. All of the practical advice and detailed information provided is with a clear focus on helping you guide your team to achieve a faster return on investment.

Migrate your data quickly and easily - no programming required

300 pp., approx. US$ 74.95
ISBN 1-59229-028-0, April 2004

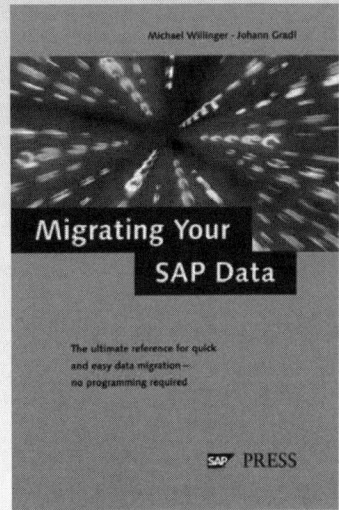

Michael Willinger · Johann Gradl

Migrating Your SAP Data

The ultimate reference for quick
and easy data migration—
no programming required

SAP PRESS

Migrating your SAP Data

www.sap-press.com

M. Willinger, J. Gradl

Migrating your SAP Data

The ultimate reference for quick and easy data migration - no programming required

Every time R/3 is introduced, data from the old systems has to be migrated into R/3. From experience we know that this takes up a large part of the time and also of the cost of R/3 introduction.
This book is a practical companion for migration projects. It book illustrates the basic principles of migration; it discusses the necessary preparatory measures for a project and shows you how to migrate your data using the means offered by the SAP-system economically, rapidly and more or less without programming effort.

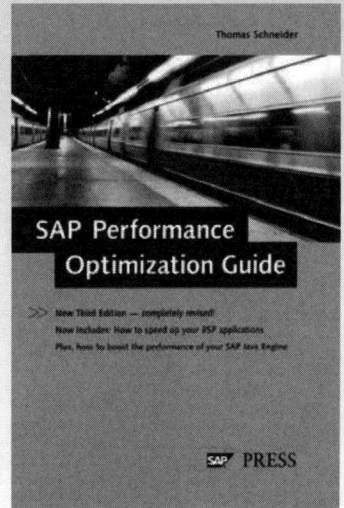

SAP Performance
Optimization Guide

New Third Edition — completely revised!
Now includes: How to speed up your BSP applications
Plus, how to boost the performance of your SAP Java Engine

SAV PRESS

SAP Performance
Optimization Guide

www.sap-press.com

T. Schneider

SAP Performance Optimization Guide

Analyzing and Tuning SAP Systems

Optimize the performance and economical running
of your SAP-System - the new edition of this book
shows you how! Whether you administer an R/3 or
one of the newest mySAP-Solutions, you learn how
to syste- matically identify and analyze performance
problems. Another focus is the adaptation of
appropriate tuning measures and verification of
success. Performance optimization includes the
technical side as well as the analysis of applications.
For the new edition the book has been thoroughly
revised and brought up to date. A new chapter
provides insight into the connection of the system to
the Internet with the help of Web AS.

Interested in reading more?

Please visit our Web site for all
new book releases from SAP PRESS.

www.sap-press.com

SAP PRESS